AMERICAN THINKING AND WRITING

by

JOSEPH M. BACHELOR
Associate Professor of English at Miami University

and

RALPH L. HENRY
Associate Professor of English at Carleton College

D. APPLETON-CENTURY COMPANY
INCORPORATED
NEW YORK   LONDON

PE 1417

.B 25

PREFACE

Amid the welter of conflicting opinions that assail our thinking in these days, Americans will agree on two basic truths: (1) our democratic way of life is now almost unique in the world and hence grows daily more precious; and (2) this democratic way is imperiled. Committed to a historically rooted belief in human freedom, we in America have come to the testing time of democracy.

There have not been wanting distinguished interpreters and eloquent defenders of the American way of life. The fifty selections of contemporary writing in this book bear witness to the worth and validity of the American tradition. There is a deep glow of pride and love of country in many of the pieces in this volume, but their prevailing tone is objective, reasoned, dispassionate. They are not emotional, not hortatory, not bombastically patriotic. The authors are firm in their belief in democracy but none the less critical of its deficiencies. The strength and weakness of America and the great issues of our time, as they affect the pattern of American life, are the concern of many of the book's most brilliant essays.

The selections in *American Thinking and Writing*—although varied in style, tone, and type—are knit together into an integrated whole. A glance at the Table of Contents will reveal many well-known names in the list of authors. But it will also indicate how the synthesis of the book moves from the breadth and sweep of the land to the people, to the social and political problems of our form of government, to the present functioning and the future ideals of the democratic system. An appeal to varied literary tastes has been made by the inclusion of formal and familiar essays, short stories, satirical sketches, public addresses, and editorials.

This book has been prepared as a text for the teaching of writing through intelligent reading. That is its primary purpose. But the compilers believe that students may learn from this volume many lessons having a special meaning at the present time.

Readers may well feel that their studies in these provocative essays have made them better Americans by confirming their faith in the inherent greatness of their native land.

Formal acknowledgment of permission to use each essay has been made at the page on which it begins. But the compilers wish, in a more personal way, to acknowledge the kindness of the following writers, many of whom graciously acquiesced in slight changes in or deletions from their articles to make them absolutely contemporary: Brooks Atkinson, Stephen Vincent Benét, Pearl Buck, W. J. Cameron, Henry S. Canby, Henry Steele Commager, W. H. Cowley, Edmund E. Day, R. L. Duffus, Irwin Edman, John Erskine, Harry Emerson Fosdick, Roy Helton, Ethel Ambler Hunter, Dale Kramer, Stephen Leacock, Ralph Linton, Walter Lippmann, John A. Lomax, Matthew Luckiesh, Della T. Lutes, Walter Millis, the Honorable Frank Murphy, William Fielding Ogburn, Donald Culross Peattie, Harriet Duff Phillips, Channing Pollock, Gene Richard, Vincent Sheean, Wallace Stegner, Benjamin Stolberg, Webb Waldron, the Honorable Henry A. Wallace, and E. B. White.

It is impossible to thank individually the editors of magazines and the editorial departments of various publishers for all their courtesies, but their helpful suggestions and generous granting of requests are none the less appreciated. The compilers do wish to thank specifically Miss Beatrice Wardell of Carleton College, for many and diverse services to the book while in preparation; Mr. Leland S. Dutton, of the Miami University Library, for his kindness in making available source materials; Mr. Edgar W. King, Librarian of Miami University, whose interest and assistance invariably solved the multitudinous perplexities and difficulties that attend a book from its inception as an idea to its appearance as a bound volume. The compilers, indeed, found so much friendliness and ready help in every direction in which they turned that they were throughout encouraged, and in the end humbled, by the sincerity and warmth of so much human good-will.

J. M. B.
R. L. H.

TO THE TEACHER

A **text** is an educational tool; a good text should be as efficient
a tool in the hands of a teacher as a saw or hammer is in the hands
of a carpenter. It is hoped that teachers of English will find
American Thinking and Writing a truly effective classroom tool.

The selections in this book, although they vary greatly in
length and style and thought, all have to do, in one way or another, with the present-day American scene. Indeed, the writing
itself is wholly contemporary and deals with contemporary problems. Most of the material is making its first appearance in text-
book form; hence the essays have a freshness that should please
teachers as well as students.

Interesting and stimulating as it is believed these essays will
prove to students, their purpose is not merely to supply reading
for English classes. Not that they will fail to provide informative
and aesthetic enjoyment as *reading*—good writing will always
do that for persons who have any appreciative responses—but
they have a further and, frankly, a more practical purpose. That
purpose is to harness a student's writing to his reading: to supply
him with specimens of various kinds of good writing as models
and to provide him with challenging ideas that will encourage or
provoke or even goad him to the expression of his own ideas.
Intellectual indifference or mental lethargy has all too often
resulted from reading which students found unrelated to their
own problems and interests. If there is any student who will not
defend—and sometimes oppose—the ideas in this book, he must
indeed be a peculiar American.

To harness writing to reading, unusually full apparatus for
teaching the essays has been supplied. The first set of questions
after each selection is for the student's own use. The purpose of
these questions is to test his reading ability. The questions are
entirely factual, not matters of opinion or controversy; if he can
answer them satisfactorily, he has read the essay intelligently and

comprehendingly. These questions are a test not only of his reading ability but also of the degree of his concentration at the time of reading each essay. If any student is unusually backward in reading ability, it is suggested that he be asked to write out the answers to the questions. This, of course, will add to his labor, but specific replies will develop his comprehension of the printed word. The ability to read intelligently is of the very essence of a student's success, not alone in English but in all his content courses. Incidentally, these questions are not intended to take any of the teacher's time nor any of the class period. The teacher should assume that the student has completed an intelligent reading of the selection assigned when he comes to class.

The questions in the second set are for class discussion. They stem directly from the essay; they ask the student's opinion about the author's ideas or about points of larger significance suggested by the essay. They are intended to elicit reactions from the student. Doubtless there will be diversity of student opinion. The purpose of the questions is not to obtain conformity of thought, but to have the student *think*. The teacher, of course, will make such selection of these questions as will put any particular class on its mettle. The reaction of each student to these discussions should provide him with something vital about which to write. Although this urge to express his ideas will not in itself guarantee good writing, it will likely result in better writing than he would do if he were not personally interested. There is, fortunately, an inevitable relationship between interest and accomplishment.

The third set of questions is of an entirely different kind: they direct the student's attention to certain rhetorical and stylistic effects in the essay and call attention to *how* the author gained these effects. They show how the author began his essay in a way to catch the reader's attention, how he organized his material, how he linked his paragraphs together, how he obtained graphicness by figurative language, how he lightened his writing by humor, how he made it pungent by satire and irony, how he drew upon personal experiences to illustrate and humanize his ideas and to make them concrete, how he summarized his thesis at the close of the essay. These questions are a kind of practical rhetoric. If the student will incorporate in his own writing the principles and devices he observes in these essays, he will be utilizing the "machinery" of successful writing; he will, in actuality, have a working knowledge of rhetorical principles and stylistic devices. But one point must be kept constantly in the foreground: the value of reading in developing the art of writing consists almost entirely in *analyzing* what is read. The student must observe that an author writes clearly because he unifies his thoughts and arranges them logically, that he makes his sentences and paragraphs "stick together," that he emphasizes certain ideas by the *way* he expresses them and by *where* he puts them in the sentences, in the paragraphs, and in the whole composition. In short, it is observing *how* good writers write, far more than reading *what* they write, that helps a student likewise to write well.

The next section of the apparatus supplied for each essay is intended to instill in the student an interest in words and to increase his vocabulary. There is a definite relationship between a student's command of words and his ability to write. It is not merely a matter of a larger vocabulary with which to express himself; it is a *feeling* for words, which gives his writing personality and individuality quite independent of the size of his vocabulary. An interest in words as an aid to good writing has all too long been neglected in books intended for instruction in English. If writing, as has been facetiously pointed out, is merely putting one word after another, good writing is the putting of the right words, one after another. The right word will always be the *inevitable* word; when a student has an unerring instinct for words, he is moving toward clear and effective composition. There is, indeed, no surer means of guaranteeing good writing than to acquire a knowledge of words. To foster this knowledge, the teacher will use these ample and diverse vocabulary exercises as will best fit the needs of the class and as time allows. Many of them may be assigned as outside work; others may be done more painstakingly in class. These vocabulary exercises are not devoid of the spirit of intellectual adventure. They should yield a maximum of vocabulary improvement for the time expended. And it may be well to remember that many an indifferent student has entered into an enthusiastic appreciation of English through the avenue of the mastery of words.

The last section of the apparatus following each essay provides theme topics based upon the essay or suggested by it. They are subjective topics which allow the student to express his personal opinions. These topics, however, are intended to be only suggestive. Class discussion will produce others by the score. If a student has something of his own that he wishes to say, he should be encouraged to "get it out of his system." The whole spirit of this book is to induce the student to think and then to express what he believes. His ideas may be immature, but if they are sincerely his own, they will gradually run into the deeper and steadier currents of objective truth. The colors in which strong personal feeling is expressed are likely to be the primary colors; but the color of perfunctory writing is forever a monotonous, neutral gray.

As a final aid to the teacher in using reading as a basis for good writing, what for want of a better name may be called a "Corrective Handbook" has been placed at the back of this text. The chart is so arranged that the teacher, in correcting a theme, can direct the student instantly to the kind of error made. For example, 1a would mean that he has written a sentence fragment. The student should turn to the handbook and from it correct his error. This handbook does not supply exercises for class work; its purpose is solely corrective. Nor does it lay claim to completeness. The common and fundamental errors made by students are included; unusual or debatable matters of usage have been omitted as irrelevant or confusingly superfluous.

Thus the purpose of *American Thinking and Writing* is to supply students with interesting reading that will be productive of good writing. The compilers hope that this volume will accomplish its objective; yet they know that these essays are at best only a tool. The real effectiveness of the book rests with the teachers who use it; a saw is merely a piece of steel attached to a piece of wood until it is in the carpenter's hands.

TO THE STUDENT

Although reading the selections carefully and doing the exercises as the teacher directs will be an essential part of your work with this book, your most vital relationship to it, and the greatest benefit you will derive from it, will be in the writing of themes. And immediately you should disabuse your mind of the idea that writing a theme is an incidental activity or a necessary drudgery—it is a privilege. Since you must either be able to express yourself effectively or suffer both socially and financially throughout your life, it is a privilege to learn how to write well. It is a privilege, also, to have a more experienced person care enough about your acquiring this ability to spend time correcting what you write and suggesting ways by which you can improve your writing. That you do not like to write themes, that you may do them poorly, that you have little aptitude in writing are sufficient reasons, in themselves, for your writing themes.

Naturally, the first question that arises is, What shall I write about? The question is basic. The compilers of this book believe that you will write a better theme about a limited, definite, concrete subject than about a broad, vague, abstract one. It should preferably have a high degree of personal element in it—something in which you have participated, something which you have observed, something about which you have well-formulated ideas. But whether or not the subject is personal, it must be limited; otherwise it cannot be treated adequately in a short theme. You should be able to state the *idea* of your subject in a single concise sentence. If you cannot do this, choose another subject.

The young writer often feels that he has nothing about which to write. To say this is to acknowledge that you have not observed, thought, felt, reacted. It is impossible that you have existed for eighteen years in a vacuum. A boy will never have a more poignant grief than that caused by the death of his dog under an automobile; the memory of your childhood Christmas tree is a more beautiful sight than the Alps will ever be; that surprise party brought you greater joy than winning ten thousand dollars on the stock market will ever bring. Nothing to write about? Enough to fill several, perhaps many, books. But you protest that your life is just like everybody else's. Nonsense. There have never been two lives in an identical pattern since the world began. If you have nothing to write about, don't let anybody know it. Inarticulateness would possibly reveal that you are uninteresting as a personality; that you are unresponsive to the myriad of stimuli all about you; that you have no opinions of your own.

But to take a concrete case. Recently a student protested that he had nothing to write about. The teacher, with an assumed casualness, asked him what he had done during the summer. He had lived on a farm and, the season being unusually dry, he had had to haul water for the cattle. How many cows were there? Sixteen—and sheep and horses, too. "Well, that couldn't have been very much of a job." "You bet it was a job! Do you know how much water a cow drinks on a hot day?" The instructor did not know. "About fifty gallons of water." It seemed incredible. The instructor made a rapid calculation, then countered, "Fifty gallons would be over a barrel and a half apiece. That would be almost as big as the cow," he continued with provocative exaggeration. "Now it hardly seems possible that—" "Well she does, too," the boy interrupted with the vehemence born of experience and possibly from the memory of endless barrels of water being dipped from a creek and hauled to a barnyard—only to disappear into the cavernous stomachs of insatiable cows. The boy also knew how much a horse drank, and a sheep, and a pig. Strangely enough, although a horse is considerably larger and heavier than a milch cow, it drinks much less water.

The boy gave a description of the creek—nostalgic to the instructor who, as a boy, had swum in one like it—and a graphic portrayal of the time he upset while getting his wagon out of the stream. The instructor sat back, possibly a little self-satisfied. "It is all very interesting, and I have really learned a great deal

—about cows. You must write it for the class." The boy looked amazed that he should write about hauling water for cows. And the class was interested and learned a great deal about cows—and about a certain boy who had before seemed uninteresting and "had nothing to write about." They felt the drudgery and heat of the summer, the excitement and humor of the toppled-over barrels, the loneliness of a farm barnyard at evening. (The instructor, incidentally, verified the water-consumption of farm animals from the Government Agricultural Reports—and the boy was right.)

Your writing, to be good, must embody a few established principles. Unity is one of the basic requirements of good writing. This requirement you will have attained for the composition as a whole if you rigorously limited your subject as suggested above. Now all you have to do with such a subject is to stick strictly to it. Let no extraneous ideas, no matter how tantalizing, interesting, or amusing, beckon you away from it. The paragraphs making the whole should be separate units of that whole. Don't develop two loosely related ideas in one paragraph nor split an indissoluble unit of thought into two paragraphs. Finally, each sentence must be a unit of thought; it must not combine unrelated ideas. Throughout, unity is *oneness* in writing.

Emphasis is the way in which a writer "manages" his writing. It is, so to speak, putting your best foot forward. The beginning and the ending of your composition are the places of importance; so the skilful writer uses them to advantage. Your chief concern at the beginning is to catch the reader's attention; you may use any legitimate means to do this. Having caught the reader's attention, you must hold it. Holding his attention will depend partly on *what* you say, but likely even more upon *how* you say it and *where* you put it. Emphasis is the art of marshaling your material so skilfully that the reader would resent being stopped before he reached the end. The close of your theme should bring the reader the sense of artistic satisfaction. A good theme doesn't just stop; it is completed. The thesis is summed up; the whole is rounded off; it is all tied up neatly. Test the theme yourself. Read the first paragraph—Are you *interested?* Read the last paragraph

—Are you *satisfied?* Similarly, the opening and the close of the paragraphs are the places of vantage, and a good writer, like a good general, will concentrate his forces at key points. To obtain emphasis, the writer must be a conscious craftsman. Since emphasis is based on values, it doesn't just happen. Emphasis is *force* in writing.

Besides unity and emphasis, good writing must have coherence. Without coherence, the thought will ride along on a bumpy road. It will jar from sentence to sentence and jolt from paragraph to paragraph. The paragraphs should be linked together by connective words (see Corrective Handbook, 6d), by transition sentences, or by the logical development of the thought itself. The sentences within the paragraphs must likewise flow along smoothly and "stick together." Coherence represents the writer primarily as a logician, in which respect it is as much akin to science and mathematics as it is to good writing. Coherence is *smoothness* in writing.

These three essential qualities of good writing are concerned with words used in sentences; but all writing finally rests on words *used as words*. That is why words are so important. You may make your writing vaguely intelligible by using an inadequate vocabulary, but you will never make your writing effective, distinctive, or individual with such a vocabulary.

Let us analyze briefly the outstanding deficiencies in student themes because of the vocabulary used: (1) the words only approximately express what the writer intends to say; (2) they are too often abstract words instead of concrete words; (3) they are too often colorless words instead of picture-making words; (4) they are the first words that came into the writer's mind and no effort was made to find the one and only right word for each individual word-choice; (5) they are too often words without connotations, that is, words with no suggestive overtones.

To illustrate what poor and good words will do to a piece of writing, let us examine the following paragraphs:

The Squire's house was two log cabins put together, and both of them were worn out; two or three skinny dogs lay asleep at the door and raised up their heads whenever Mrs. Hawkins or the children went in and out. Old stuff was in the bare yard; a bench stood near the door with a tin wash basin on it and a pail of water and a gourd; a cat had begun to drink from the pail, but that was too much work, so she took a rest. There was an ash-hopper by the fence, and an iron pot, for soft-soap-boiling, near it.

But the paragraph from *The Gilded Age*, as Mark Twain wrote it, reads as follows:

The Squire's house was a double log cabin, in a state of decay; two or three gaunt hounds lay asleep about the threshold, and lifted their heads sadly whenever Mrs. Hawkins or the children stepped in and out over their bodies. Rubbish was scattered about the grassless yard; a bench stood near the door with a tin wash basin on it and a pail of water and a gourd; a cat had begun to drink from the pail, but the exertion was overtaxing her energies, and she had stopped to rest. There was an ash-hopper by the fence, and an iron pot, for soft-soap-boiling, near it.

These two paragraphs are in large part identical, and they certainly express the same facts, but they are remarkably different as pieces of writing. The superiority of the second paragraph depends entirely on Mark Twain's use of words.

There is no easy way to acquire an effective vocabulary, nor can anyone offer facile advice that will lead you to a mastery of words. Certain wise procedures are obvious: you should look up, thoroughly understand, and use all the words you encounter which are not already an active part of your vocabulary. Further, you should use with nice distinctions the words you already possess. You should pause, in writing your theme, before you scribble down any old word, to see whether you cannot find a more exact, forceful, or graphic word. And certainly, after your first draft is written, you should go over it searchingly to see whether you cannot substitute better words for the weak and colorless ones. With assurance this much can be affirmed: there are few rewards more satisfying and profitable than those which come from the study and mastery of words.

As a final suggestion as to the best way to write a theme, you are urged to write the first draft several days before the theme is due. A "cooling time" before you copy the theme will work wonders in its improvement. Defects, not at all obvious during composition, will be startlingly patent. You can then make corrections and improvements while copying your theme, and you will be bringing to your aid the best teacher in the world—self-analysis.

Now that you have written the best theme you can, check it against the questions in the following chart. Be honest with yourself in your answers. If you have forgotten something, this check will remind you; if you can improve something, you have a final chance to do so.

Your instructor now has, presumably, the best theme you can write upon the topic assigned or chosen. You have handed in your theme as an example of your ability to write; it must now stand on its own legs as a piece of writing.

Occasionally your instructor may believe that the maximum benefit to you from a theme will come from your rewriting it. You must guard against doing this task—and let us honestly call it a task—in a perfunctory manner. Your initial interest in the subject will possibly be lacking but, if you earnestly try to improve the theme, you will find that the pleasure of original creation in writing is no greater than the *satisfaction* derived from perfecting what has been written.

Usually your instructor will indicate on the margin of the theme the corrections he wishes you to make. The Corrective Handbook, which follows the selections, will aid you in this part of your work. In it you can readily find examples of the kind of errors that occur in themes and illustrations of ways to correct them.

Spelling will likely be among the errors indicated for correction. Besides spelling the word correctly on the margin of your theme, you should copy it in your notebook (see Corrective Handbook *4a*). Spelling, like mathematics, is absolute—it is either right or wrong—and therefore can be mastered. Incidentally, while you are looking up the spelling of a word, you can make a remarkable investment, for the time expended, by noting the derivation and definition of the word. This simple habit of mastering words will prove a life asset of inestimable value.

CHART FOR CHECKING A THEME

I. *Choice of a Subject*
1. Is the subject sufficiently limited?
2. Were you interested in it enough to want to write about it?
3. Did you know enough about it to write a satisfactory theme?

II. *Unity*
1. Have you stuck strictly to the subject?
2. Do your paragraphs develop unified segments of the whole?
3. Do your sentences have singleness of thought?

III. *Emphasis*
1. Does your beginning catch the reader's attention?
2. Does your development of the subject hold his attention?
3. Does your close satisfy his sense of completeness?

IV. *Coherence*
1. Have you avoided abrupt transitions between paragraphs?
2. Do your sentences run along smoothly and logically?

V. *Words*
1. Have you eliminated hackneyed, trite, weak, colorless words?
2. Have you employed accurate, definite, forceful, graphic words?
3. Can you substitute any other words that will improve the theme?
4. Are all the words correctly spelled?

VI. *Punctuation*
1. Have you punctuated a sentence fragment as a sentence?
2. Have you joined sentences with only commas?
3. Have you used commas wherever necessary?
4. Has each sentence the correct end-punctuation after it?
5. Have you put quotation marks around quoted material?

VII. *Mechanical Details*
1. Have you written your theme on regulation paper?
2. Have you given your name, section, date, etc., as required?
3. Have you indicated the source material accurately?
4. Have you left sufficient margin for your instructor's corrections?

CHART FOR CHECKING A THEME

I. Choice of a Subject
1. Is the subject sufficiently limited?
2. Were you interested in it enough to want to write about it?
3. Did you know enough about it to write a satisfactory theme?

II. Unity
1. Have you stuck strictly to the subject?
2. Do your paragraphs develop unified segments of the whole?
3. Do your sentences have singleness of thought?

III. Emphasis
1. Does your beginning catch the reader's attention?
2. Does your development of the subject hold his attention?
3. Does your close satisfy his sense of completeness?

IV. Coherence
1. Have you avoided abrupt transitions between paragraphs?
2. Do your sentences run along smoothly and logically?

V. Words
1. Have you eliminated hackneyed, trite, weak, colorless words?
2. Have you employed accurate, definite, forceful, graphic words?
3. Can you substitute any other words that will improve the theme?
4. Are all the words correctly spelled?

VI. Punctuation
1. Have you punctuated a sentence fragment as a sentence?
2. Have you joined sentences with only commas?
3. Have you used commas wherever necessary?
4. Has each sentence the correct end-punctuation after it?
5. Have you put quotation marks around quoted material?

VII. Mechanical Details
1. Have you written your theme on regulation paper?
2. Have you given your name, section, date, etc., as required?
3. Have you indicated the source material accurately?
4. Have you left sufficient margin for your instructor's corrections?

16

TABLE OF CONTENTS

xix

This Land of Ours

THIS LAND AND FLAG

FROM

THE NEW YORK TIMES

WHAT is the love of country for which our flag stands? Maybe it begins with love of the land itself. It is the fog rolling in with the tide at Eastport, or through the Golden Gate and among the towers of San Francisco. It is the sun coming up behind the White Mountains, over the Green, throwing a shining glory on Lake Champlain and above the Adirondacks. It is the storied Mississippi rolling swift and muddy past St. Louis, rolling past Cairo, pouring down past the levees of New Orleans. It is lazy noontide in the pines of Carolina, it is a sea of wheat rippling in western Kansas, it is the San Francisco peaks far north across the glowing nakedness of Arizona, it is the Grand Canyon, and a little stream coming down out of a New England ridge, in which are trout. (1)

It is men at work. It is the storm-tossed fishermen coming into Gloucester and Provincetown and Astoria. It is the farmer riding his great machine in the dust of harvest, the dairyman going to the barn before sunrise, the lineman mending the broken wire, the miner drilling for the blast. It is the servants of fire in the murky splendor of Pittsburgh, between the Allegheny and the Monongahela, the trucks rumbling through the night, the locomotive engineer bringing the train in on time, the pilot in the clouds, the riveter running along the beam a hundred feet in air. It is the clerk in the office, the housewife doing the dishes and sending the children off to school. It is the teacher, doctor, and parson tending and helping, body and soul, for small reward. (2)

It is small things remembered, the little corners of the land, the houses, the people that each one loves. We love our country because there was a little tree on a hill, and grass thereon, and a sweet valley below; because the hurdy-gurdy man came along on a sunny morning in a city street; because a beach or a farm or a lane or a house that might not seem much to others was once, for each of us, made magic. It is voices that are remembered only, no longer heard. It is parents, friends, the lazy chat of street and store and office, and the ease of mind that makes life tranquil. It is summer and winter, rain and sun and storm. These are flesh of our flesh, bone of our bone, blood of our blood, a lasting part of what we are, each of us and all of us together. (*3*)

It is stories told. It is the Pilgrims dying in their first dreadful winter. It is the Minute Man standing his ground at Concord Bridge, and dying there. It is the army in rags, sick, freezing, starving at Valley Forge. It is the wagons and the men on foot going westward over Cumberland Gap, floating down the great rivers, rolling over the great plains. It is the settler hacking fiercely at the primeval forest on his new, his own lands. It is Thoreau at Walden Pond, Lincoln at Cooper Union, and Lee riding home from Appomattox. It is corruption and disgrace, answered always by men who would not let the flag lie in the dust, who have stood up in every generation to fight for the old ideals and the old rights, at risk of ruin or of life itself. (*4*)

It is a great multitude of people on pilgrimage, common and ordinary people, charged with the usual human failings, yet filled with such a hope as never caught the imaginations and the hearts of any nation on earth before. The hope of liberty. The hope of justice. The hope of a land in which a man can stand straight, without fear, without rancor. (*5*)

The land and the people and the flag—the land a continent, the people of every race, the flag a symbol of what humanity may aspire to when the wars are over and the barriers are down; to these each generation must be dedicated and consecrated anew, to defend with life itself, if need be, but, above all, in friendliness, in hope, in courage, to live for. (*6*)

OUTLINE

A brief outline of this editorial is given below. The writer grouped his ideas under five headings (II-VI). As an experienced writer, he likely had this outline in his mind only, not actually arranged on paper. Unless you can duplicate his clarity of thought, it will be well for you to precede your writing with some form of outline. This outline need not be elaborate, but a jotting down of your ideas in a systematic way will be helpful. Whether you do this or not, one thing is certain: you should be able to make a logical outline *from* any piece of exposition you have written. If you cannot do this, very likely your theme is vague or confused or poorly arranged. Good writing is the product of clear thinking.

I. Comprehensive Introductory Question: The flag stands for what?

II. Love of Land
Eastport—Golden Gate—San Francisco; White Mountains—Green Mountains—Lake Champlain—Adirondacks; Mississippi—St. Louis—Cairo—New Orleans; pines of Carolina—wheat of Kansas—nakedness of Arizona—Grand Canyon—New England trout stream

III. Men at Work
Fishermen at Gloucester, Provincetown, Astoria; farmer—dairyman—lineman—miner; steel makers—truck driver—engineer—air pilot—riveter; clerk—housewife and children; teacher—doctor—parson

IV. Personal Relationships
Tree—grass—valley; city street—hurdy-gurdy; beach—farm—lane—house; parents—friends—talk in street, office, store; seasons—weather; part of each of us and all of us together

V. American History
Pilgrims—Minute Men—Valley Forge; pioneers over mountains, down rivers, across plains; settlers and new homes; Thoreau—Lincoln—Lee; corruption and its opponents

VI. People on Pilgrimage
Common, ordinary people; hope for liberty, for justice, for human dignity

VII. Closing Summarizing Paragraph
Land a continent—people of every race—flag a symbol; must be defended even with life but in spirit of friendliness, hope, and courage

QUESTIONS

I

1. Which parts of the country are mentioned twice? Is any part neither mentioned nor implied? (*1*)

2. Can you identify in American history all the persons and places mentioned? (*4*)
3. What world situation did the author have in mind when he said that in America "a man can stand straight, without fear, without rancor"? (*5*)
4. Compare the last paragraph with the following statement of President W. C. Coffey of the University of Minnesota: "We are all quite ready to talk about our privileges and the defense of them, but are we not, as a nation, tending to understress the concomitant obligations, ignoring the truth that privileges cannot exist without obligations?"

II

1. The author has not mentioned America at play or at leisure: sports, automobile trips, wintering in Florida or California. If play and rest are as necessary as work, why has he omitted this phase of American life?
2. Does this editorial make you feel more kindly toward persons of different racial backgrounds, religion, color, financial or social status from your own?
3. Do you think persons reading this editorial will have a better understanding of what the flag stands for? If this is so, has the truer significance of the flag resulted from new things you learned from the editorial or from the author's recalling to your mind things you already knew? Would the editorial have been as effective if it had revealed to you a series of startling, little-known facts about America? Can you draw any conclusion from your answer about most of your own writing?

III

1. The majority of the sentences in this editorial begin with "It is." Why is this repetition, as it is used here, effective rather than monotonous? Could the author have obtained the desired accumulative effect by beginning his sentences in a great variety of ways? Formulate a statement about repetition that is effective and repetition that is undesirable.
2. What was the author's purpose in bringing together the Grand Canyon and a New England trout stream?
3. What figures of speech are illustrated by "sea of wheat" (*1*) and "servants of fire" (*2*)?
4. What effect has the author gained by not writing "It is the hope of liberty" and "It is the hope of justice"? (*5*)
5. Why did the author not write "The land, the people, and the flag"? (*6*)

WORDS

In writing, one is constantly faced with the choice of words. The words used by the writer of this editorial are at the left in the list below. A synonym, in italics, has been substituted in quoted excerpts taken verbatim from the editorial. Why, in your opinion, did the author use the word he did?

1. rolling (*1*): It is the fog *drifting* in with the tide
2. storied (*1*): It is the *fabled* Mississippi
3. lazy (*1*): It is the *indolent* noontide in the pines of Carolina
4. rippling (*1*): It is a sea of wheat *undulating* in western Kansas
5. murky (*2*): It is the servants of fire in the *smoky* splendor of Pittsburgh
6. tranquil (*3*): the ease of mind that makes life *peaceful*
7. dreadful (*4*): the Pilgrims dying in their first *rigorous* winter
8. hacking (*4*): It is the settler *chopping* fiercely at the primeval forest
9. stood up (*4*): who have *determined* in every generation to fight
10. rancor (*5*): a man can stand straight, without fear, without *bitterness*

THEME TOPICS

Before you write your theme, read "To the Student," which will be found in the prefatory matter of this book. For this and for every assignment hereafter, check your first draft with the "Chart for Checking a Theme." Then make the necessary changes to improve the final draft of your theme.

1. I Am Proud to Be an American
2. See America First
3. My Favorite State (Part of America)
4. My Idea of the Ideal American Citizen
5. Yes—It is "America, the Beautiful"
6. How to Guard against Propaganda
7. My Duties as an American Citizen
8. America—Still the Land of Opportunity
9. "Small Things Remembered"
10. The American Way Is Worth Fighting For

THE PROMISE OF AMERICA

THOMAS WOLFE

G O, SEEKER, if you will, throughout the land and you
will find us burning in the night. (*1*)
There where the hackles of the Rocky Mountains
blaze in the blank and naked radiance of the moon, go make your
resting stool upon the highest peak. Can you not see us now?
The continental wall juts sheer and flat, its huge black shadow
on the plain, and the plain sweeps out against the East, two
thousand miles away. The great snake that you see there is the
Mississippi River. (*2*)

Behold the gem-strung towns and cities of the good, green
East, flung like star-dust through the field of night. That spreading constellation to the north is called Chicago, and that giant
wink that blazes in the moon is the pendant lake that it is built
upon. Beyond, close-set and dense as a clenched fist, are all the
jeweled cities of the eastern seaboard. There's Boston, ringed
with the bracelet of its shining little towns, and all the lights that
sparkle on the rocky indentations of New England. Here, southward and a little to the west, and yet still coasted to the sea, is
our intensest ray, the splintered firmament of the towered island
of Manhattan. Round about her, sown thick as grain, is the glitter
of a hundred towns and cities. The long chain of lights there is
the necklace of Long Island and the Jersey shore. Southward and
inland, by a foot or two, behold the duller glare of Philadelphia.
Southward further still, the twin constellations—Baltimore and
Washington. Westward, but still within the borders of the good,
green East, that night-time glow and smolder of hell-fire is Pittsburgh. Here, St. Louis, hot and humid in the cornfield belly of
the land, and bedded on the mid-length coil and fringes of the

snake. There at the snake's mouth, southward six hundred miles
or so, you see the jeweled crescent of old New Orleans. Here,
west and south again, you see the gemmy glitter of the cities
on the Texas border. (3)

Turn now, seeker, on your resting stool atop the Rocky Mountains, and look another thousand miles or so across moon-blazing
fiend-worlds of the Painted Desert and beyond Sierras' ridge.
That magic congeries of lights there to the west, ringed like a
studded belt around the magic setting of its lovely harbor, is the
fabled town of San Francisco. Below it, Los Angeles and all the
cities of the California shore. A thousand miles to north and west,
the sparkling towns of Oregon and Washington. (4)

Observe the whole of it, survey it as you might survey a field.
Make it your garden, seeker, or your backyard patch. Be at ease
in it. It's your oyster—yours to open if you will. Don't be frightened, it's not so big now, when your footstool is the Rocky
Mountains. Reach out and dip a hatful of cold water from Lake
Michigan. Drink it—we've tried it—you'll not find it bad. Take
your shoes off and work your toes down in the river oozes of the
Mississippi bottom—it's very refreshing on a hot night in the summertime. Help yourself to a bunch of Concord grapes up there
in northern New York state—they're getting good now. Or raid
that watermelon patch down there in Georgia. Or, if you like,
you can try the Rockyfords here at your elbow, in Colorado.
Just make yourself at home, refresh yourself, get the feel of
things, adjust your sights, and get the scale. It's your pasture now,
and it's not so big—only three thousand miles from east to west,
only two thousand miles from north to south—but all between,
where ten thousand points of light prick out the cities, towns,
and villages, there, seeker, you will find us burning in the
night. (5)

Here, as you pass through the brutal sprawl, the twenty miles
of rails and rickets, of the South Chicago slums—here, in an unpainted shack, is a Negro boy, and, seeker, he is burning in the
night. Behind him is a memory of the cotton fields, the flat and
mournful pineland barrens of the lost and buried South, and at
the fringes of the pine another shack, with mammy and eleven
children. Farther still behind, the slave-driver's whip, the slave

ship, and, far off, the jungle dirge of Africa. And before him, what? A roped-in ring, a blaze of lights, across from him a white champion; the bell, the opening, and all around the vast sea-roaring of the crowd. Then the lightning feint and stroke, the black panther's paw—the hot, rotating presses, and the rivers of sheeted print! O seeker, where is the slave ship now? (6)

On there, in the clay-baked piedmont of the South, that lean and tan-faced boy who sprawls there in the creaking chair among admiring cronies before the open doorways of the fire department, and tells them how he pitched the team to shut-out victory today. What visions burn, what dreams possess him, seeker of the night? The packed stands of the stadium, the bleachers sweltering with their unshaded hordes, the faultless velvet of the diamond, unlike the clay-baked outfields down in Georgia. The mounting roar of eighty thousand voices and Gehrig coming up to bat, the boy himself upon the pitching mound, the lean face steady as a hound's; then the nod, the signal, and the wind-up, the rawhide arm that snaps and crackles like a whip, the small white bullet of the blazing ball, its loud report in the oiled pocket of the catcher's mitt, the umpire's thumb jerked upward, the clean strike. (7)

Or there again, in the east-side Ghetto of Manhattan, two blocks away from the East River, a block away from the gas-house district and its thuggery, there in the swarming tenement, shut in his sweltering cell, breathing the sun-baked air through opened window at the fire escape, celled there away into a little semblance of privacy and solitude from all the brawling and vociferous life and argument of his family and the seething hive around him, the Jew boy sits and pores upon his book. In shirt-sleeves, bent above his table to meet the hard glare of a naked bulb, he sits with gaunt, starved face converging to his huge beaked nose, the weak eyes squinting painfully through his thick-lens glasses, his greasy hair roached back in oily scrolls above the slanting cage of his painful and constricted brow. And for what? For what this agony of concentration? For what this hell of effort? For what this intense withdrawal from the poverty and squalor of dirty brick and rusty fire escapes, from the raucous cries and violence and never-ending noise? For what? Because, brother, he is burning in the night. He sees the class, the lecture room, the shining apparatus of gigantic laboratories, the open field of scholarship and pure research, certain knowledge, and the world distinction of an Einstein name. (8)

So, then, to every man his chance—to every man, regardless of his birth, his shining, golden opportunity—to every man the right to live, to work, to be himself, and to become whatever thing his manhood and his vision can combine to make him—this, seeker, is the promise of America. (9)

QUESTIONS

I

1. After reading the essay, state, in general terms, to whom *us* in "find us burning in the night" refers. (1)
2. Where is the seeker supposed to be sitting as he views the continental United States? (2)
3. Name the places he is directed to see as he looks eastward (3); as he looks westward. (4)
4. What personal things is the seeker directed to do to convince himself that the country is not so large that he need be overawed by it? (5)
5. How is success in money (6), in fame (7), in learning (8) represented?
6. What deduction does the author intend every American to draw from his essay? (9)

II

1. Do you think there is more opportunity for a young man or woman in America than there is in any other country?
2. Do you believe there are as many opportunities now as there were in your grandfather's day? If so, are they the same kind of opportunities? How do pioneer opportunities differ from those in a highly developed country?
3. Do you today have more or fewer chances (a) to get rich, (b) to have comforts and enjoyments, (c) to acquire education and culture, (d) to serve mankind than boys and girls had, say, fifty years ago?
4. Do you think the author's examples of successes are typical enough to prove his thesis? This thesis is not that everyone will be successful. What is it?
5. What goals have you set for your own personal success?

III

1. Why is a night-scene a better artistic medium for the author's purpose in this essay than a day-scene would have been? Think of *all* the reasons.
2. What are cities gleaming in the night symbolical of in the essay?
3. Discuss the effectiveness of the following figures of speech: the great snake (*2*), flung like star-dust (*3*), that giant wink (*3*), dense as a clenched fist (*3*), ringed with a bracelet (*3*), sown as thick as grain (*3*), fiend-worlds of the Painted Desert (*4*), ringed like a studded belt (*4*).
4. Point out at least twenty words in this essay that suggest the brilliance of lights or jewels.
5. What does the author hope to accomplish by the almost boisterous good-fellowship of the expression "It's your oyster"? (*5*)
6. What is your final, considered judgment about the style of this essay? Is the style unusually effective or too decorated? Does the author seem to enjoy his own use of language? Be prepared to defend your answer.

WORDS

Point out, from the right-hand column, the correct definition for each word in the left-hand column.

1. hackles (*2*)	1. clamorous
2. constellation (*3*)	2. something hanging as an ornament
3. pendant (*3*)	3. aggregation
4. indentations (*3*)	4. harsh sounding
5. humid (*3*)	5. mournful music
6. congeries (*4*)	6. neck plumage or ruff
7. dirge (*6*)	7. land at base of mountains
8. piedmont (*7*)	8. boiling
9. semblance (*8*)	9. group of fixed stars
10. vociferous (*8*)	10. damp
11. seething (*8*)	11. meeting together
12. converging (*8*)	12. filthiness
13. constricted (*8*)	13. contracted
14. squalor (*8*)	14. appearance
15. raucous (*8*)	15. notches

THEME TOPICS

1. The Great Middle West (Pacific Northwest, Southwest, etc.)
2. The Mighty Mississippi
3. Rock-bound New England (The Deep South, etc.)

THE U. S. A.

EDITORS OF *FORTUNE*

LESS by definition than by achievement, the United States is the greatest nation on earth. Everybody says it, everybody believes it—without quite knowing why. It isn't the greatest in size. Its continental area is less than half the size of the Soviet Union, and smaller than Canada or Brazil. Its population of 130,085,000 is small compared to 450,000,000 Chinese, 170,000,000 Russians. Per square mile it has only 43 inhabitants; in contrast the 742 persons per square mile in England seems almost fantastic.

Commonly presumed to be wealthier in natural resources than any other nation, the U. S. in some respects is probably equaled and in others exceeded by the British Empire and the Soviet Union. Furthermore, the U. S. has certain vital deficiencies. It consumes more than half the world rubber crop, grows none. It drinks half the world's coffee, and again grows none. In normal times it uses three fourths of the world's raw silk without cultivating any silk-worms to speak of. It has virtually no tin or platinum; precious little manganese, quicksilver, tungsten and nickel. It is far from independent of the outside world. (*1*)

But in spite of all lacks and unfavorable comparisons the U. S. *is* the greatest nation on earth. And its actual greatness rests not on any single asset, but on a combination: a vast land area, a great, resourceful population of diverse origins and talents; an agriculture of such richness that it embarrasses; a universal industry of cosmic dimensions; an enormous treasury of resources—all integrated under a form of government that has stimulated their optimum development. (*2*)

Just as the greatness of the U. S. is a source of wonder to the rest of the world, so the character of the U. S. people has always been a tantalizing enigma. The U. S. has been called "Uncle Shylock," but let a famine develop in Asia or an earthquake level a city in South America and Americans rush to the rescue. The U. S. is a law-abiding nation, which had 1,400,000 major crimes in 1937, and has a hard time finding jail space to house the criminals. It has 30,000,000 students enrolled in schools and colleges, but over four percent of the population is illiterate, a rate comparing unfavorably with the averages of most European countries. It has a divine faith in the power of legislation. It spends more money on making laws and governing itself than any other country, outside of the U.S.S.R., and it takes a peculiar satisfaction in circumventing or ignoring its own laws. (3)

But if Americans are too paradoxical for compact description, they can be measured in terms of their major achievement. That achievement has been the integration within the boundaries of a single, unified nation of an infinite variety of racial, cultural, economic and geographic components.

Consider the derivation of the people. At first there are the Latins, here for plunder for the galleons of Spain, or land and furs for Paris. Then there are the English, coming for freedom, finding it, losing it, and fighting to have it again. Stern, hard-muscled, tough-minded English yeomen in the North, and English Cavaliers of a quite different breed in the South. The Englishmen pushing westward out of curiosity, or because they hated the sight of the neighbors' chimneys, or because they wanted less government. By 1810 they had traversed most of the West, and by 1850 had settled most of it—in spots. All this is very new. As late as 1890 Pershing was fighting the Sioux in Dakota. Meanwhile for decade after decade more people and still more flowed in from Europe with their diverse cultures and customs. All this has been integrated, and that integration is the foundation of the nation's greatness.

Externally the nation looks like a compact, single economic unit, but a familiar inspection reveals that it is scarcely that. Indeed, it is a union composed of countless units, each with its own economy, based upon its own sources of wealth, dominated by self-interest, and competing with every other unit. (4)

More nearly European than any other U. S. region is the Northeast [east of Ohio, north of Virginia]. It has 34 cities of more than 100,000; its population of 40,000,000 occupies but seven percent of the nation's area. Yet there is nothing more rural than the New England villages where milch cows are prodded down Main Street by towheaded youngsters, and sheep crop the green plots around the monuments to those who died at Cold Harbor and Bull Run. It is a highly civilized, highly educated region, yet witchcraft flourishes in parts of Pennsylvania, where barns and houses wear cabalistic symbols designed to ward away the dreaded hex.

Economically it stands in relation to the U. S. about the way England stands in relation to the British Empire. The region is dependent on the rest of the country for its wheat and flour, and for a large part of its fresh meats, fruits, vegetables and canned goods.

To the U. S. the Northeast sells machinery, coal, steel, glass, clothing, shoes and paper. Again like England, the Northeast is the great concentration point of finance, ownership and control. Of the national income the region garners nearly 40 percent. Thus the Northeast draws financial tribute from every part of the U. S., and intellectual tribute as well. A common complaint throughout the country is, "All our smartest young people go east." (5)

The Southeast [west to the Texas line] is the precise opposite of the Northeast. It has more than twice as much land but only two thirds as many people. Of these 70 percent are rural, and their per capita income is less than half that of the Northeast. However, precisely because it has been retarded, the industrial South appears to have the greatest growth potential of any region in the U. S.

The Southeast is naturally rich. It has 40 percent of the U. S. forest land; it has bauxite, oil, natural gas, sulphur, phosphates. Around Birmingham coal crops up close to important iron deposits, and years ago Henry C. Frick predicted that by 1940

Birmingham would be a bigger steel city than Pittsburgh. It isn't—by far. But it could be.

The trouble with Birmingham—and with most southern industry—economically, is that it is owned by the North. It is a tributary region. Northern hands take the dollars out of its pockets almost as rapidly as it puts them in. Its chronic depression will not be solved by further industrialization controlled by northern capital. And while dreamily contemplating the ivy twining higher around the crumbling white columns of a gracious southern past, the rest of the U. S. would do well to remember that if the per capita income of each Southerner were raised from its present $285 to the national average of $485, the nation would have captured a new market half again as big as the entire export trade, and would be richer by billions. (6)

If Hitler annexed the Russian Ukraine to the industrial Reich, the combination would produce an economy and a territory similar in many respects to the Middle States. Of all the regions, this one is most nearly independent of the others, could most easily drop out of the Union and survive as an independent nation. One of the world's greatest agricultural sections, it ranks second only to the Northeast as an industrial region. It has few imports, many exports, and its economy has been developed to a point where it processes its own raw materials and sells both commodities and finished goods.

The region is also second to the Northeast in the extent of urbanization, its cities being strung like beads around the shores of the Lakes, from Cleveland to Milwaukee—close to the docks of the freighters that carry through Sault Sainte Marie locks more tonnage than clears the Suez or the Panama. Behind this arc of cities lies a farming checkerboard, waving with yellow corn, black with plowed earth, and dotted with fat red silos, magnificent barns. Here—in addition to some 60 percent of the nation's corn—are half the hogs and the greatest number of pure-bred, registered cattle in the U. S., half of all the creamery butter, 70 percent of the factory cheese, more than 40 percent of the milk. Here are more than a third of the chickens laying nearly 40 percent of the eggs.

Your typical farmer of the region is a staunch individualist, yet nowhere will you find a man more eager to be taught or more willing to make sacrifices for coöperative ventures. He knows soil chemistry, avidly follows the experimentation going on at his state agricultural college. He has successfully used his political power time and again. He is probably the most completely democratic individual in the entire U. S., and he knows how to make democracy work for him. (7)

West of the states bordering the Mississippi the last few vertebrae are ironed out of the land and the roads shoot westward like black arrows. Wheat stretches to the right of the road and to the left, and behind and ahead, and a few miles across the lonely flatness you see the combines spouting chaff. That treetop standing like a semaphore ten miles beyond your radiator cap means a farmhouse, and that gray smudge ten miles beyond the tree, a town. And when the wind blows hard, as it so often does, the tan dust eddies up above the tossing wheat and an iridescent curtain dims the sun.

The eight Plains states cover almost a quarter of the nation—but support only a twentieth of the U. S. people. The reason is simply that this land is not productive enough to provide a living for its inhabitants. It is certainly the least independent U. S. region.

The area's most important resource is the land itself, a resource of diminishing value. Mined for wheat during the years of the war wheat boom, the Plains states contain 165,000,000 acres of the most seriously eroded land in the U. S. By 1930 the region was growing half the U. S. wheat, and had become the largest sheep raiser, and ranked second in horses and cattle. But its cows give less milk than other cows, and its horses and chickens are valued lower at the market. Always arid, the Plains have been experiencing a chronic drought for nearly ten years, and farmers can sit on their front porches and watch their livelihoods blowing away into the sky. As land reverts to the government by default of taxes, much of it is returned to its original grass. Timothy and alfalfa replace wheat on thousands of acres, and the agronomists work ceaselessly to discover new crops suitable for the parched soil, new ways of utilizing the last drops of the scanty rain that falls. (*8*)

Politically the youngest of the regions, the Southwest is a colonial economy exporting vast quantities of raw materials, importing most fabricated goods. Texas, bigger than any European nation except the U.S.S.R. and Germany, grows more than a fourth of U. S. cotton and claims that it could supply the entire world. It furnishes close to 40 percent of U. S. crude oil. It supports 7,000,000 head of cattle. Thanks to a $100,000,000 investment in irrigation ditches, the lower Rio Grande valley has already become a large producer of oranges, lemons, and grapefruit, and a distinct worry to California citrus growers.

Nearly all of this fabulous wealth is in East and Central Texas. West Texas blends into the New Mexico-Arizona Southwest, with "centers" (not cities) separated by scores of miles of empty desert, incredible conformations of the land, always the hot sun, the high, dry air, the giant, theatrical, green cacti standing like sentries against the sky. Phoenix, where fences separate cactus desert from irrigated fields of lettuce, orange groves, and every fruit and vegetable, is a spectacular working model of what other parts of the region may someday hope to be. In addition to the $77,500,000 annual copper output, tourists constitute a main source of income in Arizona and New Mexico, approximately $48,000,000 being spent by visitors. (9)

In the Far West, Nevada and California combine to form an almost indescribable region, with the infinite variety of California on one side of the mountains and the wild Nevada desert on the other. California has the fourth highest total income in the U. S., whereas Nevada keeps herself going mainly by virtue of spinning roulette wheels and the complacent magistrates handing down three thousand six-week divorces per year in Reno, "The Biggest Little City in the World."

Since Sutter's Mill in '48, California has produced something like $2,000,000,000 in gold, and its gold production is still worth more than $40,000,000 a year—including the driblets panned by thousands of prospectors working the streams and earning from a quarter to $5 a day. But more important than the gold is agriculture. Virtually no crop refuses to grow in California, and practically no crops are overlooked, although citrus is the leading one. The state's economy is in transition between the raw-material exporting economy of the Southwest and the agricultural-industrial economy of the Middle West. (*10*)

Although the Pacific Northwest was explored by Lewis and Clark around 1805, its intensive settlement did not begin until the Northern Pacific linked Chicago with Seattle in 1883. Today this region grows over a fifth of the nation's apples, a quarter of the cherries, nearly a third of the pears, a tenth or more of the potatoes, onions, strawberries, green peas, and dry beans. However, its greatest source of wealth is its forests, representing about half the standing saw timber in the U. S. Over 50 percent of all wage earners in Pacific Northwest manufacturing are employed in lumber industries. Currently the annual cut runs ahead of the new growth by about two to one, and the region is becoming pocked with stranded communities decaying in the devastated cutover areas. Safe from destruction are 70,000-odd square miles of forest in U. S. government land—land that amounts to 48 per cent of the region's total.

The region is in competition with practically every part of the country. Its lumber competes with southeastern lumber; its wheat with the Middle West and Plains states; its orchards with the Northeast; its sheep and wool with the Southwest; and so on.

Meanwhile, the Pacific Northwest must import nearly all finished goods, as well as oil, sugar and other commodities. The region's markets are thousands of miles away, and freight eats up from a quarter to a half of the farmer's wholesale price in the East.

Conversely, the region is squeezed when it buys eastern manufactured goods. However, these are familiar troubles in a pioneer economy, and the region will unquestionably outgrow them. Its potentialities are great: it has, for example, about 40 percent of all U. S. potential water power, and vast mineral deposits of zinc, lead and silver. (*11*)

Such is the sweep and magnitude of the U. S. A. On the map this gigantic slab of earth confronts us with here a thumb thrust toward the warm Caribbean, and there a fist reaching for icebergs in the North Atlantic. Here is the cool loveliness of velvet lawns in New England, and here a black-shadowed date grove in Phoenix under a sun that burns like mustard plaster. Here are palms tossing on the Louisiana shore, and here the high Sierras with their snowy crests floating like swans in the tall blue sky. Here is New York at night, hell-red with Neon, and here is a lone rider herding sheep on an empty Wyoming plateau. Here is the whole lavish land, so vast its horizons exhaust the eye, so turbulent with beauty, ugliness, terror, and hope that it wears a thousand faces and speaks with 10,000 tongues. (*12*)

If the political boundaries of our states coincided with the economic boundaries, then the area now known as the U. S. would be far less potent, far less rich than it is. Then New England would be struggling for food, and in the Northwest an automobile would be as rare as in other agricultural countries that have difficulty accumulating foreign exchange. It is when the Aluminum Co. of America contracts for water power in Oregon that the U. S. is created. It is when the rich coupon clippers on Manhattan are taxed to help build highways in empty Nevada that the U. S. lives. Every time a freight train crosses a state line, every time a purchasing department makes up its mind to buy an out-of-state commodity, the U. S. grows greater. For in these events, as in thousands of others, one is working for all, and all for one.

This action is like that within a huge retort in which dissimilar substances mix and compound, to create a new substance greater than the sum of its component parts. That new substance is what we know as the U. S. A. This is why the U. S. has become great.

And in this compounding the U. S. citizen has come to be a veritable superman—having the largest per capita share of the world's coal and corn and iron ore and wheat and electricity and automobiles and bathtubs and radios and telephones and machines in general. (*13*)

And it is significant that all the serious problems that now confront the U. S. are problems of abundance, not poverty. They are problems of maintaining a high standard of living; of an overwhelming desire to keep democracy and make it work, even at the price of suffering. The advance of technology has been too rapid, throwing millions out of work. The productive power of labor is too great, and there is too much capital accumulation in the form of savings. The fact is that the U. S. is faced with problems different from those in almost any other country in the world, and these problems have their origins in the colossal achievements of the U. S. (*14*)

QUESTIONS

I

1. In what respects is the U. S. not the greatest nation on earth? What paradoxes are there between its production and consumption of certain commodities? (*1*)
2. Upon what does the greatness of the U. S. rest? (*2*)
3. In what ways are the people themselves paradoxical? (*3*)
4. What is the correct measurement to apply to America? Of what is the nation really composed? (*4*)
5. Give the land and climate characteristics, the economic resources and problems, and the potentials for future development of the Northeast (*5*), the Southeast (*6*), the Middle States (*7*), the Plains States (*8*), the Southwest (*9*), the Far West (*10*), the Pacific Northwest (*11*)
6. What would separate political units within the country do to it? What has their absence made the U. S. citizen? (*13*)
7. In what way are the problems of the U. S. different from those of other nations? (*14*)

II

1. This article says little of the morale and ideals of the American people. What part do you think the spiritual qualities of a people, in contrast to their material wealth, contribute to their greatness? In what way does wealth aid and in what way does it hinder the development and the preservation of self-reliance in a people?
2. It is estimated that every American has the equivalent of thirty slaves working for him. Name and explain some of the most important of these "slaves."
3. This article reveals that we are, in many ways, not a self-sufficient nation. Can you think of any practical solutions of the problem? How has war proved that we are not self-sufficient? Is the national insufficiency greater than we had assumed? What do you think our future policy in foreign trade should be?
4. Certain states have tried to tax or exclude goods coming from other states. Discuss the effect, if generally practised, of such procedure.

5. Do you believe that "All the smartest young people go east"? Do you know any persons who have done so? any students who have gone there?

6. If the country were broken up into a number of separate nations, in which one would you prefer to live?

7. How does the present-day farmer differ from his earlier prototype? In what ways is he the same? What is the conflict in interests between the farmer and the city dweller? Can you think of any solution to the problem? Do you believe the farmer has received an unfair portion of the national income in comparison with factory workers or skilled labor?

8. Does the reading of this essay leave you with a hopeless feeling that our national problems are too great to solve, or with an optimistic feeling that the future of America is secure? Analyze the reasons lying behind your conclusion.

III

1. Comment upon the language and style of writing from the viewpoint that this is primarily a factual article.

2. What are the words of transition which begin the affirmative trend of thought from the negative opening of the essay?

3. What is implied by saying that the Western plains were "mined for wheat"?

4. Why is the word *agronomists* (8) so much better as used here than its synonym *agriculturists* would have been? What does *agronomy* imply that *agriculture* does not?

5. Read aloud the paragraph beginning: "Such is the sweep and magnitude of the U. S. A." Comment upon the descriptive quality of the prose in this paragraph. If you think it is a well-written summary of the physical greatness of our country, analyze why it is so successful a piece of writing.

THEME TOPICS

1. America: An Enigma to the World
2. The Problem of American Abundance
3. My Visit to Hollywood (a Ranch, a Lumber Camp, a Factory)
4. My Racial Ancestry
5. The Corn Belt (Deep South, Rural New England, Dust Bowl, Picturesque Southwest, Fabulous California)
6. The Source of American Strength
7. Soil Reclamation (Reforestation)
8. The Best Field of Work to Prepare For
9. The Effect of Technology upon Labor
10. The American Farmer: A Coöperative Individualist

WORDS

Point out the correct synonym, from the right-hand column, for each word in the left-hand column.

1. achievement (*1*)	1. unbelievable
2. diverse (*2*)	2. eluding
3. cosmic (*2*)	3. very dry
4. integrated (*2*)	4. many-colored
5. optimum (*2*)	5. mysterious
6. enigma (*3*)	6. true
7. illiterate (*3*)	7. continuous
8. circumventing (*3*)	8. vast as the earth
9. components (*4*)	9. eagerly
10. traversed (*4*)	10. constituent parts
11. cabalistic (*5*)	11. accomplishment
12. garners (*5*)	12. puzzle
13. chronic (*6*)	13. returns to
14. urbanization (*7*)	14. self-satisfied
15. avidly (*7*)	15. unable to read
16. iridescent (*8*)	16. different
17. eroded (*8*)	17. laid waste
18. arid (*8*)	18. powerful
19. reverts (*8*)	19. traveled over
20. incredible (*9*)	20. profuse
21. complacent (*10*)	21. the best
22. devastated (*11*)	22. unified
23. lavish (*12*)	23. worn away
24. potent (*13*)	24. citification
25. veritable (*13*)	25. gathers

MAIN STREET IN 1940: SIGOURNEY, IOWA

DALE KRAMER

D URING the 'twenties a whole school of writers gained
a comfortable living by the relatively simple process of
ridiculing Main Street. Sinclair Lewis was discoverer
and a chief exploiter of the vein, his works being largely responsible for the assumption that America's commercialism sprang
from the small town. H. L. Mencken agreed but added a bitter
charge of responsibility for Prohibition.

Doubtless the arraignment was not without some justification
on both counts. A success itself, Main Street, like any self-made
man, was willing to advise others on the proper conduct of their
private and public affairs. And it was but natural that the pioneers, since prosperity came only through hard work and sacrifice, frowned on such time-wasting frivolities as whisky
drinking, dancing, card playing, and overindulgence in the reading of books.

But, when, through Prohibition, they succeeded in at least partially forcing their code on the rest of the nation, the intellectuals
of the cities rebelled, and were joined by the less inhibited sons
and daughters of Main Street who had fled their environment.
The fight became so extensive that the loudest anti-Main Street
gun, Mencken's *American Mercury*, became the 'twenties' symbol of sophistication and the founders of the *New Yorker* established the urbanity of their venture by simply casting an aspersion
or two on "the old lady from Dubuque."

Unfortunately, most of the anti-Main Street crusaders turned
to political and economic pontification after the stock-market
crash of 1929, leaving the small town and its affairs largely unre-
ported these last ten years. What, for example, was the effect

From *The Forum*, April, 1940. Used by arrangement with, and permission of, Dale Kramer.

of the depression itself on Main Street civilization? Of repeal? Of the New Deal? In short, how does the Main Street of today compare with that of the Lewis-Mencken era? (*1*)

To answer this question, the writer has examined the business, social, and cultural—with slight excursions into the political and religious—life of Sigourney, Iowa. Sigourney is a Midwestern county-seat town untypical only in that it was named after a poetess, the now almost forgotten Lydia Hunt Sigourney, sweet singer of the middle nineteenth century.

The business houses serving the town's two thousand odd inhabitants and the surrounding farm population are set in a square around a neat, green park in the middle of which rises a three-story stone courthouse, with a six-foot town clock in its tower—the traditional courthouse square. Other essentials of Main Street life necessary for the survey—neat Carnegie library, prosperous movie theatre, the dozen odd bridge and study clubs, a new liquor dispensary—are present, and a touch of color is lent by the community's proximity to two favorite place names of the old Main Street baiters: What Cheer, twelve miles to the west, and Oskaloosa, twenty. (*2*)

Main Street's economy—the manner in which it gets a living—is properly the first segment of its life to come under examination. Here one is struck by three major circumstances: the small community's relative prosperity, dependence for the latter on a myriad of federal agencies, and, last but not least, the decline of what was loosely known as Babbittry. (*3*)

It is only necessary to glance around Sigourney's square to see that businessmen are once more feeling good after the dark years of the early 1930's. At night one may count no less than twenty gleaming neon signs, and a surprising proportion of the business houses have been remodeled inside and out. The visual impression is confirmed by local bankers, who declare that a majority of businessmen are making a living out of their establishments and that a few manage to put money aside. The percentage of merchants who are solvent is about the same as in the 'twenties, but profits are generally less.

The reason put forward by these local observers for recovery is increased business efficiency. Not so long ago there was much talk of the local merchant's being driven to the wall by chain-store competition, but now he fears the chain unit no more than any other rival—although confident that his profit would be larger if the combination were legislated out of business. Careful buying, excellent display of goods, and strict cash selling have largely solved this phase of the small-town merchant's problem. (4)

The effort to dissolve another difficulty, that of out-of-town trading, has been less successful. Shopping is a major pastime of women everywhere, and those of small communities have more and more taken advantage of the automobile and hard roads to visit the larger stores of nearby cities. As trade slackens, the stocks of those Main Street merchants most affected—dealers in dry goods, wearing apparel, and furniture—narrows, accelerating the trend.

Fittingly—though it is considered a none too healthy development by most economists—the place of leadership formerly held by these businesses has been taken by dealers in the commodity chiefly responsible for their decline, the automobile itself. Sigourney has fourteen garages and service stations, some of them the best money-makers in town. Even lawyers, the writer was informed by a prominent local attorney, find a chief source of income in a motorcar by-product—litigation over highway accidents. (5)

Thus Main Street merchants showed courage and adaptability in meeting the impact of depression and the encroachment of outside competition. But, speaking generally, they refuse to recognize the extent to which the federal treasury is responsible for lifting the black fog which enveloped them at the end of 1932—an error not indulged in by such a conservative guardian of the public purse as the *Saturday Evening Post*, which often speaks bitterly of Iowa and other hinterland States which draw more money out of the national treasury than they pay in.

There have been the AAA, CWA, PWA, WPA, CCC, FSA, FCA, SSA, SERA—a mouthful for any anti-New Deal orator. They commandeered all available extra space in the courthouse, including the old Assembly Room, crowded the offices under the new post office, and finally overflowed into private buildings. But each has done its bit toward priming the town pump, and more than a little of the water flowing from the spout still comes through the top rather than from the bottom of the well.

Most important, of course, are the AAA and other agricultural agencies, for Main Street merchants are naturally dependent on the patronage of farmers. The "gentle rain of checks"—averaging about $300,000 yearly for Keokuk County—has stimulated buying, while loans from the Farm Security and Farm Credit administrations have liquefied mortgages in the banks and furnished capital for purchase of operating equipment.

Fewer funds have gone directly to town residents, but even these sums have not been inconsequential. Sigourney was one of those many communities which, in the dark days of 1931-32, attempted a public-works program of its own. Men were employed to crush road-surfacing rock in a local quarry and were paid in scrip which eventually was retired by attachment of stamps representing 2 per cent of its face value. In theory, of course, business was to be stimulated by increased buying, but actually the community was only levying on itself a tax for relief, with most of the burden falling on merchants who honored the scrip for purchases. In effect the CWA and later the WPA took over the program, only substituting specie for scrip. Men still work in the quarry, crushing rock for the roads, and their income (employment peak was thirty men, monthly wage $40.50) is equal to a small factory's payroll. Added to this is a tidy community income from the seventy-five pensions paid to Sigourney's aged, as well as from salaries of various administrative officials.

From a short-range view the importance of this federal assistance is recognized, as when fifty Sigourney businessmen journeyed to Des Moines to protest removal of the CCC camp, but politically Main Street is a dogged opponent of New Deal "spending." Although Sigourney voters, angry and frightened, turned sharply against Herbert Hoover in 1932, they asserted their basic opposition to change four years later by giving Alf Landon a majority over President Roosevelt. Since that time, charges of radicalism leveled at the New Deal have sunk deeper. Main Street merchants definitely believe themselves a part of "business" and follow the lead of their big brothers in demanding a "chance." That it might only furnish them with an opportunity once more to finance public works without the aid of wealthier taxpayers who pay taxes in neither Sigourney nor Iowa they do not consider and probably will not. (6)

But, if Main Street has returned to the standpat political conservatism of Babbitt, it has not been so quick to readopt the rococo characteristics which made him a butt for wits of the 'twenties. The luncheon clubs meet as of old, with "right thinking" still very much the byword; but the tone is subdued. The early depression years crushed Main Street's pride, of course, reducing its self-assurance, but at least equally important is the fact that in the chastening process the small community developed an ability to look more objectively at itself. For example, Sigourney remembers with more than a little embarrassment the signs, BEST LITTLE CITY IN IOWA, which in the 'twenties adorned the roads leading into town. In short, Main Street took on a degree of sophistication during the past decade—a fact which is even more evident in other phases of community life. (7)

No Sigourney hostess has yet telephoned the society editors of the *Sigourney Review* and the *Keokuk County News* to announce that a cocktail party will be held on such and such a date or has reported Martinis in the list of refreshments at a bridge afternoon. When she does, it will be an anticlimax, for the Main Street society revolution has been won. A woman may now serve and drink liquor, in moderation of course, without loss of her honor. She may also smoke, though not on the streets or in public places.

The first guns in this battle were fired some years before the crash—witness the flapper, spiked beer, necking, and the Charleston—but it was not until the old guard had been weakened on the economic front, thereby losing faith in its own general infallibility, that the youthful hordes broke down the barriers of moral righteousness. There were other factors of course, advertising not being the least. When the first photographs of women smoking cigarettes appeared on billboards ten years ago, they were defaced, but the tobacco companies persevered, spending millions in all advertising fields. Their business judgment, it is now apparent, was good. Movies, too, played an important part in routing old taboos. Women members of the audience identified themselves with the heroine in all other things, and it was only natural that they first accepted, then emulated, her cigarette and cocktail.

But not all hostesses serve liquor, and the subject is still a little touchy. Thus this writer does not wish specifically to accuse any of Sigourney's bridge clubs (Idle-A-While, Fortnightly, Matron's, Pastime, Sigourney, Pleasant Hour) of these carryings-on. But the extent to which the moral wave has receded is symbolized by the prominently placed punch bowl, with alcoholic content, at the annual New Year's Eve banquet given by members of the Lion's Club and Junior Chamber of Commerce to their wives, the high point of the social season.

Like most Main Street towns, however, Sigourney is against the sale of hard liquor over the bar and certainly would outlaw the saloon by local option if the State had not already taken the responsibility (but 3.2 beer is available at three of the five cafés). The Sigourney drinker of hard liquor must first pay one dollar for a permit book, then secure his beverage by the bottle at the State-owned liquor store, where the purchase is entered in a book. His advantage is a 25-per-cent saving over what he would pay in New York, Illinois, or other States licensing private dealers.

Oddly enough, the shift to legal whisky and gin after Repeal was slow. Two factors seem to have been responsible. First, youthful drinkers, having known little or nothing else, actually preferred the taste of near beer spiked with alcohol. Second, older men were intimidated by the indignant eyes of the moral element peering through the plate-glass window of the converted bank building, as they waited furtively for their orders to be wrapped. As a result, illegal sale of liquor flourished for some years, until the drinking of liquor became respectable and the younger generation's taste had improved. A few bootleggers still exist, but their living is a poor one, gained from sales to minors and WPA-relief clients, who are barred from the State liquor store. But even this market is cut by the ability of nearly everyone to find an obliging friend or acquaintance who will make his purchase without fee.

No one can say with exactness, of course, whether the total consumption of intoxicants is more or less than during the 'twenties, but it appears that the increase in their use by the ladies is offset by a somewhat greater sobriety in the younger generation. Graver responsibility in an uncertain world, as well as better liquor, has undoubtedly contributed to the decline of drunkenness among youth, but more important is the simple fact that drinking lacks the romance of a decade ago.

In the pre-Prohibition period, a chief topic around high schools was the merit, price, and availability of "donkey," as raw alcohol was affectionately termed. Spines of eighteen-year-olds shivered delightfully as, automobile lights cut off, they drove up dark lanes to half-abandoned farmhouses and waited breathlessly for the bootlegger's mysterious emergence from the shadows. Reports went out of "tins" of the precious liquid buried here and there by the bulk-buying thrifty, and expeditions of the unscrupulous were organized to seek them out. It was high adventure, these young men and their girls sitting in restaurants beneath the inevitable "No Spiking" signs, hands busy under the table pouring alcohol into bottles of near beer; and often, in the excitement, too much was consumed, or the varying potency of the beverage wrought havoc with the drinker's judgment. A general rowdiness resulted, particularly at dances, where it was not uncommon for the young men of Sigourney to engage in mass combat with those of some nearby town—usually What Cheer, which Sigournians always considered an underhanded settlement, its young given to playing dirty in football and its elders not above the outright purchase of referees and umpires.

This is not to say, of course, that Main Street's youth suddenly eschewed all semblance of undecorous behavior. But the jitterbug is less raucous than the flapper, the whisky-and-lime-rickey-drinking young man less rowdy than the "donkey" tippler. (8)

Since to show the effects of repeal it has been necessary to dwell at some length on the drinking habits of Sigourney's population, it would seem well at this point to strike a balance with a report of the community's less frivolous activities.

It is possible to state, for example, that, despite their loss of the cocktail war, Main Street's church societies are still stronger in point of membership than the bridge clubs. Sigourney has its Methodist Guild, St. Mary's Altar Society (Catholic), Presbyterian Kensington Society, Women's Council of the Church of Christ, Evangelical Service Circle, Baptist Sew and So Society, to mention the chief groups, while several of the churches also maintain missionary societies. In these the neighborly, helping-hand spirit of an earlier pioneer society is maintained, although it is to be expected that the quiet atmosphere of the quilting circle suffers occasional disruption as members discuss a card party which is known to be going full blast at such and such a house on that very afternoon.

In certain respects, however, the churches have accepted modernization. For one thing, the old-fashioned fire-and-brimstone revival meeting is, in general, a thing of the past; most of the younger ministers are opposed to conversion by this method. The tendency to a calmer spiritual approach has also obliterated another familiar institution, the Sunday-school "contest." There was a day when Sigourney's Methodists so aggressively competed with those of Delta, seven miles to the west, that other Sunday schools were emptied. It is natural, too, that in an age of economic upheaval the preachers are taking a greater interest in social and political problems. (9)

Fitting into the older Main Street social pattern, too, are the numerous lodges, patriotic societies, and "study" clubs. Of these, only the latter have shown an inclination to change, and a discussion of them fits more smoothly into the next section, a consideration of the reading habits and other cultural phases of Main Street life.

Succeeding generations of Sigourney's youth have pulled open the heavy plate-glass door of the red-brick Carnegie library, piled their hats and coats on the broad shelf over the radiator at the top of the short flight of stairs, and padded silently across the rubber-matted floor to the bookshelves and magazine tables. On school nights, the heavy oak tables are surrounded by boys and girls of high-school age looking up assignments given them by their teachers; armloads of books are carried home by children of all ages. But somehow the library's presence has not resulted in an appreciation of contemporary literature.

Interest in the nation's major novelists is about nil. Theodore Dreiser is represented in the library by only a single work, his nonfiction *Twelve Men;* Sherwood Anderson by only *Poor White;* Hemingway by his latest, *The Fifth Column and the First 49 Stories.* There is no Wolfe, Caldwell, Dos Passos, or Faulkner. Of the important writers only Sinclair Lewis and Willa Cather are well represented, though excluded were the former's *Elmer Gantry* and the latter's *A Lost Lady.*

The fact is that Main Street's literary affairs are inexorably dominated by that singular figure of American letters, Zane Grey. Of 104 books purchased during the first half of 1939, twelve, mostly replacements of worn-out volumes, were from Mr. Grey's pen. Other popular authors but trailing at a considerable distance are Gene Stratton-Porter, Edna Ferber, Fannie Hurst, Lloyd C. Douglas, James Oliver Curwood, and Peter B. Kyne, while Edgar Rice Burroughs would undoubtedly fare very well if the librarian had not some years ago taken a notion to censor him by the simple process of neglecting to reorder his books. These, with mystery stories, nonfiction works on aviation and exploration (Admiral Byrd's *Alone* and Anne Lindbergh's *Listen! the Wind* were in some demand), and children's books comprise most of the titles which pass over the librarian's desk at an average rate of fifty a day.

The search for signs of vegetation in this wasteland is not very encouraging, although a few are discoverable. The most important educational force is the radio, and, if the literary tastes of Main Street improve, it will be largely because this institution takes fuller advantages of its opportunities. The possibilities are demonstrated by a sharp increase in demand at the public library for titles discussed by a book commentator on the Iowa State College station at Ames. Meanwhile the women's study groups hear book reviews and occasionally discuss a short story which has been read aloud from one or another of the "quality" magazines. Sigourney has its Stitch and Study Club and Women's Club, both devoting the major portion of each meeting to literary and educational subjects, while the Alpha Delphian Chapter regularly pursues a course of study laid out by its national officers.

Against these encouraging factors is the inability of the library to stock even a fraction of the volumes in which the community should be interested, and here the depression struck the small-town reader a hard blow. Looking about for a budget item to slash, the eyes of the town council were apt to light first on the library tax levy. For example, the Sigourney library's annual pre-depression budget for book purchases was two thousand dollars, against four hundred at the present time. After the purchase of replacements, there is naturally little remaining for the acquisition of new books. In querying the Sigourney library to discover the local attitude toward John Steinbeck's social and, from some points of view, slightly salacious novel, *The Grapes of Wrath*, this writer learned that the work created no problem—for the simple reason that, having spent its half-year budget, the library's board was not considering new books.

Thus, since the taste of Main Street's reading public has not developed to a point where it will clamor on its own account for more and better fare and because local councilmen are unlikely to increase taxes for a project they are apt to consider frivolous, any hope of returning the library item in the budget to the old figure seems to lie in a possible crusade by the women's study groups. They would be irresistible in such an action. Undoubtedly some groups have already brought pressure on their local law-making bodies; others, probably, have merely failed to think of it or are unaware that budgets are but a shadow of their former substance. (*10*)

Bearing more directly on Main Street's life than the library is the moving-picture theatre, and here it is possible to present a somewhat more encouraging report. Audiences are demanding a higher quality in plot, direction, and acting.

This is not to say, however, that the movie-going public has suddenly grown sophisticated. A survey of the Garden Theatre's offerings reveals Sigourney still partial to the he-man-who-doesn't-want-to-fight-but-has-to type of drama; and, despite the undoubted spurring of liquor drinking and cigarette puffing by the cinema, Sigourney is for the wholesome maiden against the slinky city gal every time. But the manager has been forced to cease booking the Buck Jones-Ken Maynard type of thriller, and even the so-called "horse operas" of the Gene Autry school command only mild interest. Now, when a *Dodge City, Stage Coach,* or *Union Pacific*—the old formula more expertly handled—appears on the horizon, he bills it for a four-day run, certain of packed houses. Of course, a picture made from one of Zane Grey's classics is sure-fire, let the producer do his worst.

When no outdoor melodrama is available, the Garden's manager tries to get one of the highly publicized stars in something with plenty of action and not too much sex. Thus Robert Taylor (his producers knew what they were about when he was set to swapping punches on more or less even terms with Wallace Beery) is more popular than the "smoother" Tyrone Power. Sonja Henie, with her skating and artlessness, is popular, and so are Fred Astaire and Ginger Rogers, particularly when they dance. Greta Garbo, Joan Crawford, Katharine Hepburn, and Bette Davis emote too freely, embarrassing onlookers. But the Main Street theatre audience is a young one, and the advancement in its taste, although a high degree has not yet been reached, furnishes a glimmer of hope for better things from Hollywood.

On the radio, Main Street likes the favorites of the rest of the nation, with such variations as might be expected from its taste in movies. A survey of Iowa's preferences made by Kansas State College in the spring of 1939 showed Jack Benny the favorite, with Charlie McCarthy second. A slick little fellow, Charlie lost esteem the further he got from the city, the range of popularity being great even between Iowa's cities and her villages. Other national programs followed at a considerable distance, with those of the Fibber McGee type gaining as they progressed into villages and rural areas. Few rooters were found for the darling of Manhattan's intelligentsia, "Information, Please!"

Besides these, Main Street has hardly any cultural contacts. Few books are purchased, while magazine consumption ranges from pulps up the scale to slicks, with readers of the latter apt to consider themselves somewhat highbrow. Naturally there is little or no access to the legitimate theatre, and that old cultural agent, Chautauqua, has for some time been dead or nearly so. Only slightly more life remains in another summer institution: the tent show, with its red-wigged comedian, dastardly villain, and heroine of most spotless virtue. But its final doom has been sealed by the improved critical judgment resulting from a diet of movies; increasing numbers view the melodramas as farce. Sigourney's chief interest in the annual approach of Hila Morgan's show is—and in fact has been for twenty years—whether Hila, admitting the encroachments of time, has at last ceased her portrayal of sixteen-year-old innocence. (11)

The major conclusion to be drawn from all this seems to be that, during the decade 1929-39, Main Street's domination of America's moral life ended. The small community's hold was broken by a defection in its own ranks, as the radio, movie, and automobile brought the ways of the city closer and as the prestige and authority of the older generation were shattered by its inability to cope with the depression.

Paradoxically, the modernizing process was accompanied by Main Street's readoption, under the pressure of hard times, of some older and simpler values. Besides deflating "boosterism," the depression rained calamities on well-to-do and poor so indiscriminately that women felt no strong necessity for competing in "appearances," which in turn reduced jealousy and its chief by-product, gossip. It is impossible to state categorically that the size of the electric refrigerator and the make and model of the family automobile have entirely lost their position as arbiters of Main Street social standings, but their influence has been greatly reduced.

There is danger, of course, that a business boom which may still result from the increased demand of warring European nations for U. S. farm products may upset the rural community's equilibrium, calling back the breast-thumping Babbitt. Benefit of the doubt, however, should go to Main Street. Babbittry, after all, resulted largely from the businessman's overweening confidence in his own abilities, and there could be little doubt in his mind that a war boom was owing to no stroke of genius on his own part. As for hysteria, it will certainly come with war, but memory of the stupidities committed during the last conflict should serve as a powerful deterrent to new ones. For two decades Sigourney has recalled with shame the day on which a mob paraded a harmless old German around the square, a sign, I AM A GERMAN SPY, attached to his back. Since officials were hardly interested in espionage agents of that sort (his crime was a Kaiser beard), Sigourney finally placed him on a train going out of town. Moreover, the Germans of Midwestern communities, now mostly second- and third-generation stock, are known to be unsympathetic to Naziism, and are therefore unlikely to be charged with undue friendliness to Hitler.

On the other hand, neither is there much chance that Main Street will depart further from its traditionally simple way of life; Mr. Mencken, Mr. Lewis, and their fellow travelers of yesteryear will have to be satisfied with a partial rout of Puritanism and a mere beginning of interest in "cultural" affairs. Yet much of the gap between the small town and the city was closed during the past decade—as much as probably ever will be. Meanwhile, as the urban center improves its civilization, if it does, Main Street will undoubtedly advance proportionately. (*12*)

QUESTIONS

I

1. Who were the chief Main Street "baiters" of the 'twenties and what charges did they bring against Main Street? Why have its attackers ignored it during the last ten years? (*1*)
2. Why did the author choose to investigate Sigourney, Iowa, and what are the typical features of the town? (*2*)
3. What three facts does the observer note about Sigourney's economy? (*3*)
4. What is the present condition of Sigourney's business and to what may that condition be ascribed? (*4*)
5. What is the greatest difficulty Sigourney business men face? How does one of its most successful businesses help to undermine the rest? (*5*)
6. What outside agencies help to account for its prosperity, and what is the attitude of the business men toward these agencies? (*6*)
7. What change did the depression produce in the self-assurance of conservative business men? (*7*)
8. What changes have come about in the Sigourney attitude toward smoking and drinking and in the use of liquor itself? (*8*)
9. What part do the churches and their societies play in Sigourney life? (*9*)
10. What are the people's preferences in reading? How did the depression affect this phase of their cultural life? (*10*)

11. In what way has Sigourney's taste in movies improved? What are its radio preferences? (*11*)
12. What general conclusions are to be drawn from the author's analysis? (*12*)

II

1. In what way would your analysis of a small town you know differ from that made of Sigourney, Iowa, as regards smoking and drinking, reading, motion pictures, radio programs, political conservatism?
2. Do you think the depression was the main cause of the business man's not being so sure about the correctness of his ideas?
3. Do you know any specific cases in which the depression acted as a "leveling" force in your community?
4. What would you do, as a citizen of a small town, to raise its cultural standards?
5. Have you any ideas about the problem of liquor that would help toward a sensible solution of it?
6. What is your attitude toward federal agencies "pouring" money into local communities? toward WPA, CCC, NYA, old-age pensions, workmen's security?
7. What is your attitude toward chain stores? toward out-of-town shopping?
8. Do you think Babbittry is as inactive in small towns as the author of this article seems to think it is?
9. Do you think small towns are the national safeguard against too great political liberalism and moral laxity?
10. Has Mr. Kramer painted a fair picture of the small town? After reading his essay, would you like to live in such a town as Sigourney, Iowa, if an opportunity presented itself to you to settle there in business or professional life?

III

1. In what way do the first four paragraphs serve as a historical background for this essay? (*1*)
2. What is the purpose of the short paragraph at the beginning of the section labeled (*9*)?
3. What is the author's attitude when he says "A picture made from one of Zane Grey's *classics* is sure-fire"?
4. What element of humor is there in the author's calling Mr. Mencken and Mr. Lewis "fellow travelers"?
5. What devices does the author use to make his writing convincing? Point out several examples of "documentation" which he uses.

WORDS

For each word at the left point out a synonym from the five words which follow it. Be careful not to confuse similarity of sound for similarity of meaning between words. Peculiarly enough, a word of exactly opposite meaning is often taken as the synonym of a word.

1. arraignment (*1*): arrangement, indictment, harangue, settlement, inelegance
2. inhibited (*1*): free, inhabited, joyless, deserted, restrained
3. sophistication (*1*): human enjoyment, material wealth, worldly wisdom, earthly desires, mundane success
4. urbanity (*1*): influence, greed, politeness, patience, conceit
5. aspersion (*1*): abatement, abundance, abuse, astonishment, alienation
6. pontification (*1*): agreeable surprise, dogmatic pronouncement, sincere regret, startling announcement, political acumen
7. myriad (*3*): magnified, meritorious, meticulous, multitudinous, maudlin
8. accelerating (*5*): retarding, hastening, aiding, hindering, satisfying
9. rococo (*7*): raucous, potent, effete, inquisitive, ornate
10. infallibility (*8*): uncertainty, inaccuracy, nonconformity, inerrability, expertness
11. taboos (*8*): restrictions, duplications, diseases, eccentricities, desires
12. emulated (*8*): impeded, facilitated, imitated, gratified, rejected
13. intimidated (*8*): initiated, intimated, overawed, encouraged, overburdened
14. furtively (*8*) openly, secretly, confidently, hesitatingly, boldly
15. unscrupulous (*8*): unprincipled, untutored, unconquerable, unswerving, unfortunate
16. eschewed (*8*): escaped, lessened, welcomed, shunned, denied
17. undecorous (*8*): becoming, fitting, appropriate, unbecoming, flattering
18. obliterated (*9*): built up, wiped out, walled in, shut away, cast down
19. inexorably (*10*): exclusively, willingly, inflexibly, remorselessly, excruciatingly
20. salacious (*10*): saline, salutary, licentious, prudish, voracious
21. defection (*12*): defect, desertion, deduction, degradation, decision
22. paradoxically (*12*): self-contradictory, unquestionably, self-evident, unerringly, self-explanatory
23. categorically (*12*): partially, reliably, naturally, explicitly, dubiously
24. equilibrium (*12*): balance, unbalance, weight, gravity, force
25. overweening (*12*): meek, trustful, timid, ruthless, arrogant

THEME TOPICS

1. Main Street as I Know It
2. What Radio Has Done for American Culture
3. Stores on Our Main Street
4. Shopping in a Big City
5. The Drinking Problem As I See It
6. The Small Town: The Bulwark of Decency
7. Small-Town Sophistication
8. I Would (Would Not) Like to Live in a Small Town
9. Cultural Forces in My Community
10. My Favorite Radio Program

AN AMERICAN HOME

DELLA T. LUTES

TIMES there have been and many, in the years that lie between my youth in Southern Michigan and now, when memories of the homes I knew so intimately have seemed the only safe and sane anchor to cling to in a muddled world. One of these stands out with special clarity, not because it differed greatly from a hundred others, but because, thinking of it often as I have, it has become to me a symbol of what the American Home then was; of what, in spirit, it should be now; and what, if we could once get and cling to the vision, it might become again. That was the house where the Mason family lived—Uncle Jed, Aunt M'ri', and their flock of children, with an ever-fluctuating occupancy of hired men, visiting seamstresses, transient book-agents, school-teachers, tin-peddlers, and comp'ny. A plain, homely, squat old house it was—but what a home!

I can see it clear as day, brooding there beside the country road, close to the ground, a wing to the north where the spare bedroom opened off the front room, and another to the south which held kitchen and woodshed with a loft overhead where boys and hired men slept. I recall the doorstep over which gay wedding guests and faltering pallbearers' feet trod, the frost-thickened windows, and the soap-stones, salt-bags, and stone jugs heated to guard against a frigid night. Warm and glowing in the raw Michigan winters, it was yet a simple house, lacking not only the elegance but the actual space of many of its neighbors. There was just the front room, large and square, and another—long and wide, used for eating, sewing, and sitting. The front room was for comp'ny and for the girls' beaux. In this dining-sitting room were a dilapidated old lounge where Uncle Jed

From *The American Mercury*, May, 1936. Used by permission of Della T. Lutes and *The American Mercury*.

stretched himself of a winter's evening, and Aunt M'ri's rocking chair where she sat to knit mittens, wristlets, and scarves for the boys, and petticoats for the girls. Also, of course, the chunk stove, an unconscionably long dining table, and innumerable chairs of all sizes and shapes. (*1*)

Uncle Jed's was a large family—five girls and two boys, appallingly large according to the present average, but no larger than most families in that day and community. When people married they expected to have families and built their houses accordingly. The two boys—one in his early twenties and the other several years older and bordering upon the ludicrous state of bachelorhood—having finished with school, worked with their father on the farm. That was what boys expected to do until they came of age and were able to set up for themselves, either on the same farm (but in a separate house) or on a rented one until they could buy. The girls went to school as long as they cared to and then stayed at home until they married. Occasionally one more valorous than the rest cut loose from the parent branch and went out to teach "deestrick" school, but there were very few other vocations open and girls looked upon marriage and the making of a home as the natural—and desirable—consummation of life, and prepared themselves accordingly for this estate.

And that was what a home was for. That was the obligation a man took upon himself when he married—to build a refuge for those for whom he was responsible, a harbor of safety during all their youth, a sure retreat in case of later need, a haven of comfort and welcome in time of trouble. That was why homes had front rooms—to provide a place for courtings, for weddings, for reunions, for the honoring of guests, for all the essential rites and ceremonies attendant upon and necessary to family life.

Uncle Jed was a pretty well-to-do farmer and so when the older girls reached the courting age he bought a new Brussels carpet for the front room (huge, overrunning urns of roses with ivy trailing), window shades of green paper with gaudy peacocks trailing their gay tails across the bottom, and lace curtains. He had bought a melodeon some years before, and Cordelia, the eldest, had taken lessons. She played the *Battle of Waterloo* (with variations) and *Moonlight on Killarney*. A younger sister,

Flora, took singing and elocution. She often recited for company
and was in demand at school exhibitions and church affairs. Together the sisters sang *Whispering Hope, Juanita,* and *Listen to
the Mocking Bird*—the boys whistling the refrain. They had even
learned one musical duet together in which they crossed hands.
The girls worked happily about the home, sewed, pieced quilts
(still hoping, the gossips said), gathered and preserved fruits,
even went into the fields to help in times of stress, attended
church, went visiting, sang, played games, danced.

Uncle Jed and Aunt M'ri' were getting along in years. Uncle
Jed had turned most of the hard work over to the two boys and
the hired man, and the girls did the housework. Cordelia, besides
being a musician, was something of an artist and spent considerable time at her easel; Flora had her elocution to master and was
often heard declaiming from some upper room. In spite of this
there was never any confusion, never, seemingly, any work left
undone, and always an amazing quantity of food on hand. Only
a thorough knowledge of the necessary routine and a technique
resultant upon training and experience could have accomplished
such apparent wonders. The law of the house, as of all other
houses of that day, was order. The woman who did not manage
her housework according to a system was stamped as a poor
manager if, indeed, she did not fall to the lower estate of slat-
tern. There had to be order to accomplish the necessary ends of
housekeeping.

Aunt M'ri' had rheumatism and took it easy. There were, however, certain household rituals wherein she still remained supreme,
as in the making of sausage and mincemeat at butchering time,
the pudding for Christmas, and dyeing the rags for a new carpet in spring. No one else could reach the acme of perfection
in the seasoning of sausage—that exact proportion of sage to rose-
and-ivory flesh—or that transcendent flavor upon which the complete success of mince pies depends. Neither were the girls able,
try as they might, so to mingle butternut shuck and sumac bud
as to get that lovely shade of reddish brown which their mother
could do. So, Aunt M'ri' was still supreme house-mistress in her
own right, although she nodded in the sun of a winter's day,
and pottered about in her garden during the summer. (2)

Uncle Jed often drove to town. He liked to saunter into the grocery store, help himself to a link of boloney or a piece of cheese, a fist-full of crackers from the barrel, a pickle from a keg by the door, and, comfortably munching, join a group about the pot-bellied stove with a wooden spittoon at one side and a checker board lying athwart a cask on the other. Uncle Jed did not play checkers, but he liked to look on for a while. The action, however, was too slow for a man with errands to do, so after he had exchanged views on the weather, the price of hogs and wheat, picked up any stray advertising matter that might lie around the counters, and filled his pockets with purchases of candy, peanuts, and oranges, he would go his way.

He usually took to town with him a small load of grain, apples, potatoes, crocks of butter, and baskets of eggs, to exchange for a piece of beef or what groceries were needed. Possibly some spools of thread or a yard of cambric for the girls. They went themselves to do more personal trading. And quite often he carried someone home with him. It might be a friend of the family, or it might be an utter stranger. Uncle Jed's hospitality did not stop at known quantities. There was always a spare bed (according to the standards of homemaking and hospitality) and plenty to eat. There was always an invitation to the chance guest to pull up and have some dinner. "Aw—come on, no matter if you have et, you can put down a piece o' pie!" Or "Put up yo' ho'ses and stay all night." A far more common form of hospitality than is the mendacious "Drop in and see us sometime" of today, and infinitely more sincere.

Uncle Jed loved bringing someone home, especially on Saturday nights. And, as a matter of fact, the family also loved it. Along about dark they would begin to watch for him. As the piebald team hove in sight down by the cross-roads, their jogging pace quickened by the sight of home, eager faces would peer from window and door. "Has he got anybody?" "Can you tell who it is?"

He liked best to bring someone who was in need of good food and strong nourishment. Someone half ill, run down, or low in spirits. Let such a one—butcher or candlestick-maker—so much as mention a depressed state of mind or a questionable condition of health and Uncle Jed was upon him. "You come along home 'th me. Some good fried salt-pork gravy and taters 'll put flesh on yer bones." (3)

Once, having occasion to consult a lawyer—an unusual occurrence in his life—he called upon the son of an old acquaintance, a young man, unmarried, and with a shingle still swinging rather listlessly in the legal wind. The man had been ill with a bad cold, and looked wretched. He apologized for frequent use of his handkerchief and immediately Uncle Jed forgot all former reason for his visit. Nothing would do but the young man must go home with him. The lawyer demurred, made a feeble argument for business, could not think of thus thrusting himself, a stranger—

"Fiddlesticks!" Arguments fell before Uncle Jed's forceful insistence. "I'm goin' home about four o'clock. You be to Green's store—I got to get some cheese and things—"

Bundled in muffler, ear-laps, arctics, overcoat, and mittens, for this particular incident happened in winter, the young man was at Green's store at four o'clock, bag in hand, looking rather wan and sheepish, but wistful and eager as well. Arrived at the Mason Farm, the guest, a stranger to everyone in the house, was welcomed as if he had been expected for the last six months and fate hung upon his arrival. One divested him of wraps. Another drew a chair up to the stove—a fire would be laid in the front room as soon as the boys came in. Aunt M'ri' assured him that supper was all ready, just waiting for them to come. So there he sat, drowsily lolling in the downy lap of warmth and content, voices flowing melodiously about and over him, occasionally addressed to him. Was he getting warm? Wouldn't he like a drink of fresh milk? The boys were just in with it—some people who came there loved it—others couldn't bear it. Supper was all but on the table.

Uncle Jed came in, drew his old armchair to the other side of the stove, and took from his pocket the weekly paper. He had no need to talk. They had talked all the way home. He had learned from his young guest all that he felt concerned to know about the city's and the nation's problems. He had inquired regarding his family relations, manner of living, state of health, and business. He had brought him safely into the bosom of his family;

now he would, for the time being at least, feel no further responsibility toward him. A man who couldn't take care of himself, once delivered into a home like this, was poor timber for visiting.

The guest was grateful for the consideration. All he wanted, at the present time, was just this good warm fire, this old comfortable chair, the sight of these friendly faces, the smell of hot, odorous food wafting in from the kitchen.

In the meantime the boys had come in—and the hired man as well—scrubbed to luminosity, hair sleeked, pants pulled down over boots, clean wam'uses over sweaty shirts. They were introduced. They shook hands vigorously and assured the city feller that they were pleased to meet him, accompanied by shy glances that almost convinced him of their sincerity. One of them built the fire in the front room. Another helped, fetching kindling and wood to fill the box. The eldest son stood about making awkward inquiries as to the guest's health, greatly to his embarrassment. He was beginning to feel that just a place at that already bountifully-laid table would immediately put him amongst the halest of the hale; that even to speak of noisome disease would be repulsive to a lusty man—like him. Eagerly, hungrily, he awaited the call to supper. (4)

In a family the size of Uncle Jed's, where there were never less than nine at the table and usually from one to three extra, preparing any meal was a considerable undertaking. Two of the girls did the cooking. Some of the others set the table. Amongst them all there was a constant passing to and fro from kitchen to dining room, from there to the front room to watch the fire, to see that the spare bedroom was heating, and down cellar. It was like a pageant, a moving, stirring spectacle of homely family life.

With so large and so hearty a family there must of necessity be quantities of food at every meal, although supper was counted a slight one. Choice of food depended largely upon the season, but with a richly-stocked cellar in which was a variety of winter vegetables, countless jars of preserves and pickles, rows of smoked hams sewed into whitewashed bags, the ubiquitous pork barrel, with a large butt'ry in which were stored dry groceries, flour, crackers, and sugar, there was never any lack in either quantity or quality, even though diversity might be wanting.

The guest from the city, finally invited to draw up, was by this time in so febrile a state from aggravation of eye and ear and nose that he was barely able to wedge himself, a mere vacuum of human propensities, into the place reserved. Well-accustomed though he may have been in his own home to a not unplentiful supply of food, his eye was gorged, his digestion barely able to wait on appetite. But, Christian man though he may have been, it was many years since his head had lowered in acknowledged gratitude for the food he was about to eat, and he was suddenly abashed in his own ardor as Uncle Jed stood with hoary head bowed before his plate, and, lifting his hand for silence, raised his benign voice in simple supplication for a blessing on the food before them.

The guest lifted his eyes to rest with renewed deference upon his patriarchal host. His greed subsided. Food took its proper place in the category of human needs. Hospitality, friendliness, beneficence, kindliness—where, when, had he last heard these words? Appreciatively, thoughtfully, he took in the scene before him. A snow-white cloth with napkins; lustrous china, banded with gold. In the center of the table the caster—a customary accessory to table furnishing of that day—dignified, even elegant in its gleaming coat of silver, with the usual five bottles—vinegar, hot-sauce, mustard, salt, and pepper—in the revolving rack. At one end of the table a huge platter of thinly-sliced cold corned beef, wine-red, ivory-edged; and at the other a great tureen, the lifted cover of which revealed creamy cubes of potatoes drenched in golden butter; plates of hot bronze-cheeked biscuits napkin-covered and bread as well—generous slices of salt-risin' bread, freshly baked.

Neither Uncle Jed nor the hired man held much barter with biscuits. Uncle Jed's brief was not so much against biscuits as for bread. He liked salt-risin' bread because it had body to it. "So'thin' to clamp onto," he said as with evident relish he set his seventy-year-old teeth into a crusty slice. "Biscuits is all right for wimmen," conceded the hired man generously, "and children. But you take a man 'at's been out in the wood-lot on one end of a cross-cut saw all day, and he's got to have fodder 't's substantial." And so great loaves of bread came fresh from the oven on baking days—Wednesdays and Saturdays—with biscuits almost daily for the less manually employed.

Butter was put at both ends of the table, pound pats of butter, stamped with an ear of corn or a sheaf of wheat. Three times a week thick layers of cream were skimmed from long rows of tin pans into the stone churn, and from the churn, after due agitation on the part of the wooden dasher, came great lumps of yellow butter, ladled into a huge wooden bowl where it was "worked" over and over to free it from milk, then salted and moulded into pats for the table or crocks for trade. Butter, with ten or fifteen cows on the farm, was one of the most abundant of foods, and buttermilk served as fattening matter for the hogs.

Uncle Jed also kept bees, and so there was on this munificently abundant table a handsome glass dish in which lay a perfect comb filmed with transparent wax, ready to drip ambrosia at the touch of a knife. On the cover of the dish the word HONEY was stamped in fine embossed lettering. Another dish, also of glass (what would not a collector give for those things today!) held pickled pears, red-chestnut in color, glazed with syrup of nectar, and indented here and there with cloves—Aunt M'ri's pickled pears, the receipt for which has traveled down along the years. And for dessert, hot gingerbread fresh from the oven and preceded by such a heavenly aroma of molasses, cinnamon, allspice, and ginger as would start the sweat from a man's tongue. Gingerbread and whipped cream. A huge bowl, blue, with a weeping-willow beside a little bridge on its fat side, filled with it, heaped to capacity and more, its surface roughened into tiny peaks and minarets where the last few precious spherules dropped from the spoon. And even this godly dish not unaccompanied, for there was sauce. Sauce in a crystal compote upheld by lovely crystal hands, with small sauce-dishes each to receive its quota of royal damson plums and their rich red-purple syrup, tart and sweet together like the sun and rain which had brought them to perfection. And tea. Farmer folk had tea for supper. Coffee for breakfast, yes—coffee boiled in a tin pot and "settled" with a broken egg. But tea for dinner and tea for supper. Green tea, hot and strong, reduced to reason with milk and to a state of amiability with sugar. (5)

After supper the guest, in a state of mellowed somnolence, was escorted to the front room, and further honored. The family hearth, though it was but a sheet-iron chunk stove, had been lit for him. He was given the best chair. One of the girls (the eldest as being more seemly, since he was an unmarried man), showed him the newest pictures for the stereoscope. The eldest son, who had once broken loose from parental discipline and traveled as far west as Nebraska, brought forth a trophy—a buffalo's horns, polished and mounted in plush—a hatrack!

But Uncle Jed did not come in. His duties as host done, he had flopped down upon the lounge in the dining room to snooze. Neither did Aunt M'ri'. Her knitting in her hands, she drew her rocking chair a little nearer the stove, a little nearer Uncle Jed. The front room was for young folks and comp'ny. For her the comfort of the older fire, older things—each other. The hired man slid unobtrusively to a chair in full view of the front room, tilted it against the wall, and occupied himself with a toothpick.

The dishes had been washed. The girls came in. Cordelia went to the melodeon. Flora stood beside her. They all sang—a few old hymns, a few old songs. The boys replenished the fire. It was going to be a cold night. Finally the guest was asked if he would like to retire. They bade him good-night and hoped he would rest. They would call him in the morning. The eldest daughter preceded him into the bedroom, drew the shade, fussed around. One of the boys brought in a soapstone wrapped in a towel. The guest protested. He was never so pampered in all his life. As a boy he had slept in a room where snow blew in about the windows. They laughed, made friendly little remarks, bade him good-night again. Told him to leave the door into the front room open for better air and the remaining warmth....

And now he sinks into the ethereal depths of a feather bed. Lord! He had forgotten the heavenly softness of a feather bed! He draws a soft, light comfortable over his shoulders. He sniffs the odor from the sheets—lavender, as I live and breathe! And so white, so crisp, so clean, lace-trimmed (the lace tickles his nose). He sighs and burrows his face into the pillow. He is warm, content, happy. He has forgotten the strife of little men, their petty quarrels, their animosities, their greed, envy, enmity, their everlasting "lawin'." Before he left the office today he had been sunk in dejection. Partly due to illness, of course. But there had seemed so little to live for. He had not realized his own loneliness. Now he recognizes it as a cloud that has brooded over his spirits, hampered his thoughts.

But now—throughout this house—in this room and that, sleep people who are his friends. Almost, he feels—his family. They have welcomed him as one of themselves. They like him. Smiling a bit at his own sentiment he murmurs, "God bless Uncle Jed." And his last conscious thought is, "As long as there are Uncle Jeds in the world, and Aunt M'ri's—and grace before meat—" (6)

I have a neighbor today whose family numbers four. If all goes reasonably well, the man and his wife will continue to reproduce themselves for better or for worse. The eldest child, a girl, has finished with school and is working in an office. The boy is still in high school, his tenure hanging by a thread. The mother, not content with the limited income of her husband, has a part-time job outside. Their apartment consists of a living room, a small dining room, two bedrooms, a bath, and small kitchen. The boy sleeps on a cot set up each night in one place or another.

"Why don't you bring your young man in?" I have heard the father querulously ask his daughter. "I don't like the idea of you being out in a car till all hours of the night—or morning. When I was young I used to have to face the old man and all the family. And go home at ten. Hey, Mama?"

The mother sighs. The daughter sneers.

"Yeah? And did they all stick around in one room with a radio goin' and a smart-aleck kid makin' wisecracks? Not on your life."

"Well," the father regretfully admits, "we have no place to go—unless it's to bed."

"And I s'pose I can take to the street," the young smart-aleck derides. "Okay with me. I'd rather go, anyway."

Meals at this house are seldom on time, due to the irregularity of the mother's hours, and when ready they are sketchy and unappetizing. A can of salmon, potato salad from the store, tasteless bread, and a still more tasteless baker's cake. The children eat, not for pleasure, but to appease youthful hunger. Filled but never satisfied. The father eats—his inner eye envisioning the meals that graced the table of his boyhood home. Then they are off—the movies, the car, the street, or the living room and the radio. (7)

Sometimes I think the living room, that interloper which in a moment of mad modernity ousted the good old parlor and sitting room at one and the same time, has done more to cause the disintegration of family life and hospitality than any other one factor, except the complete rout of the spare bedroom. In the too-small kitchen with the unstocked cupboards which have replaced the good old butt'ry, there is neither room nor food for the impromptu guest. As for a casual overnight visitor, there is not the slightest chance. And where there were once a hundred homes like Uncle Jed's to one feeble imitation like my neighbor's, the opposite is now true. Uncle Jed's home is almost extinct, the other is found at every turn.

If America does need any one thing more than another it is a million homes based upon a modernized version of Uncle Jed's. A pantry well-stocked is a more self-respecting device any day than a cabinet furnished with a sugar bowl and spice rack. A cellar provisioned against the fangs of winter will in reality save time, energy, and money. An extra chair in the dining room, an extra bed in the house, a heart for hospitality, might do more for the peace of the world than armored cruisers or a league of something that does nothing. You cannot hate a man whom you have invited to sit at your table, and you cannot help feeling an interest in the welfare of one who has slept in your house.

No one would have us go back to the actuality of Uncle Jed's house, to its discomforts, inconveniences, and restrictions. Science and invention have brought us freedom from much that was unpleasant, from much that was actual suffering. But they have also driven out of our homes that gentle spirit of contentment in simplicity, of beneficence, of hospitality, which once made the American home. (8)

QUESTIONS

I

1. Where was Uncle Jed's home located, and what kind of house was it? (1)
2. Who were the members of the household, and what did each contribute toward making it a home? (2)

3. What was Uncle Jed's routine when he went to town, and what special guest did he bring home one winter evening? (*3,4*)
4. What were some of the good things served at the evening meal, and how was the guest entertained after supper? (*5,6*)
5. How did the home of the author's present-day neighbor differ from Uncle Jed's, and what deductions does the author draw from the contrast as to one of America's greatest needs? (*7,8*)

II

1. Did Uncle Jed's way of living have virtues not possessed in your home?
2. Do homes mean as much to us as they did to our parents and grandparents? What factors in American life have changed people's attitudes toward the homes in which they live?
3. Do you think modern girls have progressed or retrogressed in being so different from Uncle Jed's daughters? Do you know any girl who prides herself on being a good "manager" of a house?
4. Why, in present-day economy, has the country general store been replaced by other means of merchandising?
5. Was hospitality more sincere in earlier days than now? What social and economic changes are to be noted in our "visiting" habits from those in Uncle Jed's home?
6. Note that almost all that the Mason family ate—meat, vegetables, butter, bread, honey, pickles, and preserves—came from their own farm. Do you feel that we have lost something in our dependence on canned and packaged goods?
7. Name as many factors as you can that have contributed to the disintegration of the American home.
8. Do you agree that America needs most "a million homes based upon a modernized version of Uncle Jed's"? Would return to the friendly hospitality of early-day American homes aid materially in bringing peace to our troubled world?

III

1. The good artist, in writing as well as painting, uses idealization and contrast. Point out places in this essay where the author has used both to obtain the effects she desired.
2. Do you find the author's description of the Mason house vivid? Can you *see* the house? (*1*)
3. Do the descriptive phrases used of the evening meal convey sensory impressions that you can almost smell and taste? Point out all the words of this kind in section (*5*).
4. What artistic effect does the author obtain by the lawyer-guest's unfinished sentence "and grace before meat—"? (*6*)

5. What is the author's purpose in using such expressions as: "salt-pork gravy and taters" (3), "finally invited to draw up" (5), and "much barter with biscuits" (5)?

6. *Why* is the following statement amusing: "Green tea, hot and strong, reduced to reason with milk and to a state of amiability with sugar"? (5)

WORDS

Determine which of the following statements are true and which are false.

1. transient (1): A *transient* roomer lives permanently at a place.
2. unconscionably (1): An *unconscionably* long speech is likely to be enjoyable.
3. consummation (2): The *consummation* of a task is at the beginning of it.
4. transcendent (2): *Transcendent* happiness is seldom man's lot.
5. mendacious (3): A *mendacious* person is noted for telling the truth.
6. piebald (3): A *piebald* horse is dappled in color.
7. odorous (4): *Odorous* flowers have no scent.
8. luminosity (4): The *luminosity* of the sun hurts the naked eye.
9. noisome (4): Sewer gas has a *noisome* odor.
10. ubiquitous (5): A mosquito at night seems to be *ubiquitous*.
11. febrile (5): A calm person is seldom in a *febrile* state of mind.
12. propensities (5): A good mixer must have highly developed social *propensities*.
13. benign (5): A *benign* countenance is a stern one.
14. beneficence (5): A stingy man is not likely to be noted for his *beneficence*.
15. munificently (5): A generous man remembers his friends *munificently*.
16. somnolence (6): *Somnolence* induces a man to be alert.
17. ethereal (6): An *ethereal* thing is as light as air.
18. animosities (6): *Animosities* result in amiable relationships.
19. tenure (7): *Tenure* of office is the time during which a man holds it.
20. querulously (7): A discontented person is likely to complain *querulously*.
21. derides (7): I like a man who *derides* me.
22. interloper (8): An *interloper* has a right to be where he is.
23. modernity (8): Antiques are prized for their *modernity*.
24. disintegration (8) Defeat usually results in the *disintegration* of an army.
25. impromptu (8): An *impromptu* speech is a prepared one.

THEME TOPICS

1. My Grandfather's Home
2. I Stay at ——'s Apartment!
3. Modernizing the Farm House
4. Old-Time Hospitality
5. Company Is a Pleasure (a Nuisance)
6. Why the American Home Disintegrated
7. The Old Front Room
8. An Old Country Store
9. A Big Family Dinner
10. Real Homes: America's Greatest Need

ONE HUNDRED PER CENT AMERICAN

RALPH LINTON

THERE can be no question about the average American's Americanism or his desire to preserve this precious heritage at all costs. Nevertheless, some insidious foreign ideas have already wormed their way into his civilization without his realizing what was going on. Thus dawn finds the unsuspecting patriot garbed in pajamas, a garment of East Indian origin; and lying in a bed built on a pattern which originated in either Persia or Asia Minor. He is muffled to the ears in un-American materials: cotton, first domesticated in India; linen, domesticated in the Near East; wool from an animal native to Asia Minor; or silk whose uses were first discovered by the Chinese. All these substances have been transformed into cloth by methods invented in Southwestern Asia. If the weather is cold enough he may even be sleeping under an eiderdown quilt invented in Scandinavia. (1)

On awakening he glances at the clock, a medieval European invention, uses one potent Latin word in abbreviated form, rises in haste, and goes to the bathroom. Here, if he stops to think about it, he must feel himself in the presence of a great American institution: he will have heard stories of both the quality and frequency of foreign plumbing and will know that in no other country does the average man perform his ablutions in the midst of such splendor. But the insidious foreign influence pursues him even here. Glass was invented by the ancient Egyptians, the use of glazed tiles for floors and walls in the Near East, porcelain in China, and the art of enameling on metal by Mediterranean artisans of the Bronze Age. Even his bathtub and toilet

From *The American Mercury*, April, 1937. Copyrighted. Used by permission of *The American Mercury* and by arrangement with, and permission of, the author.

are but slightly modified copies of Roman originals. The only purely American contribution to the ensemble is the steam radiator, against which our patriot very briefly and unintentionally places his posterior. (2)

In this bathroom the American washes with soap invented by the ancient Gauls. Next he cleans his teeth, a subversive European practice which did not invade America until the latter part of the eighteenth century. He then shaves, a masochistic rite first developed by the heathen priests of ancient Egypt and Sumer. The process is made less of a penance by the fact that his razor is of steel, an iron-carbon alloy discovered in either India or Turkestan. Lastly, he dries himself on a Turkish towel. (3)

Returning to the bedroom, the unconscious victim of un-American practices removes his clothes from a chair, invented in the Near East, and proceeds to dress. He puts on close-fitting tailored garments whose form derives from the skin clothing of the ancient nomads of the Asiatic steppes and fastens them with buttons whose prototypes appeared in Europe at the close of the Stone Age. This costume is appropriate enough for outdoor exercise in a cold climate, but is quite unsuited to American Summers, steam-heated houses, and Pullmans. Nevertheless, foreign ideas and habits hold the unfortunate man in thrall even when common sense tells him that the authentically American costume of gee string and moccasins would be far more comfortable. He puts on his feet stiff coverings made from hide prepared by a process invented in ancient Egypt and cut to a pattern which can be traced back to ancient Greece, and makes sure they are properly polished, also a Greek idea. Lastly, he ties about his neck a strip of bright-colored cloth which is a vestigial survival of the shoulder shawls worn by seventeenth-century Croats. He gives himself a final appraisal in the mirror, an old Mediterranean invention, and goes down stairs to breakfast. (4)

Here a whole new series of foreign things confronts him. His food and drink are placed before him in pottery vessels, the popular name of which—china—is sufficient evidence of their origin. His fork is a medieval Italian invention and his spoon a copy of a Roman original. He will usually begin the meal with coffee, an Abyssinian plant first discovered by the Arabs. The American is quite likely to need it to dispel the morning-after effects of over-indulgence in fermented drinks, invented in the Near East; or distilled ones, invented by the alchemists of medieval Europe. Whereas the Arabs took their coffee straight, he will probably sweeten it with sugar, discovered in India; and dilute it with cream, both the domestication of cattle and the technique of milking having originated in Asia Minor. (5)

If our patriot is old-fashioned enough to adhere to the so-called American breakfast, his coffee will be accompanied by an orange, domesticated in the Mediterranean region, a cantaloupe domesticated in Persia, or grapes, domesticated in Asia Minor. He will follow this with a bowl of cereal made from grain domesticated in the Near East and prepared by methods also invented there. From this he will go on to waffles, a Scandinavian invention, with plenty of butter, originally a Near-Eastern cosmetic. As a side dish he may have the egg of a bird domesticated in Southeastern Asia or strips of the flesh of an animal domesticated in the same region, which have been salted and smoked by a process invented in Northern Europe. (6)

Breakfast over, he places upon his head a molded piece of felt, invented by the nomads of Eastern Asia, and, if it looks like rain, puts on outer shoes of rubber, discovered by the ancient Mexicans, and takes an umbrella, invented in India. He then sprints for his train—the train, not the sprinting, being an English invention. At the station he pauses for a moment to buy a newspaper, paying for it with coins invented in ancient Lydia. Once on board he settles back to inhale the fumes of a cigarette invented in Mexico, or a cigar invented in Brazil. Meanwhile, he reads the news of the day, imprinted in characters invented by the ancient Semites by a process invented in Germany upon a material invented in China. As he scans the latest editorial pointing out the dire results to our institutions of accepting foreign ideas, he will not fail to thank a Hebrew God in an Indo-European language that he is a one hundred per cent (decimal system invented by the Greeks) American (from Americus Vespucci, Italian geographer). (7)

QUESTIONS

I

1. How far do you read in this essay before you become aware that the author's intention is satirically comic rather than serious? (*1*)
2. State, in general terms, the point that the author makes in tracing so many of our everyday articles to their place of origin. (*1-7*)
3. The author, a noted scholar, started, of course, with an accumulation of isolated facts. How has he "humanized" these facts and by what means has he connected them into a kind of narrative? (*1-7*)

II

1. Can you think of any articles or inventions that you can prove are of American origin?
2. Do you resent the fact that our civilization is derived almost wholly from other countries? Can you think of things other nations have adopted from us?
3. Would you like to see all nations made as uniform as possible? What would be the advantages? The disadvantages?

III

1. One means by which writing may be made humorous is by expressing simple ideas in grandiose language. Discuss the following expressions from this viewpoint: precious heritage (*1*), insidious foreign ideas (*1*), potent Latin word (*2*), perform his ablutions (*2*), a subversive European practice which did not invade America (*3*), masochistic rite developed by heathen priests (*3*), the unconscious victim of un-American practices (*4*), whose form derives from the skin clothing (*4*), buttons whose prototypes (*4*), hold the unfortunate man in thrall (*4*), vestigial survival of the shoulder shawls (*4*), a final appraisal in the mirror (*4*), our patriot is old-fashioned (*6*).
2. Another means of writing humorously is to create ludicrous pictures or to portray ridiculous actions. Discuss the following: patriot garbed in pajamas (*1*), muffled to the ears (*1*), foreign influence pursues him even here (*2*), unintentionally places his posterior (*2*), sprints for his train (*7*).
3. Note how the author has followed a sequence in time and established definite locations by the following: "On awakening he glances at the clock" (*2*), "In this bathroom" (*3*), "Returning to the bedroom" (*4*), "Here a whole new series" (*4-6*), "Breakfast over" (*7*).

WORDS

Discuss the following words as the meaning of each is revealed or indicated by its etymology.

1. precious (*1*): Latin *pretiosus*, from *pretium*, "price, value"
2. insidious (*1*): Latin *in-*, "in" and *sedere*, "to sit"
3. patriot (*1*): Latin *patēr*, "father"
4. domesticated (*1*): Latin *domus*, "home"
5. abbreviated (*2*): Latin *ad-*, "to" and *breviare*, "to shorten"
6. potent (*2*): Latin *potens*, "having power"
7. ablutions (*2*): Latin *ab-*, "from, off" and *luere*, "to wash"
8. subversive (*3*): Latin *sub-*, "under" and *vertere*, "to turn"
9. invade (*3*): Latin *in-*, "in" and *vadere*, "to go"
10. masochistic (*3*): From Sacher-*Masoch*, an Austrian novelist who described the practice
11. penance (*3*): Latin *paenitentia*, "repentance"
12. nomads (*4*): Greek *nomas*, "wandering about for pasture"
13. prototypes (*4*): Greek *prōtos*, "first" and *typos*, "model"
14. thrall (*4*): Anglo-Saxon *thræl*, "slave"
15. authentically (*4*): Greek *authentēs*, "one who does anything with his own hands"
16. vestigial (*4*): Latin *vestigium*, "footprint, mark"
17. appraisal (*4*): Latin *ad-*, "to" and *pretium*, "price"
18. dispel (*5*): Latin *dis-*, "away" and *pellere*, "to drive"
19. distilled (*5*): Latin *de-*, "down" and *stillare*, "to drop"
20. adhere (*6*) Latin *ad-*, "to" and *haerere*, "to stick, cling"
21. cantaloupe (*6*): From Castle *Cantalupo*, in Italy, where first grown in Europe
22. cereal (*6*): From *Ceres*, goddess of grain and harvest
23. umbrella (*7*): Latin *umbra*, "shade, shadow"—used first as a protection against the sun
24. inhale (*7*): Latin *in-*, "in" and *halare*, "to breathe"
25. decimal (*7*): Latin *decem*, "ten"

THEME TOPICS

1. My First Shave (to be written in the "mock heroic" style of the "great" event)
2. My First Cake (same style as above for No. 1)
3. The Great American Bathroom (humor by contrast to Grandfather's tub)
4. Gadgets in Our House (humor by how they don't work)
5. Mother Drives the Car from the Rear Seat (humorous by exaggerated words and actions)
6. Before the Game (as the coach sees its importance)

7. I Catch the Bus (or Train, or Street-Car—to be made humorous by exaggerated action)
8. My Favorite Breakfast (humorous by superlative terms)
9. My Home and How I Shall Furnish It (humor by idealization)
10. Father Brings Unexpected Guests for Dinner (as Mother views and meets the emergency)

America at Work and Play

MACHINE SONG

SHERWOOD ANDERSON

IT HAS been going on now for thirty, forty, fifty, sixty years. I mean the machine song. It began away back of that. I am speaking now of the great chorus, the grand song.

I am speaking of machinery in America, the song of it, the clatter of it, the whurrrr, the screech, the hummmm, the murmur, the shout of it.

The machines talk like blackbirds in a meadow at the edge of a cornfield, the machines shout, they dance on their iron legs.

The machines have a thousand, a million little steel fingers. They grasp things. Their fingers grasp steel. They grasp the most delicate cotton and silk fibres. There are great hands of steel, giant hands.

They are picking up and are handling iron pillars, great steel beams. The hands are themselves machines. They grasp huge beams of steel, swing them high up.

Steel hands are tearing up the earth. The fingers reach down through stone, through clay and muck.

They swing great handfuls of earth and stone aloft. They carry steel beams weighing tons, running with them madly across a room.

They make bridges. They make great dams. They feed upon the power in rivers. They eat white coal.

Wheels are groaning, wheels are screeching.

It is good to get these sounds into the ears. It is good to see these sights with the eyes. See the smoke rolling up, the black smoke. See the fire belching from the great retorts. The machines are cruel as men are cruel. The little flesh and blood fingers of men's hands drive, direct, control the machines.

The machines wear out as men do. Machines are scrapped, thrown on the scrap heap.

At the edges of American cities you will see fields and gullies filled with iron and steel scraps.

There, in that gully, beneath bushes, overgrown by weeds, is an automobile that, but a year or two ago, slid smoothly over roads at forty, fifty, sixty, eighty miles an hour.

How smoothly it ran, how surely. It carried me from Chicago to Miami.

I was in Chicago and it was bleak and cold there. I wanted the sun. Cold winds blew in from the lake. My bones ached. I wanted the sun. I am no longer young. I wanted the sun.

I got into the machine. It was gaily painted. I tell you there will no man live in my day who does not accept the machine.

I myself rejected it. I scorned it. I swore at it. It is destroying my life and the lives of all of the men of my time, I said.

I was a fool. How did I know it would serve me like this?

I went to lie by the river banks. I walked in fields where there were no machines.

Is the machine more cruel than the rain?

Is the machine more cruel than distance?

Is the machine more cruel than snow?

Is the machine more cruel than the sun?

Now the machine in which I rode so gaily from Chicago to Miami, the long, graceful machine, painted a bright scarlet, now it is on a scrap heap. It is in a gully under weeds. In a few years I shall be underground. I shall be on a scrap heap.

What is worth saving of the machine, in which I rode from Chicago to Miami, passing rivers, passing towns, passing cities, passing fields and forests—what is worth saving of the machine will go into the great retorts. It will be melted into new machines. It will sing and fly and work again. What is worth while in me will go into a stalk of corn, into a tree.

I went in the machine from Chicago to Miami. Bitter winds and snow blew about me. My hands that guided the machine were cold.

It ran gaily. There was a soft murmuring sound. Something within the machine sang and something within me sang. Something within me beat with the steady rhythmic beating of the machine.

The machine gave its life to me, into my keeping. My hands guided it. With one turn of my wrists I could have destroyed the machine and myself.

There were crowds of people in the streets of some of the towns and cities through which I passed. I could have destroyed fifty people and myself in destroying the machine.

I passed through Illinois, through Kentucky, Tennessee, North Carolina and went on into Florida. I saw rains, I saw mountains, I saw rivers.

I had a thousand sensations. At night I slept in hotels. I sat in hotel lobbies and talked to men.

Today I made two hundred and fifty-eight miles.

Today I made three hundred and ten miles.

Today I made four hundred miles.

We were stupid, sitting thus, telling each other these bare facts. We told each other nothing of what we meant. We could not tell each other.

There were fat men and lean men, old men and young men. In each man a thousand sensations not told. We were trying to express something we could not express.

I am sick of my old self that protested against the machine. I am sick of that self in me, that self in me, that self in me, that would not live in my own age.

That self in me.
That self in me.
That self in me.

In my own age.
In my own age.
In my own age.
Individuality gone.
Let it go.

Who am I that I should survive?

Let it go.

Let it go.

Steady with the hand. Give thyself, man.

I sing now of the glories of a ride in a machine, from Chicago to Miami.

Miles have become minutes. If I had music in me I would orchestrate this. There would no longer be one field, one clump of trees making a wood, one town, one river, one bridge over a river.

An automobile, going at forty, at fifty, at sixty miles an hour, passing over a bridge, strikes a certain key. There is a little note struck.

Whurrrrr.

It vibrates through the nerves of the body. The ears receive the sound. The nerves of the body absorb the sound.

The nerves of the body receive flying things through the ears and the eyes. They absorb fields, rivers, bridges.

Towns, cities, clumps of trees that come down to the road.

A clump of trees comes down to the road just so in Illinois.

A clump of trees comes down to the road just so in Tennessee.

Again in Kentucky, Virginia, North Carolina.

There is a man walking in the road in Kentucky.

There is a man walking in the road in Georgia.

The car passed over a viaduct. It makes a sound.

Whurrrrr.

There are faces seen, a thousand faces. A thousand, a hundred thousand pairs of hands are grasping the steering wheels of automobiles.

I have lost myself in a hundred thousand men, in a hundred thousand women. It is good to be so lost.

Cattle, standing in fields, beside barns, in Illinois, Kentucky, Georgia, Kansas.

Bridges, rivers beneath bridges, dead trees standing solitary in fields, clumps of trees coming down to the road.

New movement.

New music, not heard, felt in the nerves. Come on here, orchestrate this.

Touch this key—a field.

That key—a sloping field.

A creek covered with ice.

A snow-covered field.

Curves in the road.

More curves.

It rains now. The rain beats against the nose of the car.

Who will sing the song of the machine, of the automobile, of the airplane?

Who will sing the song of the factories?

We are in the new age. Welcome, men, women and children into the new age.

Will you accept it?

Will you go into the factories to work?

Will you quit having contempt for those who work in the factories?

You singers, will you go in?

You painters, will you go in?

Will you take the new life?

Will you give yourself to a new age?

Will you love factory girls as you love automobiles?

Will you give up individuality?

Will you live, or die?

Will you accept the new age?

Will you give yourself to the new age?

QUESTIONS

I

1. What made the author at first rebel against the machine? What changed his attitude toward it?
2. What is the author's advice to creative artists, as well as to all of us, at the close of the essay?

II

1. What great blessings has the machine brought to civilization? Can you think of any disadvantages?
2. Many serious thinkers believe our sense of moral responsibility

in using machines has lagged so far behind our mechanical inventions that machines have become a menace to society. What is your opinion on this matter?

3. Other thinkers have suggested that science and invention "take a holiday" so that man can develop enough moral intelligence to use constructively what he already has. Would you be for or against such an idea?

4. Many pessimists believe that man will ultimately exterminate himself with his inventions. Do you think any such possibility faces us?

III

1. Point out several words in the essay that are an attempt at imitation of sound. What is the name of this figure of speech?

2. Why has the author of this essay used so many short paragraphs?

3. What is the effect of the staccato fragmentary sentences used so freely in this essay?

4. The repetition of certain words and phrases is used in this essay as a device of style. What is the author's intention in using these repetitions? Do you consider the device effective?

5. Point out a number of examples of similes, metaphors, and personifications in this essay.

6. Does the rhythm of Mr. Anderson's sentences have a subtle kinship with his subject—the *song* of the machine?

7. Does this kind of writing appeal to you? Tell why you like or dislike it.

THEME TOPICS

1. The Machine: Blessing or Menace?
2. I Accept the Machine
3. An Invention We Need
4. My Visit to a Great Factory
5. The Machine and Unemployment
6. The Old Craftsman *vs.* the Machine
7. The Machine Gives Us Leisure
8. Scrap—Mechanical and Human
9. The End of Our Old Car
10. I Like (Dislike) to Work with Machinery

ON THE ASSEMBLY LINE

GENE RICHARD

A S I walk down the steps with many others, I am disturbed by the thought that the day is only beginning. I suddenly realize in one sensation that there is no escape. It is all unavoidably real and painful. How much energy I must expend today has been predetermined by my employer. I try to disregard the thought that is causing this nervous tension which will be with me throughout the hours. Around me I sense a similar reaction. It expresses itself in silence. Men are laughing insincerely. They are ashamed of their emotion. They would rather feel that they were at peace and not a part of this herd who can hide nothing of their day from each other.

The men wander quietly into their places. The shop is beautiful. Machines, blue steel, huge piles of stock. Interesting patterns of windows are darkened by the early hour. This is the impression one gets before he becomes a part of the thing. The beauty is perceivable then. The unbiased observer cannot relate it to the subjective outlook he later acquires.

There is a shrill note. It is impersonal, commanding, and it expresses the entire power which orders the wheels set in motion. The conveyor begins to move immediately. Mysteriously the men are in their places and at work. A man near me grasps the two handles of the air wrench he holds all day long. This is the extent of his operation. He leans forward to each nut as the machine does its work. One nut—two nuts—one motor. It is not necessary for him to change his position. The conveyor brings the next motor to him. One position, one job all day.

Noise is deafening: a roar of machines and the groaning and

From *The Atlantic Monthly*, April, 1937. Copyrighted. Used by permission of *The Atlantic Monthly* and by arrangement with the author. (To be read in connection with the following essay.)

moaning of hoists; the constant *pssffft-pssffft* of the air hoses. One must shout to be heard. After a time the noise becomes a part of what is natural and goes unnoticed. It merely dulls for the time the particular sense of hearing.

Truss works next to me. We are breaking a man in. There is a lot of experimenting to find out how to divide the jobs so as to achieve the maximum of group efficiency. The job is new to me, too. We are putting fuel connections on the carburetor. Between Truss and me we do three men's work. We cannot keep up. Luckily we know enough not to take it out on each other. We cuss and work in a fit of nervousness. The nut which is supposed to be previously tightened for me won't screw down because it is a bit undersized. I try to tighten it with my fingers, but I keep slipping behind. I am losing my temper. The foreman and relief man have been filling in occasionally for the man who should be there. We just can't do it. Truss snaps out, "Hell with 'em! Let their damn motors go by if we can't get 'em!" We work and mumble curses. I finally discover how to put my wrench in the hole in such a way as to bite it into the soft brass and twist the lock nut down to where I can get a wrench on it. My ingenuity works out to save my fingers, but to my disgust is merely adding to the possibility of Truss and me doing the job without help.

"Watch your quality today, men," says Sammy, the squat line foreman. We are working so fast I don't see how anyone can think of quality. The old fellow next to me seems to be having trouble keeping up. He is supposed to run in a bolt on a clamp that I straighten and tighten with a hand wrench. When he gets behind I get behind, too. I take his ratchet wrench and do the added operation myself. I do this to two or three motors and give it back. Finally I just keep the wrench and do the added operation myself. I'll get sore each time I'm put behind anyway, so, to guarantee my own peace, I assume the extra work. He looks at me with mild appreciation, and I go on feeling that I have big enough shoulders to make it easier for him. At least I'm younger and he's probably quite tired.

Up in the lavatory I usually lean out the window for a breath of fresh air. The out-of-doors smells fresh and free and reminds me how different it was when I could be outside and away from all this overwhelming noise and steel structure. But I can't take more than two or three breaths, for I must hurry back to the call of my stimulated conscience.

Men about me are constantly cursing and talking filth. Something about the monotonous routine breaks down all restraint. The men in most cases have little in common, but they must talk. The work will not absorb the mind of the normal man, so they must think. The feeling of isolation here leads one to the assurance that his confidences will never escape. We work on and on with spurts of conversation. Suddenly a man breaks forth with a mighty howl. Others follow. We set up a howling all over the shop. It is a relief, this howling. (*1*)

As the long-anticipated whistle blows for lunch the men burst into the aisles. There is a rule: "No running." Some of the men have developed a lunch-hour walk which is hard to distinguish from a run.

I am sitting on the greasy floor of the lunchroom leaning my back against the rail at the head of the stairs. The lunchroom is a great hall with many tables for the men to eat on. At the top of the stairs is a series of cages wide enough for a man to pass through when he rings his clock card. Twenty or thirty clocks are ringing, *ding-dong*, *ding-dong*, steadily for half an hour before the men go down to work. The floor is black from the dirty shoes. Some men's shoes are so soaked with oil that the surfaces shine and ooze at each step. The general manner of dress is not neat. The average worker probably wears a pair of work pants or old pants and a blue, brown, or black work shirt. Some wear vests. An old vest will protect the shirt and make a man feel dressed. In the cooler weather the whole costume can be covered when leaving the shop. In many cases it is done in such a manner as to create the illusion that the man is dressed much better than he really is. He usually has an old hat which, although it has become worn and dirty from handling, still retains form. An old topcoat then serves to disguise the rest.

In spite of the poorly regulated lives of these men, many gain weight. There are a great number of big massive hulks. This creates the impression of power. But I seldom see a man with a well-proportioned body. Some have a high left shoulder while the right droops. Some have large gnarled hands, the fingers of which fail to respond readily. Many hands lack a finger here and there. Most of the older men have a larger amount of beef in the region of the buttocks than they need. A protruding belly is almost the rule with the men who have been here long. The stomach muscles become relaxed and deformed from standing long hours in one position. I wonder if these men can be healthy. I suspect that they all have some nature of illness. The prevalence of halitosis might be accounted for some way.

Some of these men develop a surprisingly self-important air as though they were not a part of the group. They flaunt their independence. It has had me fooled since I've been here. Their attitude is effective, yet I sense there is something in it that is off color. The place has robbed these men of their true capacities and denied them a life of growth; but it cannot force them to be humble. Their outward front expresses an ownership of all those things they haven't got. They do even the most menial jobs with an air of great responsibility. (2)

The shrill whistle blows. Some men start. It works as well as a whip. There is a rustling of clothing, a dropping of feet, and a prayer-like flow of voices as we go down the stairs.

This afternoon I am transferred to the rod department. My job is to weigh one end of the rod and stripe it with paint according to the colors indicated on the scale. There are usually a few piles of rods beside each man. The men figure it looks better to work this way. I take a rod off the pile and throw it on the scale, which is so made that the rod will sit on two pegs. The color is posted on the indicator instead of the weight, so all the operator needs to know is one color from another. I then pick up another rod, and as I take the first one off I put the next one on. While the scale is coming to a rest I paint the small end of the rod in my hand with a stripe corresponding to its weight. No time is lost. One soon gets so he can take a rod off the scale before it comes to a rest and predict where it will stop. As a matter of fact, to paint 5000 rods a day this is almost necessary.

As I am painting the small end of the rod I realize that I am not conscious of what I am doing. My accuracy surprises me. I seldom make a mistake, yet I never have my mind on my work. Perhaps this is why I am able to obtain accuracy, because my subconscious is more capable of this monotony than my personality. (3)

It is soon after lunch. Some one has heard some one who heard some one else say the line was going home at two-thirty. Gradually it becomes a subject of discussion. Karl says to the bearer of the news, "You wouldn't kid me, would ya? 'Cause that's a dirty trick." "Well, I heard a guy ask a foreman," he said. We all know a foreman doesn't usually know any more than anyone else, yet we wishfully take stock in the rumor. The spirit of some men rises. Two o'clock finally arrives and there is no word yet. Karl curses the fellow who started the rumor. We still have hope, however, because we hate to abandon any chance of such a pleasant anticipation. After two o'clock we lose spirit.

Sometimes my thoughts will not hold me down. I think about all the mean things I have done, and all the things about myself I disrespect. Or I grow angry at some person out of my past. My thoughts go on and torture me. They are thoughts which I am sure are not sane. I try to stop thinking them and find that I don't really want to. I want to think them through until they satisfy me, and hope they will not come back. They do—and the process begins all over again. I cannot think them through to any finality because my work is constantly bringing me back to consciousness. These days and hours are bad. Sometimes I can lick my anxieties and think more objective thoughts. When I have contact with outside interests I can live them through the long hours of the day. Some days I have two or three good topics for thought. Then I am at peace and will postpone each pleasant thought smugly and with anticipation. As a beginner, I would try to think how fast each period of the day would go. This is a hard thing to get any satisfaction from. The day is just so long, and one gets to be as good a time reckoner as a clock.

I find now that I can put my mind to use. I have gained one thing from this hell. I have learned discipline. I can concentrate for an hour on one subject. But my efforts are fast losing direction. I have lost contact with anything to think about.

Today I am thinking, as usual, depressed thoughts. I have heard these thoughts, some of them, expressed before, but now I am feeling them from dire reality. I have worked long hours this week. Each day I go to work in the dark and leave in the dark. I have not seen daylight since Sunday, and it is Saturday afternoon. I feel strangely unimportant and insignificant. The experiences of the day have exposed my mode of existence in such a way that I see my relative position here too plainly and deeply for my own comfort. I realize how unimportant is personal worth here. When I come in the gate in the morning I throw off my personality and assume a personality which expresses the institution of which I am a part. The only personality expressed here is the personality of the employer, through those authorized to represent him. There is no market for one's personal quality. Any expression of my own individual self beyond the scope of my work is in bad taste.

When a man insinuates here by any action that he is an individual, he is made to feel that he is not only out of place but doing something dishonorable. One feels that even the time he spends in the lavatory is not a privilege but an imposition. He must hurry back because there are no men to spare. After hours on one operation I realize that the only personal thing required of me is just enough consciousness to operate my body as a machine. Any consciousness beyond that is a contribution to my discomfort and maladjustment. I am a unit of labor, and labor is cheap. There is no market or appreciation of my worth except my self-respect. I struggle to keep it. My mood is perhaps a result of a discussion over the bench with Glen. He says, "No matter whatcha do, they gotcha licked." It makes me depressed to see him take himself so cheaply. He is convinced of his lack of value here. I feel a sudden wave of fear that I might some day feel exactly as he does. (4)

Some of the men are taking to horseplay. Horseplay among bench workers has less limitation than among line workers. The bosses are not intolerant of horseplay. It is a noticeable fact that they will tolerate it where they will deal severely with serious loafing. As we are working we are unexpectedly interrupted by the foreman. He steps up between Karl and me. While we stop work and look around, he starts slowly to pave the way for what is to be a bawling out. His Swedish accent drawls out:—

"Now listen, fellas. I don't know whether anybody ever tolja this before or whether ya know how it looks from the outside [glides his fingers over the bench in pattern of self-justification], but I'm gonna tell ya now. Now I ain't kickin' on how much work yer gittin' out er how well yer doin' it. Yer gittin' out enough perductchin and yer work's fine; but whatcher doin' is shovin' a whole buncha rods down the bench in a hurry and then gangin' up an' talkin'. Now if any one a those big shots come down 'ere an' see one guy leanin' on the bench like this, another guy over here standin' around, some guys bunched up here, an' everything all goin' ta hell, they wonder what kinda buncha guys they got down here and a hellova man runnin' it. Now I been takin' a lot up there lately an' I ain't been sayin' nothin'. Now I don't want to be a —— ——, but if I hafta I will. Those guys been comin' down here lately an' I been hearin' about it. They're kickin' an' they got a kick comin'. So —— damn it; you fellas work with me an' —— damn it I'll work with you, 'cause—well—ya see how it is, doncha? I ain't kickin' about yer work, but what I wancha ta do is—work a little slower if ya hafta and a little steadier." (5)

We start back to work in silence. It leaves a bad taste and we feel as though we really had been falling down on the job. Later we see him making the rounds, so we feel at least it wasn't meant just for us. We slip into some pretty childish ruts sometimes. We are so completely dulled by our work that trivial and boyish pranks amuse us. We cuss and talk filth.

When four-thirty finally arrives we get word that we are working until six. We have all settled into sullen moods. No one has a thing to say. We are grieved at this regular policy of detaining us without consulting us. Karl is working seriously for some time and finally drops back on one foot and bellows: "—— damn it! I'm gettin' sick of this stuff. I guess we never will get out of here before daylight." He grabs the nearest rod and slams it down on the bench. I am mad too, so I egg him on. We take it out on the most faithful man in the department. Later we take to hollering to build up a morale which will help us to lick the last hour. Finally we are walking out, punching our cards. Laughter is now sincere but weary. It is still dark on the outside. I am so dulled that I have gotten here without realizing it. I stop—ponder. I can't think where I parked my car: the morning was so long ago. (6)

QUESTIONS

I

1. What are the author's feelings as he begins the day's work and what incidents with his fellow workers show the pressure on the line? (1)
2. What information does the author give us about the men's clothes, their physiques and health, and their peculiar sense of self-importance? (2)
3. What explanation does the author give for his accuracy in his work with the rods? (3)
4. What is the nature of the author's thoughts about himself while he is working? about himself as an individual? about his self-respect? (4)
5. What is the bosses' attitude toward horseplay on the line? toward idling? (5)
6. What is the men's attitude toward working overtime? What is the significance of the author's not being able to find where he has parked his car when he looks for it at the end of the day? (6)
7. What is the psychological source of the horseplay, the loud laughter, the howling, and the profane and obscene talk of workers "on the line"?
8. Point out several incidents in the essay that show how efficiency experts find ways of "stepping up" the productivity of men "on the line."

II

1. The assembly line has made wages high and automobiles cheap. Do you think the human cost has been too great?
2. Do you think the author of this essay is typical of factory workers in general? Do you believe he has given a fair picture of work on the assembly line?
3. Is quality, in your opinion, sometimes sacrificed to speed on the assembly line?
4. Do you think "the assembly line" has become a kind of horrendous symbol of modern industry? Would you prefer the

high-tensioned, seven-hour workday of a modern automobile factory or the less strenuous fourteen- to sixteen-hour workday of the Middle Ages?

III

1. How does the first paragraph set the tone of high nervous tension for the whole essay?
2. What figure of speech is illustrated by the curious word-coinage *pssffft-pssffft?* (*1*) Is *ding-dong* an example of the same figure? (*2*)
3. How does the specific incident of the nut that wouldn't tighten color the whole first part of the essay? (*1*)
4. Comment on the realism of the "bawling out" speech of the foreman. Does the speech seem to you to be an accurate bit of writing? (*5*)

WORDS

Each word at the left and the three words that follow it are derived from the same stem. Show how the four words in each group are related to this stem in meaning.

1. escape (*1*), *cappa,* "cloak, cape": chaperone, chapel, escapade
2. predetermined (*1*), *term,* "limit": terminate, exterminate, interminable
3. tension (*1*), *tend,* "stretch": attentive, extension, retentive
4. subjective (*1*), *ject,* "throw": objective, projectile, rejection
5. stimulated (*1*), *stim,* "goad": stimulus, stimulant, instigate
6. routine (*1*), *rupt,* "break": disrupt, interrupt, bankrupt
7. isolation (*1*), *insul,* "island": insular, insulate, insulin
8. deformed (*2*), *form,* "shape": formal, conform, transform
9. humble (*2*), *humus,* "ground": humility, humiliate, exhume
10. torture (*4*), *tort,* "twist": contort, distort, tortoise
11. finality (*4*), *fin,* "end": infinite, confine, refine
12. postpone (*4*), *pon,* "place": opponent, compound, expound
13. contact (*4*), *tact,* "touch": intangible, tangent, contagious
14. depressed (*4*), *prem,* "press": compress, impress, repress
15. privilege (*4*), *leg,* "law": legal, legislation, illegal
16. imposition (*4*), *posit,* "place": opposition, proposition, supposition
17. maladjustment (*4*), *just,* "law": justice, unjust, adjust
18. trivial (*6*), *via,* "way": deviate, obvious, viaduct
19. sullen (*6*), *soli,* "alone": solo, solitude, desolate
20. morale (*6*), *mor,* "custom": moral, immoral, morose

THEME TOPICS

1. The Physical Effects of Factory Work
2. The Mental Life of Factory Workers
3. Quality *vs.* Speed
4. Management Too Far Removed from the Men
5. What Is Right (Wrong) with the Assembly Line
6. Towards a Solution of Labor Troubles
7. The Right Kind of Boss
8. A Hard-Boiled Foreman
9. The Five-Day Week Is Right (Wrong)
10. What I Think of Efficiency Experts

AMERICANA: ON THE LINE

CHRISTY BORTH

SOME can take it—and some can't," said the shop foreman. His comment referred to work on modern industry's assembly line, yet it was applicable to any activity under the sun, from the ancient job of rearing offspring to the modern one of flying the China Clipper. "The trouble is that the misfits make the most noise," he added.

The fellow's remark, I thought as I left the factory, best summed up the impressions I had gleaned from a week of interviewing automobile assembly line workers, an inquiry that I had undertaken after having read Gene Richard's article, "On the Assembly Line," in *The Atlantic Monthly*. As a man who had on three occasions worked on the assembly line, I could re-live, through Richard's prose, all the unpleasant emotions of those periods when I was an unhappy square peg in a round hole.

But, as a newspaper reporter disciplined to deal with facts and schooled to mistrust the purely subjective approach, I knew that the "real story" in this, as in any story, is less likely to be in the easy reporting of one man's view than in the more bothersome method of matching many views and presenting them as objectively and impartially as is humanly possible.

It had long seemed to me that the truth about the so-called "evils of the assembly line" was a story only partially reported because the reporting had been mainly done by persons who, possessing sufficient imagination and sensitivity to enable them to write well, were bound by their possession of these qualities to be unhappy in any repetitive and routine activity.

In making my investigation, I obtained permission to interview

From *The Reader's Digest*, July, 1937. Copyrighted by, and used by permission of, the Editors of *The Reader's Digest*. (To be read in connection with the preceding essay.)

men on the assembly line. Of the foremen I requested only that they point out men with reasonably long service records and allow me to take them from their posts long enough to answer a few questions.

In each instance I informed the worker of my purpose, told him to hide his badge if he feared to talk with that identification in view, informed him that I did not want to know his name, and made it plain that he might either answer my questions or tell me to go to hell.

I believe that, out of scores interviewed, the following are sufficiently typical to be used as a composite picture of that average assembly line worker who does his work well enough to remain on the payroll, who writes no subjective dissertations about his work, and whose presence makes it possible for one company to be proud of figures which indicate that, out of a personnel of nearly 90,000, the past year's average of daily "quits" is 20, including those who quit because Death never takes a holiday. (1)

Roy is 49 years old, and has been in the same company for 28 years. For the past ten years, his job has been that of "putting new men through the paces." "I've taught men from all walks of life," he said. "Some of them are too high-strung to work on the line. It's easy to spot them. They tighten up inside like a watch that's wound too tight and they can't get going. Most of the time you can correct it by putting them somewhere else. Sometimes a quiet talk does the trick. We have had cases where men looked like they would be too nervous for the job when they started and then surprised us by getting to be real good, so good that they kicked when we tried to shift them."

And then, unintentionally, Roy established management's selfish interest in preventing "deadly monotony." "You see," he said, "we like to shift men around because that makes them more valuable. We figure a man who can do several operations is worth more to us."

John, a Mohawk Indian who graduated from Carlisle, is one of those whom Roy said foremen like to "shift around." Aged 41, he has been 18 years in the shop, about ten of them "on the line." He was the only man I encountered on the line who had read the Richard article. His comment: "I think he was out of place on the line. If he finds his kind of work, I think he'll admit he was out of place."

"This thing is silly," said Ben, a minor plant official, after I had given him the Richard article. "If I could write, I could match this with as vicious a description of a railway mail clerk's life. Before I came here I poked letters into pigeonholes for 12 hours a day in a rolling, rocking car. I can't conceive of any deadlier monotony than that."

George, who is 72, has been "in production" at one plant for 24 years. He said he feels "like a 30-year-old" at the day's end and spends his leisure "visiting around" with friends and his two married children. "Sometimes I go to shows nights and sometimes I just sit around and talk and drink beer. I done all kinds of jobs on this here line," he said with a boastful note. "I never seen one yet that would drive a man nutty unless he was nutty to begin with. Of course I can see how a man would hate monotonous work. I don't like it myself. I did it once. I worked for the express company. It was monotonous as hell and damned heavy work. I'll take this any day."

Stan was next. He is 45, has spent 25 years on the assembly lines in one plant. "It's all one to me where I work," he said, "as long as it's on the line."

Asked if he felt exhausted at the end of the day, he grinned and shook his head. He owns his own home, drives his own car to work. That drive "clear across town through traffic," he said, "is harder than work here." Stan also has a garden. "And right now," he added, pride lighting up his features, "I'm building an addition on my house myself." That work, he said, is done evenings and on his two days of leisure each week.

Fred, who is 51 and has been on the assembly line for 25 years, provided another clue as to why some men feel that this work is not deadly monotonous. "How can it be," he asked, "when the operations are being changed all the time?"

To illustrate, Fred explained that his present job—the assembly of the transmission cover—required 30 minutes for one man handling 14 tools five years ago. "We began to figure how to do it easier," he said, "and by changing operations we got it organized so that three men do it now in ten minutes with the 14 tools distributed among us three. We're still trying to make the job easier, so how can it get monotonous if it's changing all the time?

"Whenever you find a man on a job he don't like," he added, "he ain't the man for the job. That's all there is to that."

The man called "Shorty" might well be a whining burden to society, for his legs were crushed in a Michigan mine. He is 45, married, and the sole support of three children. Although locomotion is painfully laborious, he has been five years on the motor assembly line and, according to his foreman, "hollers like hell when we try to get him into an easier job." The proffered "easier" jobs, said Shorty, are not easy for him. "I've learned to make every move count," he said, "so I never have to hurry, no matter how fast the line moves."

Al is 32 and has spent six years on the final assembly line "on all kinds of jobs." He owns his own home, has a garden, and hopes to educate his two sons. "I want them to get a better education than I got," he said. Asked if he would like them to do his kind of work, he replied, "They might do worse. I can think of a lot of worse jobs."

Al has a basement workshop and is proud of the fact that he makes all his car repairs. He reads newspapers and magazines— "Mostly light stuff," he added. "But," he said, "I never go to the movies." Asked why, he explained, "Because the stories are not real. Music, now, that's *real!* I could listen to symphony concerts every night and want more."

Informed that Richard, the author whose article had spurred the inquiry, was a musician, Al opined, "Maybe he's sour because he's sick. I think a man's health has a lot to do with his attitude to his work."

Inquiries indicated that there is little variation in apparent dissatisfaction in "productive" and "non-productive" jobs. The number of requests for transfers, I found, is proportionately the same among both groups of workers. Although most productive tasks are of the type called monotonous because they involve much repetition, actually less than ten percent of the total employes work on moving assembly lines. Moreover, many non-productive tasks, such as routine clerical jobs, might be called monotonous but are seldom the subject of heated controversy.

This was illustrated by Bert, a man of 53, doing rather heavy work on the rear axle sub-assembly line. Because he suffers from neuritis, Bert's foreman took him off the job recently, but allowed him to return "because," Bert said, "I feel more at home here."

Bert has two daughters. One of them works in the payroll department. "She thinks my job must be pretty dull," he said, "but I wouldn't have her kind of a job as a gift. It must be awful monotonous to sit at a desk all day and fiddle with a lot of figures."

Bert's recreation is his garden. "I raise some pretty fancy dahlias," he said. He was launching into a discussion of dahlia culture when the factory din was punctuated by one of those concerted yells of the men on the line—a yell which began inexplicably with one man's howl and, mounting into a concerted clamor, faded out as inexplicably as it started. Bert was asked to explain.

"I don't know why they yell," he said. "It's mostly the young fellows who do it. I used to do it myself, but I don't know why any more than I know why all the roosters start crowing when one rooster lets go. Maybe it's because you feel good."

Near by I discovered Bill, a polite roly-poly fellow aged 61, with the kind of job that the average man pictures as typical of the assembly line. Bill was fitting nuts on bolts—endlessly, and without profanity.

"Monotonous?" said Bill, squinting owlishly through shell-rimmed glasses. "Gracious, no! This is child's play." Bill said he had been doing this sort of thing since 1913, when he rented his farm near Yale, Mich., and decided to "move to town and try a hand at factory work."

"I'd much rather do this than farm," he said. "Work's not so hard. Less monotonous. Fewer hours. And you get some enjoyment out of life. Evenings and Saturdays and Sundays, the Missus and I pile in the car and drive around and visit the four kids scattered over the state."

For recreation Bill reads the newspapers and listens to the radio. "While my hands are doing this job," he said, "I can think about what I read and what I heard." The din was deafening near Bill, but he said he hadn't noticed the noise.

Yes, he had seen men who screwed nuts on bolts until they got all tightened up in a knot. "But," he added, "I've seen some of them do that and then get a holt on themselves and level off. If a man can't get along with his job, it's not the job's fault, I guess; it's the man who's wrong."

Slim is 51. He has been on the assembly line 28 years. His job is a tedious gathering together of ten wires into a metal holder. Despite his age, Slim can, according to his foreman, "assemble manifolds faster than any two men we've ever tried."

Watching Slim is like watching a nicely articulated machine— no waste effort, no superfluous movement, fascinating rhythm. His fingers are as nimble as Fred Astaire's feet. Extremely taciturn, his only comment was, "I wouldn't trade jobs with any man I ever met"—in addition to the bare facts that he has two sons, one of whom graduates this June, and that he gets his recreation working around his home, which he owns, and in driving and repairing his car.

Gus is 54, has been on the line for 25 years, and gets his recreation driving his car and summering in his lake-side cottage equipped with a greenhouse which he built himself. His job is that of filling in wherever men drop out of the line.

"I wouldn't say the line's a man-killer," he said. "I've seen men who didn't belong on the job they were trying to hold down, and I've seen them do a good job when they were transferred to some other operation. Sometimes a big husky man can't take it, and a man who looks like a weakling makes good in the same place. The trouble comes when the right job and the right man don't get together. I think there aren't many men who can't be fitted in somewhere." (2)

This belief that the misfit is a rarity is shared by Gus's foreman, who said, "What management needs most to guard against is the tough straw-boss with a corporal's complex. The Prussian kind of a fellow whose authority goes to his head can raise more hell in a shop in five minutes than you can correct in a year."

And that comment is the explanation of industry's basic fault, as set forth by William S. Knudsen, who declares that management's worst problems arise from the widening of the gulf between itself and the men. "Management has to find means for restoring the kind of contact with men that prevailed in the little shops," said this transplanted Dane who rose to management's pinnacle via the assembly line.

Henry Ford, too, understands that mass production has its evils. In pointing out how mass production had furnished man for the first time in history with the tools that were capable of banishing the threat of permanent want forever, he said: "But nothing of real value has ever been produced without pain. There are always injustices that need correcting." (*3*)

QUESTIONS

I

1. In what way is Borth's approach to the problem different from Richard's? Why are persons capable of writing likely to report unfavorably about the assembly line? How were the men assured that they could talk frankly to the interviewer? (*1*)
2. Give, in general terms, a composite picture of the situation of the men on the assembly line. (*2*)
3. Were you at all surprised that the answers were unanimously favorable to work "on the line"? (*2*)
4. What selfish reason has the management of a big manufacturing plant for preventing monotony? (*2*)
5. How much, in your opinion, did the free-time occupations and interests of the men interviewed have to do with their satisfaction with their jobs? (*2*)
6. What is management's worst problem and greatest need? What two leaders of industry realize this problem? (*3*)

II

1. Is it true that almost all jobs are full of repetitious details and monotony? Does the strong person or the weak person rebel at this fact? Analyze, penetratingly, the advantages accruing from repetition.
2. What should factories do to avoid placing men in positions for which they are not fitted? Do you think the problem ought to be approached more scientifically than the haphazard way of "hiring" a man? Would the use of scientific employment methods have any bearing on our labor problems?

3. What have the factory system and mass production done to benefit humanity?

4. Can great corporations find any way to approximate the happy condition of the old shop in which the owner and men worked together? Is the almost complete separation of management and workers the chief reason for labor troubles?

5. Discuss the truth or falsity or homely "wisdom" in the following excerpts: "The trouble is that the misfits make the most noise"; "I never seen one [a job] yet that would drive a man nutty unless he was nutty to begin with"; "Whenever you find a man on a job he don't like, he ain't the man for the job"; "I think a man's health has a lot to do with his attitude to his work"; "If a man can't get along with his job, it's not the job's fault, I guess; it's the man who's wrong"; "The trouble comes when the right job and the right man don't get together."

III

1. The "subjective approach" is likely to be that of the artist; the "objective attitude," that of the scientist. The writing of which are you more likely to enjoy? which, to believe? Does your answer hold good for this and the preceding essay?

2. Do you think the author's method of reciting "case histories" is an effective way of establishing his main point?

3. Do the bits of conversation given with the "case histories" seem to you to be authentic shop talk?

4. The author, a newspaper man, has written this article in a journalistic style. Would he have gained or lost in effectiveness by making it more "literary"?

5. Mr. Richard, in the preceding article, wanted to "tell" something; Mr. Borth, in this article, wanted to "prove" something. Discuss the articles from the point of view of these two contrasting purposes.

THEME TOPICS

1. My Experience in a Routine Job
2. Square Pegs in Round Holes
3. The Benefit of Mass Production to Mankind
4. I Would (Would Not) Accept a Job "on the Line"
5. Ways Management and Men Can Get Together
6. Repetition Is the Law of Life
7. The Unfit Make the Loudest Noise (Workers and Students!)
8. Recreation and Hobbies for Workers
9. The Scientific Placement of Men in Jobs
10. Dishonest Labor Leaders

WORDS

The meaning of the italicized words is made clearer by one or more other words in each of the following sentences. Point out these clarifying words.

1. objectively (*1*): A judge must consider each case *objectively*, without personal or emotional bias.

2. sensitivity (*1*): The *sensitivity* of the artist made him see and feel what others would not have noticed.

3. repetitive (*1*): A *repetitive* statement may be said over and over to the point of monotony.

4. composite (*1*): A *composite* picture emphasizes the truth of the whole by ignoring unimportant dissimilarities.

5. dissertations (*1*): His few sketchy ideas were later lengthened into several erudite *dissertations*.

6. inexplicably (*2*): He was never known to earn any money, yet he remained *inexplicably* well-to-do.

7. articulated (*2*): The nicely *articulated* machine ran smoothly at every joint and connection.

8. superfluous (*2*): A nervous person usually makes many *superfluous* movements.

9. taciturn (*2*): The *taciturn* man was silent, even though there was urgent reason to speak.

10. pinnacle (*3*): He gradually climbed to the very *pinnacle* of success.

THE MAN WITH A TRACTOR

MORROW MAYO

SANK drove into a field that was full of thistles, broom weeds, careless weeds, winter weeds, goat-heads, and blue weeds. The wind was out of the southwest and there were scattering clouds in the east and thunderheads to the north. Despite the rank vegetation, the truck left a trail of dust like a destroyer laying down a smoke screen.

At intervals he got out and bored into the red cat-claw land with a three-foot soil auger. When he unscrewed the auger he pulled the dark moist earth out of the auger-head, sniffed it, made little balls, and threw them to the ground. He had to drive in low, and twice the truck started to boil. He headed it into the wind, cut off the motor, and let it cool.

He finished in the northwest corner of the field and stood looking out over the woolly land. It was a beautiful half-section, so level that he could see the bottom of the weeds a mile away. There was not a tree, stump, lake, or rock in it. Sank lighted a cigarette, thinking. It was a crime to let land go like that. His hands, face, clothes, shoes, and hat were the same color as the reddish dusty top-soil on which he stood. There was plenty of deep-moisture. It would not be good farming, but a man had to do many things here that he wouldn't do if conditions were different. He got into his truck and drove to the unpainted frame house which stood near the northeast corner of the field. (1)

Sank stopped his tractor in the edge of the field, headed west. He lowered the disks of the one-way plow, socking the levers down to the last notch. He wanted to get all that stuff. In third speed, making three and one half miles an hour, he took off. The

disks cut into the earth like circle saws, throwing the soil one
way. The weeds fell as soldiers sometimes fall, going up into the
air and pitching forward head first, roots up.

He plowed until dark, walked to the house and ate his supper,
rested a little while, and returned to the field. He turned on his
lights. One bright eye gleaming on the weeds ahead, one on the
plow behind, the tractor lumbered over the land, snorting fire.

It was mighty bleak out there at night. Some wit had called
this country the Siberia of America, and he was righter than he
knew. There is not much difference between the great wheat
lands of the world: between the Siberian steppes and the Aus-
tralian prairies and the Argentine pampas and the high plains of
North America. It is different only in the Danubian countries.
All the others are vast uplands—immense, limitless, very similar in
appearance, in scenery, in vegetation; very similar nowadays,
even down to tractors and implements, and men. Blindfold a man,
take him from a tractor on one, put him on a tractor on another,
would he know the difference?

At midnight the wind shifted to the west. Going east, the dust
blew over Sank; going west, the heat hit him in the face. Horses,
no matter how many, got tired eventually. The tractor did not
get tired. It was 6½ feet tall, 12 feet long, and 8 feet wide. It
weighed 5300 pounds. The rubber tires on the rear wheels were
larger than a woman's body. Sank never wondered what would
happen if that monster got out of control, stampeded, or turned
on its driver.

It was two o'clock when he stopped. He was asleep by two-
thirty, up again before daylight. He plowed eighteen hours a
day, and finally he was through. He raised the disks and drove
to the house. It was too hot for early September. The windmill
was not turning; the sky was clear. No-weather was a weather-
breeder.

Sank slept ten hours. (2)

A blue norther had struck. The land to the south was a powder
house. The thin row of young Chinese elms bent low. Sank saw a
hawk wheel in the sky in the face of that wind. Across the great
level pasture to the east a jack rabbit was loping easily, on four
legs, on three. He ran, then coasted. The hawk folded his wings

and dropped like a small black bomb tossed from an airplane. The jack rabbit was not coasting now. He was doing forty miles an hour.

The hawk struck, staggered, rose slowly with the weight, great wings flapping. High enough in the air, he opened his talons. The rabbit fell to earth, hit the hard ground, did not move. In slow, triumphant circles the hawk descended to his dinner. (3)

Sank backed his truck into the barn and got down and closed the doors with difficulty. The wind was blowing a young gale. He backed his truck to the other end of the barn, and parked it up close to a mound of seed wheat—pure black hull wheat, strong, high in protein content, one hundred and fifty bushels of it. Near the pile of wheat Sank set up his seed wheat-treating machine.

Before he opened the half-gallon can of chemical Sank put on a gas mask. The can had a skull-and-cross-bones on it. The chemical prevented wheat from becoming infected with smut. In this country smut losses from untreated wheat sometimes run as high as fifty per cent. The fumes from that chemical will kill a man. Sank poured the thick, black, sticky liquid into the seed wheat-treating machine, started the gasoline motor, picked up a scoop, and started scooping the seed wheat into the machine. The wheat ran through the chemical, up the funnel, and poured out of the spout into the truck.

Usually Sank was just an ordinary-looking man, just an average-looking farmer, with arms and legs, a mouth and eyes, a wife and two children. Working there in that barn, the wind howling outside, in the dim half-light, with that gas mask on, and the rats scurrying around, he didn't look like a farmer. He looked like a product of a more advanced civilization. He didn't even look like a man. He looked like some horrible, sightless, anthropoidal thing with a snout.

He scooped the golden grain and it was hard work. He didn't quit until he had put it all through the machine. Then he threw down the scoop, cut off the motor, took off his gas mask, and went to the house. He noticed the thin row of young Chinese elms again. Last year the saplings had bent flat to the ground before the force of the onslaught. This year the Chinese elms were not bowing their heads quite so low. Next year... (4)

The wind had subsided as suddenly as it had struck. Sank went out and unhitched his plow, hitched the tractor to the drill, set the sprockets of the drill so that it would sow twenty pounds to the acre, and scooped the seed wheat into the drill-bins until they were level full. He oiled and watered and fueled the tractor and lubricated both tractor and drill. Then he lowered the disks, cranked the tractor, threw it into fourth speed, and took off up the edge of the plowed field, making four miles an hour, sowing wheat.

Wheat is undoubtedly the finest, most courageous thing that grows on the face of the earth. The implement drilled the seed wheat into the earth. If I were called upon to award the first prize to the best thing that grows, I should walk up and hang the gold medal over the head of a stalk of hard winter wheat. The disks made little planting furrows; the drill set down the single grains of wheat in the furrows; the drag-chains covered them over with soil. It was all mechanical. It was different from the days, from Joseph down to not so long ago, when a man dipped into a sack of seed wheat, and sowed it by hand, three scattering throws to the handful.

When Sank put the grains into the soil they were hard as rocks. Twelve hours later they were mealy. Six hours later they were sprouting. This is when the farmers say the earth is moving. Put it in a glass and you can see it grow. Twenty-four hours after Sank put the first hard grains into the soil, the brave, pale green shoots were thrusting themselves up out of the earth. There is nothing petty or knickknacky or clever or obscene about anything connected with wheat. It is clean and strong and vital. Wheat is bread. It is the staff of life. (5)

When Sank came up the east side he saw the Chinese elms. On the west side he looked at a great pasture of Argentine pampa grass. On the south side he passed a sixty-foot border of African sudan grass. Originally it had prevented the Sudan from blowing Egypt off the map. Now they have got it working in the Dust Bowl. And all about Sank were the big green Russian thistles which he had plowed up, and which would become huge tumbleweeds and go galloping over the plains like horses.

Argentine pampa grass, African sudan, Russian thistles, and Chinese elms. From the four corners of the earth. All growing together right in the Panhandle, U.S.A. Nature—if nobody else —was getting international. Nature and machinery. Neither spoke any language, noticed any color, recognized any boundary. So there was still hope for men....

It had better be noted, the metamorphosis of the man with the hoe. Millet, on canvas, caught and held that brutish, hopeless earthpecker leaning on a crude hand-tool. Markham, beholding him, appalled, asked greatly and bitterly, why and how? The tragedy of the world was summed up in that eloquent painting, those awful words. But you can't say: "Bowed by the weight of centuries he leans upon his F-30 tractor." (6)

Driving that tractor Sank didn't look like a humble and degraded tiller of the soil. He didn't look like a hay-chewing rube with chin whiskers, or a dunghill yokel, or a peasant without thought or hope. The tractor had done that. It had changed a farmer from a clod into an operator; from a dumb brute into a mechanic, all over the world. The tractor had done more to make him a self-respecting man than anything that had ever happened in the whole history of agriculture since the invention of the wheel.

The man with the tractor does not gaze on the ground. Unavoidably, by the nature of things, Sank sat and gazed at the distant horizon, which was on a level with his eyes. He gazed at it when the sky was clear and steel-blue, and when the moon set behind clouds that moved slowly in serried masses, and when the sun came up like a ball of fire, a flaming red.

Sank finished sowing his wheat. He raised the disks out of the ground and drove his tractor over the impregnated earth toward his house. It was twilight. The sky was overcast and the air was sultry. But you couldn't say "The ploughman homeward plods his weary way." Sank's eyes, gleaming through caked dirt, were red, but he showed no other signs of fatigue, though he was hot and sweaty and dirty.

He felt a drop of rain on his shoulder. Another. And then a lot more. He watched the big drops strike into the dry, thirsty soil. The rain was wet and cool. And now it began to come down in a slow steady downpour. The wheat, the earth, were drinking it up. Sank had got the job done and now it was raining. It made him feel good. Wet to the skin, water pouring down his dirty face, he sat erect in the tractor-seat, steering the juggernaut to the house. (7)

QUESTIONS

I

1. What were the characteristics of the land Sank was preparing to plant? What was he trying to find out about the land with his auger? (1)
2. Why is Sank plowing as deeply as he possibly can? How do the great wheat lands resemble one another? Why is Sank plowing eighteen hours a day? (2)
3. What bit of nature study about the habits of hawks do we learn from this article? (3)
4. Why is Sank treating his seed wheat scientifically? (4)
5. What is the author's opinion of wheat? How soon after planting did Sank's wheat germinate? (5)
6. In what way may the means used to control erosion in the Dust Bowl be termed international? How does Sank belie the old conception of the brutish worker of the soil? (6)
7. In what ways has the tractor changed the farmer? How does the close of the narrative reveal the reason for Sank's hurrying? (7)

II

1. This selection is a narrative, but it embodies the thesis of an essay. State that thesis in a sentence or two.
2. Do you know any crops which have been adopted from other countries for large-scale cultivation in America?
3. Can you name anything which grows that is finer than wheat?
4. Why do you suppose the farmer has become less and less the subject of urban humor? Where are the rubes, hayseeds, and clodhoppers?

III

1. Why does the author include the incident of the hawk and the jack rabbit? This story within a story has been made especially vivid for the reader. How is this vividness accomplished by the writer? (3)

2. What difference in connotation do the words *pampas, steppes, prairies, plains,* and *uplands* give? (*2*)
3. What is the effect of staccàto, one-sentence paragraphs like "Sank slept ten hours"? (*2*)
4. Name the figure of speech in each of the following sentences: "The truck left a trail of dust like a destroyer laying down a smoke screen" (*1*); "The weeds fell as soldiers sometimes fall, going up into the air and pitching forward head first, roots up" (*2*); "The land to the south was a powder house" (*3*).
5. Do you recognize the two famous poems quoted in (*6*) and (*7*)?
6. What symbolism lies behind the statement that the man on the tractor does not gaze at the ground but instead looks at the distant horizon? (*7*)
7. Why is the coming of the rain, just as Sank has finished sowing, like the "happy ending" to a story? (*7*)
8. In what loose way is *juggernaut* used at the close of the article, with none of the religious significance it has in Hinduism? (*7*)

WORDS

With which word or phrase that follows it does each word at the left make the best sense?

1. anthropoidal (*4*): butterflies, horses, apes, caterpillars, bees
2. obscene (*5*): houses, rivers, forests, fields, stories
3. metamorphosis (*6*): of Washington, of Cinderella, of Mohammedanism, of Canada, of Red Riding Hood
4. serried (*7*): bushel of wheat, pile of coal, reservoir of water, tails of kites, columns of soldiers
5. impregnated (*7*): with stuffed paper, with new ideas, with antique furniture, with deadly drugs, with wide avenues

THEME TOPICS

1. The Tractor on Our Farm
2. The Sower—Then and Now
3. The Good Earth
4. A Dust Storm and What It Means
5. The Farmer as a Mechanic (as a Business Man)
6. Farming and Science
7. I Once Tried to Raise ——!
8. Independent Farmers *vs.* Factory Slaves
9. Wheat
10. Where Are the Hicks of Yesteryear?

AMERICAN SUMMER

HENRY SEIDEL CANBY

IN the early eighteen-hundreds Thomas Jefferson sent abroad the skeleton of a giant moose to prove to a skeptical Europe that animals (including man) did not always degenerate in the climate of the New World. We in America have always been subject to misconceptions like that, and still are. In a battling Europe no one now doubts our power and resources, but they do suspect our nerves. They think of us as a restless nation constantly driving ourselves in the attempt to get rich, always pushing ahead with no clear idea as to where we are going, and therefore deficient in judgment and fixed purpose, and easily influenced toward any course of action which promises excitement and a release of energy.

I am paraphrasing in these sentences a dozen foreign books written in the past twenty years about America. Indeed, this conception of America is a journalist's idea, picked up from reading, or from seeing the United States in its go-getting days, or from more recent visits to the great cities in the strenuous time of the year. But there is, or was, a great deal of truth in the opinion nevertheless. As one looks back to the get-rich-quick period which began after the Civil War, or reads the biographies of the promoters, industrialists, politicians, and financiers in the robber-baron age, it is impossible not to observe a neurotic strain in American history. These would-be millionaires who never relaxed were setting a direction for the country which could only lead toward some kind of a nervous breakdown. Among the leaders there was no time for domestic happiness, no energy left for the pleasures of culture or education, no objective except more power. And the industrial and financial part of America was geared to their ideals. All this Henry Adams saw clearly, and it accounts for some of the pessimism of his famous autobiography. (*1*)

That change has come no one will deny. The fact that the go-getting predatory age has become somewhat legendary, and is having books written about it, would be proof in itself. Whatever else may be true of this country, it is not now living on its nerves.

The reasons for this psychological change are numerous—some economic, some educational. I propose to discuss here only one, but that one, in spite of its obviousness, is the least discussed of all the changes in American life. In the books on the social history of the United States which have been written in the past decades, I do not remember a single mention, except in passing, of the deep influences upon American *mores* of our new way of life in summertime. I believe that American summer is a factor of first-rate importance in understanding America as it is today.

The great change in our habits of living, and, as a result, in our psychological attitudes, has come, first, from a gradual, then, a rapid sharing of the way of life of a few by thousands and hundreds of thousands. Thanks to the automobile, thanks to a slow adaptation to climate, thanks to a wide increase in prosperity, and thanks to the unprecedented growth of our cities, something very important has happened to the life of the average American. (*2*)

Summer in America in, let us say, the eighties and early nineties, was still a climatic rather than a psychological experience. Whatever may have been true of the rich in Boston or Chicago or New York, or of college professors with a three months' holiday, the average American in a small town or city did not much change the routine of his life. Summer was just an arc in the year's cycle of routine, the season of cotton underdrawers, straw hats, and vacations. On some hot day in early June the American house of the class that regarded itself as typically American began to prepare for summer. Upholstered chairs and sofas were dressed in their summer pajamas of holland striped in cool colors, the tall parlor mirrors and the chandeliers were draped against flies, and over each bed a great canopy of mosquito netting was hung from a hook in the ceiling. Back and front doors were set ajar on chains, shutters were barred from morning to evening, and the house became a grotto of shaded light, smelling faintly of cool drinks, moth balls, and palm-leaf fans.

Yet this domestic change had little effect upon the routine of American life, which was not then represented by the rich with villas at Newport, or the small professional class in the great cities or the intellectual centers, who were already spending their month to three months in "summer homes," or in trips abroad, or on excursions into the woods like that famous earlier one of Emerson's into the Adirondacks, when he was said to have carried a gun that threw a ball from one end and shot from the other. Vacations for the vast majority of both men and women in these years were brief. A week was the usual allowance for a business man, and two to three weeks were the measure of the family's absence from home. These were spent usually at a "summer hotel" on the beach or a mountainside, where mother rocked in the long line on the columned porch and learned with surprise that home life in Michigan was much like her own; and father hurried up for a week with his outing shirt and a basket of spoiled peaches, and was back again before he had time to get sunburned. But for all the rest of the long summer, neighborhood life in city or town went on in summer as in winter, with no sharp alterations in its rhythms. Most people were at home most of the time. I find in my own memories of summer in the eighties and nineties a vivid recollection of the glories of the summer hotel, with its darky waiters, but this was an interlude only in the hot routine of summer life at home. Except for the climate, we were still Europeans in those days, thinking of summer as the time for a brief vacation, *les vacances*. It was scarcely a change in life. (3)

The change began in my own youth, just before and during the early nineteen-hundreds when, in spite of panics, price levels and wages and distributed income were all steadily rising. It was then that what had been the luxury of the rich and the opportunity of professors, ministers, and specialists in medicine began

to be adapted to American middle-class life in general. It was in
these years that working hours for the white-collar class (literally white-collared then) as well as for laborers began to be
sensibly shortened. As late as the winter of 1908, in an industrial
New England city, I would hear the tramp of thousands of
workmen before daylight on their way to a great factory, and
know that the office force too were on their way to their desks.
My father in the eighties was at his mill by seven and came home
after six. But by 1908 this was an anomaly and recognized as
such. Hours were shortening everywhere, and the one week's
vacation was lengthening to two. As a result of increasing leisure,
nearby beaches and lakes which the trolley could reach were
being looped with flimsy wooden cottages. Until the hurricane
blew them down there were thousands along the New England
coast whose architecture and decoration dated them as of the
1890-1910 era. It was in these years that summer "clubs," like the
famous Lake Placid Club, and Onteora and Twilight in the Cats-
kills, began to flourish for families who wanted to live in a
summer community which was not a row of rocking chairs on a
garish hotel piazza but a replica of the companionship of home.

The great shift came, however, with the automobile, which
made access to the summer country possible for everyone. It can
be dated roughly from the middle to the end of the war of 1914-
1918, when the automobile ceased to be a luxury and became a
public utility. In the rural Connecticut valley where I spent the
summers of the first war years, we could still be called to the windows by the cry, "There's an automobile passing." By 1919 a
car (still stored in winter) had become a familiar necessity even
for people of moderate incomes.

The first result was a wide extension of summer opportunities.
The semi-rural life of the commuter who had to live near a
railroad station became available to hundreds of thousands who
could spread into the adjoining country and give to all of their
summer life some of the attributes of vacation. Around the smaller
cities, the motor suburbs, reached by car only, began to crest
the hills and fill the valleys beyond the city line and outside of
the area of tense living.

The country regions beyond the commuting areas responded

to the new transportation with what must have seemed, to old inhabitants, incredible changes. Inns sprang up or were revived everywhere—Tumble Inn, Come Inn, Uneeda Inn, as well as the more dignified Berkeley Arms or Lion's Head. These were for the tourist, as also were the wayside cabins, by thousands, which, in a favored region like Cape Cod, filled nightly in summertime. The old homestead was brought back to paint and a hard prosperity as a tourist home. Ma kept it clean and cooked the meals for the nightly visitors. Pa cultivated the garden and, in shirtsleeves and collarless, told stories of old times to the guests, when "Americans ran this town" and Vanderbilts or Astors drove four-in-hands down the street. And so it went, except for the four-in-hands, all across America.

But much more significant for the slackening of tension in American life was the transformation of great areas, sometimes whole counties, into residential property. This was most marked in New England and in parts of the Middle States where the process had begun long before, but the habit spread westward from the Atlantic and eastward from California until every city had its hinterland within easy automobile run. In the plains States, such as Nebraska, where there was no country suitable for cool summer life, this hinterland became the Rockies, a long day's journey at top speed, but still a summer suburb of Lincoln or Topeka.

Most noteworthy was Connecticut. Its shoreline, easy of access by boat, train, or trolley, had filled up long before with the first increase of leisure for the small-income class. But now all western Connecticut, from the hills just back of the Sound up the Housatonic valley and on into Massachusetts, changed its character from a region of deserted farms and a declining agricultural life to a deer park, forest reserve, and region of converted farmhouses and new summer homes, some tiny, some immense. Land values in the back country, which had averaged about seven dollars an acre in 1920, began a slow and steady rise until, by the thirties, they had reached sixty dollars an acre for good residential sites with available water and a dirt road. In populous and easily accessible districts the increase was much greater. In Bucks County, Pennsylvania, in the North Carolina mountains,

on the Michigan lakes, on the dry heights of the Southwest, summer homes appeared where there had been only shacks or wilderness before. Thanks to the automobile, increased wealth, and
more leisure, the American of the middle class began to have
two homes instead of one and to adapt his life accordingly. Curi-
ously enough, the financial cataclysm of 1929-1932, instead of
ending this pleasant way of life, furthered it. There were thousands out of a job who found that they could live more cheaply,
at least for most of the year, in their adapted farmhouse or forest
cabin. They had kept their cars when so much else was swept
away, and, with a car, summer life in simplicity could be
stretched from April to November. (4)

The summer habits of the Americans who thought of themselves as typical had definitely changed. Vacation, even for the
bread-winners, came at least every week-end, if not every night,
and was spent on the road, or pottering about a woodland cottage, or on the beach. Activity, unless the activity of motion on
wheels, or a round of leisurely golf, was not what most of the
new summer Americans were after. They had taken off their
suspenders and put on their belts, or exchanged stockings for
socks, and, though it would have seemed incredible to an earlier
generation, were seeking just relaxation. While the English were
still taking their weeks off to climb or shoot or travel, the American, in a hot climate, was changing for the season from coffee
to iced tea, from stiff shoes to crepe soles, from a fast walk to a
slow one, from a plastered house or apartment to unsealed walls
and a porch by a lake, most of all, from a taut mind to an easy
one. He had discovered the nature of his environment, as Thoreau
urged him to do nearly a century ago, and was playing with the
American climate instead of against it. For we have throughout
most of this country an atmosphere which, from September or
October to April or May, is perhaps the most stimulating in the
world; and, from late spring to earliest fall, surely one of the
most relaxing. When the American began to relax with his
weather American summer became a national characteristic of
great social importance.

The customs of this new summer life are more familiar than its
significance. Yet I doubt whether the extent and variety of the

change is realized. I know one hard-working family—these are college people and the husband is free from routine all of the summer months—who load a flat-bottom boat in June with bare necessities and pole up an old logging backwater in Maine to an island on a remote and trailless lake, where they live like their immigrant ancestors until the frosts. And I know a woman in a publishing house, with only two weeks of actual vacation, who keeps her car ready packed at the door, and every week-end, and many afternoons in summer, points north, east, west, or south through the late afternoon until some tourist home attracts her for the night. Men who, in winter, would telephone an electrician to come to put in a double plug, tinker their free days through in the summertime, shingling, rolling logs for cabins, brushing paths, hanging doors, or drifting in sailboats off the beach. Women whose social and intellectual calendar leaves, in other seasons, no hour free between ten and midnight, in summer can be found in cottage kitchens, or bottoms up in a sparse mountain garden, nursing seedlings and pulling weeds.

Of the pathology of leisure and relaxation I do not write here. That rambling population on wheels, chugging from Michigan to Florida in search of cheap living and an occasional job, with no home but a trailer or a tent—this is as much the evidence of an economic disease as of a psychological escape from too much intensity. Nor am I trying to describe the American summer of the proletariat on Long Island or New Jersey beaches or the Chicago lake front, which deserves a chapter of its own. The changes here are just as significant, but they do not, to the same extent, represent the American character, which is still typically middle-class. Nor do I forget the farmer. For him American summer means only more work and a much needed addition to a shrinking income. I write of the Joneses—the business men, lawyers, professors, doctors, club women, bridge players, Rotarians—the three thousand dollars to fifteen thousand a year folk, who are to be seen in hotel corridors, who shop in the big department stores, live in apartments or single houses, go occasionally abroad, and are still what most writers, and especially Europeans, mean when they talk of the American. (5)

And parallel with this new summer life which the automobile, increasing means, and greater leisure made possible are two other characteristics of American summer which help to make it different from any other summer in the world. The first is the children's summer camp, which, beginning in a small way in the eighties, has become a national industry. It is probably safe to say that if the Boy Scouts, who spend only a week or two in their camps, are included, over a million American children, perhaps nearly two million, go to camp every summer. Porter Sargent's handbook listed, in 1933, 3,485 organizations and private camps for children, and of these a large number were of the now familiar variety—organized communities with counsellors, usually on a lakeshore, where children live in tents or cabins from six to eight weeks in the summer. For the children, this is just an extension of the privileges of the child of the very rich who had a lake and a cabin, fishing and sailing, on his father's private place. For the parents, it means of course a different summer life—a slackening of tension, more freedom to tour, to live away from home, to rest in farmhouses too quiet, too remote for children's happiness.

It was not the extension of leisure which caused this summer development, although the increase in American wealth made it possible. Nor was it the automobile. The children's camps are clearly a result of the growing urbanization of America. The pleasant summer life I knew as a child, in a town of shaded houses and deep back yards, with the country at the back door, and freedom to ramble, has changed for hundreds of thousands of middle-class families into packed existence in a high-built city, surrounded by suburbs, where the typical life is in an apartment or a tight-squeezed house. No place for the children there in summer except the streets, and so off they go, when their parents can afford it, to a cabin settlement in a spruce grove, with play and competition all day long and stories at night. But this is a development in *mores*, as striking in its way as the education of Persian youth, or the grand tour of the young English aristocrat of the eighteenth century. Strange that sociologists have made so little of it.

Another characteristic of American summer is the summer school, which now may mean anything from a summer session of a great university to a school of writing or dancing set up on a mountain top or in a pine grove. As the college population began to increase by incredible numbers, it was natural that the summer period should come to be used for education. Economic pressure no longer necessarily sent the youth of sixteen and over to work when school closed. And there were thousands of adults, teachers many of them, who wanted more education and could not take time for it in the busy seasons of the year. Hence the summer school, which has now become another national industry. I do not propose to enter into the complex task of describing its ramifications, but wish to note here a characteristic of all summer schools, except possibly the "fourth term" of great urban universities. Summer-school life is a summer life. Its education is usually a relaxed education, conducted in relative leisure, amidst pleasant surroundings, with, usually, an organized social life. It is essentially a blend of work and vacation, and thus another instance of the release of tension, the psychological change, which comes with American summer. (6)

I said the American summer is important psychologically. It might be more accurate perhaps to say that it is important physiologically. Our European visitors are right—the rush and strain of life in American cities, the noise, the constant telephonic interruptions, the incredible engagement lists of middle-aged women, the harassed rush-about of young mothers trying to give their children every advantage, the artificial tension of go-getting salesmen, the shrieks of newspapers, the sensationalism of the movies—this kind of life seems, and is, impossible of long continuance in anything approaching real sanity. Inner life subsides to a murmur, thoughts never range free. Of those three great physicians recommended by a medieval philosopher, Dr. Repose, Dr. Temperance, Dr. Jollity, the first never gets inside the door, the second has changed his dose to cocktails before every meal, the third sounds more like hysteria. I have lived much for many years in New York, and never remember noting in the busy seasons but one thoroughly relaxed man in a public conveyance, and he was a Negro laborer, just from the South, who began to laugh at his own thoughts, and soon had a carful of people giggling shamefacedly with him.

But this life does not have a long continuance. Our busy year, thanks to American summer, has become a nine months' year and tough nerves can stand a good deal for nine months. Nine months of strenuosity, three months of let down, if not actual vacation, that is the standard experience now of the middle-class American —perhaps of all urban Americans. (7)

There is a curious bit of evidence that in spite of the increased tempo of our nine months of bustle we are showing fewer physical signs of nervous strain than did the last generation. If there was one thing upon which Americans and their foreign writers were agreed in the nineteenth century, it was that our national disease was nervous dyspepsia. But dyspepsia is evidently subsiding, indeed it is questionable whether the youngest generation knows what the name means. The typical American is no longer lean and ribbed of face, like Uncle Sam—a sign of dyspepsia. He has become typically as paunchy as the Germans, though, fortunately, not so thick about the neck. He is round-faced and of good color. Nor are the women pinched-faced and sallow like the New Englanders of earlier years, who got their complexions from nervous tensities and not from pie. Colic, hangover, flatulence, constipation are still common, to judge from the advertisements, but that gnawing of the vitals and constant malnutrition which comes from lifelong pushing to be rich, to be successful, to keep up with the Joneses, is no longer an American plague. We lunch on the cold horrors of a soda-water counter, and still keep plump of body and active in nerve. Soda mints, which used to be kept in every vest pocket and lady's reticule, have given way to sedatives, which are intended to slow down the car before the oil gives out. We stop just short of dyspepsia now, and if our nerves suffer it is from more specialized ills.

I have little doubt that the chief cause is American summer. Reading a recent French book on America, I reflected, as every French reader must have done, that no type of man or woman could last under such compulsions to be active day and night as were described there. The answer is, that for most Americans the compulsions lose half their driving power in the summertime. The Frenchman had gone home too early. He did not wait to observe us when the summer life had let down the tensions, soothed the nerves, and brought most of us back to consciousness, at least, of the quieter rhythms of nature. Even the motorist in the summer country feels the slow curves of the hills, sees the drift of the clouds, and hears when he stops—as stop he must sometime—the quiet of fields and woods. Even the most energetic of women lets down when it is too hot to dress, too humid to play bridge or go to lectures, too relaxing to be anything but easy in body and comfortable in mind.

New York is certainly not America, but it is certainly the emphasis of America. Whatever is stirring in the American consciousness gets expression there, which is why writers and artists are drawn to a city which was never built to make them feel at home. And I think the phenomena of American summer can be seen in New York as significantly as along highways, woods, or beaches. New York is never on vacation, yet it changes for summer like a woman for a love affair. Clothes, faces, movements, voices, thoughts, all go through a seasonal alteration like the easy oncomings of middle-age. I have often amused myself on Piccadilly in London by turning the eyes of the mind to Fifth Avenue or 57th Street. Invariably my pace accelerates, I draw abreast of my fellow-walkers with a compulsive stride that leaves behind legs longer than mine. But it was a winter or autumn New York of the imagination that increased my tempo. In summer, even at the noon hour, the pace of the city relaxes. The cars on a half-empty Park Avenue burr instead of roar. On the side streets the children, in wisps of garments, have taken the sidewalks for their own, the janitor sits on his steps in his undershirt, the doorman at the apartment house has no collar under his coat, and along the window sills of the tenements the housewives lean lazy breasts. The country, so remote in winter, comes back to town on the plodding feet of horses drawing wagons of flowers for window boxes, and green vegetables. But the most noticeable evidence of American summer in the city is the outward tide toward beaches and country cottages, recreation, refreshment, and rest that, at four o'clock, begins to suck a vast population into subways, trains, and boats. It is indescribably different from the commuters' rush of wintertime, as different as is the return tide in the morning, of brown, vigorous men and women, smelling of fresh air and flowers. In their nightly absence Fifth Avenue becomes a lover's strollway, and idlers hang on the railings of Radio City and the park. And this city-wide mood of pleasant yielding to humidity, heat, and evening opportunity lasts from June to Labor Day. It is the poppy and mandragora, the bromo seltzer and alka seltzer, the soft music and mental healing of our over-strenuous American life. (8)

And now, to prove that this change in American *mores* is no reversible phenomenon but a real change from the old philosophy of the Americans of whom many died but none retired, comes the American winter holiday. The winter vacation in the South, once a luxury of the rich, then a necessity for vagabonds on wheels escaping a coal bill, has become an aspiration for most Americans. Indeed, with many it has been substituted for the summer vacation, and for very apt reasons. With life in the summer now relaxed, even in the cities; with long week-ends (Friday to Monday in many industries); with the car at the door and the family at the cottage, it seems better to keep at work through the pleasant summer life, and break the hard, go-getting winter with a week or two of complete vacation on a Southern beach. Millions already do it. And week-end vacationing has spread also to the winter. Here the point is toward north instead of south. The ski-train and automobiles, ski-loaded, take youth by tens of thousands to the snowy hills each Saturday and Sunday, and already new types of inn and tourist home have spread north of the snow-line to accommodate escapists from routine.

Skiing is for youth, and to call it relaxing is perhaps a contradiction in terms. And winter vacations in the tropics are likely to remain always a luxury. In our climate it will be summer, properly lived and played with, that will chiefly serve to ease the tension in American living. When I was a boy a soft-collared shirt was called a baseball shirt, and was *infra dig.* for adults in business or the home. A belt was something to be worn on a bathing suit, and Saturday afternoon was like any other afternoon, except for boys and girls. There was something a little indecent about a turned-over collar, even when stiff, and ladies' black, ribbed stockings showed a lumpy circle above the shoe tops, even in mid-summer. Only the children made an American summer for themselves. (*9*)

Now most of the country turns young and easy-going in summer. Or, to put it less romantically, we relax into the yielding attitudes of youth at the end of every spring in a reaction against the nervous strain of winter, and in preparation for a new year. Psychologically, New Year in the Eastern and Midwestern United States comes on the day after Labor Day—a little later in the South—on the Pacific coast, perhaps at the end of the rains. January 1st is an arbitrary date; early September is when most Americans pull their zippers, tighten their neckties, take a long breath, and begin to hustle. New jobs, new expectations, new thoughts begin for them in September. Our energies, relaxed and restored in the long summer, revive with the first red leaves on the swamp maple, and the first flocks of southward moving birds.

If the foreigners who visit us will stay until summertime, as they never do, they will learn why we still survive, grow fatter not leaner, and actually, after three centuries of pursuing manifest destiny toward the Pacific and back again, seem to be developing an experimental philosophy of life. American winter—old-style— nearly extinguished the immigrant pioneers of our first century. American summer, new-style, will quite certainly save their descendants from the nervous disintegration prophesied by every European critic who has never seen us when the nights and days are hot. (*10*)

QUESTIONS

I

1. What is the European conception of Americans, and to what extent did Americans once fit that conception? (*1*)
2. To what phase of the changed way of American life does the author intend to restrict his discussion? What factors contributed to this change? (*2*)
3. What household changes were once made for summer, and what was the typical vacation of the eighties and nineties? (*3*)
4. What changes did increased wealth, more leisure, and the automobile bring into almost every part of the United States? What peculiar effect did the depression of 1929-1932 have upon the habits of many people? (*4*)

5. How are Americans adapting themselves to the summer climate? What persons does the author exclude from his discussion, and why? (5)
6. How do children's camps and summer schools fit into the author's thesis? (6)
7. What are some of the strains that three months' vacation enables us to endure? (7)
8. What is the evidence that we are standing the pressures better? How does life in New York City reflect the changed summer tempo? (8)
9. How do winter vacations help to prove the author's point? (9)
10. When is our actual New Year's and why? What effect does the author think our changed summers will have upon our national life? (10)

II

1. Do your own or your family's summer habits fit, in any way, into Mr. Canby's thesis? Do you know people who have summer homes, who go to the lakes or mountains, who take winter vacations?
2. Had you ever given the main idea of this essay any thought before you read this article? Do you find the idea challenging, stimulating, intriguing, unimportant, uninteresting?
3. Why is it especially significant that a place like New York City slackens its pace in the summer? What difference do you notice in the habits of the people in your own community in summer?
4. Have you ever read any of the European indictments of America? Did you feel that these strictures were just or unjust? Were you benefited or made angry by the charges? Do you think European visitors are better able to judge us than we can judge ourselves?
5. Do you agree with Mr. Canby's thesis that our new American summer life will save our descendants from the dangerous physical and psychological strains of modern living?

III

1. How far in this essay must the reader go to find out that the author's real purpose is to discuss the part summer plays in modern American life?
2. Point out several of the best figures of speech in this essay.
3. What has the author's use of personal observations and experiences added to the essay: for example, his father's habits of work (4), the relaxed Negro laborer from the South (7), his own New York tempo of life transferred to Piccadilly in London (8)?

WORDS

Insert, in the blanks in the sentences below, the correct word from the following: neurotic (*1*), predatory (*2*), legendary (*2*), mores (*2*), anomaly (*4*), garish (*4*), replica (*4*), cataclysm (*4*), taut (*5*), ramifications (*6*), harassed (*7*), strenuosity (*7*), dyspepsia (*8*), flatulence (*8*), sedatives (*8*).

1. Her attire was too showy and ———— to be in good taste.
2. He was ———— by worries and debts.
3. The taking of ———— may become a dangerous habit.
4. The town was submerged by a ———— from the broken dam.
5. A ———— person should consult a nerve specialist or a psychiatrist.
6. Theodore Roosevelt was noted for his vigor and ————.
7. The ———— of a people are customs that have acquired the force of unwritten law.
8. Many persons have been considered pessimists, whereas they really suffered from ————.
9. An admiral who is afraid of the water would be an ————.
10. Jesse James has become almost a ———— figure.
11. His nerves were so ———— that he thought they would snap.
12. It is not an original, but only a ———— of the famous statue.
13. ———— gives one the feeling of uncomfortable fullness in the stomach.
14. The wolf is a ———— animal.
15. The district attorney was trying to ferret out all the ———— of the gambling syndicate.

THEME TOPICS

1. My Favorite Season of the Year
2. Foreigners Do Not Understand America
3. Building Our Summer Cottage
4. The Best Summer Vacation I Ever Had
5. Children's Camps in America
6. I Attended a Summer Camp
7. The Automobile Has Changed America
8. A Week-End I Shall Never Forget
9. We Picked the Wrong Tourist Camp!
10. The Art of Relaxing

Some Typical Americans

COUNTRY DOCTOR

DON MARQUIS

IT WAS still raining; the water had been flung turbulently down out of the sky all day long. And now it was early dusk, an October dusk, and the world outside the Doctor's windows was a chaos of cold, wind-driven rain and lowering gloom and mud, the sticky black mud of northwestern Illinois which clings and clogs and overwhelms. Dr. Stewart peered out at the village street, or as much of it as he could see through the wind-slashed crevices in the murky wall of storm, and drew the heavy shawl tighter about his shoulders, and took another sip of his hot lemonade, and breathed a little prayer that he would not have a call, especially a call out to the Swamp.

He shuddered when he thought of what the Swamp would be like tonight. Green River, which drained the vast tract westward to Rock River and the Mississippi, would be up and roaring and tearing at its low clay banks; and the swamp roads—if you could call them roads at all when the spring and autumn floods were in spate—would be roiled and brawling creeks, themselves, in places, almost rivers. And here and there would be a melancholy twinkle of light, flickering through mists and scrub timber across the bogs and bayous, from some lonely farmhouse perched on a wooded island. For scattered over the district, forty miles or so in length and half as broad, were many farmers; and even when the freshets left them only a third or a quarter of the crops they had planted, they still could live, for the land was incredibly rich.

Dr. Stewart knew the Swamp and its people, none better; for day and night, winter, spring, and fall, sick or well, he had had a good many years of it.

From *O. Henry Prize Stories of 1935.* Copyrighted by Doubleday, Doran & Company, Inc., 1935. Used by permission of, and special arrangement with, Bernice M. Marquis.

"Always ague, malaria, and influenza," he murmured. And then, with grim self-irony, "I've dumped enough quinine into that hole, myself, to pave a solid road from Dante's frozen hell to Timbuctoo, and still it shakes, shivers, and shakes." (*1*)

He shivered, himself, for he had the flu, and put another lump of soft coal on the grate fire. His office was in the front part of his residence on the main street, and presently he noticed a bedraggled object bogged down in a lake of mud across the way, and chuckled. A feeble glimmer from the post-office windows illumined its dejected contours.

"Young Dr. Hastings' horseless carriage," grinned Dr. Stewart to himself.

People still called them "horseless carriages" in the late nineties of the last century.

"I can see how Hastings might break his arm cranking the damned thing," he mused, "but how the deuce did he manage to break his leg? He's got no right to break his leg and leave all the work on Jones and me . . . and Jones just a kid out of college last spring, and me sick, and the whole damned country down with flu and pneumonia!" He snorted indignantly. "Horseless carriage! Hell!" he said.

Then he reflected, "They'll be all right when there are some decent roads for them to run on."

For he was not against progress, far from it. He had seen too much of it not to believe in its continuity. Born in Ohio the same year the British burned the White House in Washington, he had seen the country grow up, and opined that it had a healthy constitution. Ohio had been "out West" when he was a lad; he was now past eighty, and Illinois had long been "an old settled country." Nearer sixty than fifty years of practice of medicine lay between his student days and this present evening.

He shook himself, as if to shake off the sense of the gloom outside and something of the dread that had settled on his spirits— the dread of a call, in his present condition.

"I haven't got time to be sick!" he said. "People need me."

For he was a country doctor, and he did not know what it was to spare himself. He had been going hard all last winter and spring —battling through prairie blizzards, battling through flooded spring swamps, to some remote house of suffering, battling all night to save a life, and reaching home again in the dawn, to gulp down a pot of boiling coffee and take up the new day's work without an hour of sleep. His hands and feet had been frozen again last winter, but no frost had reached the stout old heart within. But now, he faced a new winter—and before it was fairly begun, here he was, sick!

He hadn't time to be sick, he told himself again, rebelliously. So *many* people needed him! There were the Simpkins children, down with the measles, for instance; and nobody knew the Simpkins constitution, or how to bring out measles on the reluctant Simpkins hide, as well as he did.

And there were the Rays, and the Tuckers, and the Prices and the Smiths—sickness in all these families, and what did the two young doctors, Hastings and Jones, know about them? Good doctors, no doubt; fine, conscientious boys—but boys. They had never fought through more than half a century of chill midnights hand to hand with death. And these were *his* people that were sick, in the village, on the prairie farms round about, out in the Swamp—*his* people, and they needed him, and what right did he have to be nursing himself here at home? It wasn't natural.

Nobody ever heard him say anything about loving these people. Nor did they talk about loving him. Nor did anybody ever hear the word "service," so popular since, from his lips. The nearest thing to an expression of affection on either side would be something like this: "Don't you love to rile Old Doc Stewart, just to hear him cuss?" But there was a pretty good understanding between the Doctor and his people. He had helped bring more than one generation of them into the world; and helped to make a little easier the way out of it for some of their fathers and grandfathers. They took him as naturally as they did sunlight and rain and the change of seasons, and, some of them, as thoughtlessly. He was the last man they paid, after settling with the grocers, the implement dealers, and for the interest on the mortgage.... (2)

A mud-splattered man on a mud-splattered horse wallowed through the mire, and came to a stop in front of his house. A second later the man hammered on the outside door.

"It's come!" groaned Dr. Stewart.

He had known it would, had "felt it in his bones." He let the man in himself, for his housekeeper was nursing a case of pneumonia in the village, and, save for her, he lived alone. He was a childless widower.

He opened the door, and one of his own Swamp Angels, as he called them, stood dripping mud and water in the entry way.

"Jason Tucker, isn't it?" said the Doctor, peering at him.

"Uh-huh," said Tucker. "Howdy, Doc?" A manner of apology, as well as mud and water, oozed from his disheveled wetness.

There was an instant's silence, while the two regarded each other by the gleam of the kerosene lamp in the narrow hallway; and the Doctor read his doom in Tucker's earnestness and anxiety.

"Is it Myra, Jase?"

"Uh-huh; her time's come," said Tucker.

"Yes; it would be about now," nodded the Doctor reflectively.

"First baby, too," said Tucker, twisting his drenched cap in his nervous fingers, till a little rivulet of water was squeezed from it and ran down to the floor. He gulped, and added, "She was an old maid when we was married. And she's got this here *la grippe* on top of everything else, Doctor. What I'm scared of is it turnin' into pneumonia, if it ain't turned already."

Then, with a quick look at the Doctor, "You're sick, yourself, Doc?"

"Not so sprightly, Jase," admitted Dr. Stewart.

There was another moment's silence. Then Tucker cleared his throat, and murmured, "Doc Hastings, he's got a busted leg. His shin bone. 'Twixt his ankle and knee. It's in a splint."

He gulped again, and added anxiously, "I seen it myself, Doc— his leg's really broke."

"Of course," murmured Dr. Stewart.

After another moment, Tucker said, "And Doc Jones, he's out on the Swamp somewheres himself, and I can't get into touch with him." He paused, and drew a long breath. "It's a turrible imposition to come to you, Doc, and you sick like you be."

The thought took shape in the Doctor's mind, though he did

not utter the words: "It's more than an imposition; it's probably my death."

For he was running a temperature, and he was weak; it meant, almost certainly, pneumonia. And then there was that pain in the cardiac region, which, he had been telling himself, was only pseudo-angina pectoris. Well, pseudo or the real thing, it didn't make much difference at his age; the fact was that the heart had been strained and enlarged, last winter. Oh, damn it! He didn't have time for all this self-diagnosis!

These were the thoughts that ran through his mind. But what he said was, "I'll go, Jase."

"Thanks, Doc; I knowed you would," said Tucker. "How you goin'?"

"Come in," said Dr. Stewart. He scribbled on a prescription pad. "Take that over to the drug store and get it filled. Get back home as quick as you can with it, and give her the dose that will be marked on the bottle." Then he answered the other's question. "Buggy," he said.

"Green River's up and a-rarin' tonight," said Tucker. "Don't trust the wooden bridge, Doc—take the iron one. It's a mile further, but it's safer."

"I've seen it up and a-rarin' before," said Dr. Stewart grimly.

The men exchanged a brief glance. Neither of them said a word of the thought in their minds, but both were thinking of the same thing. Myra Tucker was, in a way, one of Dr. Stewart's artistic creations. She had been a country school-teacher, and, four or five years before, she had been kicked by a horse and fallen down, and the horse had then trodden upon her face, breaking her nose and her cheek bones and her jaws. Dr. Stewart had practically built a new face for her, feeding her through tubes until she got the use of her jaws again, and grafting skin from her arms and legs—and this in a day before skin-grafting was generally practiced. Myra had been a pug-nosed girl of no beauty; and it had pleased the Doctor, when he made her face over, to give her a bold, aquiline nose.

This was in the days before hospitals in the country regions, or district nurses; he had done it all himself, without help. Myra had some fine, thin lines, scars, on her face after it was healed. But the new nose made a different person of her. Dr. Stewart always said he was responsible for her improved profile, and, indeed, for her marriage to Jason. That made him responsible for this baby that was trying to get itself born out there in the Swamp in the midst of such difficulties.

He chuckled under his breath at the thought, and murmured to himself, "I wonder if the baby will inherit the Roman nose I gave Myra, or her natural one?"

"What say, Doc?" asked Tucker.

"Nothing—except that Green River was up and a-rarin' the night Myra was born, herself, Jase."

"Yep," said Jase; "you borned her, Doc, didn't you?" And he disappeared into the gloom. (3)

Dr. Stewart put on his overcoat and a raincoat over that, and went to the stable, lighted a lantern, and hitched up his horse.

"Two miles north to the county line," he said to himself, "and then four miles west to the iron bridge.... Here! Damn your hide! How'd you like to get lashed in the face yourself with a wet tail? Huh?"

This was to his horse, the latest of a long line of animals familiar with mud and dust and snow.

"If you don't get over that trick of using your tail like a wind-mill every time I try to put a crupper under it, I'll...I'll"—he paused to think up a terrifying threat—"I'll sell you to a circus, where they'll make you walk a tight rope and feed you on barbed wire."

He was always making terrible promises to his horses—that they should go to the treadmill, or be manufactured into bologna sausage, or the like; but as a matter of fact he never even carried a buggy whip. His horses perfectly understood the oratorical nature of his threats. Animals worshipped the man. Stray dogs gravitated to his office in the village with such regularity that he had a theory they must have the house marked, as tramps are said to mark houses. All about the place he had nailed up tin cans to trees and posts, which he kept filled with water for the birds in hot, dry weather.

In spite of his coats and lap robe, the Doctor was wet to the

skin before he was well into the area where muddy prairie
began to merge with drowned swamp, for the wind, so to speak,
showed a diabolical cleverness in taking the rain in hand as if it
were a weapon, and slicing and slashing with it, thrusting it like a
fencer through and around and past all defenses. Half an hour of
this soaking—for the Doctor moved slowly over the wretched
roads—and he was sure that his temperature was rising.

He stopped, and thrust his thermometer under his tongue, and
read what it registered by the light of his lantern. It was as he had
suspected. But he went on; he was bound for Jason Tucker's,
and he would get there, he told himself, in spite of hell and high
water. He only hoped that he would arrive before the baby
did ... or, to put it that way, before the mother ... was gone.

Thickest night came on, and his horse had difficulty in keeping
to the road. Not that it made much difference. The going when
the animal stumbled off it, with the buggy lurching after, was
about as good. The sense of sight was practically blocked off;
and the sense of hearing brought to him little more than a mingled
tumult of waters, far and near, where creek and rivulet met and
swelled the roadside ditches, or dashed against and bit into and
tore at the gravel-surfaced road itself.

He had been traveling something more than an hour, perhaps,
when the sound of these random streams began to be merged
with a steady roaring ... Green River was ahead of him and it
was, as Jason Tucker had said, "up and a-rarin'."

He paused at the road which branched off to the wooden
bridge, and got out of his buggy, leaving the horse standing in
the road; he could trust the animal to stay quietly until he returned. He wanted to look at the condition of the wooden bridge,
himself. He splashed through the mud to the bank of the stream,
holding his lantern ahead of him, and ...

And paused just in time. There wasn't any wooden bridge! It
had gone down-stream. A line of willow trees, which he remembered as having marked the entrance to it, was not thirty feet
from shore.

He had still cherished a hope that the bridge might be there
and might be passable, for it would save him a mile or so of mud
and ruts ... half a mile to the west, and half a mile back east

again, after he had crossed the new iron bridge, to get back into the road which passed the Tucker house.

"Rarin' is right!" said the Doctor, peering out at the flood, on the surface of which his lantern cast a few dancing yellow gleams.

He looked for only a few seconds, but it was long enough to see a chicken coop, part of a straw stack, and a dead pig with all four feet sticking stiffly up in the air, go whirling by.

When he got to the iron bridge he stopped and got out of his buggy once more, for an examination. The water was boiling and spouting over the roadway on the bridge itself, but the structural ironwork looked solid and unshaken. He walked out a few yards on the bridge, stamping on the planks; there was more than a foot of water swirling over the planks; it lashed him nearly to the knees.

"Drenched from toenails to tonsils," said the Doctor to himself. And then, ironically, "The thing to do with this influenza, or grip, as they call it, Dr. Stewart, is to stay warmly in bed, with your feet dry, and avoid violent exertion of any sort; for the heart at such times is particularly susceptible to strains."

Something banged against the eastern and upstream ironwork of the bridge as he made this facetious recommendation to himself, and then crashed into splinters. The air in front of him was suddenly filled with broken timbers, and, strangely, out of the débris was propelled a speckled hen, which cried shrilly to earth and heaven and flood that she was wet, and outraged because of it, and then disappeared into the howling night. The major portion of some farmer's barn had slammed into the bridge, and the impact shook the structure. But still it seemed to withstand the shock.

Nevertheless, it was nothing to drive out upon gayly and blithely, with all that water whirling over it. The Doctor went back to where he had left his horse.

"I'll lead him across," he said to himself, and started off, his lantern in one hand and the horse with the lurching buggy following. Although the flood rushing across the bridge was not deep, it was swift, and plucked and sucked at his feet. But he went on, and the horse patiently splashed along behind.

In a few moments he paused. Where the hell *was* the west end
of this bridge, anyhow? He must be nearly across it and...

By the Great Horned Toad of Mithridates! There wasn't any
west end to it! Nothing ahead of him but water rushing across his
path! He reflected on this phenomenon of a bridge unanchored
at one end and still standing sturdily, for a moment, and then the
solution came to him. The ironwork was stout enough, but
between the west end of the bridge and what had been the shore
the flood had cut a new channel, narrow, and he did not know
how deep.

He would have to cross that, and it was nothing to be got
through in a buggy. Nor, he suspected, on foot, either. He
unhitched the horse from the buggy, tied up the traces to the
horse collar, shortened the driving reins. He'd have to mount and
ride the horse through. The buggy he would leave where it was,
and it could either sink or swim.

"Damned old worn-out buggy, anyhow," he said.

He took from the vehicle, not his bag, but a smaller, leather-
bound pocket case, with a dozen vials in it: morphine tablets,
strychnine tablets, a couple of small bottles of brandy, a hypodermic syringe, a thermometer, digitalis, other things. He put this
case in the inner breast pocket of his overcoat. The larger bag
would be in the way on horseback. The lantern he left, lighted,
on the buggy seat.

As he made the effort and mounted the horse, a sharp pain in
the region of the left breast took his breath; for a moment he
closed his eyes and hung onto the horse's mane.

"Damned old worn-out Doctor, too, I guess," he breathed,
when he could breathe again. The pang passed. He pulled himself together on the horse's back, and then said, with a resonance
in his voice, "But I'm going through!"

It was a challenge to the night and the storm and the treacherous swamp and the wind and all the physical elements; the
challenge of the old man's undaunted spirit. There were people
ahead who needed what he could do for them, and he was going
through! He had always gone through; for more than fifty years
he had been going through.

There was a cramp in his left arm. It kinked and twisted. He knew what that meant. He clung to the animal's mane with his right hand, and dug his muddy heels into its flanks. To hell with the angina! He didn't have time to stop for that. Probably it was only pseudo-angina, anyhow...gas pressing up...indigestion... it was time, at his age, he was getting a little sense about what he ate and when he ate it...he was strict enough with other people's diet....

The horse wallowed into the cut at the west end of the bridge; and if there was a shore on the other side, neither horse nor rider could see it. The Doctor felt the water about his knees... about his thighs...it was up to his seat...the horse staggered... and then...

A black choking...a frantic, lashing struggle...where was the horse? A strained, instinctive muscular reaction...a blankness... and Dr. Stewart found himself clinging to the roots of a willow tree. The rushing water still pulled at his feet and legs and sodden clothing. But he clung. He strove to pull himself up the slippery bank. But the pain...the pain in his chest...it was terrible...but he held on to his willow root...he lay, half in and half out of the water, and was lifted and threshed about by the insensate, brute flood...but he held on...he was going through! Another agonizing effort, and he felt the flood release his legs. He would lie here in the mud a while and rest...it was soft, the mud was. But that pain in his chest! It was as if it were filled with hot ashes, that shifted back and forth and burned and burned when he tried to breathe. No...hot snuff...more like snuff than ashes ...it burned and burned... burned like hot snuff would burn, if you had snuff in your lungs.

Presently he managed to get his hand into his overcoat pocket and draw out the leather-bound little case. The morphine tablets were in the first vial. He took one, and lay back in the mud.

"Must look like a damn' old white-whiskered muskrat," said Dr. Stewart to himself.

He stared up at the sky. And presently he noted something. The storm had broken. The wind was blowing a section of the heavens clear of clouds. He took another morphine tablet. A corner of the moon was clear of cloud. There was a star near it.

There was something he wanted to say to that star...he couldn't quite remember what it was. His chest was a little easier...a good deal easier...oh, yes, what he wanted to say was, if you stuck it out long enough the mud got a little warmer after a while...the tension in his chest was relaxed; that was a little warmer, too.... No; that wasn't what he wanted to say to that star! What he wanted to say to it was, "Damned funny you didn't get drowned ...neither one of us got drowned...damned funny!"

He lay back; he felt almost comfortable...although his mouth did taste like he'd swallowed a raw catfish...damned funny animal, the catfish...especially the variety known as the bullhead. He knew how a bullhead must feel in the nice, warm mud in the summertime, and it wasn't so bad.

Then, suddenly, thought returned, in its complete and cruel lucidity, and he struggled to a sitting posture, and then to his feet! Jase Tucker's wife was sick, and he had to get there! He stumbled up the bank to the road. Something was moving up there, some animal. He stood staring, trying to penetrate the night. It came nearer to him, and stopped. It was his horse, marvelously escaped from the torrent, which had scrambled free from the river and waited in the road. The animal nuzzled at his elbow, as if in relieved welcome. And his own relief was boundless—thank heaven, he wouldn't have to walk that last half-mile to the Tucker house! He doubted if he could have walked that far.

He could see the lights of the farmhouse, gleaming through the roadside trees, in the distance; and he tried to mount the horse again. But the effort brought another sharp pang in his chest, and he desisted. (4)

He put his right arm over the horse's neck and twined his fingers in the mane. His left arm was...not so good.

"If you've got sense enough to let me guide you," he told the animal, "we can still make it."

He had started out to go to Jase Tucker's place, and that was where he was going. And, supporting himself in this fashion, he made it.

"And none too soon," said the Doctor, as he pulled himself wearily up the gravel path from the road to the front door. For the screams of a woman in the vital anguish of childbirth stabbed his ears.

He opened the front door without ceremony, and stood within the little living-room—the parlor, as they called it. Myra was in the best bedroom just off the parlor. The door was open, and he went in. Jase Tucker sat in a corner. Bending over the bed where the woman lay groaning and writhing was a young man with black circles about his eyes and a two days' stubble of beard on his face; he lurched and stumbled strangely towards Dr. Stewart.

"Hello, Doctor," he said. "You got here!"

"She'll come through, Hastings?" inquired Dr. Stewart.

"If the heart lasts," said Hastings.

"Hearts are hell," said Dr. Stewart.

They delivered the baby, and not until then did Dr. Stewart's consciousness fully take note of the fact that this was, indeed, the young Dr. Hastings who was supposed to be back in the village with a broken leg.

"How the hell did *you* get here, Hastings?"

"On a horse. I told Jase I couldn't come. And then I got worried for fear *you* couldn't make it...bad night, and everything, you know...and so I came anyhow. I must have passed you on the road somewhere."

"I was in the mud," murmured Dr. Stewart. "Quite a while, I guess."

Hastings repeated, almost apologetically, "I thought you might not get here." His leg was giving him great pain. He started to speak again.

But he paused. A change had come over Dr. Stewart's face. Hastings supported him, or Dr. Stewart would have fallen. Hastings eased him to a sofa. Dr. Stewart tried to roll up his sleeve.

"Heart, Hastings," he muttered, as he fumbled with his sleeve. The younger man slid it up for him, and the needle went beneath his skin. But, oh, that choking agony...the hot ashes...the hot snuff...hot sand....

"Hastings!" he said. "Keep me alive...for a while. I haven't *got time* to be sick! I haven't *got time* to die! Not till this damn' flu epidemic is over....People need me...Keep me going!"

Pretty soon the drug began to take effect; again came the warmth, the relaxation, something more like easiness. But no strength with it. He seemed to himself to be swaying, drifting, falling, floating; carried on by a full tide. Why, he was in Green River again, he thought, and it was rushing him on...down-stream....

It was not so unpleasant now, either. But he must get through. He mustn't let himself drift like this, pleasant as it was. There were people on the other side, people who needed him. He must make an effort.

Clarity returned for a moment.

"Hastings," he said again, as if he were just now seeing the young man for the first time that night, "you got here, broken leg and all!"

And then something of resonance returned to his voice; and he sat fully upright on the couch and spoke loudly—spoke as a commanding general might, in breveting a younger officer for gallantry on a field of battle, with pride and authority and affection in his tones:

"By heavens, boy," he said, "*you're* a Doctor!"

He sighed a long, deep sigh, and relaxed. He let the tide carry him on downstream. He had time now, time to let himself be carried away. He was leaving his people in good hands.

There was the wail of a baby from the bedroom.

"Another damn' little Swamp Angel squawking," said Old Doc Stewart, and smiled; and, smiling, went on with the rushing waters. (*5*)

QUESTIONS

I

1. What was the weather at the opening of the story, and what kind of place was "the Swamp"? (*1*)
2. What was the condition of Dr. Stewart's own health, and what other doctors were available to serve the community? (*2*)
3. What was the nature of Jason Tucker's visit, and in what sense was Myra Tucker Dr. Stewart's "creation"? (*3*)
4. What adventures did Dr. Stewart have on his trip to the Tuckers'? (*4*)

5. How had Dr. Hastings "proved" himself, and why was Dr. Stewart willing to turn the swamp people over to him? (5)

II

1. Have you ever known a real country doctor? Did he in any way resemble Dr. Stewart?
2. What characteristics of medical men and of the medical profession are exemplified in Don Marquis' story? In what ways do present-day doctors and specialists often differ from the old country doctor?
3. If you were planning to be a doctor, would you choose general practice or become a specialist? What do you think of socialized medicine?
4. For which one of the professions do you have the greatest respect? Which one do you think performs the greatest service?
5. Professional men have usually been held in higher public esteem than business men. Do you think this attitude is justified? Do you think it is changing? Can you think of any of the professions that are not held in as high regard as they once were?

III

1. Analyze the first paragraph as an excellent example of giving the setting of the story. Notice how smoothly the *when*, the *where*, and the *who* of the plot are introduced.
2. One of the necessary requirements of a short story writer is the ability to create characters—in this instance, the character of Dr. Stewart. Point out all the places in the story in which you learn what kind of man he was. How has Don Marquis shown his skill in giving you this information?
3. Why does the author indicate that "love" and "service" were not the key words in the old doctor's vocabulary? What was the real impelling motive in his relation to *his* people? Why does the author establish the fact that he was a "childless widower"?
4. What do you think of the imaginative passage in which, lying in the mud, Dr. Stewart talks to the stars while the morphine takes effect? (4)
5. How does the author skilfully describe the soothing effect of the drug which Dr. Hastings gave Dr. Stewart? (5)
6. How is the last sentence an especially appropriate close for this story? (5)
7. Being an artist, Don Marquis has not moralized nor preached upon the *meaning* of Dr. Stewart's life. What satisfying aesthetic experience does this leave to the reader?

WORDS

Place the word from the left-hand column before the word or phrase in the right-hand column with which it makes satisfactory sense.

1. lowering *(1)*	1. scream
2. rebelliously *(2)*	2. nose
3. reluctant *(2)*	3. hair
4. disheveled *(3)*	4. from the cyclone
5. aquiline *(3)*	5. remarks
6. diabolical *(4)*	6. inclined subjects
7. facetious *(4)*	7. of mind
8. débris *(4)*	8. frown
9. resonance *(4)*	9. witness
10. insensate *(4)*	10. leer
11. agonizing *(4)*	11. of the drum
12. lucidity *(4)*	12. villain

THEME TOPICS

1. Our Family Doctor
2. The High Ethics of the Medical Profession
3. The College Health Service and the Students
4. I Intend to Be a Doctor (a Nurse)
5. The New Age Calls for Specialists
6. I Had an Operation
7. My First Visit to a Hospital
8. A Doctor in an Emergency (Automobile Accident, a Mining Disaster, Fire, Explosion)
9. The Doctor in War Time
10. The High Requirements of Medical Colleges

SHINING ARMOUR

CHANNING POLLOCK

HAVE you ever suspected how much your behavior, and your attitude toward life, are influenced by that of the men and women you admire in books and plays?

Well, not *yours*, perhaps, but the behavior and attitude of a good many people around you—a hundred million or so, who haven't your stamina, and your force of character. Just *everyday* people.

A long time ago, I was associated with a theatrical manager who made a five-year contract with one of the most popular actors in England. Immediately afterward, the actor got himself mixed up in an affair that gave him some very unfavorable publicity, and my employer began to regard his contract as a total loss.

"Women won't go to see that man act," he said.

I thought over the matter carefully, and decided that our one chance was to cover our actor's common clay with the gilt of romance. Nobody could deny his misconduct, but we might make it seem the peccadillo of a heedless, fearless, hard-riding, hard-living young Englishman. The only trouble was that our hero proved to be nothing of the sort. He wouldn't ride because he was afraid of the horse. He wouldn't swim because he was afraid of the water.

However, we persevered. We photographed him on horseback, and blacked out the halter by which a groom was holding the horse. We syndicated newspaper stories of his daring swim through Hell Gate. We pictured him a modern combination of Byron and Casanova; a reckless, devil-may-care breaker of hearts, and horses, and rules, and records.

And did our young actor like the picture? I'll say he did! It fascinated him far more than we ever expected it to fascinate the matinée girls. The first thing we knew, he had actually learned to ride. And then to swim, and to fence. He began swaggering a little, and to believe himself really the fearless fellow we had painted him. He grew to be what we said he was; he walked into our lion's skin, and wore it until it became his own.

Fifteen years later, when the war broke out, he won world-wide distinction in the North Sea Patrol, and more medals than a coster has buttons on his Sunday suit.

At a dinner in London, a few months ago, with a dozen guests at his table, my old friend, a little gray around the temples now, lifted his glass to me, and laughingly proposed a toast "to my creator." "The Lord didn't make me as I am," he said. "Pollock did. He gave me a role so glamorous that I've spent my life trying to fill it."

That's what a good many millions of us are trying to do— trying to be like the girl we admired in the movies, or the man in the novel who always smiled and nonchalantly lit a cigarette when he found himself facing the business end of a gun.

And that's why it's so darned important what our authors make glamorous.

Shining armour.

Crime?

Cynicism?

Sophistication?

Or what?

Last winter, Professor Richard Burton and I witnessed a typical theatrical success in New York. On her wedding night, the heroine saw someone she liked better than her husband, and went off with him. A very smart woman, that, witty and wise and so attractively worldly as to make us utterly ashamed of such oafish conduct as twenty-five years' continuance with the same helpmate.

Last week, at a movie, my wife and I and five hundred other Pomonas stared wide-eyed at a dashing young gentleman who slept on satin pillows, and left his business and his partners to be ruined while he went to Europe with a lady who thought life was just one wild party after another.

And a gosh-awful lot of us wished we might be like that, and resolved then and there to spend the rest of our lives trying to fit ourselves into the picture. Maybe we couldn't manage the satin pillows, but the cynical attitude, the ha-ha at dull care and the decencies—well, that's pretty smart, even without satin! (*1*)

Why doesn't somebody discover the glory of doing your job, and the romance of loving your wife?

What *is* shining armour?

Anne lives in Virginia; I met her when I was at school in Warrenton. She was the prettiest girl in Fauquier County—and she's still in Fauquier County, still unmarried, coaxing a living out of the farm, and taking care of a mother who has been blind thirty years, and has no one else.

John went into business with a dishonest partner, who plunged the firm into debt, and then filed a petition in bankruptcy. Working for a small salary, doing without almost everything a man can do without, John has paid every dollar, and, at fifty, is beginning all over again.

Jeannette found a job, and did the bread-winning, while her husband wrote, and failed, and wrote, and failed, and, finally, turned out the best-selling and most brilliant book of its year.

These three stories, and thirty others of the same type, have been a long time in my notebooks. "Somebody ought to write 'em," I thought. "Somebody ought to show that these are the real and representative romances and gallantries, and set us admiring and trying to emulate John and Jeannette rather than the Hair-Trigger Mikes and the Gold-Digging Gerties."

And then I met Fred on Fifth Avenue.

Fred is a linen salesman. He has never earned more than forty dollars a week in his life, and, on this salary, he and Clara have bought and own their home in New Jersey, and have sent two boys through college.

That summer afternoon in 1926, he was shabbily dressed in a shiny old suit of blue serge—and you know how blue serge *can* shine, and *where*. I asked him why he couldn't treat himself a little better, now that the house was paid for and the boys were doing well.

"I'm carrying a lot of life insurance," Fred answered. "I've got to be awfully sure that Clara's all right when I'm gone."

He turned away, rather shamefacedly. A stray sunbeam fell across his shoulders, and, suddenly, I saw, not shiny serge, but shining armour. Not Fifth Avenue, but Camelot, and a plumed knight with a sword at his side, and his lady's colors worn across his coat of mail.

"What's the difference," I thought, "between that man and Lancelot? Those heroes of the lists fought twenty minutes for the women they loved, and Fred has fought forty years. There are millions of Freds—all around us. Alexander's army marches into the subway every morning, and gives battle, and comes back at night to millions of castles, where some woman has kept the flag flying.

"That's why we continue to be a nation, in spite of the grafters, and the gunmen, and the loose ladies; and the way to show the glory of these lives is to show that there isn't any real difference between the millions of Freds and the steel-clad warriors who fought at Antioch and Carcassonne."

Shining armour!

I didn't know how much of it there was in the world until I began collecting my Annes and Johns and Jeannettes, and their adventures, and mine, to make the play that was produced last March under the title of The House Beautiful.

What was the best way to prove that there is no difference between the Freds and the Lancelots? I decided to present an everyday hero, as all of us saw him, and then as his wife saw him—a romantic wife, brought up on Idylls of the King, who translated the struggles and steadfastnesses of everyday into fundamentally identical incidents of the age of chivalry. We were to see these incidents first in serge, and then in armour. What happens to all of us now that is recognizably the same thing that happened to all of us at the Round Table? (2)

Let's see....

Twenty-five years ago, my wife and I were starting life together on two little salaries and one set of big hopes, and—what

was the first thing we wanted? A home, of course! A shockingly
bromidic desire, that, and quite too distressingly sentimental for
a Broadway that weeps over "torch songs," and accepts as new
and sophisticated the romance of the lady who has a child
by a chance visitor, and suffers the anguish of remaining with
her husband. Luckily for our race, however, interest in the
home continues to be more typical than interest in chance
visitors, and the struggle for that home is certainly one thing
that hasn't changed intrinsically since "Adam dolve, and Eve
span."

Our own struggle kept my wife with Oscar Hammerstein, who
was trying his hand at grand opera, and myself at a desk in the
Lyric Theater. I had written five plays—one a great success—
without getting very much out of any of them, and I was doing
more plays—nights and Sundays—and publicity for the Shubert
Theatrical Enterprises, and articles every month for three different magazines.

Every penny we could rake and scrape was put aside for a
home, and fifty of the real-estate agents who became a character
in the play about shining armour showed us every bit of marsh
and waste land within two hours' train ride of New York.

"Where the red barn is, that's going to be Bryant Circle—and
the new Public Library." I wonder how often we heard *that*
story!

Once, when we had prefaced our trip with the expression of
a wish for woodland, we found ourselves in a grove of fifteen-
foot evergreens. My wife leaned against one, and it fell at her
feet. Every tree in that grove had been cut down and brought
there the day before; sharpened at the bottom, and pressed, root-
less, into the ground.

We bought an acre of sand on a cliff overlooking Long Island
Sound, and signed a contract for a house. Three weeks later,
when we returned to the spot, the dwelling stood there before us.

"I'm afraid to lean against it," said my wife, remembering the
tree. My own impression was that someone had painted the building on a back drop. One side hadn't been shingled, and bore the
names of half a dozen of the biggest department stores in New
York. Advertising? Not a bit of it! Rather than buy lumber, the

contractor had done his sheathing with packing cases in which our furniture had been sent out from town.

However, to us, the place was incredibly a castle. "I can't believe we own a whole house," my wife remarked. "Sometimes I look at the faucets, in the kitchen, and say, 'Well, *they* belong to us anyway.'" (3)

Romance? Adventure? The *real* romance and adventure are in every little flat and cottage, and in every office and on every farm in America.

Times Square and Hollywood continue committed to the "kick" of that moment in which somebody pokes a pistol into somebody else's belt buckle, and somebody else escapes by deftly tossing the contents of a cigarette paper into the gun toter's eyes.

But how many of us ever toted a gun, or had one superimposed upon our belt buckles, or get more than passing excitement out of seeing it superimposed?

What happens to *us* is that we fall in love, and marry, and plan for the baby, and sit holding his hot little hand and trying to read the thoughts of the doctor.

That's true suspense, and most of us have experienced it, and understand it, and know that there is more honest-to-goodness drama in that dawn by the bedside than in whole arsenals of gangsters' guns and whole life histories of those celluloid ladies who "played with passion, and made men the dangerous toys of soul-searing ecstasy."

Tragedy? Ask the man who has lost his job.

Sacrifice? Inveigle his wife into telling you what she and the children are doing without.

Heroism? Take all the gunmen, uniformed and ununiformed, out of the newspapers, and still you'll read of twenty heroes a day, and there'll be twenty thousand who never got into the newspapers.

Have you a little hero in your home? I'll say you have! The world grows heroes fifty bushel to the acre—everyday men and women—and yet one-third of the novels published, one-half of the plays produced, and nearly all the motion pictures seem devoted to the glorification of crime and the gratification of sex.

Don't tell me there isn't material for fiction and drama in my kind of heroes. Most of the world's best literature deals with them and their stories. Dickens, Thackeray, Stevenson, Kipling, Conrad, Zangwill and Thomas Hardy; Goethe, Balzac, Zola, Cervantes, Tolstoy, Dostoyevsky—the list is endless.

Our own authors seem to have had a special flair for simple folk and simple lives—Hawthorne, Howells, O. Henry, Ellen Glasgow, Ruth McEnery Stuart, Willa Cather, Mary Stewart Cutting, and the rest.

What books and plays have wielded the most important influence? We begin with Uncle Tom's Cabin.

Indeed, as Louise Maunsell Field declares, it wasn't until the later 1920's that our literature began celebrating the weakling and the psychopathic, materialism and the meretricious.

With the vogue of the movies—or, maybe, before—virtue became stupid, and fiction one continuous parade of motor cars, machine guns and satin pillows.

Shining armour?

Or merely tin foil?

Some months ago, a motion-picture magnate wrote me, "Submerged heroes do not furnish our leading men with glamorous parts."

I wondered then whether these leading men could see anything glamorous in a U. S. Grant hauling wood or in a Lincoln splitting it, and reflected upon the changed ideals of a nation that found its idols in gentlemen whose habitual attitude left you in doubt as to whether they were trying to kiss the lady or break her back. (4)

But it was the glamour of the Grants and Lincolns, of the Bradfords, and Franklins, and Crocketts that made us great. Greatness, for nations or individuals, does not lie in admiration and emulation of gunmen and grafters and night-club hostesses and stock gamblers, nor even of those glittering gentry whose chief attainments are obsequious valets and secretaries, wild women and high-powered motors.

Not that our everyday heroes are necessarily "submerged"; necessarily little people or failures.

"What is success?" I asked in The Fool, and "What is a little man?" I asked in The House Beautiful. All the heroes in my best plays—Daniel Gilchrist, Carl Behrend, John Jones and Archie Davis—have been "little men," but they wore shining armour, and fought the good fight. The good fight needn't be Austerlitz or Armageddon.

Once upon a time, my brother "ran for" mayor of Leonia, New Jersey. The excitement over John's campaign may have been more restricted than that over Lincoln's, but it was quite as intense, and our resentment of the falsehoods circulated about him was not one whit less than or different from the resentment the Lincolns must have felt in hearing their candidate described as a "blood-thirsty despot" and "King Abraham I."

And that battle, won by "a landslide of nine votes," that willingness to lose home and friends rather than compromise with conscience, seems to me to be no little heroism, and pretty good stuff for drama, at a time when most city governments are notoriously corrupt, and many people find nothing surprising or shameful in the idea that "everybody gets his, and it doesn't much matter how he gets it."

This spirit—the ignoring of all armour that isn't gold-incrusted—seems to me one of the major dangers of the stuff we are publishing and presenting today.

Not that I take much stock in the defense that vice is generally punished in these stories, and that the criminal usually ends in prison or a welter of his own blood. *That* doesn't keep the vice and crime from being glamorous, and interesting, and exciting; and what high-spirited youth ever hesitated to embark upon a career because of its dangers?

There can be little doubt that the mirror fiction holds up to Nature reflects both ways—that gangsters in life create gangsters in plays, but that gangsters in plays also create gangsters in life, and on a much larger scale.

It is no accident that the toy one sees most commonly on the streets is a pistol.

Whatever our popular literature and drama and motion pictures make smart, and attractive, and adventurous and heroic, that is the thing the more susceptible of us are going to try our utmost to be and do.

Within a few days, a weak-chinned lad, with a high-sounding

name that he bestowed upon himself, has been condemned to the electric chair. For twenty years or more, that name has been common in tales of desperadoes.

Last week, a girl's "love life" ended in violent death. "Opening her library," the newspapers report, "the detectives found it full of murder, mystery and cheap love stories."

Did anyone ever hear of a criminal whose hero was David Copperfield, or of a promiscuous girl whose heroine was the Lily Maid of Astolat?

I hold no brief for a literature made up of prigs and ingénues, but there seems no better reason for a literature of gunmen and vamps.

When I see a motion-picture advertisement reading, "The woman every modern woman wants to be...Tarnished Lady," I say that, if that ever gets to be true, the blame will lie with Times Square and Hollywood.

And, as I started to remark, even that isn't the major danger. The major danger is the inoculation of the idea that only the spectacular can be worth doing, and that only the satin and the six-cylindered can be worth striving for.

Heroism is a triumph of brawn or marksmanship; "sophistication" is a flouting of all the sober decencies; and success manifests itself in materialistic acquirement.

And are we trying to wear that kind of tin foil?

Look at your salesgirls, and stenographers, and even at your own daughters.

The pretty young thing who officiates in our rural bakeshop can't keep her mind on the rolls for trying to project the "it" of Clara Bow. The soda-water clerk at the corner lays manicured fingers on the fizz-jerker with the gesture of John Barrymore stroking his lady's arm.

Is the bakeshop girl, or the soda-water clerk, entertaining any ambition that has to do with plain living, and high thinking, and true nobility of soul? Where d'ya git that stuff? Does she want to be a Florence Nightingale, or he an Emerson or a Roosevelt? Not on your plucked eyebrows, or your pee-wee mustache, or your patent-leather hair!

Valhalla for him is a Park Avenue flat with cubist furniture and a valet showing in the ladies, and achievement for her is a surf board, and a half-piece bathing suit, and two millionaires biting their lips at the yacht's electric-lighted landing stage and hating each other for *her*.

Shining armour!

Wasn't it worth while to write the story of Fred, and to indicate that shabby boots may be spurred? "Rags are royal raiment when worn for virtue's sake" is quoted now only in mockery, but weren't we better off when we regarded it as fine and heroic?

"This is the most sophisticated comedy of the year," a dramatic critic recently wrote in a metropolitan daily. "I have never seen another play that made marital infidelity seem so unimportant."

Shall we be a greater people for desiring that kind of sophistication?

"From the earliest times," writes Miss Field, "straight down to the twentieth century, literature was devoted mainly to the cult of the hero—the strong-hearted male fighting evil. From Hercules and other heroes of the ancient world the line runs uninterrupted as far as the later 1920's. Then suddenly it breaks. The all but complete disappearance of the hero is one of the most arresting phenomena of the present day."

He hasn't disappeared; we've only forgotten him for the gentlemen in tin foil. We've merely changed our ideas of glamour. And, in changing, I think we've made our future rather uncertain.

We're telling the cock-eyed world that sentiment is bunk; that loyalty and nobility and idealism and self-sacrifice are apple sauce; and that love is ludicrous unless it's illicit. The great thing in life is to have satin pillows. And when we all believe that, our civilization won't have the chance of the proverbial dog with tallow legs chasing an asbestos cat through the infernal regions!

Fortunately for us, we shall never believe it. Sentiment and nobility and love are immortal. That may be hokum, but it's true.

The Freds and Annes and Johns and Jeannettes are all round us. Thousands of 'em cross the ferry every morning, and come to town through the tunnels, and ride down in street cars and taxis. (5)

The story of our little house, and of the honest work and affection that went into it, and stayed there, is being multigraphed every hour, and running into millions of editions. Its heroes and heroines are so many that we don't even notice 'em.

A good many come to light whenever I produce one of these plays, and, I suppose, every author has the same experience. My files are filled with their letters.

The woman in Summit, New Jersey, who has been bending over her washtubs twenty years, and "didn't know that was poetry until you reminded me."

A newspaper editor in Tarrytown, New York, who had decided to give up the fight against a local ring of politicians. "My wife hasn't had a new dress since heaven-knows-when, and my best trousers are wearing thin. We made up our minds that someone was going to get the taxpayers' money, anyway, and we might as well catch some of the gravy. Then we saw your play, and the fight goes on. My wife says she'd rather have me *that way* than own a dozen new dresses."

There are six young men in Hinsdale, Illinois, who owe their university training to the fact that another play made a certain rich man "feel selfish," and a San Francisco clergyman, running a mission at his own expense, who had "rolled down my sleeves" and surrendered, but who saw the same play, and wrote, "I've rolled up my sleeves again, the mission stays."

Yes, books and plays *are* an influence!

The trouble is that so few of our writers and publishers and producers know shining armour when they see it. Most of them spend their lives within a mile or two of Times Square, and, to them, all the rest of America is *terra incognita*. Their associates are the "wise guys." They never met the Middle Western farmer whose own family doesn't know that an incurable malady has doomed him to death, and who, with set teeth, is trying to leave the land paid for when he goes; or the small-town bank clerk who *doesn't* falsify the books, or attempt "a killing" in Wall Street, but plods on, year after year, paying for the art education of a daughter whose clumsy daubs are laughed at even in Greenwich Village. They would consider these men dull fellows.

"You've got to have clear eyes and sharp ears to know that the whistle of the 8:20 to New York isn't really a whistle. It's a trumpet, calling the men to battle."

Moreover, it's a fixed idea of our writers and publishers and producers that people who buy books and theater tickets are moved by "the desire of the moth for the star...the longing for something afar from the field of our sorrow."

The man who walks to save carfare is supposed to be thrilled by the spectacle of a millionaire in a limousine that contains everything but a fireplace, and the woman who lives in a Harlem flat is believed to be transported by a view of a movie mansion that looks like the Grand Central Station.

The fact, I believe, is that we are most deeply stirred by the things we comprehend and with which we are familiar.

Birth, and death, and love, and hunger—these are the facts of life. Tenderness, and loyalty, and patience, and self-sacrifice, and devotion to duty—these are its natural aspirations.

There are more trumpets in the world than police whistles, and ever so many more heroes than gunmen and loose ladies.

Anyway, the gunmen and loose ladies don't matter. It's the wood haulers and the rail splitters who do, and we shall be no worse off for a return to the knowledge that *they* are the wearers of shining armour—"the little men fighting behind, who win wars."

A literature that makes their example glamorous, that highlights their kind of romance and adventure, is the literature that makes men and women fine, and nations great. (6)

QUESTIONS

I

1. What effect does the author believe books and plays have on us? What illustration does he use from his own experience? (1)
2. Why are Anne, John, Jeannette, and Fred real "heroes" to the author? (2)
3. How did the author obtain his own home? (3)
4. According to the author, with what kind of "heroes" does the really great literature of the world deal? (4)
5. What false ideals do books and movies often make attractive to the public? (5)
6. What proof has the author had that his plays motivated people's actions? Why does he have faith in the future? (6)

II

1. Why is it very important what human traits novelists and play-wrights make glamorous in their fictional characters? Are *you* one of the persons upon whom novels and movies have no influence?
2. Why do the movies so rarely discover "the glory of doing your job and the romance of loving your wife"? Do we read and see thrillers just because the happenings in them do *not* happen to us?
3. Many astute critics assert that authors use lurid material because it makes their job easier and that they avoid the commonplace because it takes great artistry to make such material interesting. Is a bandit or your father the more "interesting"?
4. To what extent do you think novels and movies are "escape mechanisms"?
5. Do cheap books and movies incite impressionable youths to lives of crime? What is the danger, even if these thrilling pieces of "literature" do show at the end that crime doesn't pay?
6. Do you think "filthy" books and "vulgar" movies should be censored? Is there danger in expecting laws to do what we ought to do for ourselves?

III

1. The whole tone of this essay is one of intense earnestness. Did you approve of the author's sincerity even when you did not personally agree with all his statements? (Incidentally, the editors can assure you that the author meant every word he wrote and a great deal more.)
2. Would a more objective presentation of the ideas have carried greater weight with you?
3. What is the symbolism of Mr. Pollock's reference to "shining armour"? What is the common theme in the stories of Anne and John and Jeannette?
4. Why does the author tell Fred's story in detail? What does the picture of Fred as Lancelot in shining blue serge do for the essay as a whole?
5. Point out several places where the author has used a kind of gentle sarcasm. Was it effective?

WORDS

Point out in what way each word in the left-hand column is connected with the opposite word in the right-hand column.

1. stamina (*1*)		1. weaving
2. peccadillo (*1*)		2. sin
3. cynicism (*1*)		3. dogs
4. oafish (*1*)		4. elves
5. bankruptcy (*2*)		5. benches
6. bromidic (*3*)		6. chemistry
7. intrinsically (*3*)		7. inside
8. superimposed (*4*)		8. placing
9. inveigle (*4*)		9. blindness
10. psychopathic (*4*)		10. mind
11. meretricious (*4*)		11. prostitute
12. obsequious (*5*)		12. following
13. promiscuous (*5*)		13. mixing
14. inoculation (*5*)		14. eyes
15. aspirations (*6*)		15. breath

THEME TOPICS

1. The Best Movie I Ever Saw
2. My Favorite Movie Actor (Actress)
3. The Social Importance of Literature
4. Real Estate Salesmanship
5. Drug Store Cowboys
6. A Quiet Hero I Know
7. Sophistication Won't Solve America's Problems
8. The Power of the Movies
9. We Must Return the Hero to Literature
10. When ———— Was Gravely Ill

CORDELL HULL: THE VANISHING AMERICAN

BENJAMIN STOLBERG

T HE typical American is today as rare as the Indian. This Republic is too vast, too complex, too sectional and too contradictory to produce a national type. A cattle man in Oklahoma, an Oregon wheat-farmer, a Georgia cracker, a Boston Brahmin, a Columbia professor, a Detroit gangster are Americans all, to a Chinese visitor who can't tell them apart. On the surface we are much alike. We go to the same movies, listen to the same broadcasts, read the same national magazines, are swept by the same crazes. But under the surface are deep regional differences. Moreover, in this age of revolutionary upheaval, American life is losing its traditional continuity. Just stop and think of Babbitt, his father and his son. Babbitt's father was born before the Civil War, grew to manhood in Reconstruction days, faced old age when Teddy Barnum Roosevelt was at his best. Babbitt himself sold Liberty bonds, lived in the fool's paradise of permanent prosperity, idolized Calvin Coolidge. Young Babbitt today is perhaps a member of the American Youth Congress, who hissed another Roosevelt for calling Russia a dictatorship and who thinks that democracy is a "bourgeois prejudice." (*1*)

Yet now and then one does run into a genuine American in the traditional sense. It is in this sense, which is indefinable but unmistakable, that Cordell Hull is a genuine American. Of course, he is not "typical." He is almost aboriginal, and his kind is rapidly vanishing.

Hull comes from the land of Chickamauga, of coon hunts, of Daniel Boone, Davy Crockett, river boats, Muscle Shoals, Look-

From *The American Mercury*, April, 1940. Copyrighted. Used by permission of *The American Mercury* and the author.

out Mountain; the land of the great frontier border leaders—
Andrew Jackson, Henry Clay, Lincoln, Andrew Johnson. In this
historic borderland, which begins at the Northern rim of the
Carolinas and stretches through Tennessee, Kentucky, Missouri,
Indiana, Illinois, the frontier tradition lasted longer than in any
other part of the country—long enough to integrate a social order
which gave us our characteristic national outlook. None of these
border leaders came from the old slave-holding aristocracy or the
rising merchant class. They all came from the frontier yeomanry,
from the families which had either prospered moderately or had
skidded down into the abject and illiterate poverty of "white
trash." In short, they represented the only social phenomenon
which is distinctly American: the rise of the Common Man and
his folk-democracy.

It is this tradition which gives Hull the characteristic folk outlook of the frontier and above all the characteristic personal
traits which it developed. Without intimating any analogy with
the genius of Lincoln, one may say that Hull's similarity to him
as a social type is amazing. First there is the close analogy in
political experience. Hull was a circuit judge in a backwoods
community. Lincoln was a peripatetic lawyer following the circuit in a community very similar, given the difference in time.
Both were young state legislators. Both were volunteer captains
in wars with which they had no great sympathy—Lincoln against
Mexico, Hull against Spain. Both went into "lawin'" without much
success, being politicians at heart. And neither of them had to
learn politics any more than a duckling learns swimming. They
were born to it—the politics of interminable discussions of a frontier democracy: of the county court house and hotel lobby, of
the country store and the small town newspaper. Politically Hull
is especially Lincolnesque: crafty, devious, infinitely patient,
always principled, courageous only when necessary but then fearless. His is not the cheap craftiness of the ward heeler. It is the
craftiness of the frontier democrat who is deeply suspicious of
the human animal, without moral indignation and without cynicism.

The best of these border statesmen based their democracy not
on the sentimental belief that all men are equally good, but on

the shrewd perception that most men's motives are equally ulterior and that they have to be protected from one another by the democratic process. Perhaps it is this insight which gives some of them that look of infinite sadness and long-suffering patience which screens their caginess so deceptively. This look of frontier *Weltschmerz*—as characteristic of Hull as it was of Lincoln—endows them with an enormous advantage in all dealings from politics to poker; Hull always looks at you as though he is ready to forgive and forget the shenanigans you have no intention of pulling. "Hull," said Frank Rice, his closest friend during the Spanish-American war, "had one great advantage in a poker game. He could look sad and beautiful and humble while he had four of a kind, timidly and carefully betting against other people's full houses." When Captain Hull returned from Cuba he had $6300, three-fourths of all the money in the Fourth Tennessee. Thirty-five years later Dr. Raymond Moley ran up against the same deceptive meekness in a political poker game with the Secretary of State. (2)

Cordell Hull was born on October 2, 1871, in Overton (now Pickett) County in middle Tennessee. He is of Scotch-Irish stock, with some English on his father's side, and a strain of Cherokee on his mother's. His father, William Hull, was a little fellow with a hair-trigger temper, a perfect shot, full of colorful excitement and hard work. When Billy Hull had saved his first thousand dollars, he bought some woodland and called it Wolf River Farm. He became a timber man, cutting logs and rafting them down the Obey River to Nashville. Elizabeth Riley Hull, the Secretary's mother, was a typical frontier woman who combined the native intelligence of Nancy Hanks with the sweet temper of Rachel Jackson. There were five sons: Orestes, Sanadius Selwin, Cordell, Wyoming, and Roy. Cordell was the steadiest of the lot. His father once said, "Cord was always like a grown man from the time he could walk." Sanadius Selwin, Nade for short, is still living in San Antonio, where he has a petty government job. He was known as the "gamblin' Hull," having supposedly lost $30,000 of his "pappy's" money in crackpot business ventures. Finally, the story goes, Cordell put a stop to it. "Why don't you git out," he said, "instead of devilin'

Pap to death?" And for $500 Nade obliged. Today Nade is proud of his brother not because he is Secretary of State, but because he could raft logs and work the farm from sunrise to sundown. "Hard work was always Cord's specialty," Nade says. The Secretary of State still puts in a fourteen-hour day.

The Hull boys went to Montvale Academy. From there Cordell went one winter to the National Normal University in Lebanon, Ohio, and then for ten months to the Cumberland University Law School in Lebanon, Tennessee, run by the Cumberland Presbyterian Church. A full-fledged bachelor of law at nineteen, he was admitted to the bar before he was twenty. In short, Hull is a self-taught man. Like most self-taught men he is not widely cultivated. But his native intelligence and tireless industry have made him a very learned man in his chosen field of economics. He also has the self-taught man's advantage of not being overawed by authority. In time he became a leading expert on taxation and the tariff. He is one of the few real scholars in this Administration.

After practising law for a couple of years in Celina, Tennessee, Hull was elected to the State Legislature, where he remained until the Spanish-American War. Then he recruited a company of mountaineers from around Celina, and joined the Fourth Tennessee Regiment as a Captain. But his fame as a military man did not rest on his martial exploits—the Fourth Tennessee got to Cuba too late to fight—but on his poker-playing and "a command of language which was the envy of all the sergeants in Cuba." The Secretary of State is still one of the most fluent private cussers in public life, specializing in original expletives and alliterative combinations.

In 1903 Hull became Circuit Judge, with headquarters in Carthage, Tennessee. The district was primitive, without a railroad in six of its eleven counties. His administration of justice was impartial, full of common sense wrapped in dull legal terminology. Once he fined his "pappy" five dollars for sitting in court with his hat on. He still likes to be called "Judge" by his friends. In 1907 Hull went to Congress from the Fourth Tennessee District, and began one of the most distinguished Congressional careers in American history. He served in the lower

House, except for one term, until 1930, when he went to the Senate. His one defeat was in 1920, due partly to the Harding landslide but mainly to neglect of his constituency in his absorption with the tariff question.

For eighteen years Hull was a member of the powerful Ways and Means Committee; and he was really the leader in the House of President Wilson's progressive economic program. He first came to national attention as the author of the Federal Income Tax Bill of 1913 and the Revised Act of 1916. He was also the author of the Federal and State Inheritance Tax Law of 1916. All these acts were rudimentary—really only revenue measures to compensate for the tariff reductions of the Underwood Act. Still, it was the first effort to provide revenue by direct taxation of wealth rather than by indirect taxation of the consumer. Above all, Hull became the great foe of protectionism. He has been leading this struggle for a quarter of a century. In this he is, of course, the traditional spokesman of the Cotton South. But his attitude on the tariff, as on all economic questions, is that of a national progressive rather than of a Southern sectionalist. Labor has always been for him. On the seven occasions when he voted against measures sponsored by labor, his vote was determined, according to the AFL, by his belief in States' Rights.

Hull has developed his original conception of tariff-reform into a philosophy of international relations which today determines his foreign policy. He is at heart a Jeffersonian free-trader in a contradictory world of increasing commercial rivalry, autarchy, and chaos. To complicate the picture, we are a creditor nation on a scale undreamed of by Thomas Jefferson. As such, we must somehow find a way for our debtors to pay us in goods. Hence Hull's program of whittling down trade barriers "heah, theah, and ever'wheah." (3)

Five hours after his inauguration, President Roosevelt swore in Cordell Hull as Secretary of State. The country was in chaos; the banks were closed, business was at a standstill, the capitalist system seemed to be in a state of gay dissolution. The brain-trusters were riding high. Most of them were consciously high-brow and "brilliant," irresponsibly "experimental," dazzled by their sudden eminence. But a majority, then as now, were of that arrested intellectual type, the Young Man of Forty, brightly stupid, ambitious, excited amateurs in politics and arrogant dilet-tantes in economics. To them Hull was an old Congressional dodo, slightly daffy on the matter of international trade agree-ments, a backwoodsman who had belatedly discovered the *laissez faire* capitalism of Adam Smith in a world of "social planning." They had lots of fun at the expense of the "good gray Secre-tary," the Honorable Mr. Milquetoast at the State Department rookery who "didn't know what it was all about" and would soon suffer the fate of Robert Lansing. In retrospect this evalua-tion of Hull by the political playboys is exceedingly funny. Today Hull is the most respected figure in Washington, re-spected for his staying power, his simple dignity, his strength of character, and his intellectual integrity.

Hull is in the New Deal but not of it. When a friend once tried to draw him out on it he said, "I 'tend to mah int'national affairs." His caution in refusing to commit himself sometimes reaches fantastic lengths. At his press conferences he has de-veloped to a fine point the art of saying nothing elaborately:

That situation is complicated by the interplay of many phases which are receiving our most careful analysis. However, each phase is made up of so many individual circumstances and conditions that we are attempting to investigate each phase of the circumstances and conditions so that we will have a true comprehension of the en-tire development.

This is a free rendition, by Harlan Miller of the Washington *Post*, of a reply by Hull to a ticklish question. And then the Secretary is apt to add a touch of irony to the confusion he has created: "We always want to be helpful to you gentl'men." When not provoked into extreme caution, his answers are likely to be direct, dry, witty, but always skillfully meaningless.

Hull's outlook on "mah int'national affairs" is determined by his policy on international trade agreements, the good neighbor policy toward Latin America, and his attitude on national de-fense. Since he became Secretary of State he has changed his mind only on the latter. Formerly an advocate of gradual inter-national disarmament, today he believes in the strongest possible national defense, with a navy powerful enough to defend this hemisphere.

But his main interest is the extension of his trade agreements. The Trade Agreements Act of 1934, of which he was the main architect, attempts to increase our foreign markets through reciprocal tariff adjustments, and gives the President the right to reduce tariffs as much as 50 per cent. A Hull agreement provides for the reduction of duties on specified commodities which a nation may sell us, in return for which we get tariff concessions from that nation for our goods. Whenever we grant a concession to any one nation, it extends automatically to all other nations, with certain explicit exceptions. Moreover, once a country signs a trade agreement with us, it must not grant preferential treatment to any other country, nor must it withhold from anyone else the lower duties granted to us. Technically this business is called, quite insanely, "unconditional most-favored-nation reciprocal trade agreements."

Under this policy our foreign trade has gone up remarkably. Today we have reciprocal trade agreements with twenty-two nations, with which we do 60 per cent of our foreign business. Hull claims that the rise of the national income from 40 billions in 1932 to 68.5 billions in 1939 was partly, but very significantly, due to this program.

Of course, the Hull policy runs up against a number of difficulties. It hurts some of our smaller industries. Reduced import duties on Argentine wheat cannot possibly help our wheat-farmers. Besides, this policy is so dismally undramatic that Mr. Hull has a hard time selling it to the American people. Finally, the most telling objection to the trade agreements is that the world is not moving that way. Within a year we have lost the Polish, Czechoslovak, and largely the Balkan and Near Eastern markets. The tendency toward autarchy is spreading. All countries at war have to adopt a more or less totalitarian economy. We ourselves are moving toward economic nationalism. That's what the New Deal, in its domestic program, is mainly about. That's why the London Economic Conference of 1933 was torpedoed by Roosevelt. Mr. Hull sailed to lower the barriers of international commerce and to stabilize exchanges, while the

New Deal was abandoning the gold standard and trying desperately to control our internal economy. In short, the Hull trade agreements policy seems irrelevant and contradictory to the economic drift of the age.

Yet it is the most enlightened international economic influence the American democracy can exercise. The collapse of the Russian Revolution, and its reactionary spread into international fascism, into "National Socialism," has shown that virulent "social planning" leads to bureaucratic state capitalism, to the totalitarian slave state. We cannot fight this totalitarian menace by ourselves moving toward a self-sufficient economy. We must avoid economic nationalism in principle, in the direction of international free trade. If the Allies win, only Hull's policy can lay the basis for some sort of peace in international relations. The increasing social controls we must develop to insure greater industrial democracy and the wider distribution of wealth cannot remain democratic and are bound to make for national socialism—unless world commerce flows freely. (4)

The fiasco of the London Conference saddened Hull but did not discourage him. In December of that year he headed the American delegation to the Pan-American Conference in Montevideo. One hour after he landed, he put on his hat and started making the rounds. Some of the Latin-American delegates he surprised at breakfast; others were still shaving. "I'm Hull from the United States," he introduced himself. And on leaving he told each of them, "Just give me a ring if you want to take anythin' up with me, and I'll be right ovah." This was not a pose. To Hull, some one said, all meetings are political meetings. That afternoon Ulric Bell, who served as the American press representative, arranged for a press conference with the Secretary. All the big-shot newsmen showed up. But Mr. Hull was nowhere to be found. Finally he came trudging in. "Where in the world have you been, Mr. Secretary?" Bell asked rather irritably. "Why, I've been to see the local President," Hull explained.

At first the Latin Americans looked at all this homespun stuff with a good deal of suspicion. But Hull kept right on behaving as though he were running for Congress from the Fourth Tennessee District. He gave a very simple reception at one of the smaller hotels. There were no splurges, no side. Finally he won the Latin Americans completely. Montevideo was a great personal triumph for Hull. He sailed home with a number of promises to confer on possible trade agreements. The subsequent Lima and Buenos Aires Conferences were almost equally successful—psychologically.

Hull today is almost the perfect symbol of the American Elder Statesman. The American people have a nostalgia for his type of Vanishing American: the backwoods politician, the common man, reared in the folkways of frontier democracy, who has risen to great heights of simplicity, dignity and moral prestige. In these days of mortal danger to our democratic institutions, Hull's traditional Americanism has an enormous appeal. (5)

QUESTIONS

I

1. Why is there no typical American? In what superficial aspects are all Americans alike? How do they change from generation to generation? (1)
2. In what way is Cordell Hull "a genuine American in the traditional sense"? How is Mr. Hull like Lincoln? (2)
3. What are Mr. Hull's backgrounds, principal character traits, and special abilities? (3)
4. How did the brain-trusters misjudge Cordell Hull? What are his views upon, and work with, such political problems as the tariff, foreign trade agreements, taxation, and foreign affairs? (4)
5. What was the ultimate effect of his "homespun stuff" at the Pan-American Conference? Why is "the American Elder Statesman" a good characterization of Cordell Hull? (5)

II

1. Do you consider Secretary Hull's work on our trade agreements with foreign countries to be his chief contribution to American statesmanship?
2. Do you think Mr. Hull's way was the best to convince Latin America of the honest motives of the United States? What do you think of the "Good-Neighbor" policy?

3. If it is true that the type of American represented by Mr. Hull is vanishing, can you account for the disappearance?

III

1. What is the purpose of the first paragraph of the essay? (*1*)
2. What advantage in economy and understanding did the author gain by the comparison with Lincoln?
3. What various means does the author use to help the reader visualize Mr. Hull's face?
4. Why has the author given brief samples of Mr. Hull's way of speaking?
5. Analyze the excerpt illustrating Mr. Hull's diplomatic art of "saying nothing elaborately." Does this seem inconsistent with the man who said, "I'm Hull from the United States"?

WORDS

For each word in the left-hand column choose the correct synonym from the right-hand column.

1. bourgeois (*1*)		1. roundabout
2. aboriginal (*2*)		2. exact
3. integrate (*2*)		3. absolute rule
4. peripatetic (*2*)		4. embryonic
5. devious (*2*)		5. unrelated
6. ulterior (*2*)		6. middle class
7. expletives (*3*)		7. amateurs
8. rudimentary (*3*)		8. homesickness
9. rivalry (*3*)		9. unify
10. autarchy (*3*)		10. favored
11. arrogant (*4*)		11. indigenous
12. dilettantes (*4*)		12. malignant
13. reciprocal (*4*)		13. selfish
14. explicit (*4*)		14. competition
15. preferential (*4*)		15. wandering
16. irrelevant (*4*)		16. mutual
17. virulent (*4*)		17. exclamations
18. nostalgia (*5*)		18. haughty

THEME TOPICS

1. A Self-made Man
2. Secretary Hull: The Vanishing American
3. The Wise Young Men of the New Deal
4. The Poker Face

5. Cordell Hull: The Elder Statesman
6. Diplomacy: Say Nothing Elaborately
7. A Man Whose Appearance Fooled Me
8. The Good-Neighbor Policy
9. I Am for (or against) High Tariffs
10. I know a Self-educated Man

WILLIAM ALLEN WHITE

WEBB WALDRON

EVERY week-day morning at eight, William Allen White, a smile on his face, hat on the back of his head, pushes through the front door of the Emporia *Gazette*, sings out a greeting to the staff in his high fluty voice, navigates the busy business department to his sanctum, throws off coat and hat, sits down at a desk awash with books, galley-proofs, pamphlets, photos, letters, magazines, and instantly begins to dictate his first editorial of the day. It may be about Dr. Higgins' zinnias, or the need of a new library for the teachers' college, or the fragrance of pawpaws, or an obituary on black Tom Williams, philosopher, jailbird and Will White's good friend, or a warning to isolationists, or some reflections on the New York wedding of a former *Gazette* reporter and the amazement of the young man's mule-skinning, bull-whacking, clod-busting, pumpkin-husking grandparents of the Kansas prairie if they could have seen their grandson carrying his bride in a swirling cloud of silk across the portal of her East Ninety-First Street mansion.

By nine o'clock, White has three, maybe four editorials dictated, off to the composing room. Then he sits back, glancing at a letter, unwrapping a new book or consorting with his soul. Gray, baldish, with just a fleck of youthful reddishness lingering in his eyebrows and at his temples, he is a little tired now at seventy-three, but with something puckish in his deceptively innocent-looking face. His office walls bear testimony to his part in our national life—photographs of Bob La Follette the Elder inscribed "To Bill from Bob," of Teddy Roosevelt "with regards of his sincere friend," of Coolidge—"I value your friendship very much." A cartoon by Rollin Kirby shows White chasing a band of Kluxers. A framed telegram from the President, "I have done it," means that F. D. R. had appointed Felix Frankfurter to the Supreme Court, as White had been urging him to do.

If you shoot a question that hits him, he will turn suddenly, his blue eyes flashing, speak vigorously, humorously, then relapse into his musing. The phone rings—a call from New York, swift discussion of policy in the campaign to aid Britain. In comes the managing editor to discuss the news story about the waterworks. Then the business manager with the report on an advertiser who is flirting with bankruptcy. Then a woman who pours out a bitter tale of domestic strife, pleads for counsel. A business man comes to discuss cattle prices. Will's office is no more than a passageway, open to the whole staff, indeed to the whole town.

"One hundred years ago and more," says Will White, "the preacher was the natural leader in his community. Later it was the lawyer. Now it is the editor." He is speaking not of the big city but of the medium-sized or small town—like his own beloved Emporia—the rich heart of America. Is he over-prejudiced in favor of his profession? Perhaps. Some editors *are* the leaders of their communities. Some aren't. Many aren't who might be. Will White emphatically *is*. How he achieved that leadership, and has held it for over forty years, is a story that touches the secret of all leadership. (*1*)

When Will was a student at Kansas University, one of his teachers said to him, "As a newspaperman, your job and your opportunity will be to make your private sentiments into public opinion." Even as a very young man politics was an essential part of his daily existence. When in his late twenties he bought the Emporia *Gazette* and set forth as an independent newspaperman, he deliberately, cold-bloodedly, he told me, picked the Republican party as a vehicle for converting private sentiment into public opinion. Not because he thought the Republicans were essentially better than the Democrats, but because in Kansas "there were more of 'em. There was no use stringing along with the Dems, they never got anywhere."

Soon after his arrival in Emporia, he got himself named chairman of the county delegation to the state Republican convention and became a force in Kansas politics. Several times he has been a delegate to national Republican conventions, has had a hand in writing Republican platforms. Though adhering to the Republican cause in state and nation, he has never given blind loyalty, and he tells why he never could—his inheritance of inner conflict.

His father was a short, pudgy, jolly country doctor, a congenital Democrat who pioneered to Kansas in the 1850's; his mother was dour Irish, spare of build, black abolitionist, Republican to the core. Will's father died when he was 14. Two years later when Cleveland was elected—the first Democratic victory after the Civil War—the Democrats of El Dorado asked his mother if she'd illuminate the house for the Democratic blowout. "The doctor would want you to," they suggested. She put a lighted candle in every window and then as the Democratic parade passed the house went down cellar and sobbed her heart out. "So, you understand," says Will, "why I never could see that one side was all black and the other all white."

Will's first newspaper job, in his teens, had been on a paper in El Dorado. His boss was perpetually running for office, trimming his paper to his own political ambitions, never getting elected, never getting himself or his paper anywhere. Out of that came a fundamental tenet of Will White's life: The way to stay in politics is to stay out of office. Once elected you are open to attack from all quarters, and you're on the way out. You and your paper are finished.

On the wall above his desk, among photographs of Presidents and statesmen, hangs the celebrated letter from Mark Hanna introducing to William McKinley the young author of the fiery and scornful attack on Populism, "What's the Matter With Kansas?" Populism, the political revolt of western farmers and laborers in the 90's, advocated many things that seemed dangerously radical then—postal savings banks, graduated income tax, recognition of organized labor in the government, more liberal currency system, federal aid to farmers. In Kansas, according to White, its manifestations were a general attack on capital, a tendency to lay all local and national ills to Wall Street, and a preference for incompetents in office.

One hot summer day in '96, during the McKinley-Bryan campaign, Will fell into a futile argument with Populists on a street corner. Enraged, he rushed back to the office and wrote his famous editorial. It got copied into a Chicago paper, came to the notice of Mark Hanna, McKinley's manager. Hanna had it reprinted as a campaign pamphlet and sent it out by the hundred thousand. For this it was perfect, because the Populists had endorsed Bryan. Hanna considered White's piece a powerful factor in McKinley's triumph, and afterward gave Will this letter of introduction to McKinley with its astonished and astonishing phrase: "He wants no office." (2)

His political power as an editor in his town, in his state and in the nation has derived largely from the fact that he has stayed out of office. Only once did he break that rule. In the 1924 Kansas campaign, Republicans and Democrats alike pussyfooted on the Klan. Aroused, White announced his independent candidacy for the governorship, stumped the State attacking the Klan's un-Americanism. He wasn't elected, didn't expect to be, but his fight gave the Klan a jolt from which it never recovered.

White has discovered still another principle of leadership—never claim credit for your good works. "If you initiate a movement in your paper," he says, "and then when it goes across yelp that you did it, why the next time you try to start something people will say, 'He's doing it to boost his paper,' and they won't take any stock in it. You lose your influence." His policy is to propose an idea, then step aside and let the community take control. (3)

White chose a small-town newspaper career because he wanted to be his own boss. After his first experience in El Dorado, he adventured to Kansas City and was a brilliant reporter and editorial writer on the Kansas City *Star*. But he didn't like it. He didn't like to have his stuff cut. He didn't like it that the business department got first crack at the free passes to shows. He wrote a charming sketch of small-town life, *The Court of Boyville*, and the managing editor turned it down. He didn't like that. So he headed back to his home state, lit on Emporia as his victim, and bought the *Gazette* for $3000 of borrowed money.

In Kansas City Will had found the girl of his choice, Sally

Lindsay, and married her, though Sally insists to this day that she did the choosing. "Will had everything I admired," she says, "and the minute I set eyes on him he had no chance." Sally became full partner on the *Gazette*. Will had employed a big Negro to help turn the presses when the power failed, as it often did. "Great Heavens, Will, who is that?" Sally exclaimed, startled, when she came to the office the first morning. "That's the power," said Will, "and I'm the glory!" When young Bill, the eldest born, came along, the baby used to lie in a clothes basket by Sally's desk while she worked.

The paper, when Will bought it in 1895, had a circulation of 425 copies, partly paid. Today it has a circulation of 7500, all paid. This figure will seem trivial to those who think in terms of big city newspaper circulation, but it means that three-fourths of the families in the county take the *Gazette*. How many newspapers, city or small-town, can show a like coverage?

One drygoods store spends more in advertising in the *Gazette* in a month today than it did then in a year. "Why," says Will, "the A. & P. alone has more goods in it today than all the grocery stores in town forty-six years ago!" And yet, the population of the county now is just about the same as it was then. The same number of people, the same number of acres under cultivation, but an amazing multiplication of wealth and comfort.

When White took over the *Gazette* it had a weekly payroll of $45, and he had to do some scratching to meet it. Today it has a payroll of $1100. Wages of printers have gone up from $8 a week to $35. "Most of my employees have better automobiles than I have," said Will, "and I'm glad of it." One man has been on the staff forty-two years, another forty-one, another forty. The shop average is seventeen years. When a person has been there twenty-five years, White awards him a bonus of $1000. Ten people have received that bonus from the *Gazette*. But if a man grows restless and wants to move on, White gets him a job on another paper—often a better job. For years White was deluged with applications from aspiring young journalists willing to work for nothing in order to gain the prestige of

having been on the Emporia *Gazette*. He used to take some of
them on, but NLRB regulations prevent him from doing so any
more. There are a dozen newspaper editors and owners in Kansas today who got their start on the *Gazette*.

Gene Lowther started carrying papers for the *Gazette* when
he was nine years old. When attending the local college he
worked for the *Gazette* as a student reporter. He went off to
Kansas University, came back as reporter, telegraph editor, then
advertising manager. Now Gene is business manager, and when
White is away he takes charge of the editorial page and writes
most of the editorials. And then there is Martha. For nine years
Martha was cook for the Whites, until Sally White persuaded
her to take a course in business college. Martha developed
an unusual aptitude for figures, now has charge of circulation at the *Gazette* and seems to be the pivot of the whole
office. (*4*)

White's deliberate return to the small town where he was
born, his success there, his integration with his community and
the fact that national fame has risen out of that integration, his
warm-hearted and personal relation to his employees—all this is
a pleasing demonstration to the small-town American that it's
better to stay at home than go to the city, and to the city man
with vague yearning for small-town wholesomeness and simplicity it makes Will White a fascinating figure.

"Did you ever have an ambition to own a string of country
newspapers?" I asked White.

"I should say not," he said. "Running a string of newspapers
is like running a string of wives. It won't work. A newspaper
should be the expression of a man. You can't put your personality into more than one paper."

The *Gazette*, being the expression of this one man White,
records in its political editorials over forty-six years the swing
of that man from smug conservatism to humble liberalism. He
once ridiculed Bryan for having said that if you legislate to
make the masses prosperous, that prosperity will pervade the
whole social structure. Now, seeing the trend toward this very
philosophy, he generally approves. But he early realized the
vice of consistency. He wrote long ago: "Of all the cowards,

of all the wobbly pussyfooters, the man who is afraid of his own record is the worst. The thing that should govern a man is not what he has said, but the truth as he sees it. Consistency is a paste jewel." (5)

There were always two lines in White's development, parallel, related, yet distinct—his genius as a newspaperman and his talent as a writer of books. Just about the time "What's the Matter With Kansas?" put him on the national map as a newspaperman, he published his first book, *The Real Issue*, a collection of sketches of small-town life. The editorial helped sell the book, and the royalties on the book helped pay off the mortgage on the paper. Since then he has published fourteen books—fiction, biography, political panorama, social comment. His most popular novel, *A Certain Rich Man*, sold over 250,000 copies. T. R. highly praised White's volume of political stories, *Stratagems and Spoils*, for their truthfulness and vigor. White's study of Calvin Coolidge and his times, *A Puritan in Babylon*, in which the Kansas editor gives a masterly analysis of the Coolidge era and reveals the glum, lean, sharp-visaged, secretive little Vermonter as a human being, sold extremely well. In short, there have been many times when success as a writer of books would have enabled him to quit the newspaper grind, but it was never even a temptation. He was rooted in his paper, his town, his community. "I might have been more famous if I'd devoted all my time to writing books, but I wouldn't have had as much fun," he says.

He is a noteworthy American, not because he has known Presidents and played a part in national political counsels, but because he has pictured in his editorials—with directness, simplicity, frequent felicity of phrase, touches of fantasy and flashes of wit—the glories, hopes, tragedies, comedies and foibles of a typical American country town. Maybe Emporia isn't typical, but we would all like to believe that our town is as sound, wholesome, generous, clean, progressive as the Emporia of William Allen White. He sets us an ideal America we'd like to live up to.

Every time he has gone beyond Emporia to do a job he thought ought to be done, he has come back to be more a part than ever of his town and people. Early this year he resigned the chairmanship of the Committee to Defend America by Aiding the Allies, telling the world that the committee needed a younger, more vigorous head. But in a *Gazette* editorial he apologized to his fellow Emporians for having devoted so much time to a cause not confined to Emporia and Kansas, confessed that of late he had not kept up his end in the Rotary Club and Chamber of Commerce, and promised that he would give the two or three years that might be left to him to chores around home.

But his organization and chairmanship of that committee was part of his lifelong fight in defense of the way of life he knows and loves. He believes that here in America, especially in Kansas, we have worked out the best system for human happiness that man has yet devised. He is fond of telling you that Kansas has few millionaires and few reliefers, and that in a town like Emporia a man and his family can have most of the conveniences common to our civilization on $1000 a year. He realizes, also, that we take our blessings too much for granted, and says that one of our important jobs is "to give to American youth the same joy and enthusiasm for freedom of speech, peaceful assemblage, free conscience, trial by jury and the benefits of personal freedom that the Germans have put into their youth by teaching them national pride, race arrogance and international hatred. "What good," he asks, "will it do to defend Britain to save our own hides and have our youth insensitive to those precious rights which our ancestors for a thousand years have bought with their blood and treasure?"

All Kansas knows about the Whites. When Bill (W. L. White) was in Finland as a war correspondent a year ago last winter, all the town knew the day and hour when he and his parents were to talk to each other by telephone. The girls in the Emporia exchange fought for the chance to handle the call. "I think," Sally White said to me, "that talking to Bill in Finland was the most adventurous thing in our lives. Wasn't it, Will?" "Yes, Sally," said Will, "I think it was." One could understand the thrill of it to them—the sheer strangeness of being able to telephone so far, the relief to know Bill was safe, and the realization that this war correspondent at the front was the baby who had kicked up his heels in the clothes-basket beside Sally's desk in the *Gazette* office while she wrote copy and corrected proof. Later they had additional excitement and satisfaction when they learned that Bill's 1939 Christmas broadcast from Helsinki had inspired Robert Sherwood to write his moving anti-war play, *There Shall Be No Night.*

On Christmas Eve a band of high-school carollers gathered under a tree in front of the White home. Sally rushed to the door and invited them in. Will, sprawled in his favorite position in an armchair in front of the fire, doing his homework for the Book-of-the-Month Club, dropped his book and hopped up as the gang streamed into the big living room. "Come on, let's sing!" he proposed eagerly. Girls and boys crowded around him at the piano as he strummed out "Holy Night," his face aglow. He was part of his town, rejoicing with it.

"Sometimes," says Will White, "I look over my shoulder and I see Bob Roberts, our gentlemanly and urbane mortician, catching up with me—but he hasn't got me yet." Emporia and the rest of the United States hope that Bob won't catch up for a long time to come. (*6*)

QUESTIONS

I

1. What are the activities and events of a typical day in William Allen White's office? (*1*)
2. Why did Mr. White choose to support the Republican Party? What political conflict was there in his own parentage? What part did one of his editorials play in a national campaign? (*2*)
3. What two principles has he followed as an editor? (*3*)
4. Why did Mr. White choose a small-town newspaper career? What part did his wife have in making it a success? To what extent has his paper prospered, and what are some of the unusual careers of persons on the staff? (*4*)
5. Why does he believe a man should not run a string of newspapers? What is his attitude toward consistency? (*5*)
6. What other activities has Mr. White engaged in besides editing a paper? What incidents show that he has always remained at heart a small-town man? (*6*)

II

1. Do you believe that the small town offers the best opportunity for success? for being your own boss? for satisfaction in living?
2. Many leaders believe that the great centers of population will, in the future, lose population and that medium-sized towns will increase in size throughout America. What do you think of this decentralization of business and industry? its effect upon health? upon economic security? upon labor problems? upon home-owning?
3. Why has the editor superseded the minister and the lawyer as the natural leader in medium-sized and small towns in America?
4. What is the secret of Mr. White's leadership? Think of the persons you know who are leaders. Can you analyze the qualities they possess which make them leaders? In minimizing or forgetting their own interests do they best serve themselves?
5. What has been the influence of William Allen White and the Emporia *Gazette* in American journalism? Do you think he ought to have accepted the "greater success" that would undoubtedly have come to him in a larger city?
6. William Allen White has been called "the Sage of Emporia." Do you consider this designation appropriate?
7. In what respects is William Allen White a typical American?

III

1. Pick out at least three figures of speech in the first paragraph of the essay. How do they help to establish the tone of the whole piece?
2. Explain the figurative reference to Emporia, Kansas, as "the rich heart of America."
3. What figure of speech is illustrated by "Consistency is a paste jewel"? What does Mr. White mean by this statement? Do you agree with him?
4. Make a list of humorous bits in this essay. How many of them are connected with Mr. White's personality?
5. Why has the author closed the essay, as he began it, with the portrayal of the human side of Mr. White? Why are the simple, domestic scene and the humorous jest at death not anticlimax?

WORDS

Each word in the left-hand column is related in some way with the opposite word in the right-hand column. With the aid of a good dictionary, explain that relationship.

1. sanctum (*1*)
2. pamphlets (*1*)
3. zinnias (*1*)
4. puckish (*1*)
5. congenital (*2*)
6. dour (*2*)
7. ambitions (*2*)
8. tenet (*2*)
9. derived (*3*)
10. candidacy (*3*)
11. influence (*3*)
12. money (*4*)
13. trivial (*4*)
14. pervade (*5*)
15. panorama (*6*)
16. felicity (*6*)
17. foibles (*6*)
18. insensitive (*6*)
19. urbane (*6*)
20. mortician (*6*)

1. religion
2. an old Latin poem
3. a professor of medicine
4. a mischievous fairy
5. birth
6. hardness
7. Roman politics
8. holding
9. river
10. whiteness
11. astrology
12. a Roman goddess
13. ancient roads
14. walking
15. sights
16. happiness
17. weeping
18. feeling
19. cities
20. death

THEME TOPICS

1. The Advantages of a Small Town
2. The Editor and His People
3. I Dared to Be Inconsistent
4. Pussyfooting Politicians
5. The Office-Seeker
6. The Secret of Leadership
7. Business Opportunities in a Small Town
8. A Big Frog in a Little Puddle
9. Hogging the Limelight
10. A Small Town I Love

WILL HOGG, TEXAN

JOHN A. LOMAX

ONE day in the early part of this century two men, father and son, sat talking together on the long veranda of the historic Varner Plantation manor house, fifty miles southwest of Houston, Texas. They were strikingly alike in stature and depth of chest, in the tawny coloring of their hair, in their wide firm mouths, their grayish-blue eyes, ruddy complexions, and deep resonant voices. The father was a man mountain, over six feet tall and weighing in his prime nearly three hundred pounds; the son was slightly smaller. Now the tired old lion, ex-Governor "Jim" Hogg, sensing perhaps the end of his days, had asked his son, Will Hogg, to leave his work in St. Louis and come home to Texas.

"Until that six months I spent talking with my father," said Will Hogg long afterwards, "I had never really known him. I had just taken him for granted. Then for the first time I understood why he had always espoused the cause of the common people, the need of battling for the weak against the strong, the necessity of free education for all, if a democracy is to survive. So I came to love more deeply this plantation, this farmhouse, and my father. Whatever little good I may do, whatever ideals may be found behind any action of mine, whatever has given my life any worth or dignity, all are due to him."

As governor of a pioneer state, James Stephen Hogg, the son of a brigadier general of the Confederacy, fostered many pioneer laws, among them the one ending the free-pass system on Texas railroads; another establishing the first Railroad Commission for government regulation of railways; still another "squeezing the mud and water" out of railroad stocks and bonds, and forbidding the further issuance of fraudulent public securities. Probably his most important law forbade the ownership of large bodies of Texas land by out-of-the-state corporations. On leaving public office Governor Hogg, like Robert E. Lee, refused handsome retainers from corporations seeking his influence, and he declined also all legal employment that involved the constitutionality, or even the interpretation, of laws regulating corporations that had been passed on his recommendation.

After the father's death the Varner Plantation became a holy place for Will Hogg and his sister, "Missima," and for the two brothers, Mike and Tom. Will once said, "I tried to fix up the old place as George Washington would do if he had a bank roll." The two towering live oaks at the entrance will long stand to remind pilgrims of two giant Texans, father and son— the spot marking for one the close, for the other the beginning, of a notable career. In making Texas a better place to live in, Governor Hogg had the aid of high office. His chief rival, Judge George Clark of Waco, once said: "He had a power of dominating his followers that I have never seen excelled in any man." His son, fired with the ideals of the father and inheriting his powers of leadership, acquired wealth that gave him independence and freedom to strike hard blows for any righteous cause. His fortune came largely through black gold, Texas oil—much of it from those wide fields upon which father and son looked as they talked and planned together on the veranda at West Columbia. (1)

Will Hogg made his home in Houston. There he became associated with J. S. Cullinan and James L. Autry, prominent officials of the Texas Oil Company. These three men refused to follow the company when its headquarters were moved to New York City. Instead, they formed a corporation of their own, the Farmers Oil Company, acquired an abandoned oil field, deepened the wells by a thousand feet or so, and struck a new oil stratum which soon poured out riches at a reported rate of sixty dollars for each dollar invested. This one venture made Will Hogg a rich man.

Late in life ex-Governor Hogg himself had become interested in oil through the discovery of the famous Spindle Top field at

Beaumont, Texas. He found bubbles coming up through the marshy lowlands of the Varner Plantation at West Columbia, fifty miles from Houston—bubbles, some said, which would burst into flames when touched by a lighted match. Here was the possibility of a heritage for his children not provided by his otherwise small estate. He bought the plantation, comprising some 5000 acres, and his will requested that his children should not sell the land for ten years. Several years after his death, during the period of the World War, one of the big oil companies explored the Varner Plantation and sank a well with an initial flow of 100,000 barrels of oil. Since that time this field has produced an estimated total of a hundred million barrels. When the first big well came in, Will cabled the news to his brother Mike, then on the firing line in France, and asked what should be done with Mike's share of the fortune. Mike cabled: "Ship me a dozen cases of eggs."

With the income from the profitable West Columbia oil field of the Hogg estate, Will Hogg became the senior partner and directing manager of Hogg Brothers, the firm including himself, Mike Hogg, Tom Hogg, and Miss Ima Hogg. At the same time he managed his own properties and served as investment trustee for other estates. Level-headed Mike, always at his side, acted as a brake to the impulsive and emotional outbursts of the dynamic and dominating elder brother. Among the early investments was an eight-story office building in Houston, the entire top floor of which was reserved for the offices of Hogg Brothers. A strip of sod several feet wide runs around the entire rim of the eighth-floor roof; here Will Hogg planted flowers and a young forest of shrubbery, perennially green in the semitropical climate. The main executive office was a big, high-ceilinged room with two capacious flat-topped desks and armchairs, one for Mike and one for Will—the latter's being a special job, oversize, because he overflowed the ordinary chair just as he overflowed everything else that he touched. Around the walls were hung Remington paintings—"The Herd Boy," "The Fight at the Water Hole," "The Cry for Help"—and near by a portrait of Governor Hogg. On a projection in one corner of the roof garden Will built a suite of rooms, bedroom, oval dining room, and kitchen, where he often entertained parties of friends and business callers. Once when a friend told Will that the gossips whispered that these rooms were used as a bagnio, he replied without rancor: "I don't care what they think or say as long as Mike and Raymond Dickson will visit my grave once in a while."

From Hogg Brothers stemmed various subsidiary corporations, the chief one, perhaps, being the Varner Realty Company, which invested mainly in Houston property and oil lands. Among the successful real-estate ventures of this company was the promotion of 2000 lots for persons of limited income. Every lot was sold and paid for under the generous terms provided. At one time the company, in partnership with Raymond Dickson, owned a large cotton warehousing and exporting business. For several years Will Hogg interested himself in the Wilson process for making women's shoes and spent a lot of money securing patents. This attempt to buck the shoe machinery monopoly, like other ventures, as he once said, "mildewed and turned green on us in the summertime." He financed and promoted the Findex system of filing and sold his interests at a profit. In partnership with one of his lawyers, David Picton, he furnished funds for making Ingleside, on Corpus Christi Bay, a deep-water port from which oil tankers daily take cargoes for the four corners of the earth. He took options on extensive coal properties in Kentucky and Tennessee and other options on gold mines in Mexico. He cherished an unfulfilled ambition to own a producing gold mine. One of the unvalued items of his final gift to the University of Texas was a batch of Cripple Creek, Colorado, gold mining stock.

"Will Hogg was no business man," contemptuously remarked the president of one of Houston's big oil companies. "All his money came through the friendship of J. S. Cullinan and from his father's land at West Columbia." Will's spacious office, to be sure, was not a place where shrewd, undercover, overreaching trades were executed. Rather it became a mecca to which traveled those who needed help, where worthy causes were aided, where were born many movements for the common good. Here was a healthy mixture of sound business judgment and high-minded business ideals, carried out by an efficient organization under the leadership of a resourceful personality. (2)

Will Hogg was still in his thirties when he attained financial independence. Although he was at the head of an organization managing the business and investments of several large estates, "I did this with my left hind foot," he said afterwards; "there was bigger game abroad." As the Houston *Gargoyle* remarked, he became a sort of "Superintendent of Everybody's Business." First and foremost was his interest in public education in Texas. He had grown tired of seeing its University kicked around. While he was yet a salaried employee of the Texas Company, he adopted a unique plan for raising Texas from the low educational brackets. He made his first "Blue Book," which called for the expenditure within five years of not less than a quarter of a million dollars "to stimulate thought and create and arouse, through bulletins and lectures, aspiration for higher education in Texas." The signers of the Blue Book were to be "good citizens of Texas who necessarily are and must be deeply concerned in the individual culture of themselves and their posterity." At the beginning he was asked what he would do if donors could not be found. "I'm worth a total of thirty thousand dollars," he replied. "That's enough to run the shebang for a year. I'll dump that into the pot and let the doubters see the results." He traveled at his own expense throughout Texas and secured subscriptions from wealthy men for more than the designated sum. Ultimately the special constitutional tax for higher education at which he aimed was killed by rivalry over the division of its income, if and when voted. The experiment failed. Nonetheless, interest in higher education was aroused, and Will Hogg became known as its ardent champion. This championship was needed when James E. Ferguson was elected Governor of Texas.

Governor Jim, the husband of Governor "Ma" Ferguson,— for whom later, through two terms, he "carried in the wood and toted the water,"—had little use for higher education. After he assumed office, Governor Ferguson declared that "too many people are going hog-wild over higher education." He, or his friends, disliked eight men on the faculty of the University of Texas, and he demanded that these professors be "fired," on the charge that they were engaged in an "unholy spree of establishing an educational hierarchy." Of Professor William J. Battle, Acting President and for twenty-eight years professor of Greek, he said to the Board of Regents, with Will Hogg presiding as chairman: "You keep that man Battle here and you lay a precedent that tells every Governor for forty years that they have no right to do as they want to." Will Hogg met this declaration of unbridled autocracy with the retort: "I for one would rather go to hell in a hand-basket than to act without investigation of charges."

Later, after Mr. Hogg's term as Regent had expired, a supine Board of Regents did discharge without any hearing six members of the University faculty. Soon thereafter the Governor vetoed the entire appropriation of $1,600,000 for the University of Texas which the Legislature had granted for two years. The University lay stricken and helpless until Will Hogg came to Austin, where, leasing a half floor of the Driskill Hotel, he spent a long hot summer. He and Chester H. Terrell, his able classmate of San Antonio, declared ruthless war on "Farmer Jim." No Governor could "put the putrid paw of politics on the University of Texas."

One impeachment charge against Governor Ferguson was followed by another. Texans had probably not been so deeply aroused since the Civil War as they were by the dramatic incidents that followed. The friends of the Governor came to Austin in crowds, among them a detachment of Texas Rangers, pistols on hip, wearing ten-gallon hats. Governor Ferguson kept one of the noted gunmen always at his side. At night two others sat in rocking chairs on the front porch of the Governor's Mansion. Former students and friends of the University rallied in support of Will Hogg and his cause. During the excitement friends urged him to arm himself against assassination. "Hell, they won't shoot." And he went on unobtrusively about his job.

He said in an interview: "How far this cheerful and constructive autocrat will be able to travel the rocky road of his mad career is measured entirely by the forbearance and apathy of the best citizenship of the state and by the trifling percentage of illiteracy and ignorance to which alone he can appeal with any assurance of temporary success.... My prediction is that he is riding to the biggest fall, personally and politically, in the short and simple annals of the misguided politicians of Texas." Again, dedicating a volume containing a stenographic report of the first impeachment investigation (the publication of which he paid for out of his own pocket), he wrote: "To the people of Texas whose Governor has disgraced and degraded our University by securing a Board of Regents a majority of whom servilely do his will; by falsely accusing members of the Faculty and having them dismissed, notwithstanding their acquittal... and when called to answer for his misdeeds announces: 'I don't have to give reasons; I am Governor'... to the people in their hour of humiliation, this record is dedicated."

"When the law gets in the way of practical business it don't mean anything," announced the Governor. The Senate thought differently when the Governor refused to disclose the source of $156,000 paid in cash to him in his office. They voted twenty-seven to four for his removal from office.

Following the Ferguson upheaval, letters and telegrams and personal appeals urged Will Hogg to permit his name to be proposed for Governor. "You won't have to run," they begged; "your name is enough." He replied: "I'm not running for office and I never will. I won't wear a ball and chain on my leg while I am fighting these coyotes who are befouling the name of the State of Texas. I'd rather be a rock-throwing private soldier with a free voice than be the mouthpiece of an organization that would tell me when to talk and what to say."

There were other times that the University of Texas watchdog showed his teeth. Will Hogg once learned that the Board of Regents had sold in secret, without competitive bids, contrary to all legal precedents, a three-million-dollar issue of bonds against the credit of the University. From New York City, Will notified four members of the Board by wire that the trade must be canceled or else.... It was canceled in great privacy, though it took these harried officials nearly a year to shake off the brokers who had bought the securities. (3)

"In a well-ordered democracy," Will Hogg once declared, "no boy or girl with brains and character should be denied the opportunity of college training. I find that nothing else gives me half the satisfaction derived from the knowledge that I have gambled on the brains and ambition of young men and young women. If I knew just when I was going to die, beyond my funeral expenses I wouldn't reserve enough money to buy a bowl of chili." At the close of the World War he authorized a University official, after pledging him not to reveal the donor, to advertise in all Texas papers that any ex-soldier who could enter the University would be provided with necessary funds. Letters came from five hundred, and more than a hundred ex-soldiers actually enrolled. He sponsored a movement that resulted in subscriptions for $300,000 to aid worthy students wishing to attend the University of Texas. For students of exceptional promise who wished to do graduate or professional work outside of Texas he privately provided funds. In most of these cases he so covered his tracks that his benefactions cannot be traced.

In 1925 a friend told him that Tom Douglas Spies wished to go to the Harvard Medical School. To him, through the University's Ex-Students Association, for four years went Will Hogg's checks to cover expenses. He never saw young Spies. In fact, he did not wish the young man to know the real source of the money. Only Will Hogg's death brought disclosure. In the *Annals of Internal Medicine* of March 1939, a committee of the American College of Physicians announces: "The Committee on Fellowships and Awards recommends that the John Phillips Memorial Medal for 1939 be awarded to Dr. Tom Douglas Spies for outstanding contributions to the science of nutrition, and particularly for his studies in the nature and character of pellagra."

In all such loans—and there were many—it was understood that the money repaid by the young graduates should go back to the University of Texas to be available for other young scientists. During his lifetime Will Hogg provided a model charter for a student loan fund and made an initial cash gift to fourteen Texas colleges. From his estate $450,000 has been put into Rice Institute in Houston, and into thirteen state tax-supported institutions of higher learning, including $25,000 to the Negro college at Prairie View—these funds to aid worthy boys and girls seeking college training. The residue of his property was transferred recently to the University of Texas. To that institution he gave much of his life; dying, he gave it nearly all his remaining accumulated wealth, estimated to exceed two million dollars. Another million he gave to education during his lifetime, two millions to allied social benefits. By his persuasive eloquence he raised two and a half millions more. Thus, through his hands for the common good has come seven million dollars. This much is known. Not even his family can tell what he gave away privately. (*4*)

In his devotion to the State and its University, Will Hogg did not fail to see the needs of his home city, Houston. Oil, lumber, and a deep-water port poured wealth into this growing industrial center. Millionaires sprouted overnight from oil fields that surround the city closely and spread for hundreds of miles around. "Through the leavening influence of beauty in our city," he once told a group of friends, "I want to help save ourselves from the crass commercialism that comes along with quickly accumulated wealth." He organized a Forum of Civics with these words from Pericles as its motto: "No Athenian should ever confess that he neglected public service for the sake of private fortune." The Forum he described as

an organization designed to stimulate civic pride and to combine many and varied forces for the betterment of our city and county. For the improvement of the community in its physical, social, educational or economic aspects . . . the enduring existence of which depends solely upon the spirit existing in the minds and hearts of the members of the Forum. . . . Underlying the stated purposes of such an organization there must be the basic desire to make this city more enjoyable, more adequately equipped, more beautiful,—and consequently more useful for everyone who lives and works therein. . . . As the budget of this organization is underwritten, the payment of dues or other pecuniary contributions are to be truly voluntary, unsolicited and unexpected.

At a cost of $50,000 or more, he and the Hogg estate financed the Forum, including 10,000 copies of a beautiful *Garden Book*, illustrated in colors, costing $10,000 and distributed free. From the Forum of Civics came the report of the City Planning Commission, W. C. Hogg, Chairman, the results of which are helping to make Houston a beautiful city. In closing this report Will Hogg wrote:—

When we build let us build forever. Let it not be for the present delight or for the present use alone. Let it be such work that our descendants will thank us for, and let us think, as we lay stone on stone, that a time is to come that these stones will be held sacred because our hands have touched them and that men will say, as they look upon our labor and the wrought substance of them, "See! This our fathers did for us."

In a signed public letter charging a popular mayor with attempting to divert to his own ends the plans of the Commission, he denounced him "for his suave sophistry, ruinous procrastination and infidelity to the city....Even if he were honest in every particular and hadn't recently lied...I would be against him for many reasons." He gave eleven reasons for opposing the official's reëlection; the last one reads: "In all my contacts with him I have never detected the slightest emotion for, or any real affectionate interest in, the finer things of city building or city service."

Throughout years of planning and discussion he was buying privately and securing options on hundreds of acres of desirable sections for city parks, his agents working quietly so as to prevent unreasonable prices. When at last the city was ready to go into the market for land, Will Hogg handed over the 1200 acres for Memorial Park at precisely the price he had contracted for, although in the meantime real-estate values had increased 500 per cent. In addition, he gave to the city $50,000 to enable it to buy a needed tract. Two other Houston parks, Herman and McGregor, owe much of their present-day beauty and completion to the insistence of Will Hogg. For a considerable period he was the anonymous donor of $30,000 a year with which to purchase crape-myrtle plants for the city parks and private homes. With each package of plants went two tags, one a pledge of the citizen to plant the shrubs on his ground, the second carrying explicit directions for planting and caring for the shrubs for two years. Will Hogg learned that the "white folks" were getting all the shrubs. Thereupon he bought thousands more which were given out only at Emancipation Park, the Negroes' recreation center, to brighten the dooryards of Houston's Negro district. The 1500-acre residential section of River Oaks, on which he expended three million dollars and out of which during his lifetime he is said to have made no profit, is one of the show places of Houston. In River Oaks, on Lazy Lane, he made his home with his sister, Miss Ima, among pine and oak trees that he had nurtured.

Houston's $350,000 Art Museum was largely the result of his intense devotion to the city's welfare. Another of his "Blue Books" listed $326,000 in pledges secured by him. When asked to lead a movement to raise funds, he would grin and say, "They want me to work on the æsthetic side. I'm glad to. The government made a mistake originally in not reserving for its own use all the wealth below the soil. What I don't pay back in taxes on the oil which should not have been mine, I'm glad to give away for the public welfare." A Houston man declared that many men of the city felt complimented when Will Hogg came along with a "Blue Book" and asked them to chip in with five thousand or so. To an oil millionaire who refused to subscribe he wired: "It's a damn shame that a man of your means, insight, and ability will stint his spiritual and intellectual growth by staying out of such an unselfish enterprise, especially when the amount and terms of payment involved are relatively ridiculous compared to the significance of your sharing in the beauty and joy of this gift to this beloved community, and may God bless you."

A home for newsboys, the Boy Scouts, the Girl Scouts, organized charity—a thousand and one causes were never denied his help. Just before his death he had evolved plans for a new million-dollar building for the Houston Young Men's Christian Association. At the same time he was busying himself with a movement to rebuild entirely the city's Negro section.

There was nothing sanctimonious about him. Humor was present in all such work. A committee of Houston ladies, soliciting money for a new building for the Young Women's Christian Association, were shocked to find Will Hogg an unsympathetic listener.

"But why?" they complained. "Everybody has told us that you are very generous."

"Ladies," he answered, "these young girls, strangers coming to the growing city, certainly need the care and protection that your organization throws about them. I find no fault with that. But why stumble along with a paltry hundred thousand dollars? The small sum you ask for is only chicken feed. I'll help you if you strike for half a million, and go after it this way...."

His enthusiasm grew as he talked. The result was that the committee left his office having surrendered the entire plan into his hands. To carry it out cost him his vacation. In a beautifully embossed blue leather-bound book, dedicated to the good women of Houston, blank spaces were left for signatures. Each signature cost its owner $5000. All that summer Will Hogg plodded about the streets of Houston, "Blue Book" under arm, on what he called a "gumshoe campaign, highjacking my friends." One lady complained that a breakfast in her home cost her $10,000; Will Hogg happened in with his "Blue Book," and before the eggs were finished she and her husband had signed up. Gradually a total sum of $850,000 was subscribed. As always, Will Hogg topped the list in amount given, though his own name was unobtrusively inserted far down the list. Not all the subscriptions came easily. The beloved Episcopal rector, Dr. Peter Gray Sears, declared that Will Hogg "cussed" the Young Women's Christian Association building into existence. (5)

There was a human, personal side to Will Hogg that always appealed to me even more deeply than his valiant, and often violent, fights for civic righteousness. His fury against any hampering of the University of Texas grew solely out of the fact that through it he believed the enlightenment of all the people might come. He had little sympathy for that love of Alma Mater that expends itself in grotesque costumes and noisy hullabaloos. As a student of the University of Texas, he had his own small circle of intimates, and at that time I knew him but slightly, though for a year we lived in the same dormitory. Despite his modesty, to me, raw and green from the country, the glamour surrounding the son of a distinguished Governor created a bar to easy friendship. Afterwards, when he became president of the Ex-Students Association, I was its salaried secretary. So, through years of association, I came to know some of the wise tenderness of the man.

Throughout the time that I was a minor official at the University of Texas, I had from him this standing order: "When any student in the University of Texas gets into trouble, help him. As long as he is on the rolls of the University he is my ward. If he needs money, lend it to him. If he is sick, get a doctor. If he gets thrown into jail, bail him out. If he dies and has no money or people, bury him. Don't wait to write or wire me; relieve the distress and then let me know at what cost. And," he added with savage grimness, "if you ever let anyone know where the money comes from I'll—I'll never send you another blankety-blank cent for any feather-headed scheme as long as I live." Recently a prominent Texas lawyer told me: "While I was a student in the University, I once borrowed enough money from you to buy a suit of clothes. I had to back out of your office. You see, I was wearing my last pair of trousers and they were gone in the rear." This gentleman never knew that it was Will Hogg's money that patched his pants.

One day Will Hogg called on a classmate in San Antonio and asked him for a contribution to the Student Loan Fund.

"Mr. Hogg," objected the man, "when I attended the University I paid my own way. I asked for no favors. I graduated, and since that time I have become well established and I have achieved some success through my own efforts. You now come and ask me to give money to that institution. I'd like for you to tell me what the University of Texas has ever done for me."

"Not a blankety-blank thing!" thundered Will Hogg as he gathered up his papers and left the room.

In Fort Worth he once invited a group of University of Texas men to lunch with him. Over the coffee he explained in detail his plans for the University of Texas, pleading for generous gifts. His earnestness failed to arouse any response except for a few small donations. Will Hogg grew angry. He was volunteering his time, paying his own expenses, even buying the lunch for the group. But the Fort Worth people were failing to do their part. Finally his scorn flamed: "You can do precisely as you please. You can give the money or not. But I'll get Fort Worth's share before I leave town. If you boys don't come across, I know where I can get it. I'm going out on the streets and collect the money from the whores and the hack-drivers. They'll help a good cause."

The conductor of the Golden Gate Limited on the run between San Antonio and Houston paused one morning to chat with a group of passengers in the smoking room. Politics was in the air, and soon the talk veered in that direction. Said the conductor, "There's one man I'd like to vote for if he would ever run for office. His name is Will Hogg, old Governor Jim Hogg's son. I never saw him but once, but what happened then was enough to win me."

"Tell us the story," suggested a passenger.

"I was pulling this same train out of San Antonio about a year ago," said the conductor. "There we had taken on a lunger who was traveling back to Alabama with his wife. He was in a bad way. Six months in the land of sunshine had failed to help his tuberculosis. He said he wanted to die in his old home. We put him in his berth. His anxious wife had reason to be uneasy, for the man died on the train before we were fifty miles out of the city.

"When I went to tell his wife that under the rules she would be required to take her husband's body off the train at the next stop, I found a big, deep-voiced man in a brown suit on the seat beside her. He wasn't saying much, only sitting around, handing her water and trying to make himself useful. When I spoke to her she broke down and began to cry. The man in the brown suit followed me into the next coach and stopped me.

"'Listen,' he said, 'you can't put this woman and her dead husband off the train in a little jerkwater town. It's inhuman and I won't stand for it.'

"'But it's the law. I have no choice.'

"'To hell with the law! My name is Will Hogg. I live in Houston. I know the head officials of the Southern Pacific, and I'll take all the responsibility. They won't touch you—I guarantee that. I'll wire ahead and arrange everything.'

"And he did. Most of the time he was back there in the sleeping car talking to that woman and trying to make her comfortable.

"When the long train came to a stop in Houston, waiting at the steps was a lovely woman with her arms full of flowers. They told me it was Miss Ima, Will Hogg's sister. They helped that strange woman off the car, and the last I saw of them Will and Miss Ima both had their arms around her, guiding her into a big automobile pulled up close to the curb."

The conductor paused.

"There's the sort of palooka that gets my vote, from United States Senator on up," he added.

One Christmas morning I visited Will Hogg at the Claridge Hotel in New York. I found him unwrapping packages. The assortment ranged from American Beauty roses to a half-dozen choice Virginia hams.

"Here's a package from home," he said. "Let's see what's in it." He unrolled six or seven silk neckties. Inside were nearly a hundred penciled signatures on a long strip of paper whose margins were splotched with smudgy fingerprints:—

Christmas Greetings—To Mr. Will Hogg
from his friends, the newsboys of
Houston, Texas

Will Hogg held aloft the ties, fingered them, and then walked over to the window and looked down on Broadway far below. He stood with his back to me for a long time. When he turned around, as if angry at his tears, he blurted out: "The damned little rascals! They ought to be horsewhipped for spending their nickels on me. I don't need any neckties. Why, by God..." He choked again and turned back to the window.

Fred Scott, for thirty-five years a redcap at the Southern Pacific depot in Houston, shook his head sadly when I asked him about Will Hogg.

"He was the Negroes' friend. We went to him with all our troubles. He would always intercede for us. Once when his cook's little boy stuck a rusty nail in his foot, Mr. Hogg took him to St. Joseph's Hospital and told them to put him in a private room and take good care of him. And they did for a long time. It cost Mr. Will a thousand dollars.

"When the train pulled in, Mr. Will would always holler out, 'Scott!' I'd come a-runnin' and take care of his valises. Every time he gave me a dollar. He was never crabbed with me. Other gentlemen were loose with their money, too, but they never said, 'Much obliged.' Mr. Will was a busy man, but he would stop and smile and say that."

Scott slumped in his seat. "Everything's as dark as an iron safe since Mr. Will's gone. We have no one to turn to. We're just lost." (6)

After days of work,—as he once put it, "days when I cook up pills to gag the local inhabitants,"—Will Hogg periodically would "light and look at his saddle." He made long visits to Hollywood and New York City. He visited South American resorts with Irvin S. Cobb, who for ten consecutive years hunted from Will's lodge at Aransas Pass. Now and then he made long, leisurely trips through Europe.

When friends were not traveling with him he picked up friends on the way. He played the game of life as lustily and with as much gusto during his vacations as he did when he kept his office force of twenty or thirty men humming while he was at home.

Will Hogg owned no golf sticks. He did not hunt or fish or ride. Fond of camping out, he busied himself on such trips as a kitchen subaltern to see that everyone had enough to eat. Alvin, a Southern Negro cook in New York City, would often be summoned to his Park Avenue apartment to cook "Mr. Will's" favorite chili con carne. Even in Paris, where his beloved chili was unknown, another Negro from the South was set up in business only because of his skill and knowledge in putting together this appetizing dish. But talkative Ike, chef at West Columbia, remained the favorite. "Ike's the best garbage cook in the world," declared Will Hogg. "You can't beat one of his meals of fried catfish, country sausage, young mustard greens, black-eyed peas or Mexican frijoles, buttermilk, with a dash of potlikker for an appetizer."

No one who reads this chronicle would believe that Will Hogg was inherently shy. He was forceful always in office conference, but public speaking filled him with terror. His few public addresses made vernacular history, some of it unprintable. He could be poetically profane, he could cuss by note, often using words that are not or should not be in the dictionary. Vivid, keen, contradictory, fiery, dynamic, rough, he was never malicious. The gruff, brusque outward manner concealed a great, sentimental, generous man within. "A man has to love him a lot to keep from killing him," sighed a suffering business associate one day.

This "tender tempest" either had to cuss things out or break down and weep like a child. (His tears choked him to silence twice as he begged the Regents not to elect a politician President of the University of Texas.) Selfishness, injustice, the hypocrisy of scheming politicians, drove him to fury. When George W. Littlefield, a millionaire stockman and banker, led the fight on the University of Texas under directions from Governor Ferguson, Will told him: "Major, I'm going to talk to you like no man ever talked to you before. You've been the bull-tongued banker in a one-horse town, sitting up in your saffron-colored cage so long that you've lost the power to tell right from wrong." Then the fearless major listened to a lurid description of his ancestry—and he didn't shoot.

Mose was Will's chauffeur. One day Mike Hogg noticed that Mose looked gloomy and down in the mouth.

"What's the matter, Mose?" inquired Mike.

"I'm just feelin' bad," answered Mose. "I ain't havin' no luck. Mr. Will ain't cussed me in a long time. You know, when he cusses me a little, he always gives me a dollar; when he gives me a big cussin', I gits five dollars. But he ain't cussed me no time lately, big *or* little... and I needs the money."

Will Hogg bequeathed Mose $1000 for each of his ten years of service to the family. A similar sum was given to each personal household servant of his home in Houston and of his New York apartment.

His friends sometimes called him "William Combustible Hogg." He was always a man's man. No one who ever knew him doubted just where he stood. Always he fought in the open. It should be added that, though his influence was often solicited, he usually avoided taking any part in political scrambles.

But he struck hard. After accusing one of his wealthy fellow townsmen of shady financial deals, he concluded his signed statement with this phrase: "A consistent and calculating career of mendacity which would belittle even Jesse James, who was romantic enough to ride a horse." There was no reply, no libel suit. No one talked back.

Nor did Will Hogg do things to be seen of men. "I don't like the blankety-blank guff of newspapers." He once threatened Odd McIntyre: "If you put my name in your column of tripe, I'll kick you so hard you'll taste leather the rest of your life."

At the close of a campaign of terrific effort for the Houston Art Museum, he got wind of a public reception to be held in his honor and fled from Houston. Another time a great gathering of citizens planned in secret a reception at the Rice Hotel to present him with a diamond-studded medal "for having rendered the people of Houston the most distinguished service of the year." To throw him off his guard a small group of prominent men, headed by the president of the First National Bank, invited him to a private dinner at the hotel. Becoming suspicious, he feigned illness and left his office early, rode home and went to bed. Nor would he budge from it.

He played at being a gem collector and a connoisseur and patron of art, and came to own eighty-five Remingtons. All his jewelry he gave away. In trying to help Maclyn Arbuckle and a group of penniless actors he fruitlessly spent a hundred thousand dollars on a moving-picture experiment in San Antonio. He angeled a Broadway show for Earl Carroll. When trouble came to Carroll he used his powerful influence to secure his release from prison. He seemed never to tire of giving. A companion told me, "One night I saw eleven panhandlers touch him in a single block in Hollywood, and each carried away something." He surrounded himself with "laughter and the love of friends." He found pleasure in giving Christmas presents though he suffered tortures when thanked for his favors. He enjoyed his playground in Old Mexico, where he and his friend, Raymond Dickson, shared ownership in a ranch stocked with thousands of cattle. Though it was twice the size of Manhattan, with a

Spanish castle in its centre, he called it "a little patch with a
sick cow and a sour well."

Irvin Cobb spoke of Will Hogg as of all men the most lovable,
most self-effacing, most generous. Ex-Attorney General Watt
Gregory said that he was the most vivid personality Texas will
ever know. O. O. McIntyre wrote in his column: "Some day
I hope to hear him shout, 'Hello, Splinters! How in hell did you
get up here?'"

As for me, I shall always like best to think of him as he stood
in his room in New York City, with tear-dimmed eyes, stroking
lovingly a handful of silk neckties which the newsboys of
Houston had sent him for Christmas. (7)

QUESTIONS

I

1. Who was Will Hogg's father and who were the other members
   of the family? (1)
2. What were Will Hogg's most important business activities? Why
   was he rated rather unsuccessful as a business executive? What
   were his real life interests? (2)
3. What was the nature of his fights for the University of Texas?
   What were some of his gifts to the University? (3)
4. What were some of his personal benefactions? (4)
5. In what ways did he show himself the public-spirited citizen? (5)
6. What incidents reveal the very human side of the man? (6)
7. What was the nature of his pleasures? At what times could he be
   sharply outspoken? What was his attitude toward personal publicity? What did his closest friends say about him? (7)

II

1. Do you think Will Hogg cared so little for money because it
   came so easily? Wherein is his attitude completely different
   from that of rich play-boys? Would there be any objection to
   wealth if men were to use it as did Will Hogg?
2. Do you think Will Hogg's reason for not running for office a
   valid one? Wherein is his reason different from that of many
   capable men who refuse to accept public office?
3. How can persons of moderate or even meager means serve the
   public good? Can we excuse ourselves from helping good
   projects because we do not have much money? What can we
   give that is even more important than money?

4. How does Will Hogg's cussing "the Young Women's Christian Association building into existence" have a delightfully "Texan" flavor?
5. President Conant of Harvard University, as well as Will Hogg, believes that "No boy or girl with brains or character should be denied the opportunity of college training." Do you think this democratic ideal can be realized? If so, how?

III

1. Is the introduction of Will Hogg through a sketch of his father an effective way of beginning this biographical essay?
2. Pick out five incidents, each of which shows a different side of Will Hogg's character. Mr. Lomax was faced with a complex and diversified personality. Is his method the best way to portray the man?
3. Can you state the headings of the outline, actual or mental, from which Mr. Lomax wrote this article?
4. Which incident in the article impressed you most? amused you most? seemed most worthy of emulation?

WORDS

For each word at the left point out a synonym from the five words which follow it.

1. espoused (1): shunned, inflamed, embraced, ameliorated, effaced
2. fraudulent (1): deceptive, grotesque, reputable, enormous, foreign
3. stratum (2): corpuscle, carrion, excess, layer, erudition
4. dynamic (2): dangerous, vigorous, fragile, inattentive, anemic
5. perennially (2): briefly, unendingly, cautiously, spasmodically, watchfully
6. capacious (2): spacious, narrow, lengthy, short, crooked
7. subsidiary (2): basic, incidental, unending, intermittent, auxiliary
8. mecca (2): subsidy, goal, knowledge, siesta, mirage
9. autocracy (3): freedom, liberality, despotism, panic, venom
10. supine (3): helpful, helpless, rugged, rough, effete
11. putrid (3): pure, decadent, poisonous, rotten, antiseptic
12. apathy (3): indifference, alertness, energy, caution, foolhardiness
13. servilely (3): slanderously, secretively, sensually, sinuously, slavishly
14. harried (3): nettled, harassed, relieved, mitigated, quenched
15. benefactions (4): incriminations, allegations, legends, legions, goodnesses
16. leavening (5): abandoning, imbuing, hibernating, capsizing, cogitating
17. crass (5): tender, tough, gross, fibrous, fragmentary

18. pecuniary (5): governmental, financial, elemental, cursory, lamentable
19. suave (5): polished, sweetened, acidulous, rough, hairy
20. procrastination (5): promptitude, profession, delay, procession, proficiency
21. infidelity (5): loyalty, sacrifice, unfaithfulness, vanity, fortitude
22. sanctimonious (5): self-conscious, self-possessed, self-righteous, self-sufficient, self-important
23. gusto (7): vigor, ennui, spite, splendor, gravity
24. malicious (7): malcontent, doleful, hateful, suspicious, subdued
25. mendacity (7): lying, veracity, voracity, languor, truthfulness

THEME TOPICS

1. I Know a Human Dynamo
2. The Public-spirited Citizen
3. The Will Hogg of Our Community
4. Natural Resources Belong to the Public
5. Educating the Right People
6. We Need a New —————— in Our Community
7. I Solicited for the Red Cross (Community Chest, etc.)
8. I Shall (Shall Not) Run for Office
9. Scholarships for Deserving Students
10. A Fearless Man I Admire

GOIN' TO TOWN

WALLACE STEGNER

AFTER the night's rain, the yard was spongy and soft under the boy's bare feet. He stood at the edge of the packed dooryard in the flat thrust of sunrise looking at the ground washed clean and smooth and trackless, feeling the cool firm mud under his toes. Experimentally he lifted his right foot and put it down in a new place, pressed, picked it up again to look at the neat imprint of straight edge and curving instep and the five round dots of toes. The air was so fresh that he sniffed at it as he would have sniffed at the smell of cinnamon.

Lifting his head backward, he saw how the prairie beyond the fireguard looked darker than in dry times, healthier with green-brown tints, smaller and more intimate somehow than it did when the heat waves crawled over scorched grass and carried the horizons backward into dim and unseeable distances. And standing in the yard above his one clean sharp footprint, feeling his own verticality in all that spread of horizontal land, he sensed how the prairie shrank on this morning and how he himself grew. He was immense. A little jump would crack his head on the sky; a few strides would take him to any horizon.

His eyes turned south, into the low south sky, cloudless, almost colorless in the strong light. Just above the brown line of the horizon, faint as a watermark on pale blue paper, was the wavering tracery of the mountains, tenuous and far-off, but today accessible for the first time. His mind had played among those ghostly summits for uncountable lost hours; today, in a few strides, they were his. And more: under the shadow of those peaks, under those Bearpaws that he and his mother privately

From *The Atlantic Monthly*, June, 1940. Copyrighted. Used by permission of *The Atlantic Monthly* and the author, and by arrangement with Brandt & Brandt, New York.

called the Mountains of the Moon, was Chinook; and in Chinook, on this Fourth of July, were the band, the lemonade stands, the crowds, the parade, the ball game, the fireworks, that his mind had hungered toward in anticipation for three weeks.

His shepherd pup lay watching, belly down on the damp ground. In a gleeful spasm the boy stooped down to flap the pup's ears, then bent and spun like an Indian in a war dance while the wide-mouthed dog raced around him. And when his father came to the door in his undershirt, yawning, running a hand up the back of his head and through his hair, peering out from gummed eyes to see how the weather looked, the boy watched him, and his voice was one deep breathing relief from yesterday's rainy fear.

"It's clear as a bell," he said.

His father yawned again, clopped his jaws, rubbed his eyes, mumbled something from a mouth furry with sleep. He stood on the doorstep scratching himself comfortably, looking down at the boy and the dog.

"Gonna be hot," he said slyly. "Might be too hot to drive."

"Aw, Pa!"

"Gonna be a scorcher. Melt you right down to axle grease riding in that car."

The boy regarded him doubtfully, saw the lurking sly droop of his mouth. "Aw, we are too going!"

At his father's laugh he burst from his immobility like a sprinter starting, raced one complete circle of the house with the dog after him. When he flew around past his father again his voice trailed out behind him at the corner of the house. "Gonna feed the hens," he said. His father looked after him, scratched himself, laughed suddenly, and went back indoors. (*1*)

Through chores and breakfast the boy moved with the dream of a day's rapture haunting his eyes, but that did not keep him from swift and agile helpfulness. He didn't even wait for commands. He scrubbed himself twice, slicked down his hair, hunted up clean clothes, wiped the mud from his shoes with a wet rag and put them on. While his mother packed the shoebox of lunch he stood at her elbows proffering aid. He flew to stow things in the topless old Ford. He got a cloth and polished the brass radiator.

Once or twice, jumping around to help, he looked up to catch his parents watching him, or looking at each other with the knowing, smiling expression in the eyes that said they were calling each other's attention to him.

"Just like a race horse," his father said once, and the boy felt foolish, swaggered, twisted his mouth down in a leer, said "Awww!" But in a moment he was hustling them again. They ought to get going, with fifty miles to drive. And long before they were ready he was standing beside the Ford, licked and immaculate and so excited that his feet jumped him up and down without his volition or knowledge.

It was eight o'clock before his father came out, lifted off the front seat, poked the flat stick down into the gas tank, and pulled it out again dripping. "Pretty near full," he said. "If we're gonna drive up to the mountains we better take a can along, though. Fill that two-gallon one with the spout."

The boy ran, dug the can out of the shed, filled it from the spigot of the sixty-gallon drum that stood on a plank support to the north of the farmhouse. When he came back, his left arm stuck straight out and the can knocking against his legs, his mother was settling herself into the back seat among the parcels and water bags.

"Goodness!" she said. "This is the first time I've been the first ready since I don't know when. I should think you'd have got all this done last night."

"Plenty time." The father stood looking down at the boy, grinning. "All right, race horse. You want to go to this shindig, you better hop in."

The boy was up into the front seat like a squirrel. His father walked around in front of the car. "Okay," he said. "You look sharp now. When she kicks over, switch her onto magneto and pull the spark down."

The boy said nothing. He looked upon the car, as his father did, with respect and a little awe. They didn't use it much, and starting it was a ritual like a fire drill. The father unscrewed the four-eared brass plug, looked down into the radiator, screwed the cap back on, and bent to take hold of the crank. "Watch it now," he said.

The boy felt the gentle heave of the springs, up and down, as his father wound the crank. He heard the gentle hiss in the bowels of the engine as the choke wire was pulled out, and his nostrils filled with the strong, volatile odor of gasoline. Over the slope of the radiator his father's brown strained face lifted up. "Is she turned on all right?"

"Yup. She's on battery."

"Must have flooded her. Have to let her rest a minute."

They waited—and then after a few minutes the wavelike heaving of the springs again, the rise and fall of the blue shirt and bent head over the radiator, the sighing swish of the choke, a stronger smell of gasoline. The motor had not even coughed.

The two voices came simultaneously from the car. "What's the matter with it?"

His brow puckered in an intent and serious scowl, the father stood blowing mighty breaths. "Son of a gun," he said. Coming around, he pulled at the switch to make sure it was clear over, adjusted the spark and gas levers. A fine mist of sweat made his face shine like oiled leather in the sun.

"There isn't anything really wrong with it, is there?" the mother said, and her voice wavered uncertainly on the edge of fear.

"I don't see how there could be," he said. "She's always started right off, and she was running all right when I drove her in here."

The boy looked at his mother where she sat erect and stiff among the things in the seat. She looked all dressed up, a flowered dress, a hat with hard red varnished cherries on it pinned to her red hair. For a moment she sat, stiff and nervous. "What'll you have to do?" she said.

"I don't know. Look into the motor."

"Well, I guess I'll get in out of the sun while you do it," she said, and, opening the door, she fumbled her way out of the clutter.

The boy felt her exodus like a surrender, a betrayal. If they didn't hurry up they'd miss the parade. In one motion he bounced out of the car. "Gee whiz!" he said. "Let's do something. We got to get started."

"Keep your shirt on," his father grunted. Lifting the hood, he bent his head inside, studying the engine. His hand went out to test wires, wiggle spark-plug connections, make tentative pulls at the choke. The weakly hinged hood slipped and came down across his wrist, and he swore, pushing it back. "Get me the pliers," he said.

For ten minutes he probed and monkeyed. "Might be the spark plugs," he said. "She don't seem to be getting any fire through her."

The mother, sitting on a box in the shade, smoothed her flowered voile dress nervously. "Will it take long?"

"Half hour."

"Any day but this!" she said. "I don't see why you didn't make sure last night."

He breathed through his nose and bent over the engine again. "Don't go laying on any blame," he said. "It was raining last night."

One by one the plugs came out, were squinted at, scraped with a knife blade, the gap tested with a thin dime. The boy stood on one foot, then on the other, time pouring like a flood of uncatchable silver dollars through his hands. He kept looking at the sun, estimating how much time there was left. If they got it started right away they might still make it for the parade, but it would be close. Maybe they'd drive right up the street while the parade was on, and be part of it. . . .

"Is she ready?" he said.

"Pretty quick."

He wandered over by his mother, and she reached out and put an arm around his shoulders, hugging him quickly. "Well, anyway we'll get there for the band and the ball game and the fireworks," he said. "If she doesn't start till noon we c'n make it for those."

"Sure," she said. "Pa'll get it going in a minute. We won't miss anything, hardly."

"You ever seen skyrockets, Ma?"

"Once."

"Are they fun?"

"Wonderful," she said. "Just like a million stars, all colors, exploding all at once."

His feet took him back to his father, who straightened up with a belligerent grunt. "Now!" he said. "If the sucker doesn't start now . . ."

And once more the heaving of the springs, the groaning of the turning engine, the hiss of choke. He tried short, sharp half-turns, as if to catch the motor off guard. Then he went back to the stubborn laboring spin. The back of his blue shirt was stained darkly, the curving dikes of muscle along the spine's hollow showing cleanly where the cloth stuck. Over and over, heaving, stubborn at first, then furious, until he staggered back panting.

"Damn it!" he said. "What you suppose is the matter with the thing?"

"She didn't even cough once," the boy said, and, staring up at his father's face full of angry bafflement, he felt the cold fear touch him. What if it didn't start at all? What if they never got to any of it? What if, all ready to go, they had to turn around and unload the Ford and not even get out of the yard? His mother came over and they stood close together, looking at the Ford and avoiding each other's eyes.

"Maybe something got wet last night," she said.

"Well, it's had plenty of time to dry out," said his father.

"Isn't there anything else you could try?"

"We can jack up the hind wheel, I guess. But there's no damn reason we ought to have to."

"Well, if you have to, you'll have to," she said briskly. "After planning it for three weeks we can't just get stuck like this. Can we, son?"

His answer was mechanical, his eyes steady on his father. "Sure not," he said.

The father opened his mouth to say something, saw the boy's lugubrious face, and shut his lips again. Without a word he pulled off the seat and got out the jack.

The sun climbed steadily while they jacked up one hind wheel and blocked the car carefully so that it wouldn't run over anybody when it started. The boy helped, and when they were

ready again he sat in the front seat so full of hope and fear that
his whole body was one taut concentration. His father stooped,
his cheek pressed against the radiator as a milker's cheek touches
the flank of a cow. His shoulder dropped, jerked up. Nothing.
Another jerk. Nothing. Then he was rolling in a furious spasm of
energy, the wet dark back of his shirt rising and falling. And
inside the motor only the futile swish of the choke and the half-
sound, half-feel of cavernous motion as the crankshaft turned
over. The Ford bounced on its springs as if the front wheels
were coming off the ground on every upstroke. Then it stopped,
and the boy's father was hanging on the radiator, breathless,
dripping wet, swearing: "Son of a dirty, lousy, stinking, corrupted . . ."

The boy, his eyes dark, stared from his father's angry wet
face to his mother's, pinched with worry. The pup lay down
in the shade and put his head on his paws. "Gee whiz," the boy
said. "Gee whiz!" He looked at the sky, and the morning was
half gone.

His shoulders jerking with anger, the father threw the crank
halfway across the yard and took a step or two toward the
house. "The hell with the damn thing!"

"Harry, you can't!"

He stopped, glared at her, took an oblique look at the boy,
bared his teeth in an irresolute, silent swearword. "Well, God, if
it won't go!"

"Maybe if you hitched the horses to it," she said.

His laugh was short and choppy. "That'd be fine!" he said.
"Why don't we just hitch up and let the team haul this damned
old boat into Chinook?"

"But we've got to get it started! Why wouldn't it be all right
to let them pull it around? You push it sometimes on a hill and
it starts."

He looked at the boy again, jerked his eyes away with an exasperated gesture, as if he held the boy somehow accountable.
The boy stared, mournful, defeated, ready to cry, and his
father's head swung back unwillingly. Then abruptly he winked,
mopped his head and neck, and grinned. "Think you want to
go, uh?"

The boy nodded. "All right!" his father's voice snapped crisply. "Fly up in the pasture and get the team. Hustle!" (2)

On the high lope the boy was off up the coulee bank. Just down under the lip of the swale, a quarter mile west, the bay backs of the horses and the black dot of the colt showed. Usually he ran circumspectly across that pasture, because of the cactus, but now he flew. With shoes it was all right, and even without shoes he would have run—across burnouts, over stretches so undermined with gopher holes that sometimes he broke through to the ankle, staggering. Skimming over patches of cactus, soaring over a badger hole, plunging down into the coulee and up the other side, he ran as if bears were after him. The black colt, spotting him, hoisted his tail and took off in a spectacular, stiff-legged sprint across the flats, but the bays merely lifted their heads to watch him. He slowed, came up walking, laid a hand on the mare's neck and untied the looped halter rope. She stood for him while he scrambled and wriggled and kicked his way to her back, and then they were off, the mare in an easy lope, the gelding trotting after, the colt stopping his wild showoff career and wobbling hastily and ignominiously after his departing mother.

They pulled up before the Ford, the boy sliding off to throw the halter rope to his father. "Shall I get the harness?" he said, and before anyone could answer he was off running, to come back lugging one heavy harness, tugs trailing little furrows in the damp bare earth. He dropped it, turned to run again, his breath laboring in his lungs. "I'll get the other'n," he said.

With a short, almost incredulous laugh his father looked at his mother and shook his head before he threw the harness on the mare. When the second one came he laid it over the gelding, pushed against the heavy shoulder to get the horse into place. The gelding resisted, pranced a little, got a curse and a crack with the rope across his nose, jerked back and trembled and lifted his feet nervously, and set one shod hoof on his owner's instep. The father, unstrung by the hurry and the heat and the labor and the exasperation of a morning when nothing went right, kicked the horse savagely in the belly. "Get in there, you damned big blundering ox! Back! Back, there! Whoa! Whoa, now!"

With a heavy rope for a towline he hitched the now-skittish team to the axle. Without a word he stooped and lifted the boy to the mare's back. "All right," he said, and his face relaxed in a quick grin. "This is where we start her. Ride 'em around in a circle, not too fast."

Then he climbed into the Ford, turned on the switch to magneto, fussed with the levers. "Let her go!" he said.

The boy kicked the mare ahead, twisting as he rode to watch the Ford heave forward as a tired, heavy man heaves to his feet, begin rolling after him, lurching on the uneven ground, jerking and kicking and making growling noises when his father let the emergency brake off and put it in gear. The horses settled as the added pull came on them, flattened into their collars, swung in a circle, bumped each other, skittered. The mare reared, and the boy shut his eyes and clung. When he came down, her leg was entangled in the towline and his father was climbing cursing out of the Ford to straighten it out. His father was mad again, and yelled at him. "Keep 'em apart! There ain't any tongue or trees. You got to keep Dick kicked over on his own side."

And again the start, the flattening into the collars, the snapping tight of the tugs under his legs. This time it went smoothly, the Ford galloped after the team in lumbering, plunging jerks. The mare's eyes rolled white, and she broke into a trot, pulling the gelding after her. Desperately the boy clung to the knotted and shortened reins, his ears alert for the grumble of the Ford starting behind him. The pup ran beside the team yapping in a high, falsetto, idiot monotone, crazy with excitement.

They made three complete circles of the back yard between house and chicken coop before the boy looked back again. "Won't she start?" he shouted. He saw his father rigid behind the wheel, heard his ripping burst of swearwords, saw him bend and glare down into the mysterious inwards of the engine through the pulled-up floorboards. Guiding the car with one hand, he fumbled down below, one glaring eye just visible over the cowl.

"Shall I stop?" the boy shouted. Excitement and near-despair made his voice a tearful scream. But his father's wild arm waved him on. "Go on, go on! Gallop 'em! Pull the guts out of this thing. Run 'em, run 'em!"

And the galloping—the furious, mud-flinging, rolling-eyed galloping around the circle already rutted like a road, the Ford, now in savagely held low, growling and surging and ploughing behind; the mad yapping of the dog, the erratic scared bursts of runaway from the colt, the mother in sight briefly for a quarter of each circle, her hands to her mouth and her eyes hurt, and behind him in the Ford his father in a strangling rage, yelling him on, his lips back over his teeth and his face purple.

Until finally they stopped, the horses blown, the boy white and tearful and still, the father dangerous with unexpended wrath. The boy slipped off, his lip bitten between his teeth, not crying now but ready to at any moment, the corners of his eyes prickling with it, and his teeth tight on his misery. His father climbed over the side of the car and stood looking as if he wanted to tear the thing apart with his bare hands. (3)

Shoulders sagging, tears trembling to fall, his jaw aching with the need to cry, the boy started toward his mother. As he came near his father he looked up, their eyes met, and he saw his father's blank with impotent rage. Dull hopelessness swallowed him. Not any of it, his mind said. Not even any of it—no parade, no ball game, no band, no fireworks. No lemonade or ice cream or paper horns or firecrackers. No close sight of the mountains that throughout every summer called like a legend from his horizons. No trip, no adventure—none of it, nothing.

Everything he was feeling was in that one still look. In spite of him his lip trembled, and he choked off a sob, his eyes on his father's face, on the brows pulling down and the eyes narrowing.

"Well, don't blubber!" his father shouted at him. "Don't stand there looking at me as if it was me that was keeping you from your picnic!"

"I can't—help it," the boy said, and with a kind of terror he felt the grief swelling up, overwhelming him, driving the voice out of him in a wail. Through the blur of his crying he saw the convulsive tightening of his father's face, and then all the fury of a maddening morning concentrated itself in a swift backhand blow that knocked the boy staggering.

He bawled aloud, from pain, from surprise, from outrage, from pure desolation, and ran to bury his face in his mother's skirts. From that muffled sanctuary he heard her angry voice. "No," she said. "It won't do any good to try to make up to him now. Go on away somewhere till he gets over it."

She rocked him against her, but the voice she had for his father was still bitter with anger. "As if he wasn't hurt enough already!" she said.

He heard the heavy, quick footsteps going away, and for a long time he lay crying into the voile flowers. And when he had cried himself out, and had listened apathetically to his mother's soothing promises that they would go in the first chance they got, go to the mountains, have a picnic under some waterfall, maybe be able to find a ball game going on in town, some Saturday—when he had listened and become quiet, wanting to believe it but not believing it at all, he went inside to take off his good clothes and his shoes and put on his old overalls again.

It was almost noon when he came out to stand in the front yard looking southward toward the impossible land where the Mountains of the Moon lifted above the plains, and where, in the town at the foot of the peaks, crowds would now be eating picnic lunches, drinking pop, getting ready to go out to the ball field and watch heroes in real uniforms play ball. The band would be braying now from a bunting-wrapped stand, kids would be tossing firecrackers, playing in a cool grove. . . .

In the still heat his face went sorrowful and defeated, and his eyes searched the horizon for the telltale watermark. But there was nothing but waves of heat crawling and lifting like invisible flames; the horizon was a blurred and writhing flatness where earth and sky met in an indistinct band of haze. This morning two strides would have taken him there; now it was gone.

Looking down, he saw at his feet the clean footprint that he had made in the early morning. Aimlessly he put his right foot down and pressed. The mud was drying, but in a low place he found a spot that would still take an imprint. Very carefully, as if he were performing some ritual for his life, he went around, stepping and leaning, stepping and leaning, until he had a circle six feet in diameter of delicately exact footprints, straight edge and curving instep and the five round dots of toes. (4)

QUESTIONS

I

1. How are we introduced to the boy, and how do we learn that something important is going to happen on this day? (1)
2. What are the various steps taken in the first attempt to make the car go? (2)
3. What final effort was made to start the car and how did it turn out? (3)
4. What personal indignity did the boy finally suffer? In what same activity, but in what different mood, do we leave him at the close of the story? (4)

II

1. Can you think of a disappointment, such as the one in this story, that happened to you in your childhood? Do you think of it romantically? sentimentally? realistically?
2. Psychologists tell us that "tragedies" to a child are not unimportant just because they are trivial. They are as important *to a child* as great catastrophes are *to men.* May not a man be better prepared by experience to endure the loss of his money than a child the breaking of his toy? Is everything important *to the person* to whom it is happening?

III

1. In the first two paragraphs occur these unusual phrases: "the flat thrust of sunrise" and "feeling his own verticality in all that spread of horizontal land." Look for other original and effective bits of writing throughout the story, particularly figures of speech.
2. Is the author's knowledge of boy psychology sound in his description of the boy's sudden zeal in washing himself really clean, his unusual helpfulness, his hustling his parents off?
3. Are all the details of cranking the car accurately handled? Do you get a picture of all three persons: the father cranking, the mother anxiously critical, the boy in an agony of stabbing fear that they won't be able to go to Chinook at all?
4. What are the basic characteristics of the man as revealed in this

story? What are the mother's chief characteristics? How do we know that each parent loves the boy?

5. The word pictures of the nervous horses being hitched to the car, the father's rage when the horse steps on his foot, the final mad chariot race around the farmyard are all vividly done. Analyze how the writer achieves such pictorial writing. Pick out the words and phrases which are most effective.

6. Note how much emotion is crowded into the boy's sudden realization: "Not even any of it—no parade, no ball game, no band, no fireworks." What kind of language best expresses pathos?

7. How has the author lessened the reader's resentment against the father for striking the boy? Is the mother's attitude toward her husband's treatment of the boy consistent with her character as portrayed throughout the story? Is the story meant to be romantic or realistic?

8. Is the description of the boy's gradual recovery well handled? What phrases picture best his mood at the end of the story?

9. Do you think the boy's making footprints a second time gives an artistic touch of unity to the story?

10. What is the main source of appeal to the reader in this story? Does it have human interest and universality?

WORDS

Each word at the left and the words that follow it are derived from the same stem. Show how the words in each group are related to this stem in meaning.

1. verticality (*1*), *vert*, "turn,": aversion, divert, traverse
2. tenuous (*1*), *tend*, "thin": attenuate, extenuate, tendril
3. immobility (*1*), *mov*, "move": movement, momentum, remove
4. rapture (*2*), *rap*, "seize": rapacious, ravish, rapt
5. agile (*2*), *ag*, "do": agitate, agent, exigency
6. immaculate (*2*), *macul*, "spot": maculate, mackerel
7. volition (*2*), *vol*, "will": voluntary, volunteer
8. volatile (*2*), *vol*, "fly": volatilize, volley
9. exodus (*2*), *hod*, "way": method, episode
10. belligerent (*2*), *belli*, "war": bellicose, rebellion
11. cavernous (*2*), *cav*, "hollow": cave, excavate, concave
12. circumspectly (*3*), *spec*, "look": spectacles, spectator, inspect
13. ignominiously (*3*), *nom*, "name": nominal, renown
14. incredulous (*3*), *cred*, "believe": accredited, credentials
15. rigid (*3*), *rig*, "stiff": rigidity, rigor
16. erratic (*3*), *err*, "wander": err, error, erroneous
17. impotent (*4*), *pot*, "power": potent, potential, omnipotent

18. sanctuary (*4*), *sanct*, "holy": sanctimonious, sanctum, sacrosanct
19. apathetically (*4*), *path*, "feeling": pathos, sympathy, antipathy
20. uniforms (*4*), *uni*, "one": unison, unanimous, onion

THEME TOPICS

1. The Party I Wasn't Invited To
2. The Day Everything Went Wrong
3. Father (Mother) Has a Temper
4. Children Live in a Controlled World
5. A Fourth of July Celebration I Remember
6. When Our Car Wouldn't Start
7. My Worst Adventure with a Car
8. The Pathos of Childhood
9. Life with *My* Father (humorous)
10. Mother Always Understood

THIS BUSINESS OF GROWING OLD

STEPHEN LEACOCK

OLD age is the "Front Line" of life, moving into No Man's Land. No Man's Land is covered with mist. Beyond it is Eternity. As we have moved forward, the tumult that now lies behind us has died down. The sounds grow less and less. It is almost silence. There is an increasing feeling of isolation, of being alone. We seem so far apart. Here and there one falls, silently, and lies a little bundle on the ground that the rolling mist is burying. Can we not keep nearer? It's hard to see one another. Can you hear me? Call to me. I am alone. This must be near the end.

I have been asked how old age feels, how it feels to be reaching 70, and I answer in metaphor, as above, "not so good."

Now let us turn it around and try to laugh it off in prose. It can't be so bad as that, eh, what? Didn't Cicero write a book on old age, to make it all right? But you say he was only just past 60 when he wrote it, was he? That's a tough one. Well, what about Rabbi ben Ezra, you remember—"Grow old along with me." Oh, he was 81, eh? No, thanks, I'll stay right here around 70. He can have all his fun for himself at 81. (1)

I was born at Swanmoor, a suburb of Rye in the Isle of Wight, on Dec. 30, 1869. That was in Victorian England at its most Victorian, far away now, dated by the French Empire, still glittering, and Mr. Dickens writing his latest book on the edge of the grave while I thought out my first on the edge of my cradle, and, in America, dated by people driving golden spikes on Pacific railroads.

It was a vast, illimitable world, far superior to this—whole continents unknown, Africa just an outline, oceans never sailed,

From *The New York Times Magazine*, December 31, 1939. Copyrighted. Used by permission of The Times Publishing Company and the author.

ships lost over the horizon—as large and open as life itself.

Put beside such a world this present shrunken earth, its every corner known, its old-time mystery gone with the magic of the sea, to make place for this new demoniac confine, loud with voices out of emptiness and tense with the universal threat of death. This is not mystery but horror. The waves of the magic sea called out in the sunlight: "There must be God." The demoniac radio answers in the dark: "There can't be." Belief was so easy then; it has grown so hard now; and life, the individual life, that for an awakening child was so boundless, has it drawn in to this—this alley-way between tall cypresses that must join somewhere in the mist? But stop, we are getting near No Man's Land again. Turn back. (2)

Moving pictures love to give us nowadays "cavalcades" of events, to mark the flight of time. Each of us carries his own. Mine shows, as its opening, the sea beaches of the Isle of Wight. ...Then turn on Portchester village and its Roman castle... Queen Victoria going past in a train, in the dark, putting her head out of the window (her eight heads out of eight windows) ...Now shift to an Atlantic sailing steamer (type of 1876) with people emigrating to Canada....Then a Canadian farm in a lost corner of Ontario up near Lake Simcoe for six years....Put in bears, though there weren't any....Boarding school scenes at Upper Canada College—the real old rough stuff...University, cap and gown days, old style, put a long beard on the president, show fourteen boarding houses at $4.50 a week....School teaching—ten years—(run it fast, I want to forget it)....

Then make the film Chicago University with its saloons of forty years ago, a raw place, nowhere to smoke....And then settle the film down to McGill University, and run it round and round as slowly as you like for thirty-six sessions—college calling in the Autumn, students and co-eds and Rah! Rah! all starting afresh, year after year....College in the snow, the February classroom; hush! don't wake them, it's a lecture in archaeology.... All of it again and again....College years, one after the other. ...Throw in, as interludes, journeys to England, a lecture trip round the empire....Put in Colombo, Ceylon, for atmosphere. ...Then more college years....

Then loud music and the great war with the college campus all at drill, the boys of yesterday turned to men.... Then the war over, lecture trips to the U. S.... Pictures of Iowa State University.... Ladies Fortnightly Club—about forty of them.... Then back to the McGill campus.... Retirement.... An honorary degree ("this venerable scholar").... And then unexpectedly the war again and the Black Watch back on the McGill campus.

Such is my picture, the cavalcade all the way down from the clouds of the morning to the mist of the evening. (3)

As the cavalcade passes down the years it is odd how gradually and imperceptibly the change of outlook comes, from the eyes of wonder to those of disillusionment—or is it to those of truth? A child's world is full of celebrated people, wonderful people like the giants and magicians of the picture books. Later in life the celebrated people are all gone. There aren't any—or not made of what it once meant.

I recall from over half a century ago a prize-day speaker at Upper Canada College telling us that he saw before him the future statesmen, the poets, the generals and the leaders of the nation. I thought the man a nut to say that. What he saw was just us. Yet he turned out to be correct; only in a sense he wasn't; it was still only us after all. It is the atmosphere of illusion that cannot last.

Yet some people, I know, are luckier in this than I am. They're born in a world of glamour and live in it. For them there are great people everywhere, and the illusion seems to feed itself. One such I recall out of the years, with a capacity for admiration all his own.

"I sat next to Professor Buchan at the dinner last night," he once told me. "He certainly is a great scholar, a marvelous philologian!"

"Is he?" I said.

"Yes," my friend continued. "I asked him if he thought the Indian word snabe was the same as the German word knabe."

"And what did he say?"

"He said he didn't know."

And with that my friend sat back in quiet appreciation of such accurate scholarship and of the privilege of being near it. There are many people like that, decent fellows to be with. Their illusions keep their life warm.

But for most of us they fade out and life itself as we begin to look back on it appears less and less. Has it all faded to this? There comes to me the story of an old Carolina Negro who found himself, after years of expectancy, privileged to cast a vote. After putting the ballot paper in the box he stood, still expectant, waiting for what was to happen, to come next. And then, in disillusionment: "Is that all there is, boss? Is that all there is to it?"

"That's all," said the presiding officer.

So it is with life. The child says "when I am a big boy"—but what is that? The boy says "when I grow up"—and then, grown up, "when I get married." But to be married, once done and over, what is that again? The man says "When I can retire"— and then when retirement comes he looks back over the path traversed, a cold wind sweeps over the fading landscape and he feels somehow that he has missed it all. For the reality of life, we learn too late, is in the living tissue of it from day to day, not in the expectation of better, nor in the fear of worse. Those two things, to be always looking ahead, and to worry over things that haven't yet happened and very likely won't happen—those take the very essence out of life.

If only one could live each moment to the full, in a present, intense with its own absorption, even if as transitory and evanescent as Einstein's "here" and "now." It is strange how we cry out in our collective human mind against this restless thinking and clamor for time to stand still—longing for a land where it is always afternoon, or for a book of verses underneath a bough, where we may let the world pass. (4)

But perhaps it is this worry, this restlessness that keeps us on our necessary path of effort and endeavor. Most of us who look back from old age have at least a comfortable feeling that we have "got away with it." At least we keep out of jail, out of the asylum and out of the poor house. Yet one still needs to be careful. Even "grand old men" get fooled sometimes. But at any rate we don't want to start over; no, thank you, it's too hard. When

I look back to long evenings of study in boarding house bedrooms, night after night, one's head sinking at times over the dictionary—I wonder how I did it.

And school days—at Upper Canada College anno domini 1882 —could I stand that now? If some one asked me to eat "supper" at 6 and then go and study next day's lessons, in silence in the long study from 7 to 9:30—how would that be? A school waiter brought round glasses of water on a tray at half-past eight, and if I had asked for a whisky and soda could I have had it? I could not. Yet I admit there was the fun of putting a bent pin—you know how, two turns in it—on the seat where the study master sat. And if I were to try that now at convocation they wouldn't understand it. Youth is youth, and age is age.

So many things, I say, that one went through seem hopelessly difficult now. Yet other things, over which youth boggles and hesitates and palpitates, seem so easy and so simple to old age. Take the case of women, I mean girls. Young men in love go snooping around, hoping, fearing, wondering, lifted up at a word, cast down by an eyebrow. But if he only knew enough, any young man—as old men see it—could have any girl he wanted. All he need do is to step up to her and say "Miss Smith, I don't know you, but your overwhelming beauty forces me to speak; can you marry me at, say, 3:30 this afternoon?"

I mean, that kind of thing in that province of life would save years of trepidation. It's just as well, though, that they don't know it or away goes all the pretty world of feathers and flounces, of flowers and dances that love throws like a gossamer tissue across the path of life.

On such a world of youth, old age can only gaze with admiration. As people grow old all youth look beautiful to them. The plainest girls are pretty with nature's charm. The dullest duds are at least young. But age cannot share it. Age must sit alone. (5)

The path through life I have outlined from youth to age, you may trace for yourself by the varying way in which strangers address you. You begin as "little man" and then "little boy," because a little man is littler than a little boy; then "sonny" and then "my boy" and after that "young man" and presently the interlocutor is younger than yourself and says, "say, mister." I can still recall the thrill of pride I felt when a Pullman porter first called me "doctor" and when another one raised me up to judge, and the terrible shock it was when a taxi man swung open his door and said, "Step right in, dad."

It was hard to bear when a newspaper reporter spoke of me as the "old gentleman," and said I was very simply dressed. He was a liar; those were my best things. It was a worse shock when a newspaper last Autumn called me a septuagenarian, another cowardly lie, as I was only 69 and seven-twelfths. Presently I shall be introduced as "this venerable old gentleman" and the axe will fall when they raise me to the degree of "grand old man." That means on our continent any one with snow white hair who has kept out of jail till 80. That's the last and worst they can do to you. (6)

Yet there is something to be said even here for the mentality of age. Old people grow kinder in their judgment of others. They are able to comprehend, even if not to pardon, the sins and faults of others. If I hear of a man robbing the cash register of the shop where he works, I think I get the idea. He wanted the cash. If I read of a man burning down his store to get the insurance, I see that what he wanted was the insurance. He had nothing against the store. Yet somehow just when I am reflecting on my own kindliness I find myself getting furious with a waiter for forgetting the Worcester sauce.

This is the summary of the matter that as for old age there's nothing to it, for the individual looked at by himself. It can only be reconciled with our view of life in so far as it has something to pass on, the new life of children and of grandchildren, or if not that, at least some recollection of good deeds, or of something done that may give one the hope to say, "non omnis moriar" (I shall not altogether die).

Give me my stick. I'm going out on to No Man's Land. I'll face it. (7)

QUESTIONS

I

1. What is Stephen Leacock's feeling about being seventy years old? (*1*)

2. In what way is the present world different from the world of Mr. Leacock's youth? (2)
3. What are the outstanding biographical facts revealed in Mr. Leacock's "cavalcade"? (3)
4. What examples of illusion and disillusionment does Mr. Leacock give to prove that we see differently in old age? (4)
5. What things of youth would he now find difficult to do and what things, difficult to youth, could he now do very easily? (5)
6. How may the way in which one is addressed tell the story of his life? (6)
7. What effect does age have upon understanding people's actions? What hopes reconcile one to the acceptance of old age? (7)

II

1. Do you believe Mr. Leacock's statement that modern life has become "this alley-way between tall cypresses"? (2)
2. Does this essay help you to comprehend why your elders sometimes do not understand youth? Can age and youth ever really see things the same way? Analyze your answer penetratingly.
3. Is Mr. Leacock giving us sound doctrine when he urges us to live day by day and not to look ahead to joys and sorrows to come? (4)
4. Do you think that restless worry about the future is the spur needed to keep us at work "on our necessary path of effort and endeavor"? (5)
5. What is apparently Mr. Leacock's view of immortality? Have you any well-formulated ideas on the subject? (7)

III

1. Mr. Leacock is a master of satiric humor and even in this rather serious essay he has followed his natural bent. Point out expressions, ideas, and incidents of humor.
2. Mr. Leacock uses a "motion-picture effect" to supply the reader with a number of biographical details quickly. Discuss the device from the viewpoint of speed, condensation, and novelty. (2)
3. The anecdote of the old Carolina Negro and his first vote is a mixture of pathos and humor. Which element do you think predominates? What application of this little story does Mr. Leacock make? (4)
4. Note how Mr. Leacock enlivens what might have been a dull account by his "ages of man." Analyze carefully why this is effective writing. (6)
5. As a summarizing comment most appropriate for characterizing

Mr. Leacock's essay, select one (or perhaps two or three) of the following words (arranged alphabetically): broad-minded, clever, comprehensive, humane, humorous, imaginative, inspiring, interesting, penetrating, pessimistic, philosophical, poetic, thought-provoking, typical, whimsical, wise, witty.

WORDS

Discuss each of the following words as its meaning is revealed by, or related to, its etymology.

1. illimitable (*2*): Latin *il-*, "not'" and *limes*, "boundary"
2. demoniac (*2*): Latin *daemon*, "evil spirit"
3. interludes (*3*): Latin *inter-*, "between" and *ludere*, "to play"
4. venerable (*3*): Latin *venerari*, "to respect highly"
5. cavalcade (*3*): Latin *caballicare*, "to go on horseback"
6. philologian (*4*): Greek *philos*, "loving" and *logos*, "speech"
7. essence (*4*): Latin *esse*, "to be"
8. transitory (*4*): Latin *trans-*, "over" and *ire*, "to go"
9. evanescent (*4*): Latin *e-*, "out" and *vanescere*, "to vanish"
10. palpitates (*5*): Latin *palpare*, "to feel, stroke"
11. trepidation (*5*): Latin *trepidare*, "to tremble"
12. gossamer (*5*): Middle English *goose summer*, November
13. interlocutor (*6*): Latin *inter-*, "between" and *loqui*, "to speak"
14. septuagenarian (*6*): Latin *septuagen*, "seventy each"
15. reconciled (*7*): Latin *re-*, "again" and *conciliare*, "to unite"

THEME TOPICS

1. I Met a Celebrated Person Once
2. Living Day by Day
3. Crossing Bridges We Never Reach
4. The Value of Illusions
5. The Old Understand Many Things
6. The Impatience (Intolerance) of Youth
7. In Defense of Youth (Age)
8. My Little Cavalcade
9. My Belief in Immortality
10. Worry (Fear) as a Spur to Accomplishment

Americans by Choice

SHORES OF DESTINATION

VINCENT SHEEAN

THE *Queen Mary* goes too fast for the sea-gulls. They can pursue it for a good part of the first day, affronting with unruffled breasts the wind and the waves that rise against them; but afterwards they wheel to their accustomed courses, and we go on with turbined majesty to the vast solitudes of the ocean. They are solitudes even here, in the main-traveled road of the north Atlantic, on a ship which is filled with passengers and crew, anxious men and women of the millinery trades returning to New York, politicians and diplomatists and business men, ladies and sailors, refugees. (*1*)

It is the British sea. This is a British ship, and on the two occasions when we pass other ships on the water they are British ships, too. The immense steamer takes to the sea in fair weather or foul with superb confidence, a monarch in his element. Hearts of oak: Britons never will be slaves.

As a matter of fact a good many of them are, and right on this ship, too, but they seem to have adjusted themselves to the position. At least they are not slaves to the foreigner, and the foreigner's submarines are not yet thick in the cold subaqueous depths where centuries have washed the bones of the British sailor. Those are pearls that were his eyes; the whole history of his country rises from the deep water, the salt and fishy depths; it comes storming down the wind, rides the wave, stings in the spray. It was here that they made the Empire, clear-eyed and short-tempered men with no gift for diplomatic language. They were pushed out of an overcrowded island and had nowhere to go except by water, so that the water became their road and

From *The Saturday Review of Literature*, July 1, 1939. Copyrighted. Used by permission of the Editors and by arrangement with Carol Hill, 22 East 40th Street, New York, for the author.

the foundation of their house, and if the house was safe it was because of the water and the men on it. A good many of them seem to be employed just now in polishing brass, carrying buckets, making life agreeable and luxurious for the idle, thoughtful, or anxious passengers who can afford to travel on this ship. Others by the hundred swelter in the jungles of machinery below; and there are hundreds more whose only duty to the sea lies in carrying a tray, sweeping a floor, making a bed. Such a world is afloat here that you can ring a bell and get very nearly anything you are likely to need; you can go shopping, you can get photographed, you can dance or swim or get your hair cut or go through a Turkish bath; there are even books and places where you can sit and read them. Only a very small proportion of the passengers who travel in this way belong to the nation which made the ship and manned it; most travelers are Americans; but there are also refugees from half the countries of Europe. They do not have quite so many bells to ring, as they are in the third class, but they keep cheerful enough: they have escaped from a kind of hell and are going to what they may think (for a while yet) a kind of paradise, and at least they are free. Among them are the bearded and black-capped Jews who can eat only at the orthodox table; but there are young and old of all nations here, dark eyes that will never see Spain again, and children who last played in the Tiergarten in Berlin. There are also half a dozen men of the Lincoln Battalion, returning belatedly to their own country from the fight down there. One of them is a tall Negro boy who left his right leg on the Ebro. (2)

Once they have passed over this sea they will feel safe, probably, and I think with altogether unwarranted optimism. What was all that that went on in Europe? they will say. We are in a new country where all are equal and every man has a chance, a country torn out of the dark wilderness by our collateral ancestors, by people just like us, by refugees.

That is the way their release will affect them, some of them. They have further discoveries to make in America, but all that lies ahead. For the moment they have escaped from the misery which politicians and profiteers have brought upon the old continent, and they are entitled to their interval of cheer before they find out that there are politicians and profiteers in America too. As they lean over the rail and look into the blue-and-white ocean, they can calculate with joy the millions upon millions of tons of water that will lie between them and the old continent, water like a rampart, setting off into the past all that was cruelty and despair in the life there. If I went over and told one of them that this was not so; that the seas had shrunk and the air itself contracted; that Europe was everywhere now, and the whole world one place; this they would certainly refuse to accept. (3)

And why not? For the most part we live by means of forgetting death. The breathless young lady in the first class who is simply *entranced* at the Orkney homespuns in the shop, and simply cannot *resist* buying a scarf, and must simply *die* if she doesn't have a cocktail at once—what else is she doing, and she no refugee at all, but a young lady of great privilege and presumable happiness? The ship and all aboard it live by passage, by transit, by putting away the past, by forgetting what has receded as well as the final harbor ahead. Between the shores of departure and destination there is time, so much time that cloud after cloud passes over the memory of unhappy things, and it is natural and inevitable to face the winds of the ocean with a great and rising hope.

The woman who eats at the next table is a golf champion. She is going to America to play golf. I have read her name in the newspapers and know by expert testimony that she plays very good golf. I don't think she is much aware of what cargo we carry. I doubt if she notices much beyond the first-class passengers (a few of them) and the stewards. Her conversation is breezy and robust, like her appearance. If she visited the refugees in the third class—as I am sure she will not—she would experience sympathy and some obscure discomfort. I can hear her saying through her teeth: "Poor devils!" Halfway up in the elevator she would forget them, intent as she is upon the problem of what she can eat. Between her regime as an athlete, her regime as a somewhat queasy passenger, and the huge, rude demands of her appetite, she is the prey to unceasing conflict, and the whack with which she sends the little white ball great distances is perhaps, after all, no special talent, but the effect of sheer physical exasperation under a trained control.

We have a general and a newspaper owner, too. The general talks gossip, nothing but gossip, although most of it is about the notable monsters of the day, Hitler, Mussolini, and the like. He has just heard this or that; he read something the other day; and is it true that—? The newspaper owner is fastidious, thoughtful, uneasy; he is the editor of a Liberal newspaper in London, and these are not the most hospitable times for Liberals. So they come to America—perhaps to reassure themselves, perhaps to assert by their presence that there are still Liberals alive on the other side of this sea of transition. (4)

I sit stretched out in a deck chair and read a book: "Les Grands Cimetières sous la Lune." The Great Cemeteries under the Moon. A terrible tale of fascism on the island of Majorca, by a Catholic, a Royalist, an extreme Conservative. He is disgusted and embittered by the sheer indecency of the fascist triumph he records, even though its proclaimed ideas are closely related to those he has adopted as his own. The white wall of the cemetery under the moon, with the dark splotches that lie along its base, the body and blood of Spain....

The passengers go by on the deck, taking their exercise: twice around is a mile. The Czechoslovak diplomat, explaining his own downfall with eager emphasis, has fallen into the toils of a lady from New York who does not exactly follow all his discourse, but finds it very interesting. She will give a wondrously garbled version of it at dinners for at least a week after she gets home again. Prague and the Ebro have receded, receded; time and the sea have covered them; men and things lie submerged; of their bones are coral made. But in this lull, this swift trajectory over the sunny water, when hope seems altogether to have vanquished memory, there is a gathering-together of forces; and I am not sure whether that sound was the creaking of the boards on the deck of the ship or the flexing of muscles, thousands of muscles, down below where the workers feed the fire. The ship is forced on over the blue sea, and in five days we do what it took another age three months to accomplish:

cross to the New World. Men and machines have so contracted space that this ocean itself no longer divides the hemispheres. It is, rather, a path for the storm that is coming, and those who have fled from the storm once will only have to face it in another place.

If it comes now who will ride it out? The seasick passengers? No: those who tend the engines, watch the sea and sky, feed the fires. (5)

QUESTIONS

I

1. How is the speed of the *Queen Mary* indicated by the sea-gulls? What kind of people are on the passenger list? (1)
2. What circumstances naturally made Britain a great maritime nation? In what way is the ship a miniature world in itself? What countries do the various refugees on the *Queen Mary* represent? (2)
3. In what way do the refugees' and the author's views of America differ? In what sense is America closer to Europe than the refugees think? (3)
4. What different types of passengers are represented by the breathless young lady, the golf champion, the general, and the editor? (4)
5. What is the nature of the book the author is reading? What is amusing about the incident of the New York lady and the diplomat? Who of the persons aboard will, in the author's opinion, best ride out the storm? (5)

II

1. Point out passages in the essay that show Mr. Sheean's realistic, not to say pessimistic, attitude. Do you agree with his opinions about politicians, profiteers, the "upper classes," the delusion awaiting refugees?
2. How have events proved the correctness of Mr. Sheean's statements that our oceans and distances are no longer safeguards? Analyze acutely the ways by which the world has become so contracted. What bearing has your analysis upon an isolationist policy for America in the future?
3. Mr. Sheean puts his faith in the workers (5) and not in the first-class passengers nor in the anxious refugees. Do you agree or disagree with him?

III

1. Do you feel a mystic symbolism in the voyage of the *Queen Mary?* Read the sentences from "The ship and all aboard it ..." to "... a great and rising hope." (*4*)
2. Point out several "purple patches" of poetic prose in this essay. Do you like the beauty and fervor of these passages?
3. From what great writer do the sentences "Those are pearls that were his eyes" and "Of their bones are coral made" come?
4. Note the extravagant vocabulary of "the young lady in the first class." (*4*) Is Mr. Sheean reporting her accurately or being slightly sarcastic? What is his attitude in suggesting that the golf champion's skill might be attributed to her diet? (*4*) In what way is his reference to the New York lady and the diplomat satiric? (*5*)
5. In what sense does Mr. Sheean call the Atlantic "a sea of transition"?
6. The author hints that the optimistic refugees are indulging a vain hope that, by fleeing Europe, they are escaping the downfall of civilization. Pick out the sentence that shows the author's pessimism most strongly.

WORDS

Select, from the right-hand column, the correct definition for each word at the left.

1. affronting (*1*)		1. nauseated
2. subaqueous (*2*)		2. sound in doctrine
3. diplomatic (*2*)		3. distorted
4. luxurious (*2*)		4. of indirect descent
5. orthodox (*2*)		5. bulwark
6. collateral (*3*)		6. beneath the surface of the water
7. rampart (*3*)		7. curve
8. régime (*4*)		8. full of comforts and ease
9. queasy (*4*)		9. particular
10. fastidious (*4*)		10. facing defiantly
11. garbled (*5*)		11. regulated mode of living
12. trajectory (*5*)		12. tactful

THEME TOPICS

1. A Refugee (or Immigrant) in My Town
2. We Live in a Contracting World
3. A Strange Person I Met in My Travels
4. A Man Who Gave Me a Ride

I *CHOSE* AMERICA

PERCY WAXMAN

IT WAS not to escape tyranny or poverty that I became an American citizen. I was born in Australia, educated there in the traditional British manner. Up to my 23rd year even the idea of renouncing allegiance to the Empire would have seemed sacrilege.

Then one day the opportunity came to take a trip around the world. I went first to the United States. After a brief stay in San Francisco I eagerly set out for Chicago, which I had been led by tourist literature to believe was a cross between Paris and Paradise. I arrived there on an April morning—and in the midst of a raging, subzero blizzard. That Arctic wilderness did not seem enticing to one who had never before seen snow. A train for New York was leaving in ten minutes, so I dashed aboard.

I immediately found myself confronted by an embarrassing situation. I had left the West Coast with only enough money to last until I reached Chicago, where I could use my letter of credit, for I had been warned that carrying money around America was highly hazardous. So after paying for ticket and berth to New York I was left with exactly seventy-five cents. It was a twenty-eight-hour run to New York and I had the hollow prospect of going all that time without food.

I asked the porter to tell the dining-car conductor of my situation and find out if I might not open an account with him based on my letter of credit. A few minutes later a middle-aged man stopped where I was sitting.

"I overheard the porter telling the conductor that you were in need of money," he said, "and I thought I'd see if I could help out."

Considerably embarrassed, I sputtered forth the reasons for my predicament, and that man, a complete stranger, loaned me $10. When I asked him to come to the bank with me as soon as we reached New York he said:

"Oh, I get off at Cleveland. Here's my card. You can send me the money when you get settled."

The fact that the man had *sought* me out to render me a kindness impressed me tremendously. I concluded that a country where such things happen to a stranger was a country well-worth knowing. One year after this incident I returned to the United States to stay. (*1*)

I have made my home here for over thirty years. During my first years in New York I took no steps to become naturalized. One day I received notice to serve on a jury. Not being a citizen, I ignored it. A few days later I was served with a summons to appear at City Hall. There I presented myself to a gentleman of the old dyed-mustache school of Tammany statesmen who menacingly demanded to know why I had paid no attention to the previous notice. Somewhat smart-alecky I asked: "What is the penalty for a British subject serving on an American jury?"

"Oh, that's it, is it?" he remarked with Irish fervor and across the face of my summons wrote "Alien" in big red letters, as if he wished to impress me with the full significance of that sinister designation.

On my way home I thought over this experience. At first with amusement, then more seriously. Here I was, living and working in America, enjoying its privileges but not sharing full responsibilities. I decided to be an alien no longer. And now after having been a citizen for almost twenty-five years I can honestly say that the longer I live here the better I like it. My love for America has nothing to do with that brand of patriotism which a cynical friend defined as "self-interest multiplied by population." (*2*)

It has often been said that Americans are dollar-chasers. But it has been my experience that one of the characteristics of Americans is the casualness with which they regard money. No people are more generous or extravagant. After having lived in many different parts of the world, I can honestly say that if I were friendless, unemployed and penniless I would rather take my chances asking for help on the corner of an American street than anywhere else on earth.

I can say these things openly where a born American might hesitate. The fact that I am naturalized gives me a sort of detached privilege to speak freely without seeming to talk about myself.

American hospitality is proverbial. Was there ever anything to compare with the open-hearted reception accorded a foreign visitor? Nothing is too good for him. No one bothers to inquire who his ancestors were. In spite of their reputed smartness, Americans are more liable to be swindled by foreigners than foreigners are by Americans.

As for sportsmanship, no people are more ready to give the competing foreigner a break. I have been a spectator several times during Davis Cup matches here and abroad. There is no comparison between the sportsmanlike attitude of the Forest Hills crowd and foreign spectators. At Wimbledon there is, to be sure, a certain aloof politeness toward American players, but at Auteuil I have witnessed vociferous demonstrations against non-French contestants that made me wonder at what moment diplomatic relations would be broken off.

This is the only country I know where unsatisfactory performers in the theater are not loudly booed. And where else but in America could the following have occurred:

Some years ago a famous English vaudeville performer came to this country with tremendous advance publicity. New York's Palace Theater was packed the day he made his debut. But his material, so popular in England, failed to click with the American audience. After his third number the actor, tears streaming down his cheeks, stepped in front of the curtain and said: "Ladies and gentlemen, I am doing my best to entertain you but apparently you do not like what I am offering. I am sincerely sorry." That audience, the so-called hard-boiled New Yorkers, touched by such manifest sincerity, cheered him, and from then on his act was a triumph.

These incidents may seem unimportant, but it is the trivial happenings, the spontaneous daily incidents that reveal a nation's character. And the character of America is something of which to be proud. In the maintenance of American ideals we who are naturalized have our part to play in gratitude for benefits received. We must do more than wave flags and sing *God Bless America*. We who *chose* America must remember that if the privileges we enjoy are worth living for, they are also worth dying for. (3)

I sometimes think that we who *chose* to be Americans and had to make some effort to achieve citizenship have the greatest appreciation of the true significance of our American heritage. In my own particular circle of friends I belong to the minority group who have read the Bill of Rights, have a nodding acquaintance with the Constitution and don't have to fake along with "Da de da da de da" when *The Star-Spangled Banner* is being sung. Born Americans have more of a take-it-for-granted attitude than the naturalized, perhaps because most of the latter become Americans to escape unhappy conditions in their native land.

On the pedestal of the Statue of Liberty are inscribed the following words written by Emma Lazarus:

> Give me your tired, your poor,
> Your huddled masses yearning to breathe free,
> The wretched refuse of your teeming shore,
> Send these, the homeless, the tempest-tossed to me,
> I lift my lamp beside the golden door.

As one of the 38,000,000 of "wretched refuse" (a rather unhappy phrase I think, Miss Lazarus) who have settled here in the past hundred years, I believe that every American should kneel daily and thank God for the privilege of living in the United States. And if this expression of gratitude applies to those *born* here it is at this fateful hour fifty times more applicable to naturalized Americans.

To me the name America symbolizes an idea and connotes a way of life. And the more I study its history the more significant becomes its genesis and the more far-reaching its destiny. It has become a trite saying that America is the land of opportunity. But it is too often forgotten that the opportunity sought by its original settlers had a spiritual, not a material, basis. This mo-

mentous fact has had an overwhelming influence in shaping the
destiny of the United States. Despite temporary checks to our
economic progress, America can never fail so long as we preserve a free educational system, freedom of opportunity, a
jealous regard for individual rights, and a constantly lessening
sense of class distinction.

This matter of class distinction has always seemed to me one
of the most important factors in the preservation of American
ideals, a factor which distinguishes this country from all lands
where hereditary privilege or a titular aristocracy exists.

In America we have a fervent loyalty to a way of life, to a
kind of society that presents definite promises to the most
humble of its citizens. In this free atmosphere is an electric
sparkle that spells hope for every legitimate ambition. And a
minimum of class distinction is our guarantee of maximum opportunity for each individual in each generation.

QUESTIONS

I

1. What are the biographical antecedents of the author, and what
   unusual incident helped influence his decision to live in the
   United States? (*1*)
2. What further incident induced the author to become an American citizen? (*2*)
3. What is the author's opinion of American generosity, hospitality,
   sportsmanship, appreciation of sincerity? (*3*)
4. What meaning did "opportunity" have to the original settlers?
   What are the four cornerstones of the "American way of
   life" which the author cites as being necessary to the survival
   and future success of our country? (*4*)

II

1. Do you know any naturalized citizens? How do their attitudes
   toward America correspond to Mr. Waxman's?
2. Are naturalized citizens likely to appreciate citizenship more
   than those to whom it is a birthright? Have you ever really
   thought about your *own* citizenship?
3. If you were going to choose citizenship in a country other than
   America, which country would it be? Give reasons.

4. Had you ever thought of America as a "spiritual" opportunity? How is *opportunity* usually interpreted in America?
5. Isn't the real reason that the stranger from Cleveland lent Mr. Waxman ten dollars the fact that he had "sized up" Mr. Waxman? Mr. Waxman's American career proves that the man was an excellent judge of character.
6. Do you know any people whose brand of patriotism can be described as "self-interest multiplied by population"? What definition of true patriotism can you give?
7. Are Americans dollar-chasers? Cite what you consider to be the best evidence in support of your answer to this question.
8. What evidence can you cite of sportsmanlike attitude on the part of American crowds at athletic contests? of individual American athletes in competition? of unsportsmanlike attitudes in either?

III

1. In what spirit does the author write "school of Tammany statesmen"? (*2*)
2. Does the word *alien* have an unfavorable connotation to you? Try to analyze closely your attitude toward the word.
3. In this essay note the use of specific incidents by the author as illustrations to drive home the truth of his general statements. Do you find these bits of narrative the most interesting parts of the essay?
4. What spot in the essay rather delightfully reveals Mr. Waxman in his role of critic and magazine editor? (*4*)

WORDS

Choose, from the second column, the synonym for each word at the left.

1. renouncing (*1*)	1. dangerous
2. allegiance (*1*)	2. very important
3. sacrilege (*1*)	3. evil
4. hazardous (*1*)	4. typifies
5. menacingly (*2*)	5. loyalty
6. fervor (*2*)	6. loud-voiced
7. sinister (*2*)	7. beginning
8. casualness (*3*)	8. profanation
9. vociferous (*3*)	9. warmth
10. symbolizes (*4*)	10. giving up
11. genesis (*4*)	11. chance
12. momentous (*4*)	12. threateningly

THEME TOPICS

1. Sportsmanship in Our School
2. A Poor Sport I Once Knew
3. True Patriotism *vs.* Jingoism
4. My Father (Grandfather) Chose America, Too
5. Generous (Extravagant, Dollar-Chasing) Americans
6. Appreciating America
7. Class Distinctions I Have Observed
8. How Foreigners Fool Us
9. We Are Too Hospitable to Aliens
10. A Man's a Man in America

THE ODYSSEY OF AN AMERICAN

EDWIN MULLER

WE who call ourselves Americans like to think that the needy and oppressed of Europe were clamoring to come to the New World in the late 1800s, and that America, benevolent and hospitable, generously opened wide the gates and let in the eager millions.

But it didn't happen quite that way. Actually, the great tide of immigration was largely the result of a high-pressure sales campaign. The steamship companies wanted the immigrants' passage money, the builders and manufacturers wanted their strong backs. But above all, the Western railroads wanted to sell to them the huge quantities of undeveloped land they owned along their rights of way.

Railroad land agents went all over Europe persuading peasants to sell their possessions and to come to America. *How to Make a Living on a Farm in Kansas* was translated into nearly every European language. The railroads found an even better piece of sales promotion than that. They translated the Constitution of the United States and spread it far and wide. It was read in little Bavarian farmhouses, in humble homes in Baltic lands, in Ukrainian huts owned by the Czar. The railroad agents were selling land, but freedom and the inspired words of the Founding Fathers were part of the sales talk.

The rulers of Europe were not pleased to see their best farmers enticed away. Germany forbade the advertising of American land. In South Russia, one Santa Fe agent kept just a jump ahead of the Czar's police. But the world's greatest real-estate promotion went steadily on. Shiploads of Germans and Slavs sailed

From *The Reader's Digest*, February, 1941, and *The Rotarian*, February, 1941. Copyrighted. Used by permission of the Editors of both magazines.

from Hamburg and the ports of the Black Sea. Presently they were loaded into immigrant trains which rolled westward to the wide, lonely plains. (*1*)

In such a train, late one Summer in the '70s, rode a small boy, whom we shall call Karl Seder. He was a towheaded youngster of 10, a nuisance to fellow travelers because he kept running back and forth across the car, trying to see out on both sides at once. He and his parents with his younger brother and sister had come from a German settlement in the southern Ukraine, near the Sea of Azov. The bronzed and stalwart father spoke little. From under her black head shawl the mother looked out a little fearfully at the unending sweep of the Kansas prairie.

To Karl it was like the ocean that he had just crossed, enormous, rolling away slowly to the edge of things. The few houses were little cardboard boxes tossed up on the crests of the long rollers. He strained his eyes half hoping, half fearing, to see bands of Indians.

Late one hot afternoon they came to the end of the journey, the town of Newton, then, in its rawest beginnings, just one street of unpainted shacks and tents. The train moved on, leaving the huddle of immigrants on their boxes and bundles. A long string of boxcars stood on a siding. In them the women and children were to live while the men went out with the land agent to locate their farms and prepare them for habitation. The Seder family was assigned half a car, divided by a canvas curtain from the family in the other half.

Next morning the father went away—and was gone for weeks. Karl wandered up and down the dusty street, peered under the swinging doors of the saloons, watched the Texas steers tossing their horns as they were driven up the chutes into cattle cars. Day after day the sun blazed down.

"Is it always so hot?" Karl's mother asked of a woman who had come over the year before. The other pointed to a six-foot fence. "In Winter the snow piles up over the top." (*2*)

When Karl's father came back to fetch his family, he had bought oxen, a wagon, and farm equipment, partly with their small funds, partly on credit from the railroad. Their goods were loaded into the wagon and covered with tarpaulin. Starting at dawn, they rode all day through the waist-high grass. It parted in front of them, closed again behind. Their only guide was a single furrow 22 miles long which the father had plowed. In the first hours they passed a few houses, then there were no more signs of man.

Near dusk they came to the end of the furrow. The mother looked around. In every direction only the empty horizon.

"Why do we stop here?"

"This is where we are to live."

She leaned against the side of the wagon and wept. There must have been a deep bitterness in her soul when she thought of the man who had persuaded them with easy-flowing words to sell their little farm on the rising ground above the Sea of Azov and come to this place. But she could not afford the luxury of yielding to despair. She sat up and wiped her eyes. Her husband, phlegmatic and silent, was already unloading their goods, the sacks of meal, the pots and pans.

She saw what she had first overlooked, the house that her husband had built. It was hard to see, for it was one of the famous sod shanties of the prairies 14 feet by 12, dug three feet into the ground and rising three feet above—a frame of rough poles with brush laid overhead, and covered with an 18-inch layer of sod. Inside was just enough room to stand upright.

She set about making a home of it.

Next morning things looked a little better. In the days that followed the father was out at the first gray dawn, working until the last of daylight, taking only a few minutes for breakfast, dinner, or supper—always cornmeal mush and bacon. He was breaking the tough prairie sod for the Winter wheat. That was their one reliance for the future.

They had brought the seed from Russia. All through the Winter evenings before their departure, Karl and the younger children had sat on the floor picking out the plumpest and firmest grains. There are 218,000 grains of wheat in a bushel; the children sorted many bushels. Now, as he helped to sow, Karl felt as if a trickle of gold was going through his fingers into the black soil. (3)

It was a time of hope. As they sat on nail kegs and packing

cases, eating the hasty meals, they talked of the future. The father spoke of going next year to the river valley ten miles away to get cottonwood timber for a frame house. The mother planned the shopping trips she would make to Newton when the money from the crops was in.

They strained to the limit of their strength to get more grain into the ground, and yet more. Karl took his turn at the plow, his head and shoulders just showing above the top of the grass.

Soon the wheat was up and the fields around the house were a bright green carpet, bordered with the dry brown prairie grass.

They found they had neighbors. Another German lived only a mile away, but it took sharp eyes to see his house, which, like their own, barely rose above the level of the grass. He rode over one Sunday, and his talk made them feel that they were part of a community. Next year, he said, there'd be a road close by, following the straight line of the quarter section. And a schoolhouse was planned not more than four miles away. That was the best news the mother had heard.

One evening Karl and his father were so intent upon their fence making, they did not notice that the great up-flaming of the prairie sunset glowed on long after it should have faded.

Karl heard the sound of hoofs, turned to see their neighbor coming on the gallop.

"Quick! Harness your oxen!"

He pointed to the west. Fire! And the wind was toward them. Long ago they should have plowed a protective belt around their land. Even now there might be time to run two or three furrows.

The oxen had been let out to graze. As always they had lain down, were concealed somewhere in the tall grass. The whole family began a frantic search. It was Karl who stumbled over them.

As the father prodded and lashed the oxen ahead of the plow, they could see the glow rise in the sky. A thin bright line appeared on the horizon, moved toward them. They began to cough from the smoke and the white fluff of ashes in the wind.

There was time for two furrows. Then at the neighbor's direction they ran along with torches, lighting fires on the far side. Those were critical moments. Here and there the new fires leaped the furrows, went licking toward the house and the wheat fields. The six of them ran from place to place with shovels and sticks, beating and stamping out the crawling flames. They hardly noticed the burns they received. Meanwhile a blackened strip slowly widened to windward.

It was enough. The roar and blaze of the big fire died at the edge of the burned strip. The house and the wheat were saved. (4)

Winter came early that year, with snow flurries in November. The father had just time to build a rough shelter for the oxen, to make a trip with the wagon to Newton for supplies. Then the real snow began. The stove, when it was kept full, warmed the sod house well enough, but they had to economize on fuel. From outside, the house seemed only a big snowdrift.

The thing that kept them going was the thought of the wheat. All the acres of green were safely covered by the snow. There it lay—their whole future—clothes and schooling for the children, a new house, money in the bank.

In the Spring they lived with their eyes on the sky. There was a dreadful fear: would this be one of the drought years of which the neighbor had told them, when the young wheat would shrivel and die? But the rains came. Even the father laughed and sang little songs. It didn't matter that water seeped through the roof, that sticky mud covered everything.

June came and they could see the wheat grow.

It was toward the middle of a hot afternoon. So sultry was it that when the cloud appeared over the western horizon, they thought it must mean a thunderstorm. But as it came nearer, they noticed something queer about it. It clung close to the ground and there was a humming sound.

Then they saw what it was. Grasshoppers—billions of them! Soon the sun and the sky were hidden; the wheat fields were a crawling, writhing carpet.

The Seders ran up and down, beating wildly with sticks and brooms. But they were like men on a beach trying to beat back the tide. A few hours later the plague had departed. Not a stalk was standing—all the wheat had been eaten level with the ground. The father and mother just stood there at the door, faces blank and staring.... (5)

It was a very durable-looking old gentleman who told me the story. Karl Seder is a little hard of hearing now, but his eyes are bright. I should say that he is still as alert as when he ran back and forth between the car windows looking for Indians. We sat in his private office, though he spends most of his time out front where he can talk with people. He is president of the bank in a small Kansas town.

"Did your parents ever make a comeback?" I asked.

"Next day my father was out breaking ground for a new crop."

They had to have some help, of course. The Santa Fe Railroad came to the rescue, as it and other railroads had for many another settler—extended long, easy credits. No charity about it; the road knew that its own prosperity was tied close to that of the colonists whom it had persuaded to come.

The Seders must be one of the best investments the company ever made. Before the 11-year credit period had expired, Mr. Seder had nearly 300 acres in wheat. The mother lived to see her grandchildren come home from college—and must have embarrassed them because sometimes she still wore her black head shawl. She spoke English with difficulty, always lapsed into German when she talked with headshakings of the sod-house days.

The banker has just a faint accent; his children have no German at all except what they learned in school. Since the grandmother died they no longer subscribe to the German-language weekly. Which is typical of how this community has evolved in one man's lifetime. (6)

Mr. Seder is one of the pillars of the town. He is a member of Rotary, and a director of the flour mill which is the town's chief industry. The deposit account in his bank in which he takes the greatest pride is that of the Santa Fe Railroad.

Multiply the Seders by thousands and you have part of the story of the building of the U.S.A.

You can't make a neat and rounded success story of it. To do that you'd have to end it in the days of the last war when the rain was soaking the prairies and the world was calling for wheat at $2 a bushel.

I asked Mr. Seder whether the immigrants and their descendants weren't worse off now than before they came. He shook his head. Times were bad, he said, but not that bad.

And as for going back where they came from—.

"I did go back where I came from," said Mr. Seder, and he looked rather grim about it.

A few years ago, instead of the round-the-world cruise his children had urged, he visited his native countryside in the Ukraine. It had not been a happy experience. Mr. Seder had tried to find two or three well-to-do farming families of whom his mother had often spoken. Without exception they had vanished—"liquidated," they call it in Russia.

According to Karl Seder there is no part of the country where the Nazi idea is more unpopular than in the German-settled part of Kansas. Nobody there wants to go back where he came from, whether Russia or Germany.

So it would appear that Americans did a good job when they went abroad to sell land, the Constitution, freedom, and opportunity. The methods may have been high pressure. But the goods sold have given satisfaction to the customers. From the customers the country has had value received. (7)

QUESTIONS

I

1. Why were immigrants wanted, and how were they induced to come to America? (*1*)
2. How was Karl Seder typically childlike on the journey to Kansas? What living accommodations did the Seder family have in Newton? (*2*)
3. What kind of house had Mr. Seder built? How did they prepare for the fall planting of wheat? (*3*)
4. What near catastrophe almost overtook the Seders? (*4*) What actual catastrophe did overtake them? (*5*)
5. To what success does the immigrant boy finally attain? Who had helped the family over the emergency? What satisfactory successes did the older Seders live to see? How is the develop-

ment of the community represented in the lives of the Seders? (6)

6. What are Mr. Seder's business activities? What is his opinion of his native country? What does he say about the loyalty of the old-time German immigrant? (7)

II

1. Do you think recent immigrants represent the same adaptability to American ideas and loyalty to America as the old-time settlers? If there is a change, can you account for it?
2. Are we fair in classing all immigrants as "aliens"? What are war conditions likely to lead to in our attitude toward foreigners?
3. Can you parallel the "Odyssey" of the Seders by the story of an immigrant family that has come under your own observation?
4. Have you ever had friends among the foreign-born? What did you like about them? What did you dislike?
5. What does this essay show about the contribution of immigrant peoples to the democracy of which they have become a part?
6. Do you think that Europe of the twentieth century is possibly weaker than in earlier centuries because of her loss of so many sturdy, resolute citizens by emigration to America?

III

1. This essay proceeds from a general discussion of early immigrants to one specific immigrant family. Why is this method effective?
2. What figures of speech are represented in the following sentences: "The few houses were like cardboard boxes tossed up on the crests of the long rollers" (2) and "The wheat fields were a crawling, writhing carpet" (5)?
3. The author has indicated a lapse of time by three dots at the end of (5). Is the omission of the details of the intervening years artistically satisfactory?
4. Try to express "a very durable-looking old gentleman" in other language. Compare your phrasing with that of the author for effectiveness and graphicness of description.
5. Does the description of the prairie fire have the element of suspense? If so, how did the author attain it?
6. The author tried to create the atmosphere of hopelessness and despair in the last paragraph of (5). Has he done so for you? Can you think of a more effective figure of speech than "like men on a beach trying to beat back the tide"? Where do we learn of the Seders' reaction to this calamity? What do the words "Next day" tell you about them?

WORDS

Playing with words is both a pleasurable and a profitable hobby. If the hobby becomes a habit, a distinctive vocabulary will assuredly be yours. Let us choose a few of the words in this article as an introduction to word-study.

1. oppressed (*1*). The stem *prem* or *press* means "to push down, squeeze." This stem naturally explains *pressure*. A *depression*, whether in the surface of the land or in economic conditions, is a "pressing down," and an *expression* is something "pressed out of" you. To *impress* a person is to "press (something) upon" him. Likewise, to *oppress* is "to press against," to *re-press* is "to press back," and to *suppress* is "to press under." Furthermore, the stem reveals the story of printing, for printing was originally done by pressing paper against a block of wooden letters and, later, of metal letters. Even in the great revolving cylinders of printing today, pressing is an essential part of the operation.

2. immigration (*1*). Latin *migrare* means "to go from place to place"; *im-* (*in-*), "into"; *e-* (*ex-*), "out." From this information give exact definitions of *immigration* and *emigration*.

3. phlegmatic (*3*). This word opens up for us a whole field of study —ancient physiology and even medicine. First find out what the "four humours" were, and from this knowledge explain the words *sanguine*, *phlegmatic*, *splenetic*, and *melancholy*.

4. economize (*5*). We take courses in political *economy* or *economics*, and we talk about the national *economy*, but all these complicated subjects have a very simple beginning. In Greek, *oikos* means "house" and *nemein*, "to manage"; so *economy* originally signified the way a Greek housewife ran her kitchen.

5. credits (*6*). *Credit*, as used in business, reveals one man's belief in another's intention to pay his bills. *Credere* means "to believe, trust," and much of the world's business is run upon this principle of faith in people's honesty.

6. liquidated (*7*). As this word is often used today, it is an example of grim understatement—a kind of euphemism. What does it mean as used in this essay? Similar examples are "the Chinese incident" and the gangster's "take for a ride."

THEME TOPICS

1. I Am Proud of My Immigrant Ancestors
2. America—The Melting Pot
3. There Were Giants in Those Days

PEASANT'S PROGRESS

EDWIN MULLER

I MET my neighbor, Nick Janeski, the other day, busy repairing his fence, a job he always does himself although he
is well into his sixties and has several hired men.

I complimented him on the new flag pole that he'd given the
school, a seventy-foot pine his men had felled.

He was pleased: "Yes. Is nice piece of timber," he agreed.

Nick's face, weathered by Connecticut winters and the July
sun, breaks up into soft crinkles around his blue eyes when he
smiles.

Nick arrived from Poland forty years ago, with $4 and a small
bundle. When he tries to describe the chaos of his arrival in
America his eyes grow troubled, he makes shrugging, helpless
gestures. The piled-up buildings, the noise, the crowding throngs
of people "dressed like the rich." Above all, the blank frustration
of having no word of English, of staring dumbly at impatient
questioners.

He carried a card bearing the address of his cousin, Stefan Du-
browski, who worked on a Connecticut dairy farm and had
promised to get him a job there. Eventually, after many mishaps,
Nick was put on the right train.

He was dog-weary, and in the pleasing stuffy warmth of the
day-coach he fell asleep. When the conductor woke him he was
twenty miles past his station.

They put him off the train, and presently he was plodding back
down the road. There may be bleaker regions than the Housatonic Valley in late November but certainly not when a chill rain
is falling, slowly changing into sleet. The abrupt, shaggy hills
must have been strange, even terrifying, to a man who had lived

all his life on the plains of Galicia. The farm-houses seemed very large compared with the hovels of his own village. He thought they were dwellings of the nobility.

When darkness fell he was driven to ask for shelter. You can't altogether blame the farmer's wife who came to the door. Nick, with his outlandish appearance and unintelligible jabber, must have frightened her. The door was banged in his face. At the next farm too he was repulsed.

He wasn't outraged. He had the peasant's feeling that trouble is the natural order—anything else would be surprising. He just plodded on.

The sleet was freezing on his clothes. At the next farm he didn't try the house, he went around back. There was a low shed—the pig-pen. Nick crept inside. Here in this strange land was something familiar—he knew pigs.

"I talk to those. They understand. Sure." Anyhow they didn't squeal and give him away. He'd had nothing to eat all day. He made a meal on an ear of corn that had escaped the pigs and huddled among them for warmth. At dawn he was on the road again.

His troubles were just beginning. He found the farm that was Stefan's address. But Stefan was gone—to the factories in Bridgeport or Ansonia, no one knew just where. This Nick learned through Wladek, another Pole on the place. There was no work for Nick.

The farmer said Nick could sleep a few nights in the barn and gave him a loaf of bread and other food. That loaf of bread seems to stick in Nick's mind more than his troubles. White bread it was—"such as the rich ate in my country," he says, still amazed after all these years.

That was a tough winter. The farmer let Nick stay on in the barn. Wladek and the few Polish hands in the neighborhood got him enough food to keep him going. Every day he tramped the roads looking for work.

He must have been desperately homesick and he got the rough edge of a good many tongues: "Here comes that damn Polack again." But soon people began to like him. He'd go to the men on the place early in the morning, bowing low with that shy,

eager smile of his, bringing out triumphantly the few words of
English he was picking up:

"Is work today?"

Sometimes there was, mostly odd jobs cutting firewood. He
was a stout man with an axe. Nobody in the township could cut
and stack more in a day.

One thing surprised him. Nearby in the valley there was a Pole
who owned his own large farm—fifty acres. Yet twenty years
earlier this man had come from Poland just as Nick had, without
friends or money. Nick, excited, kept turning this over in his
mind. (1)

In the spring he got a steady job—with Lathan Bassett, a dairy
farmer in the main valley. Bassett and his wife were getting on in
years, were having a struggle to keep up the place, which had
descended from father to son for five generations. The house,
still lovely, built in dignified old New England style, was sinking
into rackety shabbiness.

Nick worked for Bassett week-days and Sundays from five in
the morning till seven at night. It never occurred to him to complain—even to himself. That was the way things were. That's how
the peasants worked in Poland. And now in working hard he had
a purpose—ever since he'd seen the fifty acres of that other Pole.
He spent hardly a cent of his $18 a month.

Nick worked for Bassett four years, then reached for another
rung on the ladder. Thirty acres of Bassett's farm were down the
road, separate from the rest. It was poor land, unused, with boulders
thick as raisins in a pudding. Bassett willingly sold it to Nick
along with half a dozen of his young cattle for a little cash and
a note. There was a leaky barn and a one-room shack on the
property.

Anna, Nick's betrothed, was summoned from Poland. To judge
from the wedding photograph which Nick showed me proudly,
she was a husky young girl, with charm and bright-eyed suppressed gaiety. You can still see that charm in old Mrs. Janeski.
But there wasn't much scope for gaiety that first year. Two
weeks after she arrived, Anna was in the field heaving at a crow-
bar with her strong shoulders, grubbing a potato patch out of a
stony pasture. Nick was patching the roof of the barn. She heard

a startled exclamation—a sliding, scraping sound—a heavy thud. When she ran to Nick his face was twisted with pain, one leg doubled under him.

It was eight weeks before he could work again. That in plowing season, when urgent jobs crowd on the farmer. I can't tell you how Anna managed. I know she was out in the field with the first streak of dawn, worked long hours by moonlight.

To meet the first payment on the note they sold two of the cattle—were lucky not to lose the place.

Years followed, one day very like another. Work—hard, unending work from dawn to dark. Side by side in the corn rows, in the cabbage patch, milking, haying, breaking the routine occasionally by meeting other Poles of the neighborhood for dancing and gaiety. The village store got little business from them. Potatoes and cabbage, cabbage and potatoes. They never thought of eating the cash crops—milk, bull calves, eggs, went to market.

There were good years and bad. One year tuberculosis got into the herd and inspectors shot three of their best milkers. Once a neighbor let Nick have a pedigreed Guernsey cheap because it was sick. Nick nursed it back to health and sold it for $400. That was the year he was naturalized. They gradually paid off the note and there began to be money in the bank. (2)

The big milestone in Nick's career was when he took over the Bassett place. The old couple finally gave up and went to live with a son in Ohio. The ghosts of the 18th-century Bassetts must have shuddered when they saw the shabby household gear in the perfectly proportioned old rooms. Mostly the Janeski family lived in the kitchen. The move brought no improvement in their standard of living. They worked harder than ever, even though they had a hired man and the children to help. There never was much cash: "When one penny comes in, see already an expense waits for it."

There were setbacks. Lightning struck the main barn and it went up in smoke together with most of the winter's hay. Nick tried to get the stock out, but six of his cows died in their stanchions. Year by year, however, the Janeski family got ahead. Sometimes Nick would stand in his barnyard and look around at his buildings. He'd watch the herd come single file down the long meadow for the six o'clock milking. There'd be an expression of childlike wonder in his eyes.

Today Nick owns 250 acres free and clear. His barns and dairy equipment are the most modern, his herd of sixty-odd is one of the best in the township. He's a man of weight in the community.

The house isn't rackety any more. The Bassett ghosts would give their qualified approval to the way Anna's daughters-in-law have fixed it up inside.

Of Nick's boys, the oldest has gone to Danbury, where he owns and operates one of the best garages. The second son is the leading plumber in the neighborhood. His younger brother, who married a girl of the old Yankee farmer stock, is his partner.

The Janeski family has built itself solidly into this community. It wasn't easy. The old Yankee stock is still the leading group, and it has been hard for them to accept immigrant families on equal footing. But last year Steve, Nick's second son, was one of our selectmen. They watched him closely. It was freely predicted that he'd load the town payroll with Polacks. But he didn't, and he served his term to the satisfaction of his fellow citizens. (3)

In some ways Nick is still the Polish peasant, especially in his feeling that trouble rather than joy is the destined lot of man. It shows in his attitude toward the war. When Hitler's machine tore Poland to pieces Nick was grieved, not surprised. Poverty and suffering and death are the natural order—except in this astonishing land of the U. S. A. The time to be surprised is when good fortune comes.

Often, in talking with you, Nick will stop short in the middle of a sentence, look at you shyly, give a sort of delighted chuckle, and then go on. It distinctly is not a chuckle that indicates pride in his achievements. In his opinion his sons have accomplished far more than he. He doesn't see anything unusual in his record of endurance, resourcefulness, and unending toil. It's the way the peasants did in Poland. Only they got nothing out of it except a bare and precarious living.

Whereas here...

He looks around at the good things that have come to him. Not only the material ones; more important is his standing in the community, his right to be a free and equal citizen of this land. He drives his car to town. He sees the names of Mr. and Mrs. Nicholas Janeski engraved as patrons of the local Art Exhibit, sponsored by the summer colony. He can't contain his delighted amazement that there should be a land where such things can happen to a man.

Then the chuckle breaks out. Hitler has said that this country will fall apart because of the strains and cleavages between the different classes and races of which it is composed. When you observe Nick Janeski and his American children, when you see how they have built themselves into this community, you know that Hitler is wrong. If the United States ever falls apart it will be because Nick's grandchildren—and those of the native stock—will drift into assuming that good things come as a matter of course, good things that were created by the toil and courage of Nick and his like. (*4*)

QUESTIONS

I

1. With what is Nick busying himself when we first meet him? What has he done that shows his public spirit? What were his first experiences and early trials in getting a foothold in America? (*1*)
2. How did Nick's working for the Bassetts lay the foundation for his upward climb? What part did his wife play in his rise? (*2*)
3. What was the most important milestone in Nick's progress in America? What does he now possess as a result of his hard work? How have his children fitted into the American way of life? (*3*)
4. How does Nick still represent the "peasant psychology"? How is the reward in America for hard work and sacrifice different from what it would have been in the old country? What other than material successes have come to him? In what way do Nick and his family indicate that Hitler is wrong in his estimate of America? (*4*)

II

1. Does this recital of one peasant's progress here in America seem to you an isolated, carefully chosen case, or is it duplicated by thousands of men like Nick?
2. By hard labor, self-denial, and determination many foreigners succeed, whereas native Americans fail when faced with the

same problems. Should we resent or approve the immigrants'
success? Would *you* have succeeded, given Nick's hardships?
3. Would the story of the depression have been different or would
we need relief if there were more of Nick's spirit in America?
4. "Poverty and suffering and death are the natural order—except
in this astonishing land of the U. S. A." Does this statement
represent the primary cleavage between the Old World and
the New?
5. Noting the trend of the 1940's, should you say that the future
will, or will not, furnish more success stories like that of the
Janeski family? What will likely be America's future policy
toward immigrants like Nick?
6. Do you think that America will remain strong as long as the
rewards of toil and courage are guaranteed by our democratic
process of government?

III

1. Of what famous piece of English literature is the title of this
article a paraphrase?
2. The author, an experienced journalist, is a close observer of
people and things and an interpreter of the *meaning* of what
he sees. From this viewpoint, discuss the following: "Nick's
face . . . breaks up into soft crinkles around his blue eyes when
he smiles" (*1*); "the pleasing, stuffy warmth of the day-coach"
(*1*); "He was a stout man with an axe" (*1*); "was sinking into
rackety shabbiness" (*2*); "with boulders thick as raisins in a
pudding" (*2*); "with charm and bright-eyed suppressed gaiety" (*2*); "The ghosts of the 18th-century Bassetts must have
shuddered" (*3*); "The Bassett ghosts would give their qualified
approval" (*3*); "the names of Mr. and Mrs. Nicholas Janeski
engraved as patrons of the local Art Exhibit" (*4*).
3. Discuss the following as keeping before the reader Nick's point
of view: "dressed like the rich" (*1*); "dwellings of the nobility"
(*1*); "trouble is the natural order—anything else would be surprising" (*1*); "I talk to those [pigs]. They understand. Sure"
(*1*); "such as the rich ate in my country" (*1*); "when one
penny comes in, see already an expense waits for it" (*3*); "The
time to be surprised is when good fortune comes" (*4*).
4. What is the effect of the two-word transition paragraph:
"Whereas here . . ."? (*4*)

WORDS

Answer the following questions by consulting a good dictionary.
1. chaos (*1*): How is the word *chaos* related to the expression on
your face when you are surprised or sleepy?

2. arrival (*1*): Why did people originally have to travel by water when they *arrived?*
3. plodding (*1*): What does the word *plodding* suggest besides "walking"?
4. outraged (*1*): How is *outraged* connected with a mad dog's bite?
5. rackety (*2*): What condition of the steps, weather-boarding, and eaves does the word *rackety* suggest?
6. betrothed (*2*): How does *betrothed* suggest the "truth" of the promise to marry?
7. gear (*3*): Why did the author use the word *gear* rather than furniture?
8. precarious (*4*): How does *precarious* suggest the uncertainty of the fulfillment of prayer?

THEME TOPICS

1. The School of Hard Knocks
2. White Bread and Black
3. Foreigners in New England
4. A Foreigner Who Failed (a success story in reverse)
5. The Vanishing Native Stock
6. Difficulties Make Us Strong
7. Born with a Silver Spoon in His Mouth
8. New England Farmhouses (Furniture, Antiques)
9. Foreigners Are Getting All the Good Things
10. Americans Need the Pioneer Spirit

AMERICANIZATION OF AN AMERICAN

SALOM RIZK

SALOM," said my teacher, as I stood before him on a late
afternoon in our little Syrian school-house, "I have something astonishing to tell you. You are an American citizen!"

"An American citizen!"

Here was I, a ragged orphan, homeless and half starved, in a
miserable mountain village of Syria, and my teacher was suddenly telling me that I was an American citizen! America was
so many thousands of miles away and so unreal that his words
scarcely had meaning.

All I knew of myself was that I had been born here in Syria,
and that my mother had died the day I was born.

"I have been questioning people about you," my teacher said,
"and I have discovered that your father and mother both went
from here to America when they were young. They became
American citizens, married, and had two sons born in America.
Then your mother got homesick, returned here to her native
land just in time to give birth to you and die. But since your
parents both were American citizens, you are one, too!"

I had known nothing of that, nothing! I stared at my teacher
in a daze.

"Salom," he said, "America is Heaven. There everybody can
think, speak, write, worship as he wishes. There everyone has
the chance of comfort and a home of his own. You can go there,
Salom. You *must* go. I'll help you."

But the more he told of America, the more unreal it seemed.
When my mother died in giving me birth, everybody expected me to die, too. But my grandmother, who lived twelve

From *The Reader's Digest*, September, 1940, and *Scribner's Commentator*, September, 1940. Copyrighted. Used by permission of the Editors
of both magazines.

miles away, came donkey-back to rescue me. She said: "No, he shall live and I shall be his mother. His name shall be Salom 'the Rescued One.'" She took me home, but how was she to feed a motherless child in that primitive village, where there were no hospitals, no nursing homes, no doctors? In Syria it is not considered safe to feed animals' milk to a baby. Human milk is the only thing. So my grandmother would sit at the open window of her hut, with me often crying from hunger in her lap, watching the Arabs, Jews and Christians passing by. When she saw a woman with a baby in her arms, she would run out into the road and beg her to nurse me for a few minutes, and often these women did. Some of my grandmother's friends thought this was terrible. "One day he drinks Christian milk, another day Mohammedan milk, another day Jewish milk. He will be a monster." "You're wrong," my grandmother said, "he is nursed by women of many creeds, so he will grow up to one creed—humanity." (1)

For six years my grandmother cared for me like a mother. Then one sad day, she fell off her donkey and became a cripple, condemned to spend the rest of her days in bed. For a year I helped to care for her. Then, suddenly, she died, and since the house did not belong to her, I was literally kicked into the street by the owner.

I set out afoot back to my native village, to see if I could find any kin. On the way, a frightful thing happened. This was in the midst of the World War. Turks, Arabs and British had been fighting across Syria, and as I tramped along, I stumbled into what had been a battlefield a few days before. Corpses strewed the road and the fields, men from whom the clothes had been stripped by the Turks, some bodies horribly mutilated, and all rotting in the hot sun. Can you imagine anything more frightful for a boy of seven? It was like a nightmare. I ran, stumbled, fell, picked myself up and ran on, sick and sobbing. When I reached my village, I found not a house standing and all the inhabitants fled.

I took to the hills, and for years lived exactly like an animal. In the summer, I ate plants and roots, climbed trees, stole bird-eggs or little birds and ate them raw. Sometimes I sneaked up, grabbed a goat and milked its milk into my mouth or into my cap. In summer, I slept in the fields; in winter, I crawled into earthen bake-ovens for warmth. I would strip off my shirt, hold it up in front of the coals and burn out the vermin before I slept. (2)

When the war was over, the people trailed back, partly rebuilt the village, and started school again in one room built from the wreck of the old school. I couldn't go in, because the tuition was ten cents a month. I didn't have ten cents or even one cent. But I used to hang around the school when it let out, listening to what the children said, hoping to pick up a bit of learning. One morning, as I was lurking in the yard, the schoolmaster called me over. I looked like a wild animal—my only clothes a ragged pair of pants, my hair long. I was thin as a skeleton and sun-scorched to the color of earth. But when I poured out my story to the schoolmaster, and he saw how eager I was to learn, he let me come, even without money. I had no money for books, paper or pencils, so I learned by listening and practised writing with my finger in the dust.

One day the teacher gave me a stubby pencil and a sheet of white paper, the first sheet of clean white paper that I, thirteen years old, had ever held in my hand. "Now you can write," he said. So I wrote a letter to the teacher, trying to say gratitude for what he had done for me, using in it some of the Syrian poems he had taught me. The letter made the teacher think that I really had promise. He kept me after school and told me then the amazing thing—that I was an American citizen.

"You *must* go to America," my teacher repeated to me as I stood, still dazed, before him. "I have found the address of your two brothers and uncle in America. Write them a letter about yourself. I'll send it."

I did, and ten months later an answer came from my brother. He had thought me killed by the Turks. He sent money, told me to go to the American consul in Beirut, capital of Syria, tell him who I was and he would give me a passport, and arrange for me to come to America. Can you imagine my joy? Barefoot and in rags, I started for Beirut, ran and ran for three days and part of the nights, but when I got to Beirut and poured out my story and showed my letter to the interpreter at the consulate, he demanded my birth certificate. Birth certificate! I had never heard of a birth certificate. Nobody would take the word of a wild ragged boy who couldn't speak a word of English.

Day after day I went back, day after day I was rejected. "Here is that crazy Salom Rizk again," they would say. "He thinks he is an American citizen! Get out!" This went on for four years, from the time I was fourteen till I was eighteen. I lived by doing odd jobs, and spent every spare moment on the steps of the consulate, trying to see somebody, to present my arguments again. Finally something happened, for one day I was called in. Perhaps the consul had received a letter with documents. He said: "Congratulations! I am convinced that you are Salom Rizk." He shook hands and gave me a passport. (3)

I sailed for America. My teacher had tried to picture America for me in glowing words, but when I saw the Statue of Liberty, and the tall shining buildings, I was choked with astonishment. I had a million questions, but I couldn't ask one, for I still didn't know one word of English.

I was put on a train for the mid-west. It was early summer, the country was bursting with green abundance. Syria is barren, with scanty rain, and I hadn't dreamed any land could be so amazingly rich. Every farm looked to be a kingdom. At Sioux City, my brother met me and led me to his Model T Ford. To me it was a miracle machine, a new astonishment. In Syria automobiles were for the rich and for officials. That I should ever ride in one hadn't entered my head.

I got a job in a packing house. I thought that on the job I would learn English, but I didn't. And at home, where we all spoke Syrian, I learned no English. So I threw up my job, quit Sioux City, and started out on the road.

After a few days, I came to a beautiful college town that I liked immensely—Ames, Iowa. Perhaps I could get an education there. I landed a job in a Greek restaurant, washing dishes and scrubbing floors, and was allowed to go one hour a day to the public school to study English. I remember I was given a registration blank to fill out, with "name," "age," "address," "race." I knew my own name, my age, my address, but race?

What was that? I looked it up in the dictionary and found race-track, racehorse, race—human. What race was I? Finally, I wrote down "human." When the teacher saw my card, he looked over the class. "Who is Salom Rizk?" he asked. I raised my hand. "Very good," he said, "I am glad to have one human being in my class." I was only in school a few weeks, because then I got a full-time job in a shoe-repair shop, but in those few weeks I learned much—the teachers were so eager to help me. (4)

My boss in the shoe-repair place fired me so often that I decided to start a shop of my own. I had seven dollars cash. I borrowed enough more on my face to buy machines and furniture. I called my shop: "Collegiate Shoe Service—the Harbor of Lost Soles." Some of my ads in the college paper ran: "This is the most modern shoe clinic in town. Our patients are returned in excellent health, those dyed included. We have ambulance service. Salom Rizk, chief surgeon, says, 'Most fellows strive to win co-eds' hearts, I only want their soles.'" I appointed an agent for each dormitory, to advertise my service, collect shoes from their friends. Not only students but almost everyone in the community came in to help and encourage me.

One of the men I hired as a shoe-repairer was a Syrian student at the college, and I paid him extra to sit by me an hour a day while I cobbled, reading books to me. For every book, I paid him a quarter. For every new word he taught me, I paid him a cent. Sometimes I learned fifty new words a week. Here was a fine illustration of American democracy and opportunity—two Syrian orphans, each making it possible for the other to become a more useful, independent American, one by teaching the language, the other by giving a job. (5)

When I really began to understand America I had new astonishments. My first astonishment had been at *outside* facts visible to the eye—high buildings, well-dressed crowds, automobiles, magnificent schools. My bigger astonishments now were at the *inside* facts, the *inside* truths about America.

One of these astonishments came with the Presidential election. Roosevelt was running against President Hoover. It was almost unbelievable to me that the man at the head of this vast country, the commander of the army and navy, had to appeal even to me and my shoemakers and the grocer next door in order to stay in the White House. I was always imagining as the campaign got hotter that President Hoover would get tired of the accusations hurled at him and would call out the army and navy to crush those who were attacking him. One of my neighbors would say hard things against the President right before the corner cop. I was astonished that the cop didn't arrest him for criticizing the head of the government. Gradually I got it through my head that in America you can't arrest anybody for being dissatisfied with the government, because the government belongs to the people.

On election day, at the polls, the only thing they asked me was if I was a citizen, and my age, name and address. As I went to vote, the personnel director of the college walked out. I stopped in my tracks: I thought he would challenge my right to vote. What right had I to match my ignorance against a scholar's knowledge? I could barely read English. What did I know about the real questions? But he gave me only a glance. It seemed perfectly natural that I, Salom Rizk, Syrian shoemaker, should be helping choose the President of the United States.

I remember during that campaign the newspaper cartoons by "Ding,"—J. N. Darling. They ridiculed Roosevelt and glorified Hoover. When Roosevelt won the election, I thought that he would purge Ding as Hitler, Stalin or Mussolini would have done, but instead he appointed him chairman of a commission to conserve wild life! (6)

My next astonishment came with the depression. There was no plague, no locusts, no flood, no drought, only rich cornfields, and everybody—at least there in Iowa—seemed to have enough to eat. The farmers sure did. This twisted my reason, just like hunger in Syria used to twist my stomach. I said to a group of Iowa farmers: "In Syria we don't have depressions. We just have honest-to-goodness and eternal poverty, with drought, locusts, and the tax-gatherer, all against us." If the Syrian farmer had the help from the government that the American farmer gets, he would think he was in Heaven.

But my greatest astonishment was that Americans—especially

young Americans—took their blessings so much for granted. That everybody could write, and worship as he pleased seemed nothing strange to anybody. Least of all to the children who sometimes seemed to be trying not to read, and to escape what was offered them. I was so astonished and puzzled that I felt I ought to wake my fellow Americans to their blessings. When I was in school those brief weeks, the teachers had encouraged me to talk to the school about my experiences as a newcomer to this country. Later, I was asked to repeat the talk to the Ames Rotary Club. Now I expanded my talk and made its theme the contrasting of the old world as I knew it with the new world as I found it.

One of the college students who heard my talk urged me to spread it to a wider audience. First, he helped me make it better by straightening out my English and correcting my grammar. Then he drove all over Iowa and Illinois, persuading schools and civic clubs to hear my message.

I was happier than I had ever been before. At first, I spoke for nothing, then I began to get small fees. Then I sold out my shoe-shop; I would devote all my time to carrying the message of America to Americans. I bought a car to get from place to place. I used to sleep in the car, wash, shave and change my clothes at gas stations, and get my meals at lunch counters. But even by close figuring, I couldn't keep up my payments on the car. I lost it. I thought how crazy I had been to sell my shoe-shop. How presumptuous I, a Syrian shoemaker, to think I could tell Americans how to appreciate their own country. Then, at my next engagement, I put new enthusiasm into my talk, and the response of my audience gave me fresh determination to keep on. I thumbed rides or hiked from engagement to engagement. Finally, the tide turned. I have kept going; I have told my story in almost every State of the union. (7)

Not long ago I went abroad as interpreter to a group of students and traveled through the countries where dictators had ended unemployment. All I saw everywhere was poverty—people who couldn't buy salt for their daily fare of potatoes and cabbages, and for many fear and persecution with no escape but death. I came back home with the strengthened conviction that this country, even with its economic problems not all solved, its democracy not fully won, is a precious place.

Don't let anyone tell you that America is no longer the land of opportunity. Even the immigrant and refugee who hardly knows a word of English still finds it full of opportunity. But young people born here should do more than use their education to make something *for* themselves. They should make something *of* themselves, use their education not to get rich, but to enrich America. Today we are talking about defense, but America is too vital a country to be merely on the defensive. Our greatest strength is that we are still building our country. Our problems are our biggest opportunity. (8)

QUESTIONS

I

1. In what ways had Salom Rizk's infancy and early childhood been unusual? (1)
2. What terrifying and cruel experiences befell him after his grandmother's death? (2)
3. What was his background of schooling, and what difficulties did he have in obtaining a passport to America? (3)
4. What astonished him about America? about his brother's meeting him? Why did he leave his first job, and where did he go? (4)
5. How did he show cleverness in the way he ran his shoe repairing business, and how did he arrange to improve his education while running this business? (5)
6. In what ways was he puzzled by the American presidential election? (6)
7. In what manner did the American depression differ from conditions in Syria? What impelled him to speak to Americans about their blessings, and how did he fare in his public lecturing? (7)
8. With what conviction did his visit to countries ruled by dictators leave him? (8)

II

1. From this and the preceding essays, do you believe that you will likely understand immigrants better? Do you know of any of the means being undertaken in the larger cities to acquaint them with American ways of life?

2. Do you think immigrants should completely give up all their native cultural backgrounds when they settle in America? Analyze your answer carefully.
3. Of the four immigrants of whom we have read, whose success impressed you most? With which one were you most sympathetic? Which one would you rather talk to?
4. In earlier days immigrants believed that "America is Heaven." Do you think that our country is so regarded now by any foreign peoples?
5. Why were all the teachers so eager to help Salom Rizk secure an education? What relation is there generally between deserving and getting?
6. Is it true, as the author says, that we Americans take our blessings too much for granted? If this is so, what ought we to do about it?
7. Discuss the full import of the statement: "Our problems are our biggest opportunity." Is this sugar-coated optimism or philosophical truth?

III

1. By what device does the author try to get the immediate attention of the reader? He starts his story as a boy of thirteen and then goes back. Is this more effective than an adherence to a strictly chronological arrangement of the facts? If so, why?
2. In contrast to the two preceding essays, the author is here talking about himself instead of being talked about. What advantages does this give him over Mr. Muller's objective presentation? What disadvantages?
3. What is the symbolism in Salom's babyhood experience of being nursed by mothers of several different creeds? What is the meaning of his given name?
4. Point out words and expressions which show that Salom Rizk learned some of his English from the racy vernacular of conversation. Point out sentences in which the language is almost Biblical in its simplicity and dignity.
5. Did you notice in this essay any of the vividness and picturesqueness of description so characteristic of the Eastern mind?

WORDS

Answer the following questions by consulting a good dictionary.
1. astonishing (1): How is *astonishing* connected with thunder?
2. citizens (1): How does the origin of this word show where the first *citizens* lived?

3. abundance (4): How is *abundance* connected with water?
4. dormitory (5): Etymologically speaking, what is the sole purpose of a *dormitory?*
5. encourage (5): This is a beautiful word meaning "to put a heart into" one. What does *discourage* mean?
6. democracy (5): Why, from its etymology, must the people rule in a *democracy?*
7. opportunity (5): The etymology of this word suggests going to a harbor to depart for a journey. Can you explain?
8. language (5): How does *language* derive its name from one of the organs of speech?
9. schools (6): Why would all children like to go to *school* if the word had kept its original meaning?
10. grocer (6): Can you prove that a *grocer* was originally what we call a "wholesaler"?
11. campaign (6): How are the words *campaign* and *champagne* related?
12. President (6): Where, in relation to others, did a *president* originally sit?
13. audience (7): By etymology, does an *audience* come to see or hear?
14. enthusiasm (7): What highly religious idea is expressed in *enthusiasm?*
15. salt (8): How are *salt* and *salary* related?

THEME TOPICS

1. Luxuries in American Life
2. Taking Our Blessings for Granted
3. One Man, One Vote
4. Disillusioned Immigrants
5. Exploiting the Immigrant
6. Problems Are Good for Us
7. A Presidential Election
8. What America Is and Is Not
9. The Challenge to the Native-born American
10. Americans Always Meet the Crisis

Education, Science, and Culture

THE ART OF TEACHING

IRWIN EDMAN

INVESTIGATIONS by legislative and other committees and excitement over subversive textbooks have brought teachers and teaching into the news again. Teachers as teachers generally do not make the headlines. The layman remembers with vague affection or contempt two or three teachers among all those he had at school or college. He begins to think of them again when his own children go to school. He hears fragmentary admirations and disdains for teachers brought home by his sons and daughters, reports often even more casual than their reports and judgments upon movie stars, band leaders, or classmates.

The layman has always heard, and sometimes repeated, the clichés about the importance of teachers in molding the view of the growing generation. But even with the growth of parent-teacher associations, even though every one has gone to school, and a great many people have children going to school, the general public seldom reflects on the nature and the function of the teacher.

A great many people are ready to believe that a teacher is a "subversive influence" without stopping to wonder in what way a teacher has any influence at all. A hysteria runs through a city in time of crisis, and it is alleged that certain teachers with certain views or alleged views are deleterious in their effect upon youth.

This, then, is far from being a bad time to reiterate the question, asked from Plato down, as to what a teacher is and how he does what he does. For it is clear to even the most practical

From *The New York Times Magazine*, May 25, 1941. Copyrighted. Used by permission of The Times Publishing Company and by arrangement with the author.

men that a teacher does do good or ill to the souls of his pupils. But what good or ill is it, and how does he do it? (1)

The obvious function of a teacher is not his whole function. Pupils have to learn because they are ignorant, and the minimal equipment of a teacher is that he possess information and skills that his pupils do not possess. It is an old crack, invented by that old wisecracker Bernard Shaw, that those who can, do; those who can't, teach. But Shaw omitted to point out that many who can and who know can't teach; and though practical and even learned men know how to do many things, teaching is not necessarily one of them.

That is why, in a democratic society committed to teaching every one, schools of education arose. Thousands of teachers have been needed for the teaching of hundreds of thousands of pupils. Mere information is obviously not enough, or "talking books" would be our schoolmasters. The schools of education, the teachers' colleges, have tried to find formulas, methods; these are helpful where they are not merely jargon, but they are not sufficient.

Teaching has possibly the most ambiguous set of requirements of any profession in the world. Even in the elementary schools in a State like New York, teachers must know more about the world and about the sciences of human nature than a don at Oxford knew in the eighteenth century. Yet he must be much more; he must know not only his subject but his pupils' capacities; he must have the clarity of an expert expositor, the equipment of a scholar, the entertainer's sense of timing and of an audience, the communicative enthusiasm of a poet and a leader, and a passionate but reserved love of the young. (2)

It is not surprising that there are relatively few good teachers in the world. It is astonishing that there should be so many. For expertness in a field, as many people remember from taking courses with famous scholars, does not make a man a teacher. The art of teaching is an anxious and chameleon gift. The good teacher must make things clear and he must make them interesting not to the already interested and initiate but to the tyro and to the young ready to be distracted, uninterested and unimpressed. He must be able to make his subject "contagiously alive," and always without dramatizing himself.

Obviously one of the first requirements of a good teacher is clarity, the lucidity that comes from objectivity. There is a tale told of a professor who fell asleep during one of his own lectures. When asked how he managed to do that, he said: "But you have no idea how dull the lecture was!" There is another tale: one professor was so dull that even his colleagues noticed it. But students themselves are quick to notice—and to contract—the listlessness of a teacher with respect to what he is teaching. All the world loves not only a lover but the things he loves. And an obvious concern with the subject-matter, the problems, and the responsibilities of method, teaches students more than any texts could, and more than the facts with which the teacher is ostensibly dealing.

If students are quick to detect listlessness, they are quick, though not always expert, in detecting special pleading, the arguing of a case, the grinding of an axe, the propaganda for a doctrine. This is not to say that any teacher can, or should, be without human interests or devotions. But it should not be his own special doctrines that he is preaching. I know of one professor of philosophy who regards it as a criterion of success in teaching if at the end of a semester students ask him "But what is your philosophy?" The best of them will usually have guessed, but it would require a dogmatism and a provincialism ill-becoming a teacher of the young or a student of ideas to propagate a special bias or the point of view of a special group. (3)

Ambiguity as to a teacher's influence arises because of two things. In the humanistic and social sciences, teachers, like other human beings, obviously have ideas, loyalties and aspirations. These are likely to be not necessarily better or worse, but, in good teachers, more critical and less conventional than those current in any given society. A teacher hardly can help betraying, by incidental comment, by emphasis, by an epigram or even a joke, where his heart lies. But teaching is, as Socrates long ago pointed out, an art of elicitation, and the good teacher tries not to impose his own mind but to get the students to use theirs. In a democracy, as tragic events already have proved, nothing could be, from the point of view of national interest, a more important habit.

A second reason for the ambiguity as to a teacher's influence is that students learn inevitably not only from a teacher's mind but from his personality as well. A teacher is a person living in a given time in a community in which there are sharp points of conflict and sharp conflicts of interest. In a superficial sense it does not much matter, or does not seem to matter, what sort of person a teacher is.

The binomial theorem, differential calculus or organic chemistry can be taught by men and women who are neither saints nor prophets. A teacher may be quite as effective, it may be argued, in communicating the fact that "two and two are four, and neither five nor three," regardless of his personal opinions on politics or religion. But the fact remains that the very qualities which make a man a good teacher in any field—lucidity and responsibility, honesty and discipline—are not likely to consort with personal traits of narrowness or excess.

Even in the so-called purely objective sciences students learn by incidental personal example. The late Stuart Sherman, for many years one of the most influential professors of English in this country, said once that the trouble with college teachers is that they must be Caesar's wives: they must be above suspicion. It is natural enough that in a narrow community or in times of stress, suspicions arise very easily, and about irrelevant things. But one can see why. In the physical sciences, and far more so in the humanistic fields, the traits of intellectual discipline and candor are the function of many other personal traits. The habit of critical objectivity is one of the chief goods of education in a community. But the exemplification of candor and self-discipline in the personal temper of teachers is no less important than their expertness in their subjects or in their methods of teaching. (4)

What is present in the teaching of any subject is peculiarly notable in the teaching of subjects like history, the social sciences and morals. It is here that the tone and general quality of a teacher's personality have possibly as much influence as what he explicitly says. Any teacher worth his salt or his salary believes in working toward a better world. On what else is teaching based but on a faith that through the education of the young the world may indeed be a better one in the next generation? But it behooves the teacher to be clear as to the way in which the classroom may be used as the instrument for the formation of a better society.

The classroom is not the ideal soap-box; it is not the place for a private propagandizing mission. The teacher need not try to make it so. It is quite a natural symptom of the tensions of our time that a few instances, or alleged instances, of teachers using their scholarship or classrooms to vent propagandas of their own or of a political party, or a foreign ism or even an Americanism, should cause a hue and cry about subversive influences. But it would be deplorable if suspicion of propaganda should lead to suspicion of critical intelligence, the very nerve center of a democratic society, and if doctrines should be imposed on a teacher by a group or a clique or a caste.

The teacher, of course, has his responsibilities. But it is important to make clear what these are, and to whom, and to what. Are they to his pupils, to something vaguely called society, or to scholarship, to his subject? If teaching is to promote the ideal of freedom and liberty, the teacher clearly must be free to be an example of them. He must be free to teach by both analysis and example the qualities of mind that insure liberty in the world. Freedom in a democratic society can endure only with self-discipline, for a democratic society cannot tolerate dictation by main force.

The teacher must be free to follow the lead of his subject-matter. That requires the discipline of scholarship and the integrity of the love of truth. A teacher has responsibilities to these, and if he maintains these, he will, by example and by art and contagion, promote them in his pupils. The coöperative intelligence of citizens will be promoted better by illustrating and inculcating the habits of intelligence than by instilling patriotic slogans. A totalitarian government can "educate" its citizens by making them rubber stamps. This is the last thing a democracy can afford to do. Democracy may indeed be defined as a society in which, in the educational process and in the daily arrangements of life, the habit of intelligence is made universal. (5)

In the promotion of this habit in the young the teacher is, for better or worse, crucially important. And I suspect he best promotes his responsibilities to our democratic way of life and to his students if he keeps his eye on the ball, the ball being the facts as his responsible scholarship reveals them, and the consequences as disinterested thinking unravels them. For the good teacher does not seek to make disciples for a cause or converts to a creed, not even the democratic creed. He will exemplify in his teaching, and promote in his students, the habit of analysis, of seeing things in their own terms, of following the lead of a subject-matter, of distinguishing between facts and formulas, between inquiry and propaganda, however generous-minded the latter.

There need be no fear that such a conception of teaching implies lifelessness and ignores emotion. The mind, too, has its passion, and this is the one passion that the teacher can properly communicate. It is the passion that disciplines all other emotion. If emotion is not disciplined by critical intelligence, the only alternatives are fanaticisms and the fears and hates with which irresponsible feeling fills the world.

If the teacher communicates discipline of thought with clarity and integrity and the radiance of his own patent devotion, he is doing one of the essential jobs of a democracy. He is fortifying in free citizens the faith in a possible unity, not of robots, but of intelligent men. He is instilling coöperation through the discipline and love of truth which the young catch, by a kind of osmosis or contagion, from their teachers.

The teacher needs a combination of obstinacy and modesty to educate students in those habits of responsible inquiry essential to a society of free men. His obstinacy must be quite impersonal, a resolute adherence to the responsibilities imposed by his own studies. He will naturally guard jealously the privileges of intellectual freedom which are the first privileges and the first foundations to go when democracy goes. But he will be modest, too, as will any one who has a claim to learning or the spirit of learning. (6)

He will not assume he has all the answers, nor ask students to accept those currently fashionable in any clique, even an intellectual one. He will be interested chiefly in helping students to those habits of mind which will help them to answer the troublesome questions which arise in their own lives, not least those questions, social and political, which arise in our cataclysmically changing world. And for all his promotion of the habit of inquiry and criticism, the teacher will exhibit and propagate a modesty and piety not in the least inconsistent with independence of thought, a piety to the patrimony of the past, to that inherited tradition of which any teacher is both the critic and the spokesman. He will teach his students, perhaps best by example, to have a sense of the past which is part of the material that any intelligent men use in their disciplined dreams of a better world.

For the effect of a good teacher is not least that upon the imagination of his students. They will catch from him the tone with which they are likely to approach the world. Our ideals, it has been said, come from our first teachers and our first loves. Not the least function of a teacher is the sympathy he promotes with that patrimony of the past, with all its imperfections, of which we are the heirs.

The habit of critical inquiry directed toward a detailed improvement of our democratic society, a promotion of imaginative devotion to the "ingenious lovely things" of the past in art and ways of life—these are the twin businesses of teaching. They animate even specialized teaching in any field. They require the conditions of a free society to promote them. When practised by teachers with all the resources of the teaching art, of the scholar's science, and of the poet's enthusiasm, teaching comes, not least in times of crisis, close to being an essential industry. It is the industry by which alone we may insure that there will be a generation worthy of the heritage to be transmitted to it through who knows what sacrifices. (7)

QUESTIONS

I

1. To what extent does the average person remember his teachers, what does he believe about the importance of teachers, and upon what occasions is he excited about their activities? (1)
2. What is the *obvious* function of the teacher? What are his other functions? (2)

3. What two things must a good teacher do? What are some of the things about a teacher which students are quick to detect? (*3*)
4. What are the two reasons for the ambiguity of a teacher's influence? Why is a good teacher usually a good *person*? Why do the necessary qualities of a good teacher sometimes cause a community to be suspicious of him? (*4*)
5. To what extent must a teacher be free in teaching his subject? What must he not do? What will be his chief objective in teaching? (*5, 6*)
6. What nice balance will a good teacher maintain in his teaching? What will students obtain from him that is not in the subject matter he is teaching? What are the ultimate objectives of all teaching? (*7*)

II

1. Think of several of the best teachers you have ever had; several of the poorest. Has the author covered both in his discussion?
2. Granted the value of teacher-training, what is the danger of over-emphasis on method? On which part of teacher-preparation would you place the more emphasis: mastery of subject matter or skill in presenting it?
3. To what extent should teachers have "academic freedom"? Would you limit this freedom in any way?
4. To what extent should a teacher's private life be controlled by the community in which he lives?
5. "Those who can, do; those who can't, teach." Comment upon the truth or falsity of this generalization.
6. What do you understand by Socrates' definition: "Teaching is the art of elicitation"?
7. What is the difference in educational purposes and methods between totalitarian despotisms and free democracies? What is the best service that an American teacher can render democracy?
8. Have you ever had a teacher who influenced you in your choice of a life work, in becoming interested in a hobby, in the reading of good books, in emulating qualities of his personality?

III

1. How much of the essay is introduction? With what words does the main trend of the article begin?
2. Has Mr. Edman been a good teacher in presenting his material clearly, objectively, dispassionately, and interestingly?
3. In his last paragraph he points out "the twin businesses of teaching." Do you accept these two points as an adequate summary of his views on teaching expressed in this essay? (*7*)

WORDS

Discuss the substitution of the italicized synonym or synonymous expression for each of the author's words, which are given in the left-hand column.

1. subversive (*1*): *undermining* textbooks
2. casual (*1*): even more *accidental* than their reports
3. clichés (*1*): the *hackneyed remarks* about the importance of teachers
4. deleterious (*1*): are *hurtful* in their effects upon youth
5. minimal (*2*): the *least* equipment of a teacher
6. jargon (*2*): not merely *technical vocabulary*
7. ambiguous (*2*): the most *indefinite* set of requirements
8. expositor (*2*): an expert *explainer*
9. tyro (*3*): to the *beginner*
10. lucidity (*3*): the *clearness* that comes from objectivity
11. ostensibly (*3*): the teacher is *apparently* dealing
12. criterion (*3*): a *standard* of success
13. dogmatism (*3*): require a *positiveness*
14. provincialism (*3*): a *narrow-mindedness* ill-becoming a teacher
15. propagate (*3*): to *foster* a special bias
16. elicitation (*4*): the art of *drawing out*
17. irrelevant (*4*): about *unrelated* things
18. candor (*4*): intellectual discipline and *frankness*
19. exemplification (*4*): the *showing* of candor
20. contagion (*5*): by art and *zeal*
21. inculcating (*5*): *teaching* the habits of intelligence
22. crucially (*6*): *vitally* important
23. robots (*6*): not of *automatons*, but of intelligent men
24. cataclysmically (*7*): in our *disastrously* changing world
25. patrimony (*7*): that *inheritance* of the past

THEME TOPICS

1. A Teacher I Like to Remember
2. The Qualities of a Great Teacher
3. A Teacher's Best Service to Democracy
4. Dogmatic (Provincial, "Dry") Teachers
5. A Good Teacher Is a Good Person
6. The Necessity for Academic Freedom
7. I Want (Do Not Want) to Be a Teacher
8. Pedants *vs.* Teachers
9. Education in a Totalitarian State
10. The Past Is My Patrimony

AN EDUCATION TO BE USED

JOHN ERSKINE

IN our schools and colleges the stress laid upon athletics has long troubled the teachers of other subjects. With good reason educators worry about competitive sport. We regret the disappearance of the strict amateur, whatever an amateur may be, and we fear there is an essential evil in the profit which institutions of learning make, directly and indirectly, from the games.

Yet educators might well ask if there is not a profound reason why American students are devoted to athletics—a strictly educational reason which has nothing to do with finance or with the definition of the amateur. The educator may well ask whether athletics is not the only subject in the curriculum which is properly taught. The subjects which approach it in the genuine satisfactions they give are taught in approximately the same way. The teacher of any subject, even though he is a sworn enemy of what he calls the athletic craze, may well hope that that craze will continue in full vigor until all the other subjects are taught by the same system. (1)

We still teach athletics as the Greeks did, for use. If we think of the Greeks as traditional folk whose day was past long ago, and who are remembered now only in academic tradition, it is perhaps a good thing to illustrate their vital wisdom in this physical field, where we cannot be dismissed as academic or bookish. The Greeks held athletics even more highly than we do. The Olympian games were more nearly a religious ceremony than even football contests are with us, and the blight of commercialism, so far as we know, was absent. But they believed that other subjects also were of vital importance, and they taught them all so that study would result in an able performance.

St. Paul, who had been educated in the Greek way, used the Olympian games as a metaphor of life itself. The Greek boy was taught how to run a race, and immediately he went out and ran. His teachers assigned him no marks for his class work: life would give him his marks. He won the race or he lost it, and in either case he ran again.

Here is the ancient glory of athletics which survives the blights of our day. Our boys and girls are conscious of it, though they may not stop to define what enlists their admiration. When they are taught to swim they expect at once to swim. They don't want 95 per cent in swimming; they'll be satisfied only if they don't sink. The boy who is taught tennis, football or baseball wants to play. He is glad to risk a licking, because even though temporarily defeated he hopes eventually to win.

The Greeks and St. Paul thought the athletic attitude was the right attitude toward life. What better can we suggest after all these centuries? And in what other subjects—here is the mortifying question—do we impart this attitude?

Let me guard against a misunderstanding. When I express admiration for the practical education which the Greeks imparted I do not mean that only those subjects should be taught which we nowadays call practical, nor that we should omit what for us are the cultural subjects. I merely wish we, like the Greeks, taught every subject so that we could use it in life. The ideal of culture which considers a subject valuable because it is useless seems tragically absurd. We are here to live; education should teach us how. There is no time to waste. (2)

If we have a false idea of culture there is a historical explanation for it. The Greek boy studied all his subjects so that he could use them. The Romans later invented the sideline ideal of culture, and what they—and we after them—call liberal studies. Rome conquered Greece, and had a good supply of Greek slaves. These slaves had been trained in the arts and sciences. The Roman relied on the Greek slaves for his architecture, his mathematics, his sculpture, his poetry. For himself he developed a scheme of education which he called liberal—that is, a training suitable to a free man who owned slaves, and therefore expected to do no work. The appreciation of other men's work was what the Roman called culture. He beçame a good judge of athletics; that is, he was master of no sport himself, but he attended the arena, where the slaves took the exercise for him, and he liked to bet on the games. (3)

In the Renaissance men like Francis Bacon helped to restore the sciences to their Greek condition. Though we do not yet teach the sciences perfectly, they are the group of subjects which in our schools are taught most nearly, after athletics, in the Greek way. No wonder the sciences fascinate the young. When you make an experiment in the chemistry laboratory you get a result. You acquire some knowledge which is immediately available for life. You make the experiment yourself. If the teacher insists on making it for you in your presence you must forgive him: he is temporarily overtaken by the Roman idea of culture. He imagines that he is the performing Greek slave and that you are the liberal Roman gentleman accumulating culture by looking on.

There is today a new tendency back to the Greek way of teaching, but as yet it shows itself chiefly in the addition to the curriculum of courses in what we call specifically the arts. Our schools now give training in music, a practical training which ends in performance—in many cases, in very good performance. Here and there the schools teach dancing. In almost every well equipped school and college the teaching of drama is at least supplemented by the actual performance of plays. (4)

But after we have recognized the great progress in scientific education, and have saluted the recent return of the arts, what shall we say of the remaining subjects? Are they arts or sciences? I refer to the courses in languages, in English, in history, in philosophy, in economics, in the so-called social sciences. I am quite sure that all these subjects are of great importance, but I am equally certain that a Greek, if he could see how we teach them, would think us crazy. They supply no technique for living, and we don't expect them to. They are supposed to supply the Roman kind of culture.

The teaching of languages is the particular sore thumb in our so-called "cultural" scheme of education. Latin and Greek are taught, if at all, for cultural reasons. I have heard that the study of Greek will aid you toward clarity of thought and will improve your style. For Greek and Latin both I have heard the argument that without a knowledge of them you won't know the etymology of many English words. This is all true, of course, but I am unregenerate enough to think that the purpose in studying any language is to speak it and read it. I know from experience that you cannot read a language unless you can speak it. I know that our students are not taught to speak Latin or Greek. I am therefore not surprised that they can read neither language. This seems a pity, because the majority of the great books which have influenced our civilization were written in one language or the other.

If you don't want to know Latin and Greek, I shan't quarrel with you, but you ought to be content with your natural ignorance of those languages and not cement that ignorance, for cultural purposes, by studying Greek and Latin the wrong way. (5)

I'd say the same thing with even greater vigor of the modern languages. You might doubt my word if I assured you that Latin and Greek can be taught so that in a very short time they can be spoken, but in the case of the modern languages that truth is constantly demonstrated under our eyes. Immigrants with no schooling at all learn quickly to speak our language. We, on the other hand, give five or six years to the study of their language in school or colleges without acquiring the ability to express ourselves in it. Europeans more highly educated than some immigrants astound us by their command of several languages. They shame us by what seems their superior intellectual capacity. I think we ought to be ashamed, but not because of any incurable inferiority. The difference between us and the European is that, since the countries over there are small and close together, he frequently hears a foreign language, and he studies all foreign languages with the Greek purpose of using them.

Again, if you say that in the United States a knowledge of French and German is not necessary, and therefore you don't care whether your child can speak anything but English, I shan't argue with you, though I think you are wrong, but if a practical knowledge of French and German is not needed, why waste time in pretending to study those languages? Do you say, for the cultural result? I refuse to believe there is any cultural benefit from ignorance. Men and women who can speak several languages often show a self-confidence which is cultural, but those who have studied languages without mastering them are horribly embarrassed when in life some need of those languages comes up.

That we should insist on teaching languages the wrong way is all the more astonishing because the wrong way costs more than the right, and it takes a much longer time. The wrong way starts the pupil off with rules of grammar and with rules of pronunciation. Only a singularly mature and philosophical mind can get anything out of grammar in the abstract, unattached to a language, and how you can learn with profit the rules of pronunciation before you know any words to pronounce I cannot imagine.

I went through the agony myself in my school days—with the exception of one language, to which I shall refer again. I learned grammatical rules, and of course forgot them later. I learned how to pronounce vowels and consonants, but I did not at first acquire a vocabulary. For several years—that is, through school and college—I wasted hours in translation, perverting the text word by word with what I could ladle out of the dictionary. Only with difficulty did I resist the impression that every foreign language was a translation of my own.

When languages are properly taught, as on the Continent of Europe and in some rare places here, the student learns first the language—that is, the sound and meaning of the words. He hears nothing but the language he is trying to learn. In his first lesson he and his classmates master ten or a dozen important words. By dint of immediate practice they learn to pronounce the words and to write them. In the next lesson they repeat these words, and master ten or a dozen more. After a hundred lessons they have at their command over a thousand words, and since the words are scientifically selected for their usefulness, the pupils are ready to carry on a conversation.

Of course their grammar is not perfect, and they have many more words to learn, but they have the comfort of remembering that in their infancy they acquired words first and grammar later. The grammar comes naturally if you use the language with people who speak it well. If you don't use it, the grammar never comes at all.

After you have learned to speak the language in the first year of study, you should give at least another year to its literature. Under this system the student in the second year will really be able to read—put his feet up, lean back in a comfortable chair, and enjoy the book.

Two years for a practical command of a language! Ten years are sometimes needed for our method of acquiring culture while preserving our ignorance. I have had experience with both methods. I studied French in the American way from school days to the close of my graduate years, and when the government, at our entrance into the World War, asked me what I knew, I put French in the list. For that fib I was sent to the French Army. During the first two or three weeks I had an uninterrupted headache. When I woke at dawn, I got up, not to the war but to the language. But suddenly the fog cleared and I knew what the French were talking about. Why not? After my decades of school I had at last had a chance to hear the language spoken and to speak it myself. (6)

I have another and happier memory. I was taught Greek by a man who thought Greek was a language. Little Greek children had once prattled in it. Greek parents used it to joke and gossip, or to quarrel with the landlord. This singular teacher devoted part of each lesson to Greek conversation. When I went to college Greek words were easy for my tongue, and though for lack of practice I can no longer talk it, because I once could talk it I still can read it.

No language is a dead language unless you kill it. We are rapidly killing English. In the English class we teach no one to speak—we hardly make the attempt. We teach the biography of authors and we repeat the accepted critical opinions, but we don't teach literature. We don't show the student how verse is written, or prose; we don't impart the technique of story-telling, or novel-writing, or play-making. If we pretend to do these things, we omit the one element which in life is essential; we forget the audience. Many a college graduate gets A in his English course, but few know how to catch and hold a reader's attention. If you can't do that, you don't know how to write. There is no mystery about it; a vigorous newspaper editor will knock it into your head in a few weeks. In the college writing course, however, the instructor did not expect you to become a writer. He probably wasn't a writer himself.

If you go far enough in your study of history you will find out at last what the historian is doing and how he does it, but in the earlier years you may get the impression that history is a reservoir of known fact, a faithful report of the past. But history is the most meticulous form of imaginative literature. The past is irrecoverable, and history is one long reinterpretation of meager vestiges. Our present theory of any ancient person or episode may be upset tomorrow by the finding of a manuscript or by the rifling of a grave. Did your history teacher drill you in the fascinating art of interpreting unstable and insufficient evidence?

There remain in our curriculum several subjects which I shan't name, but which you can guess. The stickler for the Roman ideal of culture will confound me by asking how their value could ever be tested in practical use. I shall answer by echoing the question, how indeed! At that point our philosophies take leave of each other. If a subject is so cultural that it can never go with us into life, I would reform it or throw it overboard. I'm no friend of classroom dialectic, not even when it hides under a good name and pretends to have a humane and social purpose. What is the marginal utility of a loaf of bread? How many angels can stand on the point of a needle? I decline to guess the answers, though needles are useful and I revere the angels. (7)

QUESTIONS

I

1. Why, according to the author, is athletics the only subject properly taught? (*1*)
2. What was the Greek method of teaching all subjects? (*2*)
3. What false ideas of education, in the author's opinion, did the Romans introduce? (*3*)
4. What subjects in the present curriculum are taught most nearly in the Greek way and what other subjects, similarly taught, are being added to the curriculum? (*4*)
5. What is the author's opinion of the way the so-called cultural subjects are taught in colleges? (*5*)
6. What outstanding faults does he find with the teaching of modern languages? (*6*)
7. What was his own happy experience in learning Greek? How would he teach English? What would he do with subjects that can have no application to life? (*7*)

II

1. Do you think the author has given the correct explanation for student interest in athletics? Can you think of other reasons? Do you think the athletic attitude is the right attitude toward life?
2. Mr. Erskine attacks as a false idea of culture the belief that a subject which is useless still has value. Does his position seem valid to you?
3. What have you obtained from your own study of languages? Do you think you would have had more profit and enjoyment from them if you had learned to speak them instead of read them? Do you keep on reading them? Will you read them in the future?
4. "No language is a dead language unless you kill it." Comment upon this generalization. Do you agree with the author that we are engaged in killing English? How is this being done?
5. Have your subjects taught "for use" or those taught "for cultural value" been the more interesting to you?
6. Do you think the author of this essay has neglected the cultural, and overemphasized the vocational, values of education?

III

1. How does the author use a much debated question to catch the reader's attention and interest at the opening of the essay? (*1*)

2. Comment upon the positiveness of the ideas and the vigor of the style of this essay.

3. How does the highly personal note at the end fit in with the tone of the essay in its entirety?

WORDS

Answer the questions about the following words.

1. amateur (*1*): How is this word degenerating in popular use from its finer older meaning?

2. mortifying (*2*): How has *mortifying* become a very weak word compared to its original meaning?

3. clarity (*5*): How is the word *clarity* related to the wine *claret?*

4. unregenerate (*5*): What two prefixes does this word have, and what does each mean?

5. perverting (*6*): What part of this word has the meaning of "turn" in it?

6. meticulous (*7*): Does this word suggest "care" or "excessive care" in attention to details?

7. irrecoverable (*7*): What are the meanings of the two prefixes of this word?

8. dialectic (*7*): What is the meaning of this word as used in logic?

9. humane (*7*): What is the difference in meaning between *humane* and *human?*

10. revere (*7*) You can *love* your dog, but you can hardly *revere* him. What kind of things do we *revere?*

THEME TOPICS

1. The Athletic Attitude Is Sound
2. Athletic Coaches Are Good Teachers
3. My Painful Experience with the ———— Language
4. Education Is for Use
5. Why Science Appeals to Young Men
6. A Defense of Vocational Education (Liberal Arts)
7. The Most Valuable Foreign Language to an American
8. I Prefer (Believe in) the Cultural Subjects
9. The Economic Value of Good English
10. Why I Enjoy Athletics

SCIENCE

W. J. CAMERON

IT is rather wonderful how the constructive and nourishing things of our life hold up steady and pursue their way. Through untoward or even hostile conditions, the sciences and services that are building the future not only hold their ground, but also show a remarkable power to advance. The schools maintain their work, handing on to the coming generation all that from the past is true and tested, and whatever of the present holds useful promise for tomorrow. Teachers and learners never cease or fail. These, and the laboratory of the scientist, are *in* the world yet are not wholly *of* it, because the world they are building is yet to come.

It is entirely unnecessary to defend any of these, for *they are going on.* They move toward the same objective which none of them yet has seen but which each of them knows is the only possible one. With the supporting human instincts that never are wholly demoralized, nor even partially distorted for long, these together form the life line by which humanity holds, and finds its footing, and goes onward slowly or sprightly, step by step, in shadow and in sunshine. Such powerful human thrusts, forming the unformed world of the future, are worthy our resort to them, because of all things that we see today they are least contaminated by the terrible malady of defeatism. (*1*)

How true this is of science. No conventions held in this country are so free of defeatism as are the conventions of scientists. It is not merely optimism that inspires science—it is something better than optimism—let us call it "the glory of going on and not to die." Whenever science reaches what seems to be an end, it knows that there it will find a new beginning—a *group* of new

From Seventh Series of Talks by W. J. Cameron, 1940-1941. Copyrighted. Used by permission of R. Renaldy for the author.

beginnings. Even its "failures" are halfway stations on the highway to knowledge. Its lesser triumphs are caught up and included in its greater conquests. There is no big and little in science; all sound work is good and makes its contribution to the whole. To the scientist, the future appears under the form of great things yet to do. Its work is inexhaustible. The means to do it are inexhaustible. The benefits to be derived are boundless.

Yet, some would lay on science the guilt of having made the world a place of greater danger than it was. It may seem sheer heresy to say so, but science has made the world a *safer* place. Science *saves* more lives than its misused inventions destroy. The cost of using the fruits of science for destructive ends never was higher and steadily grows prohibitive, and the cost of using them for purposes of prosperous peace never was lower. Science gave us steel, and the phrase "cold steel" has ghastly connotations, but there is more steel in farm implements than in all the world's armaments, and more steel in railways, steamships, houses, printing presses, automobiles and industrial machinery than in farm implements. Explosives and chemical fertilizer come from the same source, but more use is made of fertilizer than of explosives. The force that propels the deadly missile also propels the automobile and everywhere on earth people prefer automobiles to bombs. (2)

Science will assure us—and very likely has already done so—of a basic economic supply. The next thing is adequate distribution, and in this job every department of human endeavor must assist.

Science has raised the level of experimental inquiry in every region by discovering a method of *discovering knowledge*, for lack of which we have moved too slowly almost everywhere; and a method of wisely *applying knowledge*, once we have found it. Life always has been full of potencies not fully developed for want of channels of expression, and such channels are now being opened through a mastery of techniques we did not know before.

So, if we look around, we shall see plenty of things going on. Their direction indicates the real state toward which the world is moving. It also indicates that the upward movement, being the only one with promise, is also the only one having permanence. (3)

QUESTIONS

I

1. What part do schools and science play in progress? (1)
2. What is the attitude of science toward defeatism? How does it contribute toward a better, not a worse, world? (2)
3. How will science contribute in guaranteeing basic economic supply, in solving problems of distribution, and in opening up new channels of progress? (3)

II

1. Do you think science has made the world a safer or a more dangerous place in which to live?
2. Can science be held responsible for the misuse of its discoveries by men and nations?
3. Do you think science will be the greatest single factor in future human advancement?

III

1. How far do we read before we find that the real theme of this essay is *science?*
2. Note the four successive paragraphs in which the word *science* is the first word or among the first words in the paragraph. What is the author's purpose in doing this?

WORDS

Each word at the left can modify in a sensible way the three words which follow it. Can you define each word at the left by examining the three words with which it may be used?

1. untoward (1): events, news, accident
2. demoralized (1): army, football team, money market
3. distorted (1): face, opinion, testimony
4. sprightly (1): step, dance, music
5. contaminated (1): water supply, food, mind
6. prohibitive (2): prices, measures, laws

THEME TOPICS

See Theme Topics for the following essay.

MODERN SCIENCE, THE HOPE OF CIVILIZATION

MATTHEW LUCKIESH

TWO persons are gazing at the night sky studded with stars. One is familiar with the facts of astronomy; the other is not. To the one, there is order in that apparent disorder. To the other, the starry sky appears as a chaos. The one knows that only a few thousand stars are visible. The other multiplies these into an uncounted myriad. Modern science, through systematic measurements, has brought order out of that confusion of stars. It can do the same for any apparent chaos of nature or of civilization, if its method and the resulting facts are adequately applied.

In unprosperous times, the muddle of our sociological world is conspicuous. But, amid all the endless talk of causes and cures, how often is the simple explanation presented? The cause of our economic chaos is lack of adequate knowledge. If so, the cure becomes obvious. The muddle of civilization has always existed, but modern science possesses the purpose and method which should eliminate the chaos eventually. It has worked wonders in the relatively small portion of civilized activities which it has already invaded. By looking at its material achievements—airplanes, radios, and the like—one is likely to conclude that this is a scientific age. But, looking at the sociological world as a whole, one must conclude that this is an unscientific world. While the physical sciences are learning the secrets of atoms and stars, economists, politicians, and governments are chipping flints in a Stone Age sociology.

Every person interested in the great currents of civilized

From *The Scientific Monthly*, March, 1934. Used by permission of the author.

progress and in sociological institutions should be interested in the purpose and method of modern science. Extensive understanding means an extensive faith; and this is essential if the necessary social inventions are to be made and applied.

On every hand are found the applications of modern science which contribute to convenience, comfort, and other joys of living. You have heard and read many stories of specific achievements of scientific knowledge and you will learn of many more. I could add another story of another success, but I shall speak of modern science, not because it needs spokesmen for itself, but because, in the extension of its purpose and method, lies the hope of civilization. (1)

Modern science is a great movement against the unknown. Its purpose is unchallengeable. It aims to understand by knowing the truth. Its method is uniquely dependable. It is a new kind of strategy which aims to establish the facts, unwarped by such human frailties as prejudice and egoism. The harvest of this movement is tested and testable knowledge, therefore, incontestable knowledge. Any of the major sciences, or uncounted minor ones, is the coördination of facts in a sector of knowledge.

The success of modern science is found not in mind but in method. Great minds are not a monopoly of any single era of civilization. Aristotle possessed one of the great minds, but, in accordance with the method of early centuries, he philosophized; he did not experiment. He believed to be true that which appeared to be true. For example, he thought that if two balls of equal size, but of unequal weight, were dropped from a height, the heavier would reach the ground first. He preached what he believed but had not proved. For many centuries that statement was accepted as truth until Galileo tried the experiment. He dropped the two balls from the leaning tower of Pisa and they reached the ground at the same time. This was the real beginning of a systematic accumulation of tested knowledge. The movement of modern science is not without its speculations and theories. But these are tentative and are labeled so. They are accessories after the facts. They are temporary lines of communication to be modified as rapidly as new facts require. The facts always remain supreme in modern science.

No idea or movement—not even a child—has a perfectly definite time or place of birth. Its ultimate beginning is somewhere in the mists of uncertainty. But everything has a practical beginning—a point where it began in earnest. So it is with modern science.

In Europe the Middle Ages were dark indeed. Civilization was struggling in its usual confusion. War and religion were the two outstanding occupations. Eventually, religion celebrated its survival with an intense fervor which built the great cathedrals. But, with all its good intentions, men's minds were more or less shackled by the dominance of man-made precepts, edicts, and beliefs. Freedom in thought and action had feebly struggled for centuries. A declaration of independence in these matters was awaiting the next great revolution in civilization. It was a natural result of the great awakening which we term the Renaissance. Ridding their minds of the mists of centuries of philosophical dreaming, thinking men declared that nature could be understood and was worth understanding. (2)

Modern science is just as much a human movement in the midst of humanity as any other movement. It has the same right to a symbol and a shrine as other movements. Born in the late Renaissance, Galileo was the right man, in the right place, at the right time. He was the first outstanding exponent of scientific method wherein is found the irresistible power of modern science. By his achievements in thought and action he gave the first great impetus to the movement which we call modern science—and he symbolizes it so well. To pay him homage, let us transport ourselves to Florence, Italy. Here, amid the tombs and statues, the palaces and art galleries, our imagination revives the human struggles for freedom of expression in all its senses. We seek out a modest church and enter the dim interior. The shadows, reminiscent of the glorious era of the Renaissance, are peopled with the spirits of great men, and we remember best the good ones. After a few paces, we find ourselves on a spot that preëminently deserves the glorification of modern civilization. We stand between the tombs of Michelangelo and Galileo. It is impressed upon us that the city which gave the greatest gift to Art also gave the greatest gift to Science. As we stand there with deepening reverence, we note that Michelangelo died the year that Galileo was born. In our imagination we see the failing hand of that superb creator of the beautiful passing the scepter from art to science. In our imagination we hear Michelangelo saying: "The Renaissance artists questioned the old and created the new. They have shown that the world may be beautified superficially. But knowledge alone can supply the understanding which will reveal the third dimension as well. And only perfect and complete understanding can beautify the world through and through."

The substance of that imaginary statement by the old Michelangelo to the young Galileo should be the theme of the lives of all who are a part of the movement of modern science. It might well be the theme of life for everyone, for to understand is a high purpose. Furthermore, understanding, born of incontestable knowledge in all the sciences—physical, biological, and sociological—is the only dependable cure for all the ills of ignorance—and this means most, if not all, ills of individuals and of civilization. In reality, or in imagination, all civilized persons should visit that spot in that church in Florence. It is the shrine of modern science. While there, they might pledge themselves to learn to separate incontestable facts from the common confusion of prejudices, assertions, preconceptions, beliefs, and even superstitions.

Modern science, with its cold facts and calculating method, is generally supposed to be devoid of beauty and human interest. This is not true. Any science is an array of cold, lifeless details; but so is any other structure, even the human being. The parts of a huge locomotive, when strewn on the floor of the factory, are uninteresting. But assemble the parts and put the locomotive into action. Then who will say that it is without beauty and human interest! The greatest masterpiece in painting consists of an array of material facts. The master, while painting it, was building a structure. His method was cold and calculating; every stroke was deliberate.

In the great movement of modern science are found the same intense loyalties, heroisms, and sacrifices as in any other movement. Certainly, it is unexcelled in the beauty of its fairness and purpose. Certainly, it recognizes no insurmountable barriers. Certainly, it is unlimited by boundaries, for its natural domain is the boundless unknown. All this is expressed in beautiful lines by Tennyson:

> Flower in the crannied wall,
> I pluck you out of the crannies,
> I hold you here, root and all, in my hand,
> Little flower—but if I could understand
> What you are, root and all, and all in all,
> I should know what God and man is.

Modern science may not reach that far-off goal, but it moves irresistibly toward it. (*3*)

QUESTIONS

I

1. What fundamental thing does science do, and what, according to the author, will its method do for our social problems? (*1*)
2. What is the *method* of modern science? Wherein did Galileo's procedure differ from that of Aristotle? When did science, as we understand the term, begin? (*2*)
3. How does Galileo symbolize modern science? What, in the author's opinion, is the only dependable cure for the ills of ignorance? How are art and science related? What are the *beauties* of science? (*3*)

II

1. Why have the physical sciences so far outstripped the social sciences? How does the "material" with which the social sciences work complicate the problem? (Read the following essay *What Life Means—an Answer in Nature* for a partial answer.) Do you think that sociology, let us say, can ever be an *exact* science?
2. Man is an emotional, as well as a reasonable, animal. Is he more likely to be actuated by what he scientifically knows or by what he emotionally feels? Do you think there is even an approximate solution for the problems which man faces?

III

1. Do you consider the introductory paragraph of this essay effective? What device has the author used to catch the interest of

the reader at the very beginning? From our observation of various beginnings, can you formulate any ideas about how to start your own compositions in an attention-catching manner? Unless you are a genius—there have been only a few since the world began—the way to learn to write is to *observe*.

2. From what area of human activity does the phrase "accessories after the fact" come? What is its original meaning? What is its applied meaning in this essay?

3. Do you think the lines from Tennyson's poem summarize well the profound relationship between Nature and Man and God which the author has pointed out in this essay?

WORDS

What stem has each of the words at the left in common with the words that follow it?

1. astronomy (*1*): aster, disaster, asterisk
2. sociological (*1*): social, associate, dissociate
3. conspicuous (*1*): prospector, speculation, auspicious
4. eliminate (*1*): preliminary, limitation, illimitable
5. achievements (*1*): chief, captain, chef
6. strategy (*2*): stratagem, strategic
7. frailties (*2*): fragile, frangible, fragment
8. prejudice (*2*): judicial, judicious, adjudge
9. egotism (*2*): egotistic, egocentric, egoism
10. sector (*2*): insect, segment, dissect
11. precepts (*2*): accept, preconception, susceptible
12. edicts (*2*): addict, contradict, predict
13. exponent (*3*): compound, expound, propound
14. impetus (*3*): appetite, compete, centripetal
15. superstitious (*3*): obstacle, substance, stable

THEME TOPICS

1. My Favorite Science
2. The Optimism of Science
3. The Scientific Method
4. The Ordered World of Tomorrow
5. Science Will Yet Save the World
6. The Evil Uses of Science
7. Science in Modern War
8. The Beauties of Science
9. Science and Our Social Problems
10. Science and Religion

WHAT LIFE MEANS—AN ANSWER IN NATURE

DONALD CULROSS PEATTIE

BLACK headlines bring Europe and Asia close to every home in America. The thunder of the presses echoes the thunder of cannon, and for men of good-will the shadow of war darkens all that makes life worth living.

But we forget that homo sapiens is not the only animal with a stake in this business of living. We forget the great natural world, all the life of the planet which does not know we are here or is not overjoyed by our presence in it. Speaking of civilization imperiled, we shudder with horror at going back to the beasts' way, without considering the way of the beasts, which is cleanly and reasonable, free of dogmas, ideologies, political hate and religious intolerance.

In a growing tension of fear, we begin to think that it is the end of the world which may be coming. But a million times the world has come like this to Autumn, the planet leaning into the arms of the longer nights, turning the warm cheek of harvest to the languor of Indian Summer noons. And it will happen again, a million times—peace on the farms and plenty in the bin. (*1*)

I do not deny that the headlines, the bulletins, the broadcasts speak of a danger dreadfully real. But it would be well for us all to be reminded of other and more enduring realities, lest we lose fortitude and hope. I for one had had enough of news when I recently took a train from California to New York, and I determined not to let war share my seat with me. All the way across the continent, for three days and nights, I was shut up alone in a compartment, with nothing to look at except all of America.

From *The New York Times Magazine*, October 8, 1939. Copyrighted. Used by permission of The Times Publishing Company and by arrangement with the author.

What I saw was the desert, where the plants struggle bravely for, and somehow find, a living. And I saw the Rockies, which are older than the memory of the most long-ago of wars. And the Great Plains, where the first windbreaks cast the blessing of shade.

Then came the windmills, the big barns, the silos of Kansas, the pleasant farmhouses, the first apple trees, the first hardwoods on the river banks, in the full green glory of Summer's height. Could this be, could it ever have been, "the Dust Bowl"? There had been terrible days then, terrible scenes, death to cattle, ruin for men, immigration, the end of the world—for Kansas. Here, in the gathering dusk, it lay at peace, fertile, rich, undespairing. (2)

From Chicago I went to visit a prairie grove outside the city, where I had spent three years in making a naturalist's intensive study of one square mile of land. I drove out in a car and stepped into the woods, in my city clothes, bringing with me all the mentality and artificiality of a city man.

In five minutes I had lost all that. I was back again in the world that to me seems more real than the harsh man-made world which men like to call reality. I heard the clamor of the crows, warning the woods that one of the not-to-be-trusted two-legged things was coming. A woodchuck dodged back into his hole just where there had been a woodchuck for generations; a big heron rose out of an inmost wood slough and flapped heavily across the trees. I had entered a world where man is only an interruption.

When I had roamed an hour, and filled my mind with the woods, I sat down on a log and began to try to orient my philosophy. A long time I sat with my hands between my knees, looking down at this honest soil just thinking about the millions of beings that inhabit a square foot of it. There are bacteria in it, good soil bacteria causing no pathology, which take the nitrogen out of the air and turn it into nitrates that nourish the grass and the trees. There are others that break up the nitrates and loose them to the air again.

There were earthworms under my feet, penetrating the soil, aërating it, bringing it laboriously to the surface from richer depths. Down there the pine mice had their dwellings and run-ways and hideouts. They eat the bark from the roots of the hawthorns, slowly killing them, so that, from the point of view of a hawthorn tree, and speaking humanly, pine mice must be deplorable. To the owl they are squeaking food, and to one another just fellow-pine mice. Nature has neither conscience nor moralities.

A squirrel scolded at me from overhead. How often I had seen the fox squirrels biting off the tips of the oak buds just when they were tenderest in Spring! True that this damages the oak. But of all afforestation agents the squirrels are the most useful. In burying acorns and forgetting where they hid them they are the best friends of the oaks, and an oak, a fine old burr oak like this one above me, is the friend of man. (3)

But all such moralities are just as man-made as a concrete road. Nature is not to be judged by them; nothing in it is either good or bad. Nature is just living, and it is good to live and to be alive, good enough for any chipmunk or gentian. It is even good to die, since death is a natural part of life. It is a merciful necessity in a world which would only starve and crowd and smother itself if there were no death, no return of the borrowed capital of living matter to the great clearing house of the mold.

It was right to die, here, and good to live, and in every wild-flower there were symmetry and balance; in every scampering quadruped there was the tingling adventure of hour-to-hour existence—felt intensely, thought about never. Toil of the leaves, craft of the carnivorous predator, fertility of the herbivores, bird song at dawn and evening, candid beauty of flowers—they all made sense, struck balance, brought peace to the fagged soul and mind. How good the air smelled here! How high and taut was the arc of the sky!

One square mile of land—not scenically sensational land, not even some sort of wild-life sanctuary, but just a prairie grove—and it was inhabited, I estimate, by a round million of living, breathing, reproducing, dying beings, not counting the useful bacteria, in number beyond all calculation. It had solved for itself the problem that men are finding insoluble—that of supporting itself.

More exactly, men are finding that one country cannot support itself while another ruins its financial digestion by overproduction. The wood knew neither ill. Inexorable laws swung into operation every day to counteract such loss of vital equilibrium. Every problem of living was solved here, and even the wars of the ants disturbed nobody seriously. Probably without these wars there would be too many ants. (4)

But could you transfer the solutions of the little wood to the fierce jungle of human hates and competitions? Men, unfortunately for themselves perhaps, are not beasts. An economist could learn nothing from the most admirable Exhibit A in which there is no money in circulation. A pacifist and a militarist alike can make nothing out of brute creation, where all fighting is either to obtain mates or to take over the enemy bodily for the indispensable purpose of eating him.

There simply aren't any "causes" in Nature, and no organized armies except those of the ants, which, it should be noted, are also civilized beings, with objectives in their wars, like ours, quite ignoble: that is, they fight either to steal the stored wealth or the territory of their rivals, or to make slaves of them.

There is nothing instructive to the criminologist in a domain where each species obeys undeviatingly that pattern of behavior which is law to each species after its kind. What can the moralist find to reform in a world that knows no alcoholism, no drug addiction, no prostitution; where there are no lies told because nobody can speak words, and the one who is stolen from is at fault, not the thief? The brute beasts are little helpful toward their brother man writhing in the coils of his own problems. They have nothing in common with us, except those of them who also love their mates and their children, who toil at their little industries, and die stoically. They have most of our virtues. And few of our vices. (5)

As I sat, looking down at the ground, a wasp came dragging something past my feet. As she tugged at the caterpillar she seemed also to be fighting with it, turning it over, seizing it here and there, hunting apparently for some vulnerable spot.

Presently she found it, and suddenly arched her abdomen and ran her sting into the hapless victim. She injected the paralyzing poison several times, and now, with the prey unable to struggle, she could transport it with some speed. The caterpillar was still too heavy to lift, but the wasp—a beautiful creature with copper-colored wings, steel-blue body and yellow legs—could only make progress by half walking, half fluttering. Her burrow was close at hand, and with horror and admiration I watched her drag the victim, conscious probably, but unable to stir a muscle, into her den. In perhaps a minute the wasp emerged, pulled and pushed and kicked some stones and earth over the entrance, and flew away. In that interval underground she had probably laid her eggs upon the caterpillar. When they hatched they would find their food ready for them. She, the mother, had laid up their provision for them, had done her thoughtless, heartless duty, and was off about her life.

Here was a typical event in Nature, horrifying if you take the grub's point of view; simply instinctive, even devotedly maternal, from the wasp's. In man's interest the deed was a beneficial one, since most caterpillars are destructive to vegetation. But it came to me there that the wasp, herself a frail creature, had but one superior implement in this world—her saber-like sting. With that, and her great eyes, and her fertility, she masters her world, and whatever she does in her world is right. (6)

What is man's one great implement? A gun? Not so. Where will he be when all the iron in the world (the store is finite) is gone? A machine? We may come out on the other side of the machine age, just as we have abandoned every other age of man.

Man has but one supreme weapon and that is his intelligence. It is what Nature gave him to recompense him for a rather frail and disease-susceptible body. Intelligence is his all; and all his woes come from the perversion of it, the failure to use it for the very thing for which it is intended—to look ahead and see the consequences of his acts. The hope of man is man—who has so far been his own despair.

I looked at my watch. It was time to be going, and I began to hunt for the wood path that would lead me to the road, that would take me to the car, that would hie me to the train that was to bring me to New York. Intelligence has made all those roads. Intelligence would bring the train in on time, would serve me in a hotel, would meet me in my business conferences and take me back to California.

In Nature is found no comparable intelligence, only a dim groping of reason, at best. In my prairie woods, instinct is the greater law, and its ruling is inexorable. Yet still the thoughtful turn back now and again, not only to escape the confusion of the world they have made themselves, but to rediscover old certainties. (7)

Nature is more than a refuge in times of acute distress, more than fresh air for smoke-filled lungs, more than quietude for ears in torture. Nature is the common way of living, and as such it is our touchstone.

The birds in the leaves, the snake under the stone, the spider running zigzag down her shining orb web, are all bound to the same struggle to which we are captive. Our hungers, however we dress them or hide them, are one with their simple hungers. Like them, we strive and suffer in a blind loyalty to the futurity of the race. In the enormous complex of beast, man, plant, insect, fish and blind worm, the detail is infinite. But the underlying great principles are the same for all of us.

And in the wood our brothers do not question. Yet they answer our question. The cotton-tail dashing from the weasel in great heart-bursting bounds of terror, the turtle sunning himself on a log, the thrush at evening, turned toward sunset, letting fall his pure syllables of praise—all these affirm that life is worth the living.

For them the wood is a harsh world, despite the peace that we find in it. The cornered shrew cannot escape the owl's talons. The kinglet is left by a butcher bird to dangle on a thorn, his torn feathers blowing in the soft Autumn breeze. The woods are not peaceful to those for whom the leafy places are life's battleground. Yet for the precious gift of life every creature there will fight to the last breath in him. They all know that life is hard, and, as dumbly and fiercely they proclaim, by their devotion to it and its laws, that life is good.

Yet they must live it out, with all its pains and struggle, without that great hope which has been vouchsafed almost uniquely to our species. This is the concept of coöperation, of brotherhood, of civilization. True that we bungle it daily, horribly. And Nature cannot help us—not directly. We are too strong, and too spoiled, for that.

But we should do well to heed her testimony. All the non-human rest of the animal world pursues its difficult and danger-ous course without despair. The plants seize light's primal energy and turn it to their peaceful uses, as they have done since before our day and will continue to do, whatever wars we wage.

In the Autumn sunlight is an impartial ripening kindness; in the first Autumn wind is a quickening inspiration for all. Daily the headlines cry their threats and disasters, but he who dis-covers once again in Nature the universal love of living can go forward into our stormy world with a better courage and some of Nature's eternal and indestructible peace in his heart. (8)

QUESTIONS

I

1. What is the author's opinion of the beasts' way of life? of war's bringing finality to life? (1)
2. What is the effect on the spirit of viewing great natural phe-nomena like the desert, the Rockies, and the Great Plains? (2)
3. What can man learn from the life cycle of wild animals? What makes the laws of animal living so much simpler than those governing human life? (3-5)
4. What is the lesson in the incident of the wasp and the cater-pillar? (6)
5. What is man's one supreme weapon? How is it both his greatest strength and his greatest weakness? (7)
6. What proof do we find in Nature that "life is good"? (8)

II

1. Mr. Peattie's thesis is that human beings can learn from Nature "the universal love of living" which will fortify us to endure the vicissitudes of living in a warring world. Have you found such assurance on a walk in the country, a day in the woods or along a stream? Can you analyze the feelings such an ex-perience brought you?
2. If man's intelligence is his supreme weapon, how must he change his use of that intelligence to assure himself satisfactory life on this planet? Why has man's intelligence failed to eliminate war from his group life?

3. Comment upon the philosophical truth of the following statements: "Nature has neither conscience nor moralities" (3); "Death [is the] return of the borrowed capital of living matter to the great clearing house of the mold" (4); "Nature is the common way of living, and as such it is our touchstone" (8).

III

1. What device does the author of this essay use to catch attention in the very first sentence? (1)
2. Point out several of the best descriptive passages in this essay. Note also some of the figures of speech. Can you analyze what makes Mr. Peattie's style of writing so pleasing to the reader?

WORDS

Choose from the second column the correct synonym for each word in the left-hand column.

1. imperiled (1)	1. motherly
2. dogmas (1)	2. preyer
3. ideologies (1)	3. unworthy
4. languor (1)	4. first
5. fortitude (2)	5. bravery
6. orient (3)	6. requite
7. symmetry (4)	7. unknowable
8. carnivorous (4)	8. woundable
9. predator (4)	9. relentless
10. herbivores (4)	10. adjust (oneself)
11. taut (4)	11. endangered
12. insoluble (4)	12. vegetable-eaters
13. ignoble (5)	13. guaranteed
14. undeviatingly (5)	14. unswervingly
15. vulnerable (6)	15. theories
16. maternal (6)	16. balance
17. recompense (7)	17. tenets
18. inexorable (7)	18. flesh-eating
19. vouchsafed (8)	19. lassitude
20. primal (8)	20. tight

THEME TOPICS

1. Pleasures of an Amateur Naturalist
2. My Favorite Birds
3. An Insect Battle I Once Observed
4. What I Have Learned from Animals

5. Snakes (Spiders, Centipedes): Man's Coöperating Friends
6. Intelligence—Man's Supreme Weapon
7. Instinct—the Law of Animal Life
8. Nature Knows No Moral Laws
9. The Simple Life Is Best
10. Nature and Religion

OUR WIDENING AMERICAN CULTURE

FREDERICK LEWIS ALLEN

UNDER pressure of more dramatic affairs, we Americans are, I believe, failing to notice a salient—and cheerful—fact about our country: the flowering, or at least the budding, of an American culture of which we may well be proud.

This flowering is unlike any previous one in history. We must not expect to see duplicated here what happened in the Athens of Pericles or the Florence of the Medici, or, for that matter, in nineteenth century England or France. For the essence of what is happening in America is that it is new, that it takes unprecedented forms, and that it is manifold.

I realize that anybody who speaks in such terms as these may seem to be—in the expressive phrase of the day—sticking his neck out. In the American culture of 1940 one can find plenty of evidences of undisciplined or corrupt taste. Listen to some of our radio programs; read the concentrated pap which passes for fiction in many of our magazines for the millions; sit through some of the Class B pictures at the movies; or look at the monotonous suburban developments and devastated regions which lie at the edges of our American cities, and you may well wonder what in heaven's name I am talking about.

Nevertheless I stand by my guns. I think this country is making cultural progress in a new and exciting way. (*1*)

To most people "culture" may suggest a gentleman sitting in his library with a volume of Montaigne in his hand, a glass of old port at his elbow, and a quotation from the original Greek on his lips—familiarity with, and appreciation of, old and tested things. But culture may also mean the natural feeling for beauty that went into the building of old New England houses and Pennsylvania barns—a sense of order and graciousness, whether cultivated or instinctive, and whether accompanied by wide learning or not. And any culture is sterile which is not animated by the creative impulse. The periods which we think of as the great flowerings of culture were periods not merely of appreciation but, preëminently, of production; indeed, any culture is sterile which is not animated by the devouring curiosity of the discoverer and the fierce energy of the experimenter.

In these latter aspects American culture is showing special progress. Whereas no other cultural flowering in history has involved more than a small fraction of the population, today millions of Americans are becoming more sensitive to beauty, and in them creative energy is stirring. (2)

Look, for example, at music—from that same radio that brings us so much shoddy entertainment. Toscanini's weekly symphony concert is enjoyed by an audience of four and a half million. It would take 60 Yale Bowls to seat this astronomical number of listeners. Walter Damrosch's NBC music appreciation hour is heard each week by several million. Have any such opportunities for the masses to hear good music ever before existed—and been taken advantage of? And it has all come about in the past 15 years. Incidentally, the highly intelligent "Information Please," which recently won an award by *The Saturday Review of Literature* for distinguished service to American literature, is said to be heard by 12,000,000 members of that radio public which we used to be told had 13-year-old minds!

Participation in the *making* of music has sharply increased, too, even though the piano is no longer a standard household ornament. Note some 35,000 school orchestras. Note how many of our school and college glee clubs have become choruses singing fine music. Recently I heard the madrigal club of a small West Virginia college lead off, not with "The Bullfrog on the Bank," standard for 30 years ago, but with the classic chants of Palestrina. The extraordinary growth of such institutions as the Berkshire Music Festival is another agreeable sign of our musical times.

Next, consider reading. It is true that book sales have shown little increase during the past generation. But there can be small doubt that the books which now sell most widely represent, on the average, a considerably higher level of quality. There is a world of difference between the solid fiber of John Steinbeck's *The Grapes of Wrath* (the leading fiction best-seller of 1939) and the sentimental gush of Florence Barclay's *The Rosary* (which topped the lists in 1910 and 1911, against stiff competition by Harold Bell Wright's *The Winning of Barbara Worth*). We must remember, too, that the book as a form of entertainment must now compete with the radio and the movies; while the book-reading public is now underpinned—and presumably reduced—by a gigantic magazine-reading public.

Fifty years ago there was not a single magazine in the United States with a circulation of a million. Now there are twenty-six. Many of the most popular periodicals are full of literary marshmallows and shy at ideas which might possibly offend a perceptible number of readers or advertisers; yet I think it is safe to say that if we take these magazines as a group, and think how many good things are to be found in them, they offer a creditable exhibit of mass reading. There has been nothing in Europe to compare with this vast magazine public; and those European magazines which have long been famous for their high quality—such, for instance, as *Punch*—have had tiny audiences by any American standards.

Turn to the fine arts. Popular magazines like *Life* are now reproducing paintings by old masters and contemporary Americans. *A Treasury of Art Masterpieces* (price $10) is a recent best-seller. There has been a notable increase in the sale of good color reproductions of masterpieces for home decoration. Our museums are becoming active agencies for adult education, and their turnstiles are clicking. The recent Picasso exhibit at New York's Museum of Modern Art was attended by 99,503 people during its fifty-one days; the Italian masters, at the same museum, were seen in seventy-three days by 277,794 people—an astonishing record.

Remarkable, too, is the growth in educational opportunity. If many of our universities have elephantiasis—and also footballitis—this is because the number of students in American colleges and universities has increased tenfold since 1900. The inspiring fact that millions of Americans have wanted a higher education for their children has put a heavier load on the educational machinery than it could carry without creaking here and there. Yet our professional schools have been strikingly improved; American medical education, for example, has been revolutionized for the better in the past fifty years. And those new patrons of education and science, the great foundations, are contributing hundreds of millions both to lift the standards of teaching and research and to seek out young talent and give it the chance it deserves. I have heard it stated, by people who should know, that there is now small chance that any young man of authentic scientific genius, whether in Pennsylvania, Georgia, or South Dakota, will go unassisted if he needs assistance.

Do not forget what the WPA has done for men who had not sold a picture for years—and were given postoffice murals to paint; for half-starved musicians who found themselves playing to big audiences in WPA orchestras. Call this boondoggling if you will; but does it not represent a new conception of the responsibility of the public to see that potential artists have a chance to be artists, no matter what their circumstances?

Yes, the democratic base of our culture has been widened. (3)

I should also like to remind you how many new arts have sprung up beside the seven arts of tradition. Let us forget for a moment the traditional assumption that one measures the state of a culture chiefly in terms of such familiar vehicles as books, plays, paintings, sculpture, architecture, and music. Let us assume that other vehicles may offer a means of expressing the impulse to create and enjoy beauty, and let us look about us.

New arts? One thinks immediately of the movies, which after a long period of high technical competence and singular evasion of reality are now showing signs of growing up: witness that documentary masterpiece, "The River," and such recent pictures as "Rebecca," "The Grapes of Wrath," and "Wuthering Heights." One thinks with even more assurance of that remarkable subdivision of the movies, the animated cartoon drama, realizing that in Disney we have an artist using a medium which hardly existed twenty years ago.

Note the remarkable increase of interest in photography; hundreds of thousands of people, old and young, are taking pictures —and developing them in their own darkrooms, in the true spirit of the amateur in the arts.

Drive over the magnificent parkways in the outskirts of our cities, and see how engineer and landscape architect have joined hands to create majestic avenues in peculiarly 20th-century style. Look at our new bridges and dams, works of art as well as of utility. Is there any one of us who looks at, let us say, the George Washington Bridge without a lift of the heart at the extraordinary beauty, especially at night when the great sweep of its cables is picked out with lights?

To look at some of the photographs in Walter Dorwin Teague's new book, *Design This Day* (such as the pictures of New York's Bronx-Whitestone Bridge, with its clean, undecorated, soaring arches, or of a new Texaco gas station) is to feel that this is the sort of thing we Americans do best, this is where our own peculiar genius has full play.

Do not the incredible effects achieved in lighting the New York World's Fair demonstrate the exciting possibilities of another virtually new art—that of lighting with color?

Think of the strides made in applying the principles of functional design. No automobile manufacturer decides upon his new model nowadays without anxious consideration of the way purchasers will react to the grace and sweep of its lines. And I wonder if until the past decade a designer ever planned a railroad train as a harmonious unit, as some new streamliners were planned.

Note the gay use of color in the equipment of a modern kitchen. Look at some of Frank Lloyd Wright's or Albert Kahn's factories; why, even factories and their machinery—or the best of Woolworth's glassware—are being built as if intended to be looked at! The packaging of goods has been revolutionized. Little by little we are re-learning that useful things can be beautiful, learning that millions of people like them to be beautiful. Pull out a pile of magazines of twenty years ago and lay them beside their counterparts of today; in type and format the advance has been remarkable. Their improvement has extended to books and even to the designing of letterheads; if you occasionally receive, as I do, a letter from an office which has not changed its letterheads within the memory of the oldest employee, you will wonder who could ever have hit upon such an absurd combination of discordant types.

We see, too, the beginnings of an art essentially new to America in town and regional planning. The overall design in New York's Rockefeller Center and our beginning attempts—as at Radburn, New Jersey—to lay out villages on new patterns for the motor age are steps toward the development of new techniques for harmonizing and rationalizing the work of architects, landscape architects, engineers, and what we might call social engineers. Contrast the ramshackle hodgepodge of old-style amusement parks with the efficient beauty of Jones Beach, Long Island, where 100,000 people may park their cars and bathe and picnic without traffic jams or overcrowding and, miraculously, without littering the oceanside!

I live in New York near an avenue of department stores whose windows provide an ever-changing spectacle of bold patterns in color and light and ingenious, imaginative compositions; and as I stroll up this avenue at night, I notice how many other strollers are enjoying the show as one might enjoy a visit to a gay museum. A generation ago nobody dreamed of arranging the round-eyed manikins in shop-windows with an eye to color harmonies and compositional effects.

It never occurs to most people who revel in the shopwindow effects of 1940 that they are rendering art judgments. They think they are outside the sacred enclosure of the arts. But they are inside it all the time. For the fences have been moved. (4)

Very rapidly we Americans are getting away from the Colonial attitude. Already it is a long time since we took it for granted that American novels should be respectable imitations of the best English works. It is several years since most of our literary emigrés returned from Montparnasse to discover that America was a good place to write in and about. Now we know we have our own traditions in a literary sense, we are grown up. And we are beginning, too, to be far less subservient in other arts. If we still make pseudo-Venetian furniture in Grand Rapids, still design bank buildings to look like Parthenons, we are apparently approaching the end of this phase. Our new streamlined trains are not Byzantine, or Louis XV, or Dutch Colonial.

I do not say that this national cultural independence is wholly good. The classicist will hasten to remind us that there is little to be gained by throwing away the past—and of course he is right. And we want no tariff walls against the best modern products of foreign civilizations. Our American culture must not try to walk alone, without benefit of the past or of the contributions of its neighbors. Yet what is to grow in our soil must be what is adapted to that soil. We may compare, we may learn, but I am glad we are coming to build for ourselves. For that is the only way in which anyone can build greatly.

One closing word: If I have said little about the peaks of our cultural landscape, if I have dodged the question whether our finest products in arts and letters are better today than they used to be, or better than they are elsewhere, this, I must confess, is because I would prefer to dodge a question on which there would inevitably be endless wrangling. One may be conscious, as one drives across country, that one is climbing on to rising ground, and yet lack the surveyor's instruments to judge the precise altitude of the surrounding summits. I prefer to focus your attention upon the undeniable groundswell of the land all about us.

Whether or not the very finest things that we produce are better than they used to be, we Americans are a distinctly more mature people, a more culturally enlightened people, than we were a generation ago; and we appear to be better off for the participation of the millions in cultural things that were once considered chiefly the affair of the few.

Whenever I hear anybody lamenting a supposed lack of authentic contemporary American masterpieces, I am tempted to quote to him those familiar lines of Arthur Hugh Clough's:

> In front the sun climbs slow, how slowly!
> But westward, look, the land is bright! (5)

QUESTIONS

I

1. In what way is the flowering of American culture different from the great cultures of the past? What are the most obvious examples of "undisciplined or corrupt taste" to be found in the American scene today? (*1*)
2. What do most people think of when "culture" is mentioned? What is Mr. Allen's broader meaning for the word? (*2*)
3. What evidence is there of advancement in music, reading, and education? (*3*)
4. What new arts and interests in culture are growing up in America? (*4*)
5. In what way are we showing our independence in culture? What dangers are there of our developing too great independence in our national culture? How has the base of American culture broadened? (*5*)

II

1. Can you advance, from personal observation, evidence for the truth of the following statement: "Today millions of Americans are becoming more sensitive to beauty, and in them creative energy is stirring"?
2. Do you think regional and town planning will increase in the America of tomorrow? What is the field of the "social engineer"?
3. Mr. Allen's thesis is that millions of Americans are now inside "the sacred enclosure of the arts" and that they are rendering art judgments all the time without knowing it because "the fences have been moved." Do you accept the thesis?

III

1. How does Mr. Allen apologize for writing "sticking his neck out"? (*1*) What does he mean by the expression "literary marshmallows"? (*3*) From what field does "elephantiasis" come, and what is the humor of Mr. Allen's use of it here? (*3*)
2. Point out several of the best figures of speech in the essay.
3. Point out some of the best bits of satirical humor which lighten the style of the essay.

WORDS

Explain the meaning of each word in the left-hand column as it is used in the activity, art, study, etc., given in the right-hand column.

1. salient (*1*)
2. sterile (*2*)
3. animated (*2*)
4. astronomical (*3*)
5. murals (*3*)
6. functional (*4*)
7. format (*4*)
8. rationalizing (*4*)
9. compositional (*4*)
10. *emigrés* (*5*)

1. military fortifications
2. biology
3. cartoons
4. time or figures
5. painting
6. medicine
7. book-making
8. psychology
9. fine arts
10. citizenship

THEME TOPICS

1. I Listen to the Symphony (Opera)
2. I Prefer Popular Music
3. The Dance Band I Like Best
4. My Favorite Radio Program (Magazine, Novelist)
5. Useful Things Can Be Beautiful
6. Design in Buildings (Clothes, Automobiles, Packaging)
7. Color in Electrical Displays (Show Windows, Modern Kitchens)
8. An "Eye-Sore" in My Home Town (humor by exaggeration)
9. Ye Little Gift Shoppe (satire on pseudo-culture)
10. "Culture" in My Christmas Presents (humorous)

Some Things to Think About

FIRE ALWAYS MAKES ROOM FOR ITSELF

W. H. COWLEY

I TAKE for the text of this convocation address an old Japanese proverb which reads: "Fire always makes room for itself." We are today witnessing a calamitous demonstration of the truth of that proverb. London is in danger of being destroyed, not because of the battering of demolition bombs but rather because of the fires caused by incendiary bombs. Since fire always makes room for itself, the London fire-fighters must control the huge blazes being lit every night by raiding airplanes or London is doomed.

I cite the danger of fire in London to illustrate the soundness of the Japanese proverb and to apply it to the relationship of education to the crisis we face in America and throughout the world. My thesis is that colleges and universities must rededicate themselves to nurture the fire of the spirit else we shall not be equal to the tremendous responsibilities which the world situation has catapulted upon us. Fire always makes room for itself, be it a physical or an emotional fire. In democratic countries we are staring into catastrophe because our emotional fire has been but a flicker compared with the huge flame of sulphuric energy which has been bursting forth from the totalitarians. Unless we become aroused as they have been aroused, we shall most certainly be enslaved by them, and we shall see the Anglo-Saxon tradition of freedom chained if not slaughtered outright. (*1*)

The problem of emotional fire in the crisis we face has numerous facets, and it is possible to discuss but one of them. I devote myself, therefore, to the relationship of educational philosophy to our national welfare. I begin by making what may seem to many of you to be a brash statement. It is this: a large share of the spiritual and emotional poverty which has characterized American life in recent decades is the direct result of misconceived and destructive educational doctrines. In colleges and universities we have been following false gods, and because of our adherence to them we have almost smothered the fire that should give education its heat and power, its light and its leading.

One doctrine has in particular been crippling us: the doctrine of intellectualism. In my judgment we must cut our colleges and universities free of this false educational concept or as a nation we shall sink into insignificance if not into slavery.

Intellectualism is the concept which asserts that education is concerned only with the intellectual development of students, and that social, physical, emotional, and spiritual education should be left to other institutions—to the boy scouts, the Sunday School, the church, and the junior league. This doctrine is widely held by college professors, and the president of one of our great universities has achieved national prominence in recent years by espousing it with all the power of his potent pen and with all the force of his platform skill. (2)

May I begin an analysis of intellectualism with some history? Until the time of the Civil War American colleges followed the British educational tradition and sought to educate the whole student. Educators were interested in the student's mind, of course, but also in his morals, in his manners, in his religion, and in his sense of values—indeed in everything that contributed to a complete or a whole education. During the middle of the last century this concept of education began to be abandoned. America had been changing from an agricultural and maritime to an industrial society. It needed trained engineers, agriculturalists, architects, chemists and dozens of other varieties of professional and business men for whom the old-time college provided no training. Obviously, a new type of higher education had to be provided; and since England offered no models, educators turned to Germany, which had developed broader curriculums and a new variety of university, a university devoted to intensive specialization in all the modern arts and sciences.

The adoption of German methods by such leading educators as President Eliot of Harvard, President White of Cornell, and

President Gilman of Johns Hopkins produced a growth and development in higher education of tremendous importance. The reorganized universities and the newly-established technical and professional schools, which these leaders of 19th century education and their associates headed, trained the men and women to build the nation's railroads, exploit its mines, ferret out the basic physical and chemical facts upon which modern industry is built. They also trained more and better-trained lawyers, physicians, engineers, and professional and business men of all kinds. Because they looked to Germany and followed its educational example, America met the opportunities of the 19th century and grew in wealth and strength beyond the wildest dreams of former generations.

But this material development is not the whole story. The ten thousand Americans who between 1850 and 1940 returned from Europe with German Ph.D.'s brought back with them something else besides preëminent skill as specialists. They brought intellectualism, and they saddled it upon the American college. German universities, after the crushing defeat that Napoleon administered to their fatherland early in the century, threw overboard all interest in students as individuals. They sought to raise a race of intellectual supermen, and they consciously concentrated all their energies upon the minds of students. What a student did between the time he matriculated and the time he took his examinations, no one in German universities knew or cared. Where he lived, the condition of his health, his social life, his physical and spiritual growth—these were of no interest to the German academic authorities. They considered their job to be the training of superior minds, and they conducted their universities as if nothing else counted.

This is the doctrine that German-trained professors brought back to the United States, that they foisted upon the American college, that they promoted until we tossed into the discard the tradition of wholeness and completeness that Anglo-Saxon educators had cherished for centuries. Germany has made a huge contribution to the intellectual education of America, but for this help we have paid a staggering price. Impelled by German examples we have stressed the training of the minds of students, and we have fallen into the calamitous error of assuming that the intellect dominates life, that the intellect is our chief personal and social instrument, that the intellect is the only concern of education. (*3*)

Merely to state the doctrine of intellectualism constitutes a refutation of it, but I should like to discuss three of the major arguments against it. So strong is the hold which intellectualism has upon us that its fallacies cannot too often be exposed nor too frequently ridiculed.

The first argument comes from biology. After a century of amazingly illuminating research biologists have arrived at a new and far-reaching generalization, a new orientation. Historically biologists concentrated their attention upon discernible differences in the *parts* of organisms and the functioning of these *parts*. Recently, however, a growing number of biologists have asserted that *parts* must be seen in relationship to *the whole organism*. Thus they hold that it is impossible to understand the functioning of, say the lungs, except in relationship to the sympathetic nervous system, and indeed, to every other part of the organism. This point of view is called organismic or holistic biology. John Scott Holdame, eminent British biologist, describes it in these words:

> The organism maintains itself as a whole. It is not a mere federation of individual cells acting mechanically like a machine, but is, on the contrary, a closely unified organization whose nature is such that each part or even each cell partakes of and contributes to the life of the whole. The behavior of an individual cell is unintelligible apart from its being also an expression of the life of the higher organism as a whole. The individual cells as such express in their genesis, behaviour, and deaths, the life of the whole organism.

The bearing of this observation upon intellectualism is obvious: the mind cannot—except in the laboratory—be abstracted from the rest of an organism. Educators cannot wisely, therefore, devote all their energies to the minds of students and neglect their bodies, their social development, their systems of values, their spirits. Such a concept of education is biologically ridiculous. American higher education, largely controlled during the past seventy years by intellectualists, has remarkably multiplied our intellectual and our material resources; but because it has frowned upon and neglected all objectives except the development of the intellect, we have become impoverished in all other directions—particularly in emotion and spirit.

This statement sets up the second count against intellectualism: the time-honored philosophical and psychological postulate that the intellect is never the master of the spirit but always its servant —in brief, that the mind takes its direction and its energy not from within itself, but from the purposes and systems of values of the entity which we call the Self. Thirty years ago in a powerful address Woodrow Wilson dramatically expressed this judgment in these words:

We speak of this as an age in which mind is monarch, but I take it for granted that, if that is true, mind is one of those modern monarchs who reign but do not govern. As a matter of fact, the world is governed in every generation by a great House of Commons made up of the passions; and we can only be careful to see that the handsome passions are in the majority.

Woodrow Wilson's epigram that "the world is governed by the passions" checks with everyone's commonsense interpretation of his own experience. Attitudes, sentiments, values, purposes— these are the controlling factors in the behavior of us all. The fact is admitted by everyone except the professors and administrators who have been blinded by intellectualism. We shall equate education with reality only when we take President Wilson's advice and rededicate education to the task of seeing that "the handsome passions are in the majority." That is the supreme task of education, not the training of students' minds.

May I make it entirely clear that I am not being critical of intellectual development. Indeed, colleges and universities must be the place *par excellence* in our society for the highest intellectual achievement. I give way to no one in my insistence that the college has failed if it does not effectively train the minds of the students. I insist, however, that we must go a great deal further, that we must recognize that intelligence is not enough, that men are not mere thinking machines, and that to train the minds of students and to neglect their spirit is to give them stones for the bread they seek.

The distinction which the intellectualists make between the intellect and the emotions throws into relief the third of the three arguments against their doctrine of which I would speak. The first argument stems from biology, the second from philosophy and psychology, and this third comes from logic. The intellectualists have fallen into error which logicians call the disjunctive fallacy and which laymen call the either-or fallacy. Thus intellectualists assert that education must be one thing or the other —intellectual or anti-intellectual. This is a splendid example of the crooked thinking produced by the disjunctive fallacy. It's like asserting that all men are either tall or short, fat or thin, black or white, good or bad, brilliant or stupid, charming or gauche, egotistic or modest, etc., etc.

It would seem to be impossible for any intelligent individual to fall into the clutches of this fallacy, but the fact is that the intellectualists have done exactly that. They say in effect that colleges must devote their energies entirely to the intellectual development of students and that it is impossible—or at least undesirable—to give time and thought to student social life, to athletics, to the persistent problem of personal purposes and values which every college student faces. In a word, they assert that the college must concentrate all of its attention upon intellectual training or else become a mere country club. They insist that the college must be either tall or short: tall and intellectual or short and country clubbish. They admit no possibility of a middle ground where the whole student is educated—socially as well as intellectually, in spirit as well as in a professional specialty.

It would be interesting to explore the implications of this disjunction as it affects fraternities, athletic teams, and student life in general. I prefer, however, to discuss a much larger question: the bearing of intellectualism upon the spirit, upon the spirit of faculty members and therefore upon the spirit of students. (4)

In his brilliant address given before the American Philosophical Society last spring one of our outstanding American poets, Archibald MacLeish, deplores the disappearance of fire, of passion, and of broad social purpose from among college professors, scholars, and writers. He entitled his address "The Irresponsibles" and described and criticized them in this passage:

The irresponsibility of the scholar is the irresponsibility of the scientist upon whose laboratory insulation he has patterned all his work. The scholar in letters has made himself as indifferent to values, as careless of significance, as bored with meanings as the chemist. He is a refugee from consequences, an exile from the responsibilities of moral choice. His words of praise are the laboratory words—objectivity, detachment, dispassion. His pride is to be scientific, neuter, skeptical, detached—superior to final judgment or absolute belief....

It is not for nothing that the modern scholar invented the Ph.D. thesis as his principal contribution to literary form. The Ph.D. thesis is the perfect image of his world. It is work done for the sake of doing work—perfectly conscientious, perfectly laborious, perfectly irresponsible. The modern scholar at his best and worst is both these things—perfectly conscientious, laborious, and competent: perfectly irresponsible for the saving of his world.... He has his work to do. He has his book to finish. He hopes the war will not destroy the manuscripts he works with. He is the pure, the perfect type of irresponsibility—the man who acts as though fire could not burn him because he has no business with the fire. He knows, because he cannot help but know, reading his papers, talking to his friends—he knows this fire has consumed the books, the spirit, everything he lives by, flesh itself, in other countries. He knows this but he will not know. It's not his business. Whose business is it then? He will not answer even that. He has his work to do. He has his book to finish.

This is as pointed an indictment of intellectualism as anyone has written since Tennyson in 1830 deplored the spiritual and emotional poverty that had come to dominate Cambridge, his Alma Mater. The verse Tennyson wrote is perhaps an even more stinging rebuke. Here it is:

Therefore, your halls, your ancient colleges,
Your portals statued with old kings and queens,
Your gardens, myriad-volumed libraries,
Waxed-lighted chapels, and rich carven screens,
Your doctors, and your proctors, and your deans,
Shall not avail you, when the day-beam sports
New-risen o'er awakened Albion—No!
Nor yet your solemn organ pipes that blow
Melodious thunders thro' your vacant courts
At noon and eve: because your manner sorts
Not of this age, wherefrom ye stand apart,
Because the lips of little children preach
Against you, you that do profess to teach
And teach us nothing, feeding not the heart.

Because the great majority of men and women who teach in our colleges and universities are consciously or subconsciously giving their allegiance to intellectualism, we have fallen into the bog of irresponsibility which MacLeish deplores. In Tennyson's words we are not feeding the hearts of our students. We are feeding their minds, but we ignore their spirits, their passions, their latent fire. (5)

Thus intellectualism has crippled us not only educationally but also in our national life. For decades we have been graduating young men and women who have been taught to look at everything intellectually, to be objective, to weigh all the evidence, to see both sides of every question, to be supercritical, to hold judgments in abeyance. This is all very well in the abstractions of science, but where the values of our civilization are at stake, it is criminally destructive. It has made of us a skeptical if not a cynical people. It has lulled us into a false impartiality. It has made us apathetic about our heritages of democracy, of freedom of speech and of the press. It has driven us individually and collectively into a selfish hunt for security. In brief, it has deprived us of emotion, of enthusiasm, of national spirit and passion.

It would obviously be an over-simplification to lay our current spiritual poverty entirely at the door of intellectualism, but that intellectualism has played a large part there can be no question. It has made of us spiritual neutrals in a world where everything we cherish is being viciously attacked. If we continue in this frame of mind we'll soon be ripe either for subjection by passionate Nazism or by some native leader who will make capital of our spiritual starvation and lead us to God-knows-what extremes of uncontrolled emotional debauch. That is exactly what has happened in Germany. Hitler succeeded in enlisting the enthusiasm and the devotion of German university students to his hooked-cross banner because they were fed up with the bloodless objectivity of German professors, and in a few short years Germany swung from the extreme of intellectual objectivity to the opposite extreme of emotional drunkenness. The same fate awaits us unless we achieve a balance between intelligence and spirit. Neither can be neglected. We must have both. We must denounce and renounce the coldness of reason alone and the hotness of passion alone. Unless in our colleges and our universities and in our national life we reaffirm and reëstablish the place of spirit, we shall sink to a shadow of our powers. We must temper spirit with reason, of course, but we must disavow the intellectualistic doctrine that reason is sufficient. Instead we must give the place of honor to the driving force of spirit without which intelligence drugs us into torpor and emotional impotence.

Because of the inroads that intellectualism has made, the world situation which threatens our national life comes in the nick of time to save us from spiritual atrophy. Once again we have national cohesion, a consuming enthusiasm, a great passion to unite us. It will purge us of our impurities and reinfuse spirit into our cold, intellectualistic hearts. We shall pay a large price in wealth and perhaps in lives. If such sacrifices will reëstablish our national spirit and kill off intellectualism, the price will not be too great.

The future of the country will soon be in the hands of the young men and women who are students in our colleges during these present years. We are a great and wealthy people in things material. Whether or not it is great and wealthy in things spiritual depends upon you. Thomas Huxley expressed the situation clearly when he came to this country in 1876 to speak at the founding of Johns Hopkins University. This is what he said:

I cannot say that I am in the slightest degree impressed by your bigness, or your material resources as such. Size is not grandeur, and territory does not make a nation. The great issue, about which hangs a true sublimity and the terror of an overhanging fate, is what you are going to do with all these things.

"What are you going to do with all these things?" This is the question which faces the nation and every college man and woman. It cannot be answered in intellectual terms alone. It must be answered in terms of spirit. It must be answered by our response to the challenge that totalitarianism has thrown at us. Fire always makes room for itself. We shall be equal to the challenge only if we fight the fire of the dictators with a greater and more powerful fire burning in each of us—a fire consecrated to the protection of the Anglo-Saxon tradition both in government and in education. (6)

QUESTIONS

I

1. How does our "emotional fire" compare to that in totalitarian countries? (1)
2. What concept of education, according to the author, has been crippling us? (2)
3. Why did American educators in the nineteenth century turn to the German universities? What (both good and bad) did the fostering of this type of education do in the United States? (3)
4. What is the "biological argument" against intellectualism? What is the philosophical and psychological view of the relation of the mind to the spirit or soul—"the entity which we call the Self"? What is the "disjunctive fallacy" and how has its "crooked thinking" been detrimental to education? (4)
5. What is the gist of Mr. Archibald MacLeish's attack upon American scholars and writers in his address called "The Irresponsibles"? Which line of the Tennyson quotation is the most "stinging rebuke" to the intellectuals? (5)
6. What has been the effect upon democracy of too much intellectualism in education? What must we add to our education to make it sound? (6)

II

1. Do you think colleges should concern themselves with more than the intellects of their students? Some of our universities have been called "intellectually solvent, morally bankrupt." What do you think of such a statement?
2. What part do you think emotions play in your life? Do they control your life more than your intellect, as Woodrow Wilson says they do? (4) What do you understand by the "handsome passions"?
3. Mr. Cowley says that Hitler was possible because German youth was emotionally starved. Do you think there is danger of our going on an "uncontrolled emotional debauch"?
4. In your opinion, how much of youth's so-called "wildness" may be attributed to the starvation of the nobler emotions?
5. Do you know college or university teachers who may be called "irresponsible" because they too narrowly appeal only to the *minds* of their students? who are too "busy" to take any real interest in you?

6. What type of educational institution in America, in your opinion, is doing most to "feed the spirit" in teaching its students? Is there any danger that such institutions will coddle their students too much? become educational "country clubs"?

7. Mr. Cowley, who is the president of Hamilton College, believes that intellectualism has crippled our American education by quenching its passionate zeal for all-around human improvement. How completely do you agree with him?

III

1. At what point in this essay does the author first state his main thesis? What is the last sentence of the introduction of this essay?

2. Quotations may be dragged in or they may belong so inherently in a piece of writing that their introduction has been called an "art." How do you classify Mr. Cowley's quotations?

3. It has been said that the truth of an idea "may be gauged by the objection raised to it." Discuss Mr. Cowley's address from this point of view.

WORDS

First, determine all the words in this list which you are *sure* you know. For those of which you are uncertain, turn to the place in the essay in which the word is used and see whether you can ascertain its meaning from the context. Finally, look up those words the meanings of which you are certain you do not know. This is the correct procedure in learning words: never turn to a dictionary until you have tried to learn the meaning of a word yourself. Too ready dependence upon the dictionary does not lead to word-mastery.

1. calamitous (*1*)	10. maritime (*3*)	19. gauche (*4*)
2. demolition (*1*)	11. foisted (*3*)	20. insulation (*5*)
3. incendiary (*1*)	12. fallacies (*4*)	21. dispassion (*5*)
4. nurture (*1*)	13. orientation (*4*)	22. latent (*5*)
5. catapulted (*1*)	14. organismic (*4*)	23. abeyance (*6*)
6. facets (*2*)	15. holistic (*4*)	24. apathetic (*6*)
7. brash (*2*)	16. postulate (*4*)	25. debauch (*6*)
8. espousing (*2*)	17. entity (*4*)	26. torpor (*6*)
9. potent (*2*)	18. equate (*4*)	27. atrophy (*6*)

THEME TOPICS

1. Intellect Mills *vs.* Country Clubs
2. Deficiencies in My Education

3. The Factual (Enthusiastic, Inspiring) Teacher
4. The Handsome Passions
5. Intellect: The Balance Wheel of Life
6. Emotions: The Driving Force of Life
7. I Am Not Afraid of Being Enthusiastic
8. Emotional Debauch: The Fruit of Emotional Starvation
9. A Teacher I Should Have Liked to Know
10. A Defense of Education at My College

THE INNER THREAT: OUR OWN SOFTNESS

ROY HELTON

WHAT is happening to our civilization has become abundantly clear in the past decade. The events of this year, however frightful they are, and however harrowing to our humanity, have but added a footnote.

It may be there are some today who still do not believe that anything is happening to us or has happened to us. There have always been wars, and there have always been economic depressions after wars. They say that, and they are comforted by the fact that the things we experience have familiar names, even though those names are dreadful. What these optimists neglect to consider is that both wars and depressions are growing in violence. The war of 1914 was the bloodiest and most violent war in human history. Yet this present war exceeds it in every dimension but that of time. Nothing like this war was ever seen on earth before. That also was true of the international economic depression which began in 1929. One is making no very rash guess to assume that following this war there will ensue a depression in Europe whose depth will be beyond all past experience. That is a relatively safe guess.

This is therefore no time to pull one's words. Unless we are very wise we too shall be engulfed in that general economic prostration which, in a few years, after this war is over, will be worse than any war.

The real danger is a more serious business even than war. Human civilization is changing its form under the pressure of machinery. Only the most heroic defense can prevent darker ages descending on our race than man has experienced in a thousand years. That defense is possible and it must be made, and made in this country by us, the only people strong enough and rich enough and free enough and, with those endowments, also intelligent enough to face the most vital issue that has arisen in our history. To face it means a change of direction, and a change of direction is a thing all people resent; but not to face it means far more devastating changes within one human lifetime. Can we be more forehanded than our neighbors across the seas? Can we awake sooner than they did to the nature of what threatens democracy? Can we escape underestimating our enemy? We shall not escape that if we consider our enemy to be Hitler or Mussolini. Mussolini and Hitler will die. The fabric they are creating will collapse to destroy the future of Germany, and Italy. But what they mean will not die.

It is very rare that any people is wise enough to look past men into meanings. But we must. For our civilization to survive it must turn its democratic energies toward strength and away from comfort. That is the hard truth which confronts our world and our lives. Every civilization that has avoided facing that truth when the hour came has perished. (1)

For twenty-five years the feminine influence on Western life has mounted into a dominance over every area but that of politics, and even there its power is absolute as to the direction of our purposes. Unquestionably we are a politer people than we were at the turn of the century. The cuspidor has been eliminated from all but the most reactionary of our remoter hotels and barrooms. The cigarette has largely replaced the cigar and the plug. With infinite patience and resolution men have been maneuvered into a position where it is impossible for them to think of anything but women and their wants between the end of each day's work and its beginning the following morning. And it is those wants which with increasing authority have given form to our culture.

Only a fool would say that the result has been unpleasant. We live in a far daintier world than did our fathers, but also a far less virile world. Under urban conditions (and like Great Britain, most of France, Belgium, and Holland, we are now definitely an urban people) women have far more of the rewards of our civilization than men and they completely shape its ideals. Their influence is constant: on the children in the home, in the schools, and then through the period of courtship and marriage. Moreover, our urban population is predominantly a female population and, as any mail-order catalogue will reveal, it is the urban population which sets the direction of public habit and taste.

The theory that opportunity is dead has, no doubt, always existed in human history. It is a distinctively female idea. It holds the family together. It prevents the hardship of changes and migrations. Matriarchies always arise, as in China, where opportunities are believed to be dead and where men can be convinced that this is so. The patriarch flourished only among pioneers. All modern Western democracies have become state matriarchies within the past generation. The government is the general *Alma Mater*. But for the survival of whatever is enclosed by the sheltering arms of the state such a process is finally worthless.

Who can regard the history of European civilization for the past two years without perceiving that both France and Great Britain have acted on a female pattern and a female philosophy? I am not speaking of the individual and general heroism and fortitude of their armies, but of their official appeasements and submissions, of their thinking and their policy, of their lack of defensive aggression, and of their ability to struggle only when locked in the ravisher's arms, and then the complete and abject submission of France.

The recognition of the fact that women hold the purse strings of the nation has profoundly altered the development of our industry and commerce. Nearly all devices now in general use are being marketed on their feminine and juvenile appeal. Luxury or its imitation is a paramount sales argument.

None of these changes since 1900 is of itself undesirable, but their gross effect is to produce a female world.

Now women are very fine creatures and creatures of superb courage, and no man who is not capable of appreciating that fact has a right to speak out at all. But biological and economic realities, as ancient as humanity, compel them to a selection of values of prime importance to themselves: shelter, comfort, and every attainable advantage for their young. Those are all proper ideals but not adequate to create an enduring society without an equal force in the distinctively male values of enterprise, adventure, and power. The balance of those two sets of factors makes civilization. When the female influence climbs too far into the ascendancy we have comfort, and its sequel, degeneration. When the male influence comes into ascendancy we have war and destruction.

That is the lineup today in Europe and there is nothing in the past five hundred thousand years of man's history on this earth to indicate that these fundamentals of human nature will ever change. Nor should they. What is needed and what alone can save this civilization is for us to use these facts instead of attempting to deny them. (2)

The atmosphere of bright illusion which enveloped France and Great Britain and the United States concerns itself almost wholly with a future of ease and luxury for all men, a future of unlimited power and unlimited manufactured goods and food conveyed through the air, or over sixteen-lane super-speed highways, to eager billions of almost exclusively consuming people whose needs are satisfied by automatic machinery. This vision has been lately heightened by the discovery of an isotope of Uranium which offers a slight possibility of providing the future with an unlimited supply of energy.

Now waiving the fact that today the United States actually does possess unlimited power, actually has the physical substance of that dream, can produce and frequently has produced far more energy than we have yet found any use for, and is using less energy than often in the past when we had fewer people, the dream itself is the thing to examine. Is that a male or a female dream? Is it the father bird or the mother bird who shapes that dream? Is it she who sits on the nest and is perforce a consumer, or he who goes out and collects the worms who can explain what that dream is for and what instinct its realization would serve?

Regard it carefully and you will see that every form which the world of tomorrow takes, in fiction, in the daily comics, in grave economic literature, or in the visions of democratic government, is entirely a female dream.

In the model house of any builder's exhibit the male element of family life appears to be a shameful mystery for which no provision can decently be made without killing a sale. This is equally true of our model futures. The male economic function is taken over by Uranium 235, and there is nothing left for men to do but to grow long hair or shake their fists at the planets. A Mr. Lipstick is the end product of our modern industrial romancing; but the future, we may be sure, will not work out along those lines. A female world dream cannot survive in a competitive reality, and that is probably not a fact which humanity should deplore.

We have already lost faith in that dream, and it was not Hitler who destroyed our faith. The world period from 1890 to 1914 was an era of almost frantic prediction, but within the past five years constructive prophecy has perished as a literary and economic mode.

It survives only in politics for the two months preceding each election. In fact the classical world of tomorrow is already an anachronism. It exists only in the past. For we have had that world. In every essential feature it was realized in 1929. Such revamped versions as sometimes appear add nothing to what is past. They merely substitute lucite and cellophane for glass to enclose the hothouse cities of their vast heavens on earth.

It must be remembered that this nineteenth-century dream of tomorrow was one in which male constructive efforts were utilized to attain an essentially female ideal. But that was merely a transition. We lost that kind of a future in 1930, and turned from idealizing the creation of a mechanized paradise to the wholly feminine dream of security for our domestic comforts.

Security is the woman's wish, and has always had to be. Its adoption as a goal by men and nations was the final signal of the turning point in the sex of our democratic civilization, and of its future helplessness against any male purpose. (3)

Anybody in Europe, with half a mind, knew that Germany has been preparing for war on a colossal scale since 1934. In every year since that year her expenditures for arms and munitions of war have been twice those of France and Great Britain combined and, roughly, five times that of the United States. No nation spends twenty billion dollars of self-denied wealth and luxury for a bluff.

Meanwhile the democracies of Europe, not because they were democracies, but because their concept of civilization was that of the victor and not that of the vanquished, all played while Germany worked. By that I mean they followed their rich and comfortable neighbor to the west in turning the resources of civilization toward luxury and ease, and joined her in a wonder why creating devices for luxury and ease did not seem to give employment to all their people.

Great Britain and France, each with two-thirds the population of the old German Reich, had far more automobiles than Germany allowed herself and far more of the comfortable little gadgets on which we, most of any nation, have based our lives, though neither Great Britain nor France had as many motor cars or as many gadgets as do the citizens of the State of New York. Even so it was too many for their good. For the danger of technology to man is not merely the creation of tanks and guns by an enemy, but what the absence of any serious purpose save the pursuit of objects of minor luxury can do to the human spirit.

The worth and permanence of democracy cannot be insured by guns, tanks, or dive bombers, but only by our hardihood as a people. Those devices, however necessary, are a mere skin that like the human skin can protect from external infection. They do not insure the life of what lies within. Most people die with whole skins, from internal causes. At no time in history has any civilization or any form of government successfully protected itself without strengthening its own fibers. Walls always fail to do the job alone. If outward strength were all that was necessary for survival the dinosaur would still be roaming the hills of Wisconsin. Great navies and overwhelming air defenses may indeed help us, but not for long. Depend on them, as the British have depended on their fleet and the French on their Maginot line, and what is behind them will share the fate of the dinosaur.

Such defenses have a rigidity which does not meet the conditions necessary for survival. (4)

What are the evidences of those internal weaknesses which will destroy democracy if we are not resolute to overcome them?

(1) We have not been willing to face the cost of living as a free people. We borrow and borrow instead of paying and paying. In our national economy we are like the shiftless poor or the wastrel heirs of great fortunes. We do not care to face financial truth, and pull in our belts to free ourselves from the peril of our accumulating mortgage on the American future. Our leaders assure us that all will be well, but we know in our hearts it cannot be true. Some kind of prodigious crash is ahead of us. We are following ways that cannot go on to a happy ending. We know that, just as the British knew and the French knew that Hitler was staking the whole future of his nation on war and yet were unwilling to face that effort for themselves, so that today the valor of their sons has been wasted against steel walls.

Debt has betrayed the democracies of Europe, as for a long time it has been clear that it would; for they were so burdened with the accumulated obligations of the past that they dared not tax or borrow adequately to face the necessities of present self-protection. Down that path we also are traveling fast.

(2) We are a nation of city dwellers. We are largely a sedentary people. For exercise mature Americans move faster and travel farther under cover and on the seats of their pants than the citizens of any other nation in the world. They spend more time in enclosed rooms than any race that ever survived in all history. The British come next, and the French come third. Prewar Germany with sixty-six million people—the greatest technicians of modern times—had fewer passenger motor cars than the State of Pennsylvania.

(3) We indulge our children illimitably. Instead of rearing a race of lusty, weather-conditioned sons and daughters of democracy, we exhaust our private purses to buy gasoline for our racing youth, and strain the resources of our schools and colleges to erect stadia unparalleled since the days of degenerating Rome. We have carried the spectator sports to an excess never witnessed in human life since the days of Augustus. It is true that our

younger sons and daughters romp and play like natural human kind, but once in the standard assembly line we have constructed to provide for our future, they must sit out the best Saturday afternoons in the year while twenty-two picked men provide emotion, the sense of achievement, as well as vicarious exercise for twenty-two thousand rooters.

(4) We have constructed motor roads to the tops of our mountains. In our magnificent outdoor training grounds of democracy we have done everything possible to remove any incentive for mature people to use human activity for pleasure. Folk too indolent to climb a seven-foot stepladder can ascend Mt. Mitchell, Mt. Washington, Clingman's Dome, or Pikes Peak, sitting down.

Any intelligent program for the defense of democracy and the protection of vital natural resources would impose a rising tax on the consumption of gasoline for pleasure that would compel our people to reëxamine their feet. Would we ever do that? Is democracy as dear as parental- or self-indulgence? Time will tell. Shall we ever put a weekly twenty-mile walk into our school curricula? Shall we ever get our twenty-two thousand spectators into the field and turn our twenty-two gladiators into spectators? If we do not do it ourselves Mars will, rising from within or without. For the past twenty years American civilization as represented by its great middle class has appeared to pursue no ideal more world-shaking than the attempt to get harder and harder butter on softer and softer bread. It was so also in the democracies of Europe. To those mild ideals treason is inevitable in the face of a more masculine purpose. To tie such a male purpose to democracy is the only way democracy can survive. Purpose in others cannot be fought with any number of billions of dollars borrowed from our children. It cannot be defeated negatively or defensively. Purpose is the only force that will fight purpose. But to say that we are gathering our forces in the defense of freedom is not enough. It is what freedom is used for that must give us all the strength we can ever have. If we need our freedom to save our pet luxuries, to indulge our children, to invent social or economic devices by which we can evade the task of finding work for all men and women, then there is no health in us and democracy will pass into the historic record as another noble experiment defeated by the indulgences of men. (5)

Our weakness lies also in the nature of what we live for. Our children must have good health and good food. That much is sound enough, and something to fight for and work for. They must also have better clothes than their mothers and fathers had. What we call our standard of living demands that. What we mean of course is our standard of indulgence. They must be constantly amused with moving picture shows. They must be educated, but school work must not be so difficult for them as it was for their parents. They must learn without that distress which learning has always until lately occasioned all the sons and daughters of men. The difficult subjects in the secondary schools must be made electives so that they may be avoided by all to whom they are unpleasant. The school our children attend must have a victorious athletic team so that our sons and daughters may avoid any possible taint of inferiority. At sixteen the youth must be presented with a driver's permit and be allowed to join the motoring set. Thereafter we are not to be perturbed by their returning at later hours than we permit to ourselves.

They must go to college. We did not raise our boy to be a plumber or our daughter to sully her sweet hands with domestic toil. They must go to a good college, one that pays top prices for its football stars. They must join a Greek Letter Society or our pride is humbled and their lives made tragic. There must be a more abundant social life at this institution of higher learning. Not that there do not remain a number of old-fashioned institutions in which such creamy conditions do not obtain. Our children graduate if they can and we try to find them a husband or a job.

We also live for the motor car and its rear vestibule, the home, where there is bridge on certain evenings, though we are all too tired for serious reading, and there is bed with its mild comforts, and on the Sabbath a three-hour drive after we have inspected the forty pages of comics provided with the Sunday paper and digested a large meal. There must be various appliances or it is not a home. There is also for us perhaps golf, if one is adventurous, and work and life insurance, and a ball game, and a little fishing, and a mortgage and the undertaker.

It is all good enough, but it is not enough. It will not survive in any world where a people concentrates its national spirit on a pursuit of fitness and power.

For our nation to be safe to face dangers from any quarter, and strongly bred to stand up against any wind of fate, our over-solicitous maternalism to our children must end. And what is more, they will like it better than the softness that at present prevails. Our public humanities must be maintained, but they must spur, not lull, the unfortunate and the unhappy. Our help to the underprivileged must be an urge and not a sedative. We must devise uses for older men and women, so they can contribute to our general strength and not merely sap the energies of the young. Our young men and women must be hardened by work and weather to meet every possible storm. Our lawmakers must attain the courage to compel us to pay for the necessities of government by adequate taxes.

So and so only can we meet the hurricane that is gathering over our civilization, threatening all human freedom and all democratic forms of government. (6)

This crisis may pass. Hitler may fade out of the world's eye like a blown dip. He cannot win this war. He can only humiliate his enemies, and that project has already cost too much in lives. He is no master of the miracle of creating wealth for Germany by the devastation of all her chief customers and suppliers, and the wasting of her own resources in devices which add nothing to the necessities of Europe. All that Germany could achieve from the very outset was to make her future worse than her past, worse in every way, economically, socially, and humanly.

Hitler is an anachronism, dealing with twentieth-century facts on an eighteenth-century plan. His technic is superb. He put strength into his nation but strength to an end that will fail. In our lifetime Germany will never recover from these victories. When that fact is realized a sudden warm sense of security may flush the cheeks of our democracy. Behind our barrage of arms we may enjoy a delicious respite and invent new pleasures, but the dangers will grow, and unless we meet them the fate of France will sometime overtake us in the night.

For be sure of this: In a world of power the gracious, the genteel, the sheltered life has of itself no force. It has no vital consequences. Couple democracy to those ideals, and you marry it to death. Whatever survives between now and the year 2000 will be something tough.

We are a great people. Without any undue access of patriotic vanity that has been proved a few times. We made democracy work under grave handicaps in a new world. We did not invent industrialism, but we mastered it, and directed it, and achieved with it more common good than any other people. It would be pleasant to live back in the eighties of the past century, when all that lay ahead in a man's lifetime was growth, prosperity, and mechanical wonders, realizing all the dreams of Jules Verne.

Ours is a different fate. Upon the maturity of industrialism has descended a great terror. Force of purpose implemented by machines is different from any force ever unleashed before by human will. It is impersonal and hence logical and terrible to the flesh-and-blood man, which is not machinelike. It can be fought and fought under democracy, but only by a better purpose and a stronger will. That purpose cannot arise out of our passion for Sunday driving. That will cannot be conjured from our desire to blast Hitler, so he may leave us alone to golf and the movies and the garden plot and bridge. It can arise only from the resolution to raise up on this continent the strongest, ablest, hardiest, and most intelligent race of men and women that ever inhabited the world. Only through that goal can our democracy survive. And one hint of "and also universally enjoying every modern convenience" added to that ideal will blow it into complete futility. That, in my judgment, is the extent to which our direction has to change. (7)

QUESTIONS

I

1. How are present wars and depressions different from those of the past? What dangers, worse than wars, face us? What must we turn our democratic energies to in order to save ourselves? (1)

2. What is the difference between the feminine and masculine influence on civilization? In what ways has the civilization of the democracies been feminized? (2)
3. How have feminine desires been the basic force in American life? (3)
4. What was Germany doing while the democracies were enjoying comforts? (4)
5. What indictments does the author bring against debt, urban life, indulging youth, lack of exercise? (5)
6. What weakness is there in the very things we live for? What must we do to be able to face danger? (6)
7. In what way is Hitler an anachronism? What, according to the author, is our only hope of survival? (7)

II

1. By the criteria the author sets forth in this article, do you think you are "soft"?
2. Give your opinion of the following: "For our civilization to survive it must turn its democratic energies toward strength and away from comfort" (1); "We live in a far daintier world than did our fathers, but also a far less virile world" (2); "Whatever survives between now and the year 2000 will be something tough" (7).
3. Do you observe a feminizing influence at work in our present-day American society? What specific evidences of this influence can you cite?
4. Can you offer any rebuttal to the author's pointed criticisms of the softness of our collegiate life? (6)
5. Refute as many of Mr. Helton's arguments as you can.

III

1. Point out several places in the essay where the author makes his case stronger by acknowledging the good side of what he is opposing.
2. Where, in word or idea, has the author used sarcasm as a means to "point" his argument?
3. Where does the author warn the reader that he is going to discuss the problem in a downright manner?
4. Mr. Helton received a great deal of correspondence about this essay and was answered by other magazine articles. Had you been the author, would you have been pleased or angered by this response to your essay?

WORDS

From harrowing (*1*), maneuvered (*2*), virile (*2*), matriarchies (*2*), patriarch, (*2*), appeasements (*2*), paramount (*2*), ascendancy (*2*), anachronism (*3*), colossal (*4*), technology (*4*), wastrel (*5*), prodigious (*5*), sedentary (*5*), illimitably (*5*), vicarious (*5*), indolent (*5*), sully (*6*), sedative (*6*), futility (*7*), select the right word for the blanks in the following sentences.

1. Theodore Roosevelt was a man of ———— energy.
2. An ———— person never has things done on time.
3. Julius Caesar talking over the telephone would be an ————.
4. Moses might well be considered ————.
5. The ———— of his attempt to win became more obvious.
6. The ———— and spendthrift soon squandered his inheritance.
7. Chamberlain's series of ———— did not avert war.
8. A bomb raid is a ———— experience.
9. He would do nothing to ———— the good name he bore.
10. The skilful lawyer soon ———— the prisoner into an admission of guilt.
11. A bookkeeper has a ———— position.
12. My mother has never indulged me ————.
13. It is of ———— importance that he pay the debts immediately.
14. The pain was relieved by a ————.
15. Children enjoy the thrill of ———— danger.
16. The pyramids are ———— structures.
17. Advances in ———— have resulted in much unemployment.
18. Countries in which women rule are ————.
19. Whether warships or planes have the ———— in war is debated.
20. Only ———— men can endure life at the South Pole.

THEME TOPICS

1. Houses Are Built for Women
2. Men Want Adventure
3. Women Demand Security
4. College Has Its Serious Side
5. American Boys Are (Are Not) Soft
6. The Lost Art of Walking
7. Parents Should (Should Not) Indulge Youth
8. The Worship of the Gadget
9. I Don't Like Hard Studies (Teachers)
10. What Survives Will Be Tough

WE ARE NOT POOR

ETHEL AMBLER HUNTER

IN a country where everyone worried frenziedly about the Depression, like a puppy with a bone too big for it, and where the doleful refrain of "these hard times" echoed from every street corner and bridge table, it might be well to look our poverty in the face and see of what it is made. If it bids fair to be permanent—an "equalitarian destitution," as William Church Osborn has called it—we must, I think, plan how we can manage to endure it.

The fact, however, that a large part of our population is considerably better off than the entire populations of most other countries seems to suggest that perhaps we are not so unfortunate as we think. At least it is true that we have no need for many of the things we crave—some of them are actually bad for us—and, in comparison with other peoples and other times, we certainly are not poor. Of course I except those on the very edges of the pit: the wandering youths thumbing their way around the country from one job to another; the inmates of cellars and flop-houses; the desperate fringes of society. But the great majority of the 130,000,000 of us, especially those who were well off in 1929 when dividends were large and salaries generous, are not poor—not in the true sense of the word, which is destitution.

We *are* poor in the sense of want—we want everything the other fellow has, and if we cannot have it we loudly cry poverty. Poverty is the prevailing excuse for every evasion of debt and duty, used when hard, unpleasant work is offered or when the time comes to contribute to funds for churches, community chests, and hospitals. For example, a young couple in our neighborhood recently asked their landlady to reduce the rent of their house. The landlady was old, ill, and wholly dependent upon the rents of her two small properties; her life was restricted to constant penny-pinching for food and fuel. The young people thought they were having a hard time, too. They just couldn't make their salary go around, they explained, and the only possible place to reduce expenses was the rent. They couldn't even afford to have a baby. (This last was calculated to reduce the old lady to a mush of sentimental generosity.) But the old lady remembered the parties, sometimes two or three a week, which required a lot of expensive liquor; the stream of delivery boys from the butcher, grocer, and florist; the new car, bought long before the old one was shabby; the week-end trips, and the new fur coat. It seemed to her that the economy might well be made elsewhere than in the rent.

Another young couple nearby are also among the so-called poor. The husband has had no luck as a salesman and the young wife supports them, for the most part, by secretarial work. They owe nearly everyone in town, and recently allowed the bank to take their house, which by that time was perhaps half paid for. Yet they have a car (a good one), send their boy to summer camp, take trips during the wife's vacation, and dress well. Certainly they are not poor, and had they belonged to the "poor" of twenty or thirty years ago they would have gone without the things I have mentioned rather than owe money or lose their home. They would have cut the pattern according to the cloth, and gone without the things outside the design.

Then there are Allan and Mary, an older couple with children growing up, a strong taste for gay life, and, alas, a small income. At least it seems small to them; they assert with wry smiles that they are the "new" poor, by which they mean the "high" poor. They need so many things, including modish clothes, cocktail parties, and their lovely furnishings. Mary says it costs her eight dollars a month to keep her hair decent, and—would you believe it!—Betty, now in high school, must have her hair done too. All the other girls do. The fact that soap and water and a scrupulously clean hairbrush will keep the hair neat and shining seems to be forgotten; but it is true, as many other generations of women with handsome hair have proven.

On Saturday afternoons in our town, scout leaders find it impossible to organize hikes to places of historical interest, even with refreshments offered free; for Saturday is Movie Day for the children, and this includes the children of those on Relief who, like their parents, attend with surprising regularity. When reminded of the educational and healthful features of the hike, parents reply that their youngsters are following a serial and could not possibly miss a chapter. Out-of-work adults, bitter and discouraged, may need the anodyne of the movies, as social workers say, but why spend money to stupefy children with such tiring and unrewarding excitements?

The truth of the matter is that the movies are just another of the feverish extravagances stimulated by contemporary high-pressure salesmanship, which is also responsible for the great demand for glossy new cars, elegant refrigerators, abundant cosmetics, and similar luxuries-not-necessities for which our "poor" pay a staggering yearly bill. Since 1932 the American public has decreased its gifts for support of churches by 30 per cent, for general benevolences 29 per cent, for community chests 24 per cent, and colleges 18 per cent. At the same time, however, expenditures for the luxuries mentioned above, and for theaters, cigarettes, automobiles, liquor, jewelry, radios, and other dispensables, have soared by 25 per cent to as much as 317 per cent; and much of this money was spent by our "poor" people. But how much regard for thrift, self-reliance, and quiet happiness can you expect to find among these poor when they see the more fortunate plunge into installment buying, restless gadding about, and extravagances of all sorts? The poor of our time have been nurtured on the heady doctrine that "We're as good as they are, any day." (1)

Years ago, when Americans had fewer luxuries and often ran short of necessities, we were not, strange to say, nearly so self-conscious about poverty. When I was a child, few thought they were poor, although today everyone in that same neighborhood— my own family among them—would be so labeled. There's no denying that my family and neighbors were poor so far as material possessions went. We had no electric or gas lights, no refrigerator, not even an ice-filled one. Perishables were kept in the cellar or down the well. Clothes were washed on Monday in two wooden tubs in the kitchen; then the tubs were put away until Saturday, when they were used for the weekly bath. Of course we had no bathroom! Today I smile at the thought of how dreadful everyone thinks the little houses out back must have been! We had, at most, two pairs of shoes, a best pair and an everyday pair. We had a coat; not a raincoat or a winter coat or a sport coat or a fur coat—just a coat. Some of us did have a school coat as well as a best one, but not many were so lucky.

My father sometimes had no work for months at a time. The shoe factory where he lasted shoes was more seasonal than factories are today, and being laid off was the expected, though nonetheless dreaded, thing. There was coal to buy, and food and taxes and interest on the mortgage and sometimes a doctor's bill. Yet we never felt poor. We expected to get along and did. Paying the bills was planned far ahead, and paid they were, let the chips fall where they would. Nothing was bought that we were not sure we could pay for, and consequently merchants trusted us. I can remember feeling very rich and luxurious when I had an egg for breakfast, and oranges were a treat saved for sickness and Christmas stockings.

Quite a contrast, these memories, to a scene I saw in the A & P store yesterday! A pleasant-faced, elderly woman stood haggling over a small bit of meat with the embarrassed clerk. She wore a lovely summer suit, modish shoes, and one of those knowing little hats *not* from the bargain basement. Yet she explained in an anxious voice that she must get the most she could for the money. Times were so hard that she had dismissed one of the maids and she would do without her trip South. The butcher looked at the stingy cut of meat. "Shall I carry it out to the car?" he asked her blandly. She colored a little and then picked up the package.

I would not be as poor as that pathetic creature for all the world! (2)

One thing which, I believe, made us happier when I was young was that almost forgotten commodity, "elbow-grease." When applied with skill it gave to personality a polish strongly resembling the much-admired "poise" of today. After doing a good job we could look anyone in the eye with pride, or face any situation with interest and courage. But our wise-cracking, forlorn recipients of welfare haven't work; not of a kind they will consider. Most of them dodge wood-cutting, ditch-digging, and snow-shoveling, though they can offer a nifty tap-dance, can croon, or run adding machines. Their daughters are adept, too, at these devices for easy earning, and refuse housework or clerking with uplifted, helpless hands.

Using oil lamps isn't being poor, nor is going without white coats or cars or permanents. Living in a cellar is, and so is insufficient milk for the baby, or the responsibility for sick, indigent parents. The greatest calamity, however, is *feeling* poor—the beaten spirit, the petty stinginess to keep up a good outside show.

A sturdy sense of well-being *can* be cultivated and the will-to-do restored. I know that the modern diet does not include the rough foods of my youth. But there are still apples; there are still milk and eggs, sunshine and fresh air, soap and water, books, friends, fields to walk in, streams to fish in, woods to roam. If we could only find another god than the "good car"; other happiness than that found in costly and exhausting amusements and expensive (or expensive-looking) clothes.

If we can't go back to something simpler and more wholesome, or forward to something finer, then the whole race of Americans as the world thinks of them—the American of robust humor, courage, and the ability to turn in casually a tremendous amount of excellent work—will have vanished from the earth. Then, indeed, we shall be poor. (*3*)

QUESTIONS

I

1. What examples does the author give to prove that we are poor in the sense of things we *want* but not poor in the real sense of the word? (*1*)
2. Why does the author consider that she was not poor with the very limited comforts of her childhood? (*2*)
3. What does the author recommend as at least partial solutions of the problem? Under what conditions, in her opinion, shall we really be poor? (*3*)

II

1. "We want everything the other fellow has, and if we cannot
   have it we loudly cry poverty." Is this a true picture of
   Americans today?
2. Do you agree that Americans spend too much money on luxuries?
   Do you know people who overspend for the sake of keeping
   up appearances? Do you justify or condemn them?
3. What part has high-pressure salesmanship had in stimulating
   Americans to extravagant wants which keep them poor?
4. What is your candid opinion of installment buying?
5. The author accuses many Americans of dodging "elbow-grease"
   work. Is the charge true?
6. Democracy encourages people to aspire to the higher, more
   pleasant tasks in life, to raise themselves above the hard, unpleasant ones. Parents desire their children to have easier lives
   than they have had. Yet there is much hard, unpleasant work
   always to be done. What conclusion do the opponents of
   democracy draw from this anomaly?
7. "The greatest calamity is *feeling* poor—the beaten spirit, the
   petty stinginess to keep up a good outside show." Do you
   agree with this point of view?
8. Do you accept the conclusion of this essay—that the American
   must work harder, must deny himself more, and must be
   more thrifty if he is to survive?

III

1. What device does the author use in the first paragraph to introduce her subject? What is the first statement of the author's
   main thesis that you find in the essay?
2. The author depends for much of her proof upon cases illustrating
   her points. Can you produce similar cases? Can everyone? If
   this can be done, are her points proved?
3. Note the way the author has obtained coherence in each succeeding paragraph in (1). Point out the word or expression or
   idea that joins each paragraph with the preceding one.

WORDS

Indicate which of the following statements are true and which
are false.

1. doleful (1): We have *doleful* faces when we are happy.
2. equalitarian (1): An *equalitarian* division would give each person
   the same amount.

3. modish (*1*): *Modish* styles are worn by smartly dressed women.
4. scrupulously (*1*): Merchants trust a *scrupulously* honest person.
5. anodyne (*1*): An *anodyne* is an irritating agent.
6. stupefy (*1*): Cold weather will *stupefy* flies and snakes.
7. perishables (*2*): Oysters, as food, may be classed as *perishables*.
8. blandly (*2*): *Blandly* can be used as a synonym of "suavely."
9. adept (*3*): A mendacious person is *adept* in lying.
10. indigent (*3*): An *indigent* person belongs to the well-to-do class.

THEME TOPICS

1. Our Neighbors Try to Keep Up with the Joneses
2. Spending More Than You Make
3. Elbow-Grease
4. Our Wants Make Us Poor
5. The Real Poor (Just a Bum, Share Croppers, Indigent Old Age)
6. What Can We Do Without?
7. Two Cars in Every Garage
8. Thrift: A Lost Art in America
9. An Extravagant Person I Know
10. The Hair Brush *vs.* the Beauty Parlor

WE MUST NOT SIT WISHING

HARRIET DUFF PHILLIPS

MILLIONS of words concerning the defense of democracy, and the part women can play in that defense, have poured from the lips of lecturers to women's club groups in the last year. Millions more will be poured forth in the coming year.

We women have declared ourselves to be a united group, ready to defend the patterns of freedom which we believe have made our nation great. Our hearts are behind the cause to which we have devoted so many words. But just what are we doing to accomplish our ends? Just what are we doing besides nodding approval to the visiting lecturer's inspiring words?

I am afraid that in contemplating the gigantic task before us we have lost sight of the things in front of our very noses. We talk of democracy, but many of our clubs are in themselves not democratic. I will go further than that. In some communities the woman's club, instead of being a democratizing force, is actually a dead end of democracy. (1)

A member of a woman's club in a mill town close to my home city of Pittsburgh whispered to a recent visitor, "Our members are the Four Hundred of the community. We have a limited membership." There was a smug pride in her voice. Yet if anyone had asked her or her fellow club members what was the most important work before that organization they would have answered without hesitation, "Keeping our democracy alive. Guarding our country against foreign isms."

These women, wives of minor executives and white-collar workers in the great steel mills, cannot see that by their own attitude they are making other women feel that democracy does not exist in their town. In the streets where there are smaller, shabbier homes than theirs are other women who once went to school with them, whose children are now in school with theirs. The names of these other women are Baminowsky, Demetrious, Callimando, instead of Thompson and Hillman and Smith. They too want good schools for their children and a decent community for them to live in. But, because their immigrant parents do not speak good English, because their fathers and husbands and brothers labor in the mills, there is no place for them in the woman's club.

"Why, we do everything for them!" a club woman, indignant at criticism concerning the lack of democracy in her club, will tell you. "We gather money for the library their children use; we have helped establish parks and playgrounds and free baby clinics." All this is true, but in a democracy it is necessary to bring citizens into the group, that they may help to do things for themselves and not have everything done for them.

Visit with me the woman's club in any one of a dozen mill towns lining the flats and hillsides along the Monongahela, Allegheny, and Ohio Rivers that triangle the city of Pittsburgh. You will find few if any foreign names on the woman's club lists. Talk to the women—the American-born women with the "queer" foreign names—and they will shrug their shoulders and say, "They don't want us."

The reason for the growth of this caste division in industrial communities, in other sections of the country as well as in Pittsburgh, is not difficult to find. In the early days the "foreigners" who did the hard labor in the mills spoke little or no English, had customs strange to the older Americans. They were "Hunkies," people you didn't bother about except in a Lady Bountiful spirit of "helping" them. Today many of those still referred to as "foreigners" are American-born and American-educated. They are high-school graduates, and have American ideals, and have learned American standards of living. Many of them want to have a part in the building of their community.

Yet more and more, as the woman's club movement comes into maturity, established clubs are becoming exclusive instead of inclusive. Groups organized on a purely social or vocational basis have the privilege of doing this, immune from criticism; but a woman's club, organized on the basis of community service, has not. Although it is much easier for a club to function smoothly if the membership is on the same economic and intellectual plane, such a club is not fulfilling a democratic purpose and can easily become a handicap instead of an aid in community development.

Several women with whom I have discussed this subject have remarked, "But those women wouldn't be comfortable with us." Then, as though dismissing the subject, they have added, "And they probably couldn't afford to join." (2)

A few years ago Mrs. Martz, a widow from a poor section of my own community, came to see me. For years she had cleaned offices at night to earn a living for her children, but now at last, she told me, "things were easier." Her children were grown up. Her mother had died and left her a few hundred dollars. With that small legacy she had paid off a little debt and bought a black silk dress, a coat and a decent hat, of her own choosing. She told me all these things in such a way that I knew she was leading up to something.

Suddenly she said, "Do you think the ladies in your club would stand for a working-woman member? I'm afraid to ask any of them but you. If only you'd be willing to put up my name!" She was twisting her new black gloves nervously in her fingers.

I told her I should be proud to propose her name. She was beaming as she left the house. "Please let me know as soon as the ladies decide whether I can come in," she said, starting down the walk.

"Come in"—I have never forgotten those words, for I know so many women who would like to "come in" but who have never been invited. For two years my new friend was the first at every meeting. For two years she sat in the same seat in the second row of chairs, but never said a word, just drank it all in. Then one day the president announced plans for a dinner to raise scholarship funds. Mrs. Martz was on her feet in a second. "Mrs. President," she said, "if you'll let me be chairman of the dishwashing committee, I'll feel honored." A year ago Mrs. Martz was dying and almost her last words to her daughter were "Don't forget to tell the club ladies to come to my funeral." Mrs. Martz had "come in."

There was the woman who, after a speech on democracy by a visiting lecturer, murmured, "Marvelous, we must work to keep our democracy," then went home and scolded her eleven-year-old daughter because she had brought home to play with her the little Italian girl whose father ran the grocery store down the street.

Recently I suggested to a club that it have a young Negro girl sing for it—she had an exquisite voice and may some day be another Marian Anderson. But having a Negro come into a club meeting would have offended a particularly influential member, so the girl who could interpret God's world with a voice like a bird was not given a place on the program. I could give example after example to prove my point, examples that I have gathered from personal experience through traveling up and down my state visiting clubs. (3)

It seems to me that if we are sincere in our pledge to aid in the defense of American democracy we must begin in small things in our everyday life. We must stop thinking of democracy as that misty, intangible something talked about on the platform, and realize that democracy is Mrs. Dirinsky washing clothes so that her daughter can finish college; it is the elevator boy in a department store writing notes for his book during his lunch hour; it is the tired clerk going home in the streetcar at night wondering how he can stay awake long enough to go to that community council meeting.

We must not sit wishing after an inspirational talk on democracy and its survival—wishing that we might do something outstanding and big, for there are few such opportunities. We must think and act for our nation through our daily living, where every woman is important if she lives and speaks democratically in her own community. (4)

QUESTIONS

I

1. What is the inconsistency among women's clubs in the theory and practice of democracy? (*1*)
2. What elements of a caste system are there in women's clubs? How may "doing everything" for the less fortunate persons of a community not really be the best kind of democracy? What defense do women who exclude the less fortunate advance? (*2*)
3. What do the cases of Mrs. Martz, the woman who scolded her daughter for playing with an Italian child, and the exclusion of the Negro girl singer prove? (*3*)
4. Where must we really begin to practise democracy? (*4*)

II

1. Have you observed cases of sharp social distinctions in your own community? Do you belong to any "caste" organization? Are we all snobs in one way or another, in spite of any theories we may hold?
2. What is your candid opinion of lectures and lecturers? How may they do good? How may they be a mere anodyne for action?
3. Is it your observation that women's clubs are not democratic? Should they be proud or ashamed of a "limited membership"? Why should women's clubs be more democratic than "groups organized on a purely social or vocational basis"?
4. How are the public schools probably the most democratic institution in America?
5. How may we actually hurt people by "doing everything" for them? What is a better long-range policy?
6. The question of excluding from women's clubs American-born, American-educated women of foreign lineage and of the working class is a question of immigrant assimilation. What do you think should be done?
7. Would you invite a talented Negro singer or a political radical to appear on a program of your organization?
8. Do you agree with the author of this essay that democracy begins at home—in the small happenings of everyday life?

III

1. What is the significance of the title of this essay—"We Must Not Sit Wishing"?

2. What method does the author use to make her arguments concrete?

WORDS

This lesson should be undertaken more in the spirit of adventure than of work. For each word in the left-hand column, there is a word in the right-hand column giving the *idea* behind its etymology. For instance, you have already had *immigrant*, as derived from *migrare*, "to wander." Hence 7 is related to 15. Do not look the words up until you have tried to see the connection between the word and the idea in its etymology.

1. defense (*1*)	1. living
2. inspiring (*1*)	2. judgment
3. contemplating (*1*)	3. sending
4. visitor (*2*)	4. flags
5. hesitation (*2*)	5. harbors
6. executives (*2*)	6. sitting
7. immigrant (*2*)	7. public service
8. criticism (*2*)	8. seeing
9. graduates (*2*)	9. flowing
10. standards (*2*)	10. beech tree
11. exclusive (*2*)	11. sticking fast
12. vocational (*2*)	12. touching
13. immune (*2*)	13. breathing
14. dismissing (*2*)	14. shutting
15. section (*3*)	15. wandering
16. influential (*3*)	16. steps
17. intangible (*4*)	17. striking
18. book (*4*)	18. cutting
19. survival (*4*)	19. temple
20. opportunities (*4*)	20. calling

THEME TOPICS

1. In Defense of Snobs
2. I Shall (Shall Not) Join a Woman's Club
3. The Good Our Woman's Club Does in Our Community
4. Hurting People by Helping Them
5. The Real Way to Help People
6. Democracy Begins in My Room
7. A Good (Poor) Lecture I Heard
8. Our Exclusive Set
9. Our Democratic Public Schools
10. The Four Hundred of ———— (name of town or community)

AMERICA'S GUNPOWDER WOMEN

PEARL S. BUCK

SOME months ago I had the temerity to write an article entitled "America's Medieval Women." These women have had their full revenge on me, not, as I had hoped they would, by much disagreement with me, but by the most dismaying agreement expressed in so many letters, so much talk, and—whenever I had to speak in public—such urgent requests that I go on about women that I wonder why I ever began it.

And yet now, completely aware of my own folly in pursuing a course which can lead to none of the peace which I love above all things, here I go on again, not with any hope of accomplishing anything by doing so, but merely because I find there is still something more I want to say about women.

I observe of course that American women are not born all alike, whatever they achieve in this direction afterward. By nature they seem indeed among other possible classifications, to fall into three congenital groups. The first one is the talented women, or women with a natural vocation. This group is, naturally, a small one; for the women who are in it must have besides their talent an unusual energy which drives them, in spite of shelter and privilege, to exercise their own powers. They are single-minded creatures and they cannot sink into idleness or fritter away life and time or endure discontent. They possess that rarest gift, integrity of purpose, and they can work, day upon day, mentally and spiritually, as well as physically, upon the one necessity. Such women sacrifice, without knowing they do, what many women hold dear—amusement, society, play of

From *Harper's Magazine*, July, 1939. Copyrighted by Harper & Brothers. Used by permission of *Harper's Magazine* and David Lloyd, 49 East 34th Street, New York, for the author.

one kind or another—to choose solitude, and profound thinking and feeling, and at last final expression.

"To what end?" another woman may ask. To the end perhaps of science—science which has given us light and speed and health and comfort and lifted us out of physical savagery; to the end perhaps of art—art which has lifted us out of mental and spiritual savagery.

I remark, however, in passing that I observe also that it is notable in the United States when a woman, even of this small talented group, chooses to spare herself nothing of the labor which a similarly talented man performs for the same ends. Why should this be unless perhaps it is because we are accustomed to expect so little from a woman?

The second group of women is, though far larger than this first one, yet like it in having a vocation; but here it is the vocation of the home. In this group is the woman who is really completely satisfied mentally and spiritually with the physical routine of motherhood and the activity of housekeeping. When her children grow up she begins again with her grandchildren. Her brain has been literally encompassed by the four walls of her home, and is engrossed and satisfied with its enclosed activities. As long as her four walls stand she is contented, busy, useful—a sweet, comforting, essential creature who perfectly fulfills her being and her function, who brings nothing but simple happiness to those about her, though only so long as she gives them freedom to come and go as they will and does not limit them by her own simplicity.

But both of these, the woman born talented and the woman born domestic, may be dismissed from mind for the moment. In the first place, important as they are, their combined number in proportion to the whole number of women is very small, and in the second place they are safe and stable citizens, since they know what they want to do and are doing it—in short, they are contented; and any contented person is safe and relatively sane.

There remains a third group, a very large one, and these are the ones I call the gunpowder women. Here are millions of America's women, all those whose families are not undergoing actual adversity, who are not compelled to earn money to keep from starvation, who have no definite talent or vocation, who have only a normal interest in home and children so that when these are adequately tended they still have surplus time, energy, and ability which they do not know how to use. To make conditions more difficult for them they have usually a fair or even an excellent education and brains good enough at least to be aware of discontent.

It is these gunpowder women who suffer most under the burden of privilege which American women have been given to bear.

I set this sentence alone, I throw it like a rock, though I am aware that thus unexplained it will hit some gunpowder woman and, if it does not hurt her, at least it will make her angry. But I take the risk because the very existence of these gunpowder women is a result of this heritage of privilege which so oppresses American women. The talented woman can ignore the oppression and go on doing what she was made to do, as a man does. And a born housekeeper, if her disposition be amiable, as, thank God, it more often is than not, is a comforting and comfortable soul who cannot be spoiled by privilege, since she is happy in her work. But here is this other and far more frequent woman, able, free, educated, who really quite often wants to contribute something directly to her world and not merely through husband and children. She seldom can, however. Privilege denies it— she is so privileged that her world makes no demand upon her. More than that, no one even expects anything of her. Her very friends discourage her, though they be her fellows in discontent. If she tries tentatively to do something a little more serious than her fellows are doing they cry at her, "My dear, aren't you *wonderful!*"—meaning, "Why on earth do you do it?"—meaning, "Aren't you queer?"—meaning, "You think you're smart!"— meaning, indeed, all those things which discontented helpless women do mean when they see one of their number behaving as the rest of them do not and being, therefore, a reproach to those who do nothing. (*1*)

For the vicious result of privilege is that the creature who receives it becomes incapacitated by it as by a disease. Privilege is a serious misfortune anywhere and the more serious because

American women do not realize that the privilege they boast is really their handicap and not their blessing. I am sure they do not realize it, because in the agreement and disagreement I had with my former article nearly all the women said, reproachfully, if they disagreed, "You seem to forget that women in America are the most privileged on earth," and, apologetically, if they agreed, "Of course I know women in America are the most privileged on earth, but——"

And every time this was said, in either fashion, a certain bit of Chinese history came warningly into my mind. This is the history:

Centuries ago when astute China was about to be conquered by the naïve and childlike Manchus, the Chinese used a weapon which gave them the final and actual victory, though the Manchus never knew it. When they were conquered the Chinese said, in effect, to the Manchus, "You are our superiors. Therefore we will perform all unpleasant tasks for you. You shall live in palaces apart and there enjoy yourselves. Sums of money will be set aside for you. You need not labor or strive. We will do everything for you. We want you only to be happy and enjoy yourselves."

The Manchus were delighted with this. They laid aside their weapons, went joyfully to the fine palaces the Chinese gave them, and began to spend their lives in pleasure. In a short time the Chinese were ruling their own country again as they always had and the Manchus were as good as dead. Easy food and drink and plenty of leisure had reduced them to complete ineffectuality, just as the Chinese had planned it.

Now, therefore, whenever I hear an American woman begin brightly, "Well, anyway, we are the most privileged..." I remember the Manchus and am troubled. There is something sinister in this matter of privilege.

And yet it is true—I cannot deny it, though I wish I could—the women of the United States are the most privileged in the world. We have never even had a very serious struggle to achieve our privileges, at least any struggle comparable to that of women in other enlightened countries. Privileges have been bestowed upon us, thanks largely to the inflated value which pioneer times gave to American women. That inflation still lasts, although happily it is decreasing. For the moment when American women hit what commercially is called an all-time low they will be forced to wake up, and then perhaps they will put an honest value on themselves, and thus the struggle which other women have made or are making will begin and the result ought to be valuable to everybody. But that moment has not yet arrived, and meanwhile women go on under the handicap of privilege.

Of course many women in other countries, not understanding any more than we do the effect of unearned privilege, envy American women.

I suppose thousands of Oriental women have said to me at one time or another, "How lucky you are to be an American woman! You have freedom and equality with man. Your parents do not groan when you are born and your brothers do not look down on you as less than they. You can go to school. You need not even marry if you do not wish to—at least, you need never marry someone you do not like."

I agreed to all of this and I still agree to it. I had rather be an American woman than a woman of any other country in the world because everything lies ahead of us still, as women. But if I had a chance now at those Oriental women, after these years spent among my own countrywomen, I'd answer something like this:

"You know, it's true we are very free. We can be anything we like, we American women—lawyers, doctors, artists, scientists, engineers, anything. But, somehow, we're not!"

"You're not!" the Oriental woman would say, astonished. "Why not? Do you mean the doors are open and you don't go out?"

"Well, we go out—" I would have to acknowledge. "I suppose most of us go out in some sort of work if we don't marry first; but we secretly hope to marry first, so that we need not, or we want to work just a year or two, and then come back into the home and shut the door and be secure in the old way."

"Don't you want to be independent, to be free to come and go as you like?" the Oriental woman cries. "Ah, if I could support myself, know I need not obey father, mother, husband, son all my life—"

"Oh, we American women don't obey anyone," I tell her quickly. "Our husbands support us in the home, but we don't obey them. We do come and go as we like. Of course we work in our own way at house and children, and for a few years we are even quite busy. But we have a great many ways to save labor, and the schools take our children early and then we have a great deal of leisure—at least, *you* would think us very leisured."

"Then what do you do?" the Oriental woman asks blankly.

"We amuse ourselves somehow," I reply.

"You are fed and clothed for that?" she asks.

"Yes," I reply. "Many of us—and we all expect it."

She cannot understand this, and indeed it is difficult to understand and I cannot explain it to her. Why, in a country where everything is free to women and women are so privileged, is it remarkable when a woman is first-rate in anything? But it is. Thanks to our privileges which compel us to no effort, it is the truth that men excel us, numerically as well as actually, at everything except childbearing, and doubtless if men had to bear children they would soon find some better way of doing it. And women, seeing themselves outstripped without understanding why they are, and yet feeling themselves as able as men, grow discontented and join the crowded ranks of the gunpowder women. (2)

The home of course has been the stronghold of this privilege. Behind its sheltering walls women have taken full advantage of every privilege—the privilege of security, the privilege of non-competitive work, the privilege of privacy. Yes, of privileges women have had plenty, and yet most of them have been denied the one great blessing of man's life—the necessity to go out into the world and earn their bread directly. And this one blessing is worth all privileges put together; for by it man has been compelled to put forth his utmost effort, whetting his brain and sharpening his ambition, and so he has accomplished much.

For Nature is not unjust. She does not steal into the womb and like an evil fairy give her good gifts secretly to men and

deny them to women. Men and women are born free and equal
in ability and brain. The injustice begins after birth. The man
is taught that he must develop himself and work, lest he and his
woman starve. But the woman is taught merely to develop such
things as will please the man, lest she starve because he does not
want to feed her. Because of this one simple, overwhelming fact,
men have been the producers, the rulers, and even the artists.

For necessity makes artists too. Many a talent is born without its mate, energy, and so comes to nothing unless energy is
somehow created to develop the talent. Necessity is the magic of
this creation for the man; for if he has talent he will, if driven
desperately enough, apply his compelled energy to his talent and
become at least a fair artist—for genius still remains the combination of highest natural talent and highest natural energy of a
quality which functions without outside stimulus—and this combination is rare.

"But," a gunpowder woman retorted to this yesterday, "a man
can combine his talent with his bread-winning." She looked
round on the walls of her comfortable prison. I could feel her
thinking, "If I had been free I might have been a great painter."

To which I retorted, "How do you know it is not as easy to
combine housekeeping and art as it is to make art a business?
You have never tried it because you never had to."

No, the man is lucky. By compulsion of society and public
opinion, if he has any ability and pride, he simply must work.
Nothing excuses him. Home cannot be his escape. And in desperation he somehow begins to try to make a living by what he
wants to do. And whether he succeeds or fails in it, he has no
refuge from work, hard and endless, and full of insecurity. He
bears, indeed, the brunt of that heaviest load of all—insecurity.

The curse of too many women has been that they have this
privilege of refuge in the home. Behind closed doors they may
or must work, it is true, but according to their own hours and
ways. They escape all the discipline of concentration upon one
task, often uncongenial, hour after hour, year after year, the
mental discipline of hard creative thinking, the ruthless discipline
of social organization. I have been both breadwinner and housekeeper, and I know that breadwinning is infinitely more tedious,

more taxing, more nerve-racking, than housekeeping. Indeed, cooking, cleaning, caring for children, if you know necessary bills are pretty certainly going to be paid, is almost a soporific and as good as play after the insecurity of competition in business and the arts. For safe in the home a woman becomes used to flitting from one thing to another, and her mind forgets or never learns how to concentrate or perhaps to work at all. There, leaning upon another's efforts, she becomes lazy, if not physically lazy, lazy in that core of her being which is the source of life and development, so that when her children are grown—and in a few years they are—and her mechanical tasks are over, she is fit for nothing more. She has excused herself from a life of labor because of these short-lived tasks, which, necessary as they are for a time, should never have been considered adequate for her whole self. (3)

The truth is that although women are needed today in every sort of life in the United States they do not even see they are needed. They have become so corrupted by privilege that they stare out on events and conditions around them with the same unseeing, lackluster eyes with which women in India have looked out of the windows of their zenanas. The Indian woman was not educated and she could not pass out of her door uncovered, and this American woman is free to come and go and she has been given what education she wanted, and yet there is the same look of defeat in her eyes that there is in the Indian woman's. Neither is fulfilling that for which she was born; but the American's discontent is keener because she knows it, whether she will acknowledge it or not, and the more clever she is, the more educated, the more of a gunpowder woman she is.

I do not in the least blame her for being a gunpowder woman. I can only sympathize with all her small daily explosions, her restlessness, her irritability, her silliness, her running after this and that in heroes, in arts, in clothes, in love, in amusements, her secret cynicisms and her childish romanticism, her fears and her explosions too of daring which accomplish so little because they never go far enough. She is unpredictable, not from a calculated desire to charm, but because she really does not know what to do with her inner self.

And why should she know? Why should so much more be demanded of her, if she does anything, than is demanded of a man? A man is educated and turned out to work. But a woman is educated—and turned out to grass. The wonder is not that she is unpredictable but that she is not insane. Nothing is arranged for her as it is arranged for the man who under the rule of society, by a series of efforts combined with ability, has his life laid out for him. I say that if a gunpowder woman with no boss to tell her what to do, with no office to schedule her days and force her to activity, with no financial necessity compelling her, no creative demand driving her, no social approbation urging her, if this woman can be her own taskmaster and fulfill herself by some accomplishment, then she is a creature almost superhuman. It is too much to ask of her very often, and when she achieves something she ought to be greatly praised.

For consider, please, the advantage a man has in our country over a woman. I repeat, for it is the key to all his success, a man must work or he starves. If he does not actually starve, at least society looks down upon him and makes him ashamed. But a woman within her home may live an absolutely idle existence without starving and without being despised for it. Yet an idle woman ought to be despised as much as an idle man for the good and happiness of all women if nothing else. Anyone who takes food and clothing and shelter for granted, even though it is given by one who loves to give it, and makes no return except privately to an individual, ought to be despised. A woman owes something to the society which gives her husband a chance to earn for her, and social pressure should compel her to make that return.

And yet this woman has not even the help of that social pressure. Society pays no attention to her so long as she "behaves herself" and stays at home. She is that most unfortunate of persons, idle because nothing is demanded or expected of her, and yet unable to be happy because she is idle. No wonder discontent is her atmosphere, that "discontent of women" which a visitor from Europe once said struck him "like a hot wind" when he landed in the United States. What is discontent but spiritual gunpowder of the fullest inflammability? Only the stupid woman can avoid it.

When I consider this handicap of privilege, then, which has produced these gunpowder women in my country, I cannot find a single word of blame for them. I know that men would never have risen to their present preëminence in all fields if they had had such a handicap—if, in short, they had not had the advantage of the compulsory discipline of work. I am sure that men would behave certainly no better than women if after the wife was off to office and the children to school, the man were left alone in the house. If he could sit down and read a mystery story at ten o'clock in the morning, he too would do so although a busy world hummed about him. He would curl his hair or waste an hour on his fingernails if there were no one to tell him it was not the time for that sort of thing. He would, it is true, have as she does a deadline to meet in the late afternoon, but with no one to check on him to see how time-wasting he was in getting there, he would waste as much time. He could even be as poor a housekeeper as she sometimes is and no one would blame him very much. His wife would merely work a little harder so as to be able to hire a cook. No, without the discipline of regular labor, of fixed hours, of competitive standards, the man would be where the woman is now.

If women excel in nothing it is at bottom as simple as this, and not because men's brains are better than women's. It is a pity, for these gunpowder women are as much a lost source of power in the nation as are the flood waters that rise and rush over the land to no useful purpose. Spoiled, petty, restless, idle, they are our nation's greatest unused resource—good brains going to waste in bridge and movies and lectures and dull gossip, instead of constructively applied to the nation's need of them. (4)

"What can we do about it," some of them cry at me, "if that's the way things are?" "Nothing," is my reply, "nothing at all, unless it happens you also want to do something. Nobody will make you do anything. It all depends on how much of a self-starter you are whether or not you can overcome your handicap. Nobody will help you to set about finding out what you want to be or help you to be it. For I don't want to stress doing something as much as *being* what you want to be. Mere activity is the occupation of monkeys and lunatics. Still, unfortunately, doing and being are very closely tied together, and unless you are doing what you secretly want to do, you aren't able to be the sort of person you want to be."

Yet perhaps it is too much to demand of women that, without any help or encouragement, and indeed often with active discouragement and ridicule, they put aside privilege and take their place in the world's work as ordinary human beings. The Manchus could not do it. They too went on helplessly living in their palaces and houses, and then one day the Chinese realized there was no use in feeding them any more since they were no use to anybody, and so they put them all to death in a quiet, matter-of-fact way, and that was the end of the Manchus in China.

Of course exactly that will not happen to women anywhere unless some too enterprising male scientist succeeds in creating life without the help of the female. Women would then doubtless have a very hard time convincing the invincible male that there was any real reason for their further existence. But I hope that long before then the gunpowder women will have come to such a unified state of combustion out of sheer boredom that they will refuse to tolerate their condition of privilege any longer.

For the vital difference between the privileged Manchu and the privileged American woman is that the clever Chinese allowed the Manchu no modern education. He was born into his ivory tower and never left it. But the privileged American woman enters hers when she reaches her majority, and she takes with her the influences and the memories of a world in which she had a vital part in her youth and school years, and consequently she never becomes quite tame. If education improves enough, or if society suddenly develops a new need for women, the gunpowder may work more quickly than it is working now merely through the medium of individual discontent. The best thing of course that could happen to American women would be to have some real privation and suffering come upon us because we are women, instead of all this privilege. But we have had no such suffering and are not likely to have any. Everything has been too easy for us and is too easy now. We do not feel anybody's wrongs because we have never been severely wronged, except by all these privileges.

I am aware that at this point there are those who will insist that I am unrealistic when I say that the best thing that could happen to American women would be to lose their privileges—that, in the first place, when adversity comes upon a family the woman has plenty of work to do, and second, if women should go out in any large numbers to find jobs, men would promptly pass laws to prevent women holding jobs. To which I reply, first, if she can be occupied thoroughly at home, let her be, and second, laws discriminating against women on a large scale would be a splendid thing for women—especially for American women, spoiled and wilful, but high-spirited daughters of the same fathers as their men. If laws so discriminated on any large scale, then gunpowder women would rise up against them, and this revolt would do them infinite good. It would bring them out of their seclusion into the life of the nation. In demanding their rights as human beings they would realize at last that they had to *be* human beings as well as women to secure and hold that which they demand. And having fought for something, they might go on from there.

As things are, the only real hope for the progress of women generally is in those women who because of some personal necessity do work and take an active share in the life of the world, who are participants and not parasites. The working woman—may her number increase!—will not perhaps ever fight for women, but perhaps she will fight to right a wrong near her, and by her work, even now, all women are brought more actively into the life of the world. (5)

For I am convinced there is no way of progress for women except the way men have gone—the way of work or starve, work or be disgraced. A good many women are plodding, willingly or unwillingly, along that way, learning to take what they get and do with it, to live with hazard and competition, to push past failure and begin again, to keep their mouths shut instead of spilling over into talk or a good childish cry—in other words, they are becoming mature individuals in their own right.

It is a hard road for long-privileged creatures, and one is alternately amused and angry to see many of them avoiding it and retreating again into the home. The newest generation of women, frightened by the realities of depression and economic struggle, are clamoring afresh for marriage and the home, and today marriage competition is keener than ever. Women's interest in work and a profession has not been lower since the pioneering fight for women's rights was won than it is now. Indeed, it seems that the newest generation of women, having seen a glimpse of reality in the depression years, are in definite, full retreat into the safety of femininity, into the easy old ways of living to please one man, and catching him and persuading him to do the work for two. That more women now than ever before take it as a matter of course that they must find jobs and earn their living is meaningless so long as so many of them secretly hope to give up these jobs as soon as they marry—"stop work" as they put it—and go back to the traditional place in the home. Mind you, there are ways and places and times when a woman can find a full job in her home. But to one such woman there are fifty who do not and cannot, and there is no use in pretending they are earning their keep as human beings.

"Why earn if I don't have to?" someone asks. Well, why, if not simply to see if women do not feel happier, as men do, in using all faculties and capabilities? I am always glad when I hear a woman has to earn her own living. I scorn the usual talk, "Poor thing, she has to go out and work after all these years of being provided for!" Who gave anyone the right of being provided for all those years when everywhere in the world people have to work? Yet this is not the important thing. The real point upon which this woman is to be congratulated when she does have to work is that at last compulsion is upon her to exert her body and mind to its utmost, so that she may know what real fatigue is and honest exhaustion and the salutary fear that maybe she is not good enough for the job which brings her bread, and above all, know the final inexpressible joy of complete self-forgetfulness which comes only in soul-fulfilling work.

Work is the one supreme privilege which too many women in America with all their extraordinary unearned privileges never know. And yet it is the one privilege which will make them free. (6)

I ought really to stop here. It is a good stopping place. But I am uncomfortably aware of women who will cry out when they read this, "Why don't you tell us what to do? It is easy enough to say something is wrong, but the useful thing is to say what will right it."

To which I answer, nothing will right it for everybody at once. The most tragic person in our civilization is the middle-aged woman whose duties in the home are finished, whose children are gone, and who is in her mental and physical prime and yet feels there is no more need for her. She should have begun years before to plan for this. Her mind at least should have been working toward it at all times when her hands were busy. It is as difficult for her to begin something now in middle life as it would be for a middle-aged man to change his profession. How can she reëducate herself at fifty?

And yet I do not know that she is more piteous than the many young women, educated for nothing in particular, who now out of school are trying to find out what they are for. For the most part of course they occupy themselves in the enormously competitive marriage business which they carry on, unaided, in spite of their inexperience. If they marry, they follow the path the fifty-year-old woman has gone and arrive at the same dead end. The gunpowder group is made up of all of them, young and old.

"But what can we do?" When they are pricked, thus they bleed.

Well, what can women do in the United States, women who do not have to do anything?

I wonder if they realize, in the first place, how the United States looks to someone coming here freshly for the first time? It has of course many aspects. But all of these blend into one general impression. It looks like a bachelor's house. One does not see the much-talked-of "woman's touch" anywhere. It looks what it is—a country men have made alone. There are things and places of great beauty in it—and everywhere ugliness and untidiness and carelessness. It is a man's house, well furnished and with good pictures and rugs and considerable comfort, but there is dust and the rugs have not been swept under since they were put down, and things are lying about and there is disorder and lack of organization. I have driven through cities and towns and villages in many parts of the United States and thought to myself, "Can it be possible there are any women living here? How can they let this place be so hideous?" Billboards and tawdry stands, dirty streets and unpainted buildings, staring signs and dumps and filthy water—the much vaunted feminine instincts for beauty and organization and cleanliness seem not to extend beyond the four walls of immaculate individual homes. Women have the zenana outlook here too, it seems—these things outside the home are not their business.

I have not gone anywhere in the country without seeing something vitally necessary for women to do and which is not done—and without finding, too, these gunpowder women fuming with discontent because there was nothing to do. Can the American woman not see? It is simply foolish to list the things waiting for them to do. There is nothing they cannot do if they only would. They can make cleanliness and beauty in town and countryside in small ways and large, they can improve housing, plan houses and build them, go seriously after government positions, get better laws made and kept, improve conditions locally and nationally for children, investigate and change obsolete education in schools and text-books—work for women is everywhere. Who said men's brains were better at politics and government than women's? Yet only yesterday an able woman, working for her political party, sat in my office and told me disconsolately that women were given only petty offices in the party, assistant something-or-other, vice-presidencies on small committees, where their only duty was to obey the man above them. And why should obstetricians be men, or dentists or scientists or architects? I heard a famous gynecologist say last week that gynecology could never be perfected until women entered the field seriously, for no man could ever understand completely what child-bearing was or a woman's needs at that time. Business has been built almost entirely without the practical, constructive hands of women. If women had not been so hidden in the home we might never have had this accursed relation between capital and labor, not because women's influence would "exalt" a work-a-day world in the ridiculous sentimental sense in which some women like to think it would, but merely because women are more practical about human relations than men are, more sensitive to justice in diverse claims, and above all, far more experienced in adjustment and compromise. They should be better bargainers than men.

But all this sort of thing is obvious and every member of a woman's club must be familiar with it. Modern young women of energy are indeed fairly sick of hearing of such work and damn it as "uplift," without, however, I observe, having done anything about it. They let their interest, if they have any, be expressed in individual competence and achievement, too personal to allow of general suggestion here. Such individuals should take a good aptitude test and find out their own capabilities. My point still stands—to the newcomer, the United States presents the aspects of a bachelor's house. Woman's influence has everywhere been lacking. Whatever has developed in the life of the nation has developed without her brains and her effort. I do not put any stock in this matter of her inspiration of man in his home. It seems not to have had much actual effect. He has done as he wanted to do, with or without it. I suspect woman's inspiration of man has been a good deal of what men call "kidding the little woman along." How can one inspire when one does not understand through ordinary participation? (7)

Of course if women's work in the nation has scarcely begun, I am too much of a realist to believe that, were it all done, the nation would be completely changed for the better. Some things would be much better and some might be worse. The great change would not be in what women accomplished. It would be in the women themselves—that is, the gunpowder women. The talented women of the first group and the homemakers of the second group would be about as they are. Nothing will change them much. But the gunpowder women would be no longer fussing and fretting. Their energies would be happily released elsewhere than on harassed husbands and overwrought children.

But I refuse to be too cynical. I do believe the whole nation would be better off if women would do the work waiting to be done, and not only because these women themselves would be happier and their relations with men more satisfying than they now are. I believe that by using the energy now idle and the brains now disintegrating in that idleness women could immeasurably improve all conditions in our country, if they would. And, I repeat, it is perfect nonsense for any woman to ask what there is for her to do. There is everything for her to do. If she wants a small job, let her look around her village or her neighborhood. If she wants a big job, let her look around her State, or think as largely as her nation or even realize there is a world beyond. Let her remember she can do anything she wills to do. Not to see the infinite number of things to be done is to prove the damage that privilege does to the perceptions; not to do after she sees, is to prove the damage already done to the will.

Is it hopeless? For the women resigned to privilege, it is hopeless—for these women give up even discontent and pass into nothing. It is not necessary to give them a group to themselves. Having died, they simply await burial.

But for the gunpowder women there is every hope. I listen to their discontent with all the excitement and delight that a doctor knows when he hears the murmur and feels the beat of an uncertain heart, however fluttering and unstable, beneath his instrument. I know this, at least—as long as a woman complains, she is a gunpowder woman—and still alive. (8)

QUESTIONS

I

1. Into what three groups does the author divide women and what are the chief characteristics of each group? (1)
2. In what way is unearned privilege a disadvantage to gunpowder women? Why is it difficult for an Oriental woman to understand the privileged American woman? (2)
3. Why have men accomplished more than women? (3)
4. What kind of things does the gunpowder woman do to relieve her restlessness? In what way is the world arranged to man's advantage? (4)
5. According to the author, what would be the best thing that could happen to privileged women? (5)

6. In what direction are women headed at the present time? What one supreme privilege do many American women never know? (*6*)
7. What kinds of things are there for gunpowder women to do? (*7*)
8. What could these women accomplish for themselves and for the nation? Why does the author still have hope for them? (*8*)

II

1. Do you know women who fit into each of the author's classifications? Which group do you most admire? Which group do you think the most fortunate?
2. Do you accept the dictum "Necessity makes artists" as the reason why men outdistance women in most fields of endeavor?
3. Do you think Pearl Buck justified in severely criticizing such a large proportion of American women? Has she overestimated the number of women who belong in the gunpowder class?
4. Can you offer further suggestions as to what these women can do to improve their present situation of useless inactivity or their petty whirl of trivial social pleasures?
5. Comment upon the following excerpts from the essay: "The vicious result of privilege is that the creature who receives it becomes incapacitated by it as by a disease" (*2*); "Men and women are born free and equal in ability and brain" (*3*); "Women are more practical about human relations than men are ... [and are] far more experienced in adjustment and compromise" (*7*).
6. How do you account for the fact that the famous chefs in great hotels are men, the outstanding designers of women's dresses are men, the most successful decorators of homes are men?
7. Would you vote for a woman if she were running for the presidency of the United States?

III

1. What is the significance of the word *gunpowder* as used in this essay to describe certain women in America?
2. To what extent has the author drawn upon her years of living in the Orient for viewpoint? for illustrations?
3. What effect did the author hope to gain by setting one sentence off by itself as a paragraph? (*1*)
4. What is the effect of the first sentence of (*7*): "I ought really to stop here"?
5. Point out places where the author, in the midst of her strictures, insists that she is not *blaming* the gunpowder women. Are you convinced that she is viewing the subject dispassionately and objectively?

WORDS

Discuss the meanings of the following words from the viewpoint of their etymologies.

1. temerity (*1*): Latin *temere*, "rashly"
2. congenital (*1*): Latin *con-*, "with" and *genere*, "to beget"
3. incapacitated (*2*): Latin *in-*, "not" and *capere*, "to take, to hold"
4. astute (*2*): Latin *astus*, "craft"
5. naïve (*2*): Latin *nativus*, "innate, native"
6. ineffectuality (*2*): Latin *in-*, "not" and *ex-*, "out, from" and *facere*, "to make"
7. sinister (*2*): Latin *sinister*, "left" (the evil side)
8. soporific (*3*): Latin *sopor*, "heavy sleep" and *facere*, "to make"
9. compulsory (*4*): Latin *con-*, "with" and *pellere*, "to drive"
10. invincible (*5*): Latin *in-*, "not" and *vincere*, "to conquer"
11. adversity (*5*): Latin *ad-*, "to, toward" and *vertere*, "to turn"
12. parasites (*5*): Greek *para-*, "beside" and *sitos*, "food"
13. salutary (*6*): Latin *salus, salutis*, "health"
14. tawdry (*7*): From Saint Audrey (at whose fair cheap laces were sold)
15. immaculate (*7*): Latin *im-*, "not" and *maculare*, "to spot"
16. disconsolately (*7*): Latin *dis-*, "deprived of" and *consolari*, "to console"
17. obstetricians (*7*): Latin *ob-*, "before" and *stare*, "to stand"
18. gynecology (*7*): Greek *gyneco-*, "woman" and *-logy*, "study"
19. disintegrating (*8*): Latin *dis-*, "apart" and *integer*, "whole"
20. neighborhood (*8*): Anglo-Saxon *nēah*, "near, close" and *gebūr*, "farmer" and *-hood*, "state of being"

THEME TOPICS

1. Woman's Place Is in the Home
2. A Great Woman Scientist (Writer, Singer, Actress)
3. It's a Man's World
4. Women in Politics
5. American Women Are Lucky (Pampered, Privileged, Restless)
6. A Gunpowder Woman in Our Town
7. Man's Privilege of Having to Work
8. Men Are Not Superior Creatures
9. What I Want My Husband (Wife) to Be
10. The Future of Women in America

THE DECISION IS SIMPLE

BROOKS ATKINSON

TO BE confused is to be weak. To be weak is to be lost. Yet many people profess to be confused by the shrieking world that is erupting all around them. "I don't know what to believe," they say, or "I can't make head or tail of anything." Perhaps some of the confusion derives from an unwillingness to face the stark facts, and their appalling consequences to us as well as to other nations in the world. But no one except a vain or superficial man would imagine that his mind is perfectly clear about peace, war, and the other great issues of the day. For the simple fact is that no one is master of a world that has plunged out of control, least of all the neurotic despot who symbolizes for most of us the grim and gruesome drive for world conquest. No one now can control the evil that has broken out of the charnel houses and is spreading across Europe and Asia and leaping across the oceans to our hemisphere.

But it seems to me that the confusion is superficial, a matter of policy—rather than fundamental, a matter of morals. It derives chiefly from politics, which is subtle and mischievous, and economics, which is intricate and open to dispute. Neither politics nor economics is an integral part of the world of God and nature in which we move and have our being. We must not be guided by them. Politics is a game of wits played on or just under the surface, dealing in half truths and deliberate misrepresentations and maneuvering for advantages. It is a game of barter and deception. Strictly speaking, there are no honest politicians. Our happiness, our lives, are largely affected by politics, particularly by political blunders like the long series of evasions and intrigues that concluded with the declarations of war in September of 1939.

But the cynical, beady-eyed world of politics is not the one you and I inhabit in our relations with our neighbors and friends. The political world is not a complete expression of human nature. Nor is the economic world a complete one. It is not a part of human life. It is the technique of the production and distribution of wealth, and the busy, smoky, clattering little area it occupies is hedged around with property. It does not represent anything fundamental in human nature. If we were condemned to live all our lives in the economic world we should have to get on without drama, music, literature, and dancing, without love and friends, without birds and trees, without the grandeur of the sea. The freedom of spirit, which is the vital part of human creation, has finer-spun spheres of influence to occupy than the economic world. Although the ordeal of the world now is at least in part a clash of opposing economies, that is not the reason our hearts stand still when we read the news from Britain, China, and the Near East. Politics and economics clutter our minds a good deal more than we wish they did, but they do not come out of our souls and they are only casually related to the fulness of life we have an instinct for living. (1)

When evidence appears to be confusing, it is wise to make simple decisions that represent the integrity of our characters. Wise decisions harmonize with the fundamental truths of human nature. Now, the basic questions that people are asking themselves today are moral ones. In the last analysis, we are concerned with what is right and wrong. I am not talking of personal morals, which involve matters of taste, local custom, and religious creed; I am referring to social morals. They are the standards of behavior that men, living together in social groups, have evolved out of their consciousness and unconsciousness as the working truths of mankind. Social morals have an ancient lineage that goes back further than the laws of Moses. Social morals derive from the belief that men have unlimited capacities for growth out of barbarism into consciousness, out of the appetites of animalism into nobility. By certain fundamental agreements, involving justice, mercy, freedom of thought and expression, social groups nurture and cultivate the growth of mankind. The moral nation is the one that guarantees the freedom of the people, safeguards the health of the population, educates and cherishes the children, fosters art, spreads knowledge, endeavors to promote honest dealings between individuals and groups, lives as a good neighbor with other nations, tries constantly to widen and deepen its understanding with faith in the destiny of mankind.

In the superficial worlds of politics and economics nearly all the current questions can be argued. We can easily confuse each other over a great many plausible questions—whether economic necessity forces Japan to dominate the East, whether Germany has an ethnographic right to draw boundaries according to racial strength in adjoining countries. These questions and questions like these can be argued until everyone loses his convictions.

But the moral test is not open to argument. Even in a headlong world we can find a solid place on which to stand if we ask ourselves what is right and wrong in human conduct; and I think the basic factors in the current world situation are beyond questioning. To put everything in the simplest moral terms—it was wrong for Japan to grab Manchukuo in 1931 and to spread like a scourge through China, contemptuously bombing civilians in the cities that have resisted; wrong for Italy to ravage Ethiopia, wrong for Germany and Italy to conspire against the legitimate government of Spain, wrong for Germany to roll tyrannically with a clatter of guns and rifles into Austria, Czechoslovakia, Poland, Norway, Sweden, Denmark, Holland, Belgium, Rumania, Bulgaria; wrong for Russia to engulf the small Baltic states and to crush the national independence of the Finns. These things are wrong, not because they violate international law, but because they have struck at the spirit of man, which is the creative force of the world. They have stained civilization red by the inhumanity of their motives and methods.

It will be noticed that the sequence of evil has constantly increased in horror and contempt: that the Japanese defended the larceny of Manchukuo as law-enforcement against bandits in 1931, but that Germany did not feel required to defend her treacherous conquests of Denmark, Norway, Holland, and Belgium in 1940. For evil feeds on evil and the cunning hand acquires skill in murder. The course of events from 1931 to 1940 points the way that the coming years will follow if thieves, murderers, and despots are not curbed. These things are wrong: there are blunt words for them with moral overtones—pillage, rapine, slaughter, treason, savagery. The blood has spattered around the world; the air aches from suffering; the patient earth is scorched and blistered and has meekly opened to receive her dead. This is the moral indictment.

Granted that these are perversions of the moral code of social living, what is the next step? Many people feel especially confused here. But in the sphere of morals a man does not bargain with thugs and murderers for his personal safety. (Incidentally, it does him no good.) For the man of moral integrity lives day by day according to a code of honor without regard for his personal advantage. He stands for what is honorable and tries to promote honorable actions; he opposes with his full strength actions that are dishonorable. When his brothers are viciously assaulted, driven from home and herded in bleak barracks, robbed, starved, tortured, and killed, he does not consider the consequences of what he says and does. Whatever violates the code by which he lives with his fellows is his business and he dedicates himself to correcting it. For the moral code is not a system of etiquette for polite social usage. It composes the fundamental truths of humanity and justice, wrung out of the painful experience of mankind since civilization began, and founded on the faith that men can flourish on love and enlightenment. (2)

All this comes painfully close to home. If the democratic way of life were not a moral concept of human relations it would not be worth preserving. If freedom were not creative, and the vital source of the present and future, it would not be worth the staggering price we must pay to retain and strengthen it. To look on democracy simply as a form of government is to underestimate the fulness of the life it nourishes. It does not merely preserve our liberties; it enriches our spirit. It is part of the moral wisdom of the ages—men living together with mutual respect in the tradition of a common destiny. Far from being one stage in the development of civilization or a lucky set of laws, it is a fundamental idea, and it cannot be regarded as moribund or inefficient because it has not yet been achieved.

I am surprised now and then to see people shaking their heads ruefully over matters of principle that should make them hold their heads high. For a century and a half we have been establishing in this country a working democracy without the curb or impediment of a ruling class. We were lucky in the beginning. Class distinctions and feudal ideas had not time to become embedded in our soil. If the slate was not entirely clean when the Constitution was written, it was cleaner of privilege than any other slate of that time, and wiping it clean in 1787 was a fairly painless process. In a century and a half there has never been a time when any considerable body of the country looked back longingly at the old ways of Europe.

Although we have never achieved full democracy we have progressed steadily in that direction with a robustiousness that at times has seemed comic to sophisticated worldlings. The tone has often been grandiloquent, for the free American loves to sound off. But the progress has been astonishing. See how the wealth of the country has been developed. See how widely education has been spread. Contrast the confident tone of labor today with the meekness of factory workers a century ago. Contrast working conditions today with those that existed early in your own lifetime. I remember the early morning whistle and the servility of factory workers in my home town when I was a boy. The progress toward the "dignity of man," as it is somewhat fatuously described today, has been swift and far-reaching and is still running in the progressive direction.

Everyone ought to feel encouraged by something that is right from the moral point of view and that also happens to work. Everyone ought to be proud. But I occasionally encounter the faint-hearted. After all these decades some people have missed the main point. Some weeks ago a financier said to me, half in reverie, I hope: "Perhaps democracy has fulfilled its function. Other forms of government have collapsed in the past, and there is no reason to believe that democracy is any exception. Perhaps we are too prejudiced to see what fascism has to offer in an industrial civilization." Well, it is discouraging to encounter that much obtuseness at this late hour in the day. If democracy has fulfilled its function, the financier is through. But why should we take the low view? Why not take the high view, which is this: If democracy has outlived its usefulness, Christ was the most calamitous of false prophets, Lincoln was an eloquent nit-wit, and we have been tragically misguided as a nation. If democracy has outlived its usefulness, slavery is the highest state to which man can aspire. (3)

Most of us understand that the ordeal of the world today is not only a war but a revolution. The violence that explodes and blazes in strange places is not the wilful invention of one fiend in military dress but an agonizing readjustment in the lives of nations. The same readjustment, incidentally, has been going on here amid considerable screaming. But let us not helplessly regard violence as the way civilized nations normally put their house in order. The violence of the past nine years in Asia and Europe has not emanated from any nation that has been founded on the democratic tradition of seeking and obeying the accumulated common sense of a well-informed populace. Violence is barbaric; it represents either a collapse or a lack of mind and moral integrity. In spite of the fact that violence wears a look of injured righteousness, it is purely and desperately destructive. It is not a philosophy of community living, but a brutally real force in the current world, and an attitude of benign laissez-faire cannot stand up against it. To meet it we must strengthen ourselves with more of the muscle and fiber that already have given us the widely-recognized strength of today. What the idealists of the eighteenth century created out of faith in man's infinite capacities must be more abundantly fulfilled. Our system of government needs profound and radical development in the direction of total democracy.

In a general way, what we have now is political and religious democracy—wonders a century ago but commonplace rights of the individual man in the United States of today. People speak freely in public and in the press. People assemble openly to discuss public policy, criticizing the chief executive sometimes with unnatural passion. All men—not merely men of property, as it used to be—vote on election day with moving solemnity and they instinctively accept the common verdict. Moreover, people worship in churches of their own choosing without fear of persecution, and there is no official church. Although occasional abuses break out against these forms of liberty, the people as a whole loathe intolerance. Throwing eggs and fruit at the opposing candidate shocks people deeply and arouses a storm of protest. Disfiguring synagogues, forming secret anti-Catholic organizations, are flagrant violations of the democratic faith, and they are commonly hated. On the whole, we have achieved political and religious democracy because they are morally right. They also work, which, as it happens, is no part of the moral question, although it is conspicuously encouraging. (4)

But no democracy can be regarded as fulfilled until everyone participates equally. No freedom is absolute unless it is extended to all people, and until everyone has equal freedom of action. I assume that no one believes we have developed democracy that far in this country. The Negro race, with a population of 12,-000,000, was established here by our ancestors under conditions we have since repudiated, but it is still held in economic and social bondage through the ancient evil of race prejudice. The free action of the Jews in our society is curtailed by race prejudice. Race prejudice is fomented by vicious journals sold in the public streets. Moreover, many white Americans are living mean and meager lives. Thousands of tenant farmers are caught between the grindstones of an industrial economy, and are existing in wretched conditions without hope. Thousands are scratching land that has been worn out for decades. Thousands have been dispossessed from dead land by the baking sun and the blistering winds and have crawled out of the inferno of dust storms toward land that looks green. More than four million families are subsisting below the minimum standards of safe diet on a food expenditure of $1.06 per person a week. Even in these abnormal times of rearmament, 6,500,000 out of an estimated working population of 55,000,000 are unemployed and sustained by makeshift programs that are commonly held in disfavor. England's economy has not supported its entire working population for more than two decades. Ours has failed in its primary function—that of supporting the entire population—for one decade. To millions of Americans, therefore, democracy is a hypocritical word; it tastes sour on the tongue. To have such a large portion of the population cut off from the basic principle of the country is a dangerous practical weakness. From the moral point of view it is wrong.

These festers on the body of the country are not all of a kind and cannot be cured by the same therapy. Like an old canker that sleeps in the system, breaking out at recurrent intervals, race prejudice is a virulent form of ignorance. It can be fought only with knowledge and moral teaching. Although it cannot be cured in any man's lifetime it can be steadily alleviated. Teaching, which is the active form of faith, digs deeper and deeper into the consciousness of every generation.

But the spread of economic democracy among people able to work is capable of quicker fulfilment. For this is a matter of economics, which is not a part of human vitality, but a technique of the production and distribution of wealth, and it has no relation to human life apart from what we choose to give it. Fortunately, it can be changed any time it does not meet the democratic needs of the country, and it can be changed by lawful process if the people will it that way. Geoffrey Crowther, editor of *The Economist* of London, estimates that a half of the national income in normal times would guarantee adequate living conditions to every person in that country, and probably the same proportion of income would do the same job here. The price would be cheap in comparison with the good it would create. People are more frightened by economic changes than by any other. They accept without protest the principle of drafting an army, although it infringes remarkably upon personal liberty. But the prevailing system of economics involves property, which in turn represents to most people at least the illusion of security; and people hang on to property rights with a kind of ominous desperation.

From the moral point of view, which is the foundation of the democratic way of life, we have first to ask ourselves what is right and wrong. Is economic freedom as essential to democracy as political and religious freedom? Is it right from the moral point of view to keep millions of people ill-fed when the granaries are choked with unsold surpluses, or to have millions of people living in primitive conditions when in normal times the production capacities of industry are only partly used? Are human needs more vital than property rights?

For all this is an essential part of the warfare that has been raging with increasing cruelty all over the world for about eight years, driving millions of people into forlorn exile, sentencing whole populations to slavery at the point of a rifle, defiling the wonders of the deep with the broken hulls of ships and the cold bodies of sailors; murdering men, women, and children in convulsions of terror; crushing the truth that we have labored for centuries to lift out of the darkness. Are these things right or wrong? We cannot foresee the result of the steps we take to resist and stop them. But people who are not degenerate know what direction those steps must take. (5)

QUESTIONS

I

1. What is the author's opinion of economics and politics as related to our lives? What would life lack if it were entirely economic? (1)
2. What is the nature of the real problem that faces us? Why can there be no confusion in our thinking about dictator nations? (2)
3. What is democracy besides a form of government? Why is the author surprised at people who doubt democracy? (3)
4. Why have the democracies not been responsible for any of the violence at work in the world? To what extent have we attained democracy? (4)
5. What are some of the tasks remaining for democracy to accomplish? By answering what simple question can we decide our policy of action? (5)

II

1. Have you been prone to think that politics and economics are more fundamental in your life than the author says they are? Do you agree with him that, in a way, all politicians are "dishonest"? How must we interpret "dishonest" as used here?
2. "The moral test is not open to argument." What, then, must a man of moral integrity do to oppose local, national, or international dishonesty?

3. Have you heard statements that suggested that democracy has outlived its usefulness? What is your candid opinion on this point?
4. What nice distinction does the author make between personal and social morals? (2) Are they, in your opinion, completely separated or interrelated.
5. Do you think that race hatred and democracy are incompatible?
6. Can America have real democracy as long as the prevailing economic system, embodying a faulty balance between production and distribution, fails to guarantee adequate living conditions to large segments of our population?

III

1. By reference to the current universal chaos and confusion which beset the world, the author achieves two results: he catches attention and he introduces his subject. Discuss this as an excellent type of beginning.
2. What is the effect of the word *wrong* several times repeated in (2)?
3. The author's thesis is revealed in his statement that the moral point of view—What is *right*? What is *wrong*?—is the foundation of the democratic way of life. Do you consider that this thesis has been established by Mr. Atkinson in this essay?

WORDS

One can learn much about words by capitalizing the knowledge he already possesses. This exercise offers an opportunity to learn as much as you can about the following words from what you already know. Of course, your final resort will be to the dictionary.

1. stark (1): The common expression "stark naked" will probably aid you.
2. neurotic (1): *Neuritis*, or even *nerve*, will help you.
3. charnel (1): If you know the expression "carnal pleasures" or remember the word *carnivorous*, you have a slight cue.
4. lineage (2): It is the "line" of birth and -*age*.
5. animalism (2): Your knowledge of *animal* will define this word for you.
6. larceny (2): Other words offer little assistance with this word, but *latro*, in Latin, means "robber."
7. rapine (2): You have already had *rapere*, "to seize."
8. moribund (3): *Mortal* and *mortality* will help you.
9. ruefully (3): The common expression "You'll rue the day" may suggest the meaning for you.

10. robustiousness (*3*): *Robust* will give you this word.
11. grandiloquent (*3*): You know *grand*, and *elocution* will tell you the rest.
12. servility (*3*): *Servitude*, or even *servant*, will help you.
13. fatuously (*3*): Other words offer little assistance with this word, but *fatuus*, in Latin, means "foolish."
14. obtuseness (*3*): Your knowledge of an *obtuse* angle will help you.
15. calamitous (*3*): *Calamity* will define this word for you.
16. emanated (*4*): There is little help on this word, but *manare*, in Latin, means "to flow."
17. flagrant (*4*): Badness is now the basic idea in the word, but it comes from Latin *flagrare*, "to burn."
18. repudiated (*5*): Frequently used of nations *repudiating* their debts.
19. fomented (*5*): The change in meaning of this word can best be traced in a dictionary.
20. therapy (*5*): You often hear in radio commercials of the *therapeutical* value of certain medicines.
21. virulent (*5*): You possibly know the word *virus*, "poison," which gives the cue.
22. alleviated (*5*): *Levity* will give you some help.
23. infringes (*5*): You have had *frangible* and *fragile*, which give the cue.
24. ominous (*5*): *Omen* is at the basis of this word.
25. degenerate (*5*): From your knowledge of the verb *degenerate*, you can derive the adjective.

THEME TOPICS

1. Right Is Right and Wrong Is Wrong
2. Personal Morals *vs.* Social Morals
3. Moral Decisions Should Be Simple
4. Race Prejudice and Democracy
5. A Doubting Thomas I Know
6. The Economic World Is Not All
7. The Moral Indictment against Japan (Germany, Italy)
8. The Game of Politics
9. I Want (Do Not Want) to Be a Politician
10. Democracy's Strength in a Crisis

MATERIALISM AND IDEALISM IN
AMERICAN LIFE

GEORGE SANTAYANA

THE language and traditions common to England and America are like other family bonds: they draw kindred together at the greater crises in life, but they also occasion at times a little friction and fault-finding. The groundwork of the two societies is so similar, that each nation, feeling almost at home with the other, and almost able to understand its speech, may instinctively resent what hinders it from feeling at home altogether. Differences will tend to seem anomalies that have slipped in by mistake and through somebody's fault. Each will judge the other by his own standards, not feeling, as in the presence of complete foreigners, that he must make an effort of imagination and put himself in another man's shoes.

In matters of morals, manners, and art, the danger of comparisons is not merely that they may prove invidious, by ranging qualities in an order of merit which might wound somebody's vanity; the danger is rather that comparisons may distort comprehension, because in truth good qualities are all different in kind, and free lives are different in spirit. Comparison is the expedient of those who cannot reach the heart of the things compared; and no philosophy is more external and egotistical than that which places the essence of a thing in its relation to something else. In reality, at the center of every natural being there is something individual and incommensurable, a seed with its native impulses and aspirations, shaping themselves as best they can in their given environment. Variation is a consequence of freedom, and the slight but radical diversity of souls in turn

From *Character and Opinion in the United States.* Reprinted by permission of Charles Scribner's Sons, the American publishers of this book.

makes freedom requisite. Instead of instituting in his mind any comparisons between the United States and other nations, I would accordingly urge the reader to forget himself and, in so far as such a thing may be possible for him or for me, to transport himself ideally with me into the outer circumstances of American life, the better to feel its inner temper, and to see how inevitably the American shapes his feelings and judgments, honestly reporting all things as they appear from his new and unobstructed station. (*1*)

I speak of the American in the singular, as if there were not millions of them, north and south, east and west, of both sexes, of all ages, and of various races, professions, and religions. Of course the one American I speak of is mythical; but to speak in parables is inevitable in such a subject, and it is perhaps as well to do so frankly. There is a sort of poetic ineptitude in all human discourse when it tries to deal with natural and existing things. Practical men may not notice it, but in fact human discourse is intrinsically addressed not to natural existing things but to ideal essences, poetic or logical terms which thought may define and play with. When fortune or necessity diverts our attention from this congenial ideal sport to crude facts and pressing issues, we turn our frail poetic ideas into symbols for those terrible irruptive things. In that paper money of our own stamping, the legal tender of the mind, we are obliged to reckon all the movements and values of the world. The universal American I speak of is one of these symbols; and I should be still speaking in symbols and creating moral units and a false simplicity, if I spoke of classes pedantically subdivided, or individuals ideally integrated and defined. As it happens, the symbolic American can be made largely adequate to the facts; because, if there are immense differences between individual Americans—for some Americans are black—yet there is a great uniformity in their environment, customs, temper, and thoughts. They have all been uprooted from their several soils and ancestries and plunged together into one vortex, whirling irresistibly in a space otherwise quite empty. To be an American is of itself almost a moral condition, an education, and a career. Hence a single ideal figment can cover a large part of what each American is in his character, and almost the whole of what most Americans are in their social outlook and political judgments. (2)

The discovery of the new world exercised a sort of selection among the inhabitants of Europe. All the colonists, except the Negroes, were voluntary exiles. The fortunate, the deeply rooted, and the lazy remained at home; the wilder instincts or dissatisfaction of others tempted them beyond the horizon. The American is accordingly the most adventurous, or the descendant of the most adventurous, of Europeans. It is in his blood to be socially a radical, though perhaps not intellectually. What has existed in the past, especially in the remote past, seems to him not only authoritative, but irrelevant, inferior, and outworn. He finds it rather a sorry waste of time to think about the past at all. But his enthusiasm for the future is profound; he can conceive of no more decisive way of recommending an opinion or a practice than to say that it is what everybody is coming to adopt. This expectation of what he approves, or approval of what he expects, makes up his optimism. It is the necessary faith of the pioneer.

Such a temperament is, of course, not maintained in the nation merely by inheritance. Inheritance notoriously tends to restore the average of a race, and plays incidentally many a trick of atavism. What maintains this temperament and makes it national is social contagion or pressure—something immensely strong in democracies. The luckless American who is born a conservative, or who is drawn to poetic subtlety, pious retreats, or gay passions, nevertheless has the categorical excellence of work, growth, enterprise, reform, and prosperity dinned into his ears: every door is open in this direction and shut in the other; so that he either folds up his heart and withers in a corner—in remote places you sometimes find such a solitary gaunt idealist—or else he flies to Oxford or Florence or Montmartre to save his soul—or perhaps not to save it.

The optimism of the pioneer is not limited to his view of himself and his own future: it starts from that; but feeling assured, safe, and cheery within, he looks with smiling and most kindly eyes on everything and everybody about him. Individualism, roughness, and self-trust are supposed to go with selfishness and a cold heart; but I suspect that is a prejudice. It is rather dependence, insecurity, and mutual jostling that poison our placid gregarious brotherhood; and fanciful passionate demands upon people's affections, when they are disappointed, as they soon must be, breed ill-will and a final meanness. The milk of human kindness is less apt to turn sour if the vessel that holds it stands steady, cool, and separate, and is not too often uncorked. In his affections the American is seldom passionate, often deep, and always kindly. If it were given me to look into the depths of a man's heart, and I did not find good-will at the bottom, I should say without any hesitation, You are not American. But as the American is an individualist his good-will is not officious. His instinct is to think well of everybody, and to wish everybody well, but in a spirit of rough comradeship, expecting every man to stand on his own legs and to be helpful in his turn. When he has given his neighbor a chance he thinks he has done enough for him; but he feels it is an absolute duty to do that. It will take some hammering to drive a coddling socialism into America.

As self-trust may pass into self-sufficiency, so optimism, kindness, and good-will may grow into a habit of doting on everything. To the good American many subjects are sacred: sex is sacred, women are sacred, children are sacred, business is sacred, America is sacred, Masonic lodges and college clubs are sacred. This feeling grows out of the good opinion he wishes to have of these things, and serves to maintain it. If he did not regard all these things as sacred he might come to doubt sometimes if they were wholly good. Of this kind, too, is the idealism of single ladies in reduced circumstances who can see the soul of beauty in ugly things, and are perfectly happy because their old dog has such pathetic eyes, their minister is so eloquent, their garden with its three sunflowers is so pleasant, their dead friends were so devoted, and their distant relations are so rich. (3)

Consider now the great emptiness of America: not merely the primitive physical emptiness, surviving in some regions, and the continental spacing of the chief natural features, but also the moral emptiness of a settlement where men and even houses are easily moved about, and no one, almost, lives where he was born or believes what he has been taught. Not that the American has jettisoned these impedimenta in anger; they have simply slipped from him as he moves. Great empty spaces bring a sort of freedom to both soul and body. You may pitch your tent where you will; or if ever you decide to build anything, it can be in a style of your own devising. You have room, fresh materials, few models, and no critics. You trust your own experience, not only because you must, but because you find you may do so safely and prosperously; the forces that determine fortune are not yet too complicated for one man to explore. Your detachable condition makes you lavish with money and cheerfully experimental; you lose little if you lose all, since you remain completely yourself. At the same time your absolute initiative gives you practice in coping with novel situations, and in being original; it teaches you shrewd management. Your life and mind will become dry and direct, with few decorative flourishes. In your works everything will be stark and pragmatic; you will not understand why anybody should make those little sacrifices to instinct or custom which we call grace. The fine arts will seem to you academic luxuries, fit to amuse the ladies, like Greek and Sanskrit; for while you will perfectly appreciate generosity in men's purposes, you will not admit that the execution of these purposes can be anything but business. Unfortunately the essence of the fine arts is that the execution should be generous too, and delightful in itself; therefore the fine arts will suffer, not so much in their express professional pursuit—for then they become practical tasks and a kind of business—as in that diffused charm which qualifies all human action when men are artists by nature. Elaboration, which is something to accomplish, will be preferred to simplicity, which is something to rest in; manners will suffer somewhat; speech will suffer horribly. For the American the urgency of his novel attack upon matter, his zeal in gathering its fruits, precludes meanderings in primrose paths; devices must be short cuts, and symbols must be mere symbols. If his wife wants luxuries, of course she may have them; and if he has vices, that can be provided for too; but they must all be set down under those headings in his ledgers.

At the same time, the American is imaginative; for where life is intense, imagination is intense also. Were he not imaginative he would not live so much in the future. But his imagination is practical, and the future it forecasts is immediate; it works with the clearest and least ambiguous terms known to his experience, in terms of number, measure, contrivance, economy, and speed. He is an idealist working on matter. Understanding as he does the material potentialities of things, he is successful in invention, conservative in reform, and quick in emergencies. All his life he jumps into the train after it has started and jumps out before it has stopped; and he never once gets left behind, or breaks a leg. There is an enthusiasm in his sympathetic handling of material forces which goes far to cancel the illiberal character which it might otherwise assume. The good workman hardly distinguishes his artistic intention from the potency in himself and in things which is about to realize that intention. Accordingly his ideals fall into the form of premonitions and prophecies; and his studious prophecies often come true. So do the happy workmanlike ideals of the American. When a poor boy, perhaps, he dreams of an education, and presently he gets an education, or at least a degree; he dreams of growing rich, and he grows rich—only more slowly and modestly, perhaps, than he expected; he dreams of marrying his Rachel and, even if he marries a Leah instead, he ultimately finds in Leah his Rachel after all. He dreams of helping to carry on and to accelerate the movement of a vast, seething, progressive society, and he actually does so. Ideals clinging so close to nature are almost sure of fulfilment; the American beams with a certain self-confidence and sense of mastery; he feels that God and nature are working with him.

Idealism in the American accordingly goes hand in hand with present contentment and with foresight of what the future very likely will actually bring. He is not a revolutionist; he believes he is already on the right track and moving towards an excellent destiny. In revolutionists, on the contrary, idealism is founded on dissatisfaction and expresses it. What exists seems to them an absurd jumble of irrational accidents and bad habits, and they want the future to be based on reason and to be the pellucid embodiment of all their maxims. All their zeal is for something radically different from the actual and (if they only knew it) from the possible; it is ideally simple, and they love it and believe in it because their nature craves it. They think life would be set free by the destruction of all its organs. They are therefore extreme idealists in the region of hope, but not at all, as poets and artists are, in the region of perception and memory. In the atmosphere of civilized life they miss all the refraction and all the fragrance; so that in their conception of actual things they are apt to be crude realists; and their ignorance and inexperience of the moral world, unless it comes of ill-luck, indicates their incapacity for education. Now incapacity for education, when united with great inner vitality, is one root of idealism. It is what condemns us all, in the region of sense, to substitute perpetually what we are capable of imagining for what things may be in themselves; it is what condemns us, wherever it extends, to think *a priori*; it is what keeps us bravely and incorrigibly pursuing what we call the good—that is, what would fulfill the demands of our nature —however little provision the fates may have made for it. But the want of insight on the part of revolutionists touching the past and the present infects in an important particular their idealism about the future; it renders their dreams of the future unrealizable. For in human beings—this may not be true of other animals, more perfectly preformed—experience is necessary to pertinent and concrete thinking; even our primitive instincts are blind until they stumble upon some occasion that solicits them; and they can be much transformed or deranged by their first partial satisfactions. Therefore a man who does not idealize his experience, but idealizes *a priori*, is incapable of true prophecy; when he dreams he raves, and the more he criticizes the less he helps. American idealism, on the contrary, is nothing if not helpful, nothing if not pertinent to practicable transformations; and when the American frets, it is because whatever is useless and impertinent, be it idealism or inertia, irritates him; for it frustrates the good results which he sees might so easily have been obtained. (4)

The American is wonderfully alive; and his vitality, not having often found a suitable outlet, makes him appear agitated on the surface; he is always letting off an unnecessarily loud blast of incidental steam. Yet his vitality is not superficial; it is inwardly prompted, and as sensitive and quick as a magnetic needle. He is inquisitive, and ready with an answer to any question that he may put to himself of his own accord; but if you try to pour instruction into him, on matters that do not touch his own spontaneous life, he shows the most extraordinary powers of resistance and oblivescence; so that he often is remarkably expert in some directions and surprisingly obtuse in others. He seems to bear lightly the sorrowful burden of human knowledge. In a word, he is young.

What sense is there in this feeling, which we all have, that the American is young? His country is blessed with as many elderly people as any other, and his descent from Adam, or from the Darwinian rival of Adam, cannot be shorter than that of his European cousins. Nor are his ideas always very fresh. Trite and rigid bits of morality and religion, with much seemly and antique political lore, remain axiomatic in him, as in the mind of a child; he may carry all this about with an unquestioning familiarity which does not comport understanding. To keep traditional sentiments in this way insulated and uncriticized is itself a sign of youth. A good young man is naturally conservative and loyal on all those subjects which his experience has not brought to a test; advanced opinions on politics, marriage, or literature are comparatively rare in America; they are left for the ladies to discuss, and usually to condemn, while the men get on with their work. In spite of what is old-fashioned in his more general ideas, the American is unmistakably young; and this, I should say, for two reasons: one, that he is chiefly occupied with his immediate environment, and the other, that his reactions upon it are inwardly prompted, spontaneous, and full of vivacity and self-trust. His views are not yet lengthened; his will is not yet broken or transformed. The present moment, however, in this, as in other things, may mark a great change in him; he is perhaps now reaching his majority, and all I say may hardly apply today, and may not apply at all tomorrow. I speak of him as I have known him; and whatever moral strength may accrue to him later, I am not sorry to have known him in his youth. The charm of youth, even when it is a little boisterous, lies in nearness to the impulses of nature, in a quicker and more obvious obedience to that pure, seminal principle which, having formed the body and its organs, always directs their movements, unless it is forced by vice or necessity to make them crooked, or to suspend them. Even under the inevitable crust of age the soul remains young, and, wherever it is able to break through, sprouts into something green and tender. We are all as young at heart as the most youthful American, but the seed in his case has fallen upon virgin soil, where it may spring up more bravely and with less respect for the giants of the wood. Peoples seem older when their perennial natural youth is encumbered with more possessions and prepossessions, and they are mindful of the many things they have lost or missed. The American is not mindful of them. (5)

In America there is a tacit optimistic assumption about existence, to the effect that the more existence the better. The soulless critic might urge that quantity is only a physical category, implying no excellence, but at best an abundance of opportunities both for good and for evil. Yet the young soul, being curious and hungry, views existence *a priori* under the form of the good; its instinct to live implies a faith that most things it can become or see or do will be worth while. Respect for quantity is accordingly something more than the childish joy and wonder at bigness; it is the fisherman's joy in a big haul, the good uses of which he can take for granted. Such optimism is amiable. Nature cannot afford that we should begin by being too calculating or wise, and she encourages us by the pleasure she attaches to our functions in advance of their fruits, and often in excess of them; as the angler enjoys catching his fish more than eating it, and often, waiting patiently for the fish to bite, misses his own supper. The pioneer must devote himself to preparations; he must work for the future, and it is healthy and dutiful of him to love his work for its own sake. At the same time, unless reference to an ultimate purpose is at least virtual in all his activities, he runs the danger of becoming a living automaton, vain and ignominious in its mechanical constancy. Idealism about work can hide an intense materialism about life. Man, if he is a rational being, cannot live by bread alone nor be a laborer merely; he must eat and work in view of an ideal harmony which overarches all his days, and which is realized in the way they hang together, or in some ideal issue which they have in common. Otherwise, though his technical philosophy may call itself idealism, he is a materialist in morals; he esteems things, and esteems himself, for mechanical uses and energies. Even sensualists, artists, and pleasure-lovers are wiser than that, for though their idealism may be desultory or corrupt, they attain something ideal, and prize things only for their living effects, moral though perhaps fugitive. Sensation, when we do not take it as a signal for action, but arrest and peruse what it positively brings before us, reveals something ideal—a color, shape, or sound; and to dwell on these presences, with no thought of their material significance, is an aesthetic or dreamful idealism. To pass from this idealism to the knowledge of matter is a great intellectual advance, and goes with dominion over the world; for in the practical arts the mind is adjusted to a larger object, with more depth and potentiality in it; which is what makes people feel that the material world is real, as they call it, and that the ideal world is not. Certainly the material world is real; for the philosophers who deny the existence of matter are like the critics who deny the existence of Homer. If there was never any Homer, there must have been a lot of other poets no less Homeric than he; and if matter does not exist, a combination of other things exists which is just as material. But the intense reality of the material world would not prevent it from being a dreary waste in our eyes, or even an abyss of horror, if it brought forth no spiritual fruits. In fact, it does not bring forth spiritual fruits, for otherwise we should not be here to find fault with it, and to set up our ideals over against it. Nature is material, but not materialistic; it issues in life, and breeds all sorts of warm passions and idle beauties. And just as sympathy with the mechanical travail and turmoil of nature, apart from its spiritual fruits, is moral materialism, so the continual perception and love of these fruits is moral idealism—happiness in the presence of immaterial objects and harmonies, such as we envisage in affection, speculation, religion, and all the forms of the beautiful.

The circumstances of his life hitherto have necessarily driven the American into moral materialism; for in his dealings with material things he can hardly stop to enjoy their sensible aspects, which are ideal, nor proceed at once to their ultimate uses, which are ideal too. He is practical as against the poet, and worldly as against the clear philosopher or the saint. The most striking expression of this materialism is usually supposed to be his love of the almighty dollar; but that is a foreign and unintelligent view. The American talks about money, because that is the symbol and measure he has at hand for success, intelligence, and power; but as to money itself he makes, loses, spends, and gives it away with a very light heart. To my mind the most striking expression of his materialism is his singular pre-occupation with quantity. If, for instance, you visit Niagara Falls, you may expect to hear how many cubic feet or metric tons of water are precipitated per second over the cataract; how many cities and towns (with the number of their inhabitants) derive light and motive power from it; and the annual value of the further industries that might very well be carried on by the same means, without visibly depleting the world's greatest wonder or injuring the tourist trade. That is what I confidently expected to hear on arriving at the adjoining town of Buffalo; but I was deceived. The first thing I heard instead was that there are more miles of asphalt pavement in Buffalo than in any city in the world. Nor is this insistence on quantity confined to men of business. The President of Harvard College, seeing me once by chance soon after the beginning of a term, inquired how my classes were getting on; and when I replied that I thought they were getting on well, that my men seemed to be keen and intelligent, he stopped me as if I was about to waste his time. "I meant," said he, "*what is the number* of students in your classes."

Here I think we may perceive that this love of quantity often has a silent partner, which is diffidence as to quality. The democratic conscience recoils before anything that savors of privilege; and lest it should concede an unmerited privilege to any pursuit or person, it reduces all things as far as possible to the common denominator of quantity. Numbers cannot lie: but if it came to comparing the ideal beauties of philosophy with those of Anglo-Saxon, who should decide? All studies are good—why else have universities?—but those must be most encouraged which attract the greatest number of students. Hence the President's question. Democratic faith, in its diffidence about quality, throws the reins of education upon the pupil's neck, as Don Quixote threw the reins on the neck of Rosinante, and bids his divine instinct choose its own way. (6)

The American has never yet had to face the trials of Job. Great crises, like the Civil War, he has known how to surmount victoriously; and now that he has surmounted a second great crisis victoriously, it is possible that he may relapse, as he did in the other case, into an apparently complete absorption in material enterprise and prosperity. But if serious and irremediable tribulation ever overtook him, what would his attitude be? It is then that we should be able to discover whether materialism or idealism lies at the base of his character. Meantime his working mind is not without its holiday. He spreads humor pretty thick and even over the surface of conversation, and humor is one form of moral emancipation. He loves landscape, he loves mankind, and he loves knowledge; and in music at least he finds an art which he unfeignedly enjoys. In music and landscape, in humor and kindness, he touches the ideal more truly, perhaps, than in his ponderous academic idealisms and busy religions; for it is astonishing how much even religion in America (can it possibly be so in England?) is a matter of meetings, building-funds, schools, charities, clubs, and picnics. To be poor in order to be simple, to produce less in order that the product may be more choice and beautiful, and may leave us less burdened with unnecessary duties and useless possessions—that is an ideal not articulate in the American mind; yet here and there I seem to have heard a sigh after it, a groan at the perpetual incubus of business and shrill society. Significant witness to such aspirations is borne by those new forms of popular religion, not mere variations on tradition, which have sprung up from the soil—revivalism, spiritualism, Christian Science, the New Thought. Whether or no we can tap, through these or other channels, some cosmic or inner energy not hitherto at the disposal of man (and there is nothing incredible in that), we certainly may try to remove friction and waste in the mere process of living; we may relax morbid strains, loosen suppressed instincts, iron out the creases of the soul, discipline ourselves into simplicity, sweetness, and peace. These religious movements are efforts toward such physiological economy and hygiene; and while they are thoroughly plebeian, with no great lights, and no idea of raising men from the most vulgar and humdrum worldly existence, yet they see the possibility of physical and moral health on that common plane, and pursue it. That is true morality. The dignities of various types of life or mind, like the gifts of various animals, are relative. The snob adores one type only, and the creatures supposed by him to illustrate it perfectly; or envies and hates them, which is just as snobbish. Veritable lovers of life, on the contrary, like Saint Francis or like Dickens, know that in every tenement of clay, with no matter what endowment or station, happiness and perfection are possible to the soul. There must be no brow-beating, with shouts of work or progress or revolution, any more than with threats of hell-fire. What does it profit a man to free the whole world if his soul is not free? Moral freedom is not an artificial condition, because the ideal is the mother tongue of both the heart and the senses. All that is requisite is that we should pause in living to enjoy life, and should lift up our hearts to things that are pure goods in themselves, so that once to have found and loved them, whatever else may betide, may remain a happiness that nothing can sully. This natural idealism does not imply that we are immaterial, but only that we are animate and truly alive. When the senses are sharp, as they are in the American, they are already half liberated, already a joy in themselves; and when the heart is warm, like his, and eager to be just, its ideal destiny can hardly be doubtful. It will not be always merely pumping and working; time and its own pulses will lend it wings. (7)

QUESTIONS

I

1. From what viewpoint does the author ask the reader to consider the observations he makes in this essay? (*1*)
2. In what ways are Americans basically similar, so that the author may select one as being typical of all? (*2*)
3. What is the typical American's attitude toward the past and the future? toward other people? toward doting on things? (*3*)
4. What has been the effect on the American temperament of having a vast continent to move around in? How has the American's practical sense affected his attitude toward the refinements of life? In what patterns does his imagination work? What is the nature of his idealism? (*4*)

5. How is his inquisitiveness limited? What are the proofs that he is young? (5)
6. In what way is idealism inherent in all material things? What is the typical American's attitude toward money? toward quantity? toward quality? (6)
7. In what things does the typical American show his idealism? In what things does he grope toward idealism? (7)

II

1. Do you think Mr. Santayana has stated the most typical characteristics of the modern American? Would you have omitted some that he has included? Would you add any essential ones to his?
2. Discuss the following comments about the American: "In his affections the American is seldom passionate, often deep, and always kindly" (3); "The American is imaginative; for where life is intense, imagination is intense also" (4); "Understanding as he does the material potentialities of things, he is successful in invention, conservative in reform, and quick in emergencies" (4); "To be poor in order to be simple, to produce less in order that the product may be more choice and beautiful ... is an ideal not articulate in the American mind" (7).
3. Discuss the following quotations for their philosophical import: "Comparison is the expedient of those who cannot reach the heart of the things compared" (1); "Variation is a consequence of freedom, and the slight but radical diversity of souls in turn makes freedom requisite" (1); "Elaboration, which is something to accomplish, will be preferred to simplicity, which is something to rest in" (4); "They [the revolutionists] are therefore extreme idealists in the region of hope, but not at all, as poets and artists are, in the region of perception and memory" (4); "The charm of youth, even when it is a little boisterous, lies in nearness to the impulses of nature" (5); "People seem older when their perennial natural youth is encumbered with more possessions and prepossessions" (5); "Nature cannot afford that we should begin by being too calculating or wise, and she encourages us by the pleasure she attaches to our functions in advance of their fruits, and often in excess of them" (6); "Humor is one form of moral emancipation" (7); "All that is requisite is that we should pause in living to enjoy life, and should lift up our hearts to things that are pure goods in themselves, so that once to have found and loved them, whatever else may betide, may remain a happiness that nothing can sully" (7).

III

1. Point out several excellent examples of transition sentences (usually at the beginning of the paragraph) by which Mr. Santayana knits together the parts of this essay.
2. Indicate several short expressions, in the nature of side remarks, in which the author reveals a gentle humor or delicate satire.
3. Comment upon the figurative language in the following: "The milk of human kindness is less apt to turn sour if the vessel that holds it stands steady, cool, and separate, and is not too often uncorked" (3); "We may relax morbid strains, loosen suppressed instincts, iron out the creases of the soul, discipline ourselves into simplicity, sweetness, and peace" (7).
4. Explain the following allusions: "He flies to Oxford or Florence or Montmartre to save his soul" (3); the story of Rachel and Leah (4); "the Darwinian rival of Adam" (5); "as Don Quixote threw the reins on the neck of Rosinante" (6); "the trials of Job" (7); "lovers of life... like Saint Francis or like Dickens" (7).

WORDS

Mr. Santayana's writing combines the thinking of a philosopher with the imagery of a poet. It will pay you to look up the following words carefully, then to study them in their context in the essay, and finally to use as many of them as possible in your own writing.

1. anomalies (1)	21. jettisoned (4)	41. prepossessions (5)
2. invidious (1)	22. impedimenta (4)	42. tacit (6)
3. expedient (1)	23. pragmatic (4)	43. automaton (6)
4. radical (1)	24. precludes (4)	44. ignominious (6)
5. diversity (1)	25. illiberal (4)	45. desultory (6)
6. requisite (1)	26. potency (4)	46. fugitive (6)
7. ineptitude (2)	27. premonitions (4)	47. peruse (6)
8. irruptive (2)	28. accelerate (4)	48. travail (6)
9. pedantically (2)	29. irrational (4)	49. envisage (6)
10. vortex (2)	30. pellucid (4)	50. precipitated (6)
11. figment (2)	31. a priori (4)	51. diffidence (6)
12. irrelevant (3)	32. incorrigibly (4)	52. irremediable (7)
13. atavism (3)	33. inertia (4)	53. emancipation (7)
14. contagion (3)	34. frustrates (4)	54. ponderous (7)
15. subtlety (3)	35. oblivescence (5)	55. articulate (7)
16. categorical (3)	36. axiomatic (5)	56. incubus (7)
17. placid (3)	37. comport (5)	57. cosmic (7)
18. gregarious (3)	38. accrue (5)	58. morbid (7)
19. officious (3)	39. seminal (5)	59. plebeian (7)
20. doting (3)	40. perennial (5)	60. veritable (7)

THEME TOPICS

1. The Kindly Americans
2. American Idealism
3. The American Worship of Quantity (Bigness, Money)
4. I Am (Am Not) a Typical American
5. American Idealism Is Practical
6. Americans Are Adventurous (Self-Confident, Optimistic)
7. American Inventive Genius
8. The Noble Impulses of Youth
9. Quality—the American Need
10. Yes—America Is Still a Young Country

THE HARD WAY IS THE ONLY ENDURING WAY

WALTER LIPPMANN

I THINK I am speaking for all of you when I say that we have come here in order that we may pause for a moment in which to fortify our faith and to renew our courage and to make strong our spirit.

I am speaking solemnly because in this, the most solemn hour of the history of the modern world, no one will imagine he can divert himself by forgetting it. I do not know whether we shall see again in our lives a peace that we shall believe can last. But what we can have, though the world roars and rages about us, is peace of mind, a quiet place of tranquillity and of order and of purpose within our own selves. For it is doubt and uncertainty of purpose and confusion of values which unnerve men. Peace of mind will come to men only when, having faced all the issues clearly and without flinching, they are decided and resolved.

For myself, I like to think these days of the words of Washington which Gouverneur Morris reported, words spoken when the constitutional convention in Philadelphia seemed about to fail: Washington, said Morris, "was collected within himself. His countenance had more than usual solemnity. His eye was fixed, and it seemed to look into futurity." It is (said he) "too probable that no plan we propose will be adopted. Perhaps another dreadful conflict is to be sustained. If, to please the people, we offer what we ourselves disapprove, how can we afterward defend our work? Let us raise a standard to which the wise and honest can repair. The event is in the hands of God." (1)

Upon the standard to which the wise and honest will now

An address delivered at Cambridge, Massachusetts. Copyrighted. Used by arrangement with, and permission of, the author.

repair it is written: "You have lived the easy way; henceforth, you will live the hard way." It is written: "You came into a great heritage made by the insight and the sweat and the blood of inspired and devoted and courageous men; thoughtlessly and in utmost self-indulgence you have all but squandered this inheritance. Now only by the heroic virtues which made this inheritance can you restore it again." It is written: "You took the good things for granted. Now you must earn them again." It is written: "For every right you cherish you have a duty which you must fulfill. For every hope that you entertain you have a task that you must perform. For every good that you wish to preserve you will have to sacrifice your comfort and your ease. There is nothing for nothing any longer."

For twenty years the free peoples of the Western World have taken the easy way, ourselves more light-heartedly than any others. That is why we are stricken. That is why the defences of Western civilization have crumbled. That is why we find ourselves knowing that we here in America are the last stronghold of our civilization—the isolated and beleaguered citadel of law and of liberty, of mercy and of charity, of justice among men and of love and of good will.

We mean to defend that citadel; we mean, I believe, to make it the center of the ultimate resistance to the evil which is devastating the world, and, more than that, more than the center of resistance, we mean to make it the center of the resurrection, the source of the energies by which the men who believe as we do may be liberated, and the lands that are subjugated redeemed, and the world we live in purified and pacified once more. This is the American destiny, and unless we fulfill that destiny we shall have betrayed our own past and we shall make our own future meaningless, chaotic, and low.

But we shall not resist the evil that has come into the world, not prepare the resurrection in which we believe, if we continue to take, as we have so persistently, the easy way in all things. Let us remind ourselves how in these twenty years we have at the critical junctures taken always the road of least effort and the method of the cheapest solution and of the greatest self-indulgence. (2)

We participated in a war which ended in the victory of the free peoples. It was hard to make a good and magnanimous peace. It was easier to make a bad and unworkable peace. We took the easiest way.

Having sacrificed blood and treasure to win the war, having failed to establish quickly and at the first stroke a good and lasting peace, it was too hard, it was too much trouble to keep on trying. We gave up. We took the easy way, the way that required us to do nothing, and we passed resolutions and made pious declarations saying that there was not going to be any more war, that war was henceforth outlawed.

Thus we entered the twenties, refusing to organize the peace of the world because that was too much trouble, believing, because that was no trouble at all, that peace would last by declaring that it ought to last. So enchanted were we with our own noble but inexpensive sentiments that, though the world was disorganized and in anarchy, we decided to disarm ourselves and the other democracies. That was also the easy way. It saved money. It saved effort.

In this mood we faced the problems of reconstruction from the other war. It was too much trouble to make a workable settlement of reparations and of the war debts. It was easier to let them break down and wreck the finances of the world. We took the easier way. It was too much trouble to work out arrangements for the resumption of trade because it was too much trouble to deal with the vested interests and the lobbyists and the politicians. It was easier to let the trade of the world be strangled by tariffs, quotas and exchange controls. And we took the easy way. It was easier to finance an inflationary boom by cheap money than it was to reëstablish trade based upon the exchange of goods. We indulged ourselves in the inflationary boom and let it run, because it was too much trouble to check it, into a crash that threw about twenty-five million here and abroad out of work and destroyed the savings of a large part of the people of all countries.

Having got to that, it was too hard to liquidate the inflation. It was easier to cover the inflation up and pretend that it did not exist. So we took the easier way, we maintained the tariffs, we maintained the wage-rates, we maintained the costs and expenditures of the boom, and thus made it impossible to recover from the crash. And the failure of the recovery produced at the foundations of Western civilization a revolutionary discontent. It was easy to be frightened by the discontent. So we were properly frightened. But it was hard to make the effort and sacrifice to remedy the discontent. And because it was hard we did not do it. All that we did was to accuse one another of being economic royalists on the one hand, economic lunatics on the other. It was easier to call names than it was to do anything else, and so we called names.

Then out of this discontent there was bred in the heart of Europe from the Rhine to the Urals an organized rebellion against the whole heritage of Western civilization. It was easy to disapprove, and we disapproved. It was hard to organize and prepare the resistance: that would have required money and effort and sacrifice and discipline and courage. We watched the rebellion grow. We heard it threaten the things we believe in. We saw it commit, year after year, savage crimes. We disliked it all. But we liked better our easy-going ways, our jobs, our profits, and our pleasures, and so we said: It is bad, but it won't last; it is dangerous, but it can't cross the ocean; it is evil, but if we armed ourselves, and disciplined ourselves, and acted with other free peoples to contain it and hold it back, we should be giving up our ease and our comfort, we should be taking risks, and that is more trouble than we care to take. (3)

So we are where we are today. We are where we are because whenever we had a choice to make, we have chosen the alternative that required the least effort at the moment. There is organized mechanized evil loose in the World. But what has made possible its victories is the lazy, self-indulgent materialism, the amiable lackadaisical, footless, confused complacency of the free nations of the world. They have dissipated, like wastrels and drunkards, the inheritance of freedom and order that came to them from hardworking, thrifty, faithful, believing and brave men. The disaster in the midst of which we are living is a disaster in the character of men. It is a catastrophe of the soul of a whole generation which had forgotten, had lost, had renounced the imperative and indispensable virtues of laborious, heroic and honorable men.

To these virtues we shall return in the ordeal through which we must now pass, or all that still remains will be lost, and all that we attempt, in order to defend it, will be in vain. We shall turn from the soft vices in which a civilization decays, we shall return to the stern virtues by which a civilization is made; we shall do this because, at long last, we know that we must, because finally we see that the hard way is the only enduring way. (4)

QUESTIONS

I

1. What peace can the individual obtain for himself amid confusions? What was Washington's attitude toward the kind of action that should be taken in a crisis? (1)
2. What has been our attitude toward difficult problems? What noble service does the author think we shall yet perform for ourselves and for the world? (2)
3. What are the steps in the "easy way" which we in America took between 1920 and 1940? (3)
4. How are all the democratic nations responsible for present world conditions? What does the author affirm must be our attitude? (4)

II

1. Do you agree that Americans have been too complacent and have "dissipated, like wastrels and drunkards, the inheritance of freedom"?
2. Mr. Lippmann criticizes modern Americans as not like our "hardworking, thrifty, faithful, believing and brave" forefathers, "laborious, heroic and honorable" men who set up a stronghold for civilization in the Western World. What defense can you offer for us?

III

1. The author has employed many stylistic effects to make this piece of writing clear and forceful: short sentences, parallel constructions, and repetitions. Point out examples of these devices.
2. What is the value of using the personal pronoun *you* at the beginning of the first quoted sentence in (2)?

WORDS

Answer the following questions.

1. divert (*1*): Which direction in the "turning" does the *di-* in *divert* indicate?
2. beleaguered (*2*): Has the word *beleaguered* any etymological connection with the word *league?*
3. citadel (*2*): What does this word tell us about ancient cities?
4. subjugated (*2*): How is the expression "to bear the yoke" almost a translation of the etymology of this word?
5. junctures (*2*): Does this word usually refer to time or place? To which does *junction* usually refer?
6. magnanimous (*3*): If *magnify* means to "make great" and *unanimous* means to be of "one mind," what does *magnanimous* mean?
7. enchanted (*3*): To *enchant* was originally to put under a spell by what means?
8. anarchy (*3*): If *anemia* means "not having blood" and a *monarchy* is the "rule of one person," what does *anarchy* mean?
9. reparations (*3*): What kind of things are *reparations* usually intended to "repair"?
10. inflationary (*3*): What do *inflationary* measures and *inflating* your tires have in common?
11. liquidate (*3*): Etymologically speaking, what violent clash of ideas is there in the expression "to liquidate the inflation"?
12. amiable (*4*): Is an *amiable* person pleasing or displeasing?
13. lackadaisical (*4*): Is a *lackadaisical* person energetic or listless?
14. catastrophe (*4*): Which direction does the *cata-* in *catastrophe* indicate?
15. imperative (*4*): What is the *imperative* mood in grammar?

THEME TOPICS

1. Our Policy of the Easiest Way
2. America's Responsibility for the World Crisis
3. American Leadership in the World of Tomorrow
4. "I Offer Only Blood and Sweat and Tears"
5. The Path of Least Resistance
6. America—the Citadel of Freedom
7. America Refinding Her Soul
8. Is America Decadent?
9. "America Can Be Tough"
10. "We Can Not Only Take It but We Can Give It"

IN DEFENSE OF DEMOCRACY

FRANK MURPHY

IN MY settled conviction the finest contribution which America has made to civilization is our loyalty to the idea of civil liberty. Common sense dictates that with virility and courage we must prepare ourselves to guard all the magnificent physical and spiritual resources that make up our national heritage. But, while we must be strong to protect our democratic heritage, we can and must still recognize that the heart and soul of our heritage is the civil liberty of the individual, and that in protecting our physical wealth we must not destroy our spiritual wealth of freedom. For civil liberty is still the finest possession of the American people. It is still that priceless thing without which life loses its dignity and becomes only a hopeless form of spiritual slavery. And, by the same measure that civil liberty is precious to us, we must be willing and determined to defend it against the forces that threaten to destroy it.

I am especially concerned with our defense from internal aggression. For we cannot be unmindful of the fact that the present attack on peace and liberty in Europe originated in the internal aggression of powerful groups against the democratic authority of their own lawfully established governments. But in our zeal to protect ourselves from internal aggression we must be on guard that we ourselves are not guilty of aggression against the civil liberties of our own citizens. We must not fall victim to the infection of despotism that in recent years has been sweeping the world. For, if we suppress civil liberty, we suppress democracy itself. In our own land this generation has seen a little of what happens when a crisis develops and the government is not prepared to protect its people against internal attack. I have in mind

First printed as a pamphlet by the American Council on Public Affairs, Washington, D. C. Copyrighted. Reprinted by permission of the author.

the period of the World War and some of the wrongs against
liberty that were done in the name of patriotism. Let me make
it plain that I am not assuming the role of the "second-
guesser" who always knows afterwards what should have been
done in a particular situation. I am speaking only as a citizen and
public servant who earnestly hopes and confidently believes that
we, the American people, will profit by our own wartime mistakes and, even more, by the mistakes of other democracies that
no longer live to tell the story. (1)

I believe we all should recognize that, however tragic the
wrongs that were done, they sprang from misdirected zeal rather
than evil intent. We should remember that in the feverish wartime atmosphere (an atmosphere which inevitably is dangerous to
liberty) average citizens, normally calm and reasonable, became
so imbued with the rightness of their cause that opposition or
criticism was intolerable to them. Not only could they brook no
open disagreement with national policy, but the failure of others
to share their own attitude became in their eyes evidence of lack
of patriotism.

From suspicion and distrust it was for some people an easy step
to violence and vigilante activities. In some communities irresponsible extralegal organizations assumed functions that belonged
properly to the civil authorities. And in some cases the civil
authorities themselves were carried away by a hysteria of fear.
Defenseless men and women were mistreated by such groups on
mere suspicion. On many occasions the constitutional right of
peaceful assembly was violated, and homes were invaded and
searched in the dark of night for evidence of disaffection and dis-
loyalty. In their zeal to help defend their country, well-meaning
people resorted to methods which in the calm of peacetime would
not be considered.

Even if we recognize—as we must—that this condition was not
general, it is a picture that friends of democracy have every reason to regret. But I want to emphasize how much I believe that,
instead of viewing it with rancor toward anyone, we should keep
two things carefully in mind. First, we should remember that
much of this was done sincerely in the name of patriotism and
national defense. Second, we should keep in our minds and hearts

a firm resolution that, while making the security of the country our first and greatest concern in this troubled hour, we will injure not one of the qualities that have made this nation the strongest haven of democracy and freedom on earth.

I know there are sincere individuals who earnestly believe that in a period like the present, it is not possible to maintain both civil liberty and a strong defense against internal attack at one and the same time. They are convinced that we must choose between the temporary suppression of civil rights and a weak and ineffective internal defense. I do not believe that we face any such choice. I do not believe that a democracy must necessarily become something other than a democracy in order to protect its national interests. I am convinced that, if the job is done right, our people need not suffer the tragic things that have happened elsewhere in the world and that we have seen, in less degree, even in this land of freedom. We can prevent and punish the abuse of liberty by sabotage, disorder, and violence without destroying liberty itself.

At the time of the World War the country's defense against internal attack was not fully prepared, and events took their natural course. The civil authorities were not trained for their new responsibilities. The door was wide open for irresponsible organizations to set themselves up as agencies of law enforcement. That is precisely what happened. Today the picture is quite different. The delicate business of combating espionage has been coördinated under the Department of Justice. Under responsible direction, it will be carried on, not by overzealous, inexperienced laymen, but by men who have been equipped for the work by careful training—training that includes instruction in the rights of the citizen as well as in methods of crime suppression. And we have every reason to expect them to be worthy of their training and instruction.

This work should be done and will be done by responsible employees of the Federal Government, acting in coöperation with the duly constituted law-enforcing agencies of state and local governments. There will be no alignment with agents of vigilante groups or private industrial organizations which are concerned primarily with industrial disputes and labor problems.

Enforcement officials will themselves obey the law of the land.

I believe that in this way we can eliminate at least the occasion for many of the wrongs that were done under the stress and strain of the World War. But, at the same time, I recognize that preparedness on the part of the Federal Government is not by itself a guaranty that these things will not happen again. To meet the double responsibility of self-defense and preservation of civil liberty, we need from every state and local government and, preëminently, from every citizen, an equal determination that this responsibility shall be met.

We need, and we earnestly ask, from every citizen and every government an unswerving resolve that, for as long as this crisis endures, we will keep our heads—that we will not abandon our Bill of Rights—that, whatever measures we may adopt for our defense against subversive activities, we will use them just as calmly and judiciously as we do firmly and resolutely. (2)

But, given a thoroughly prepared internal defense, given the proper mental attitude of calmness and cool reasoning, we need something more. We need a sound sense of direction—a clear understanding of our own policy and our own position.

First, we need to remember that in an emergency it is right and just for our democracy to be on guard not only against internal attack by foreign agents but obstructive activities by people in our own ranks as well. We have a right to expect that, once a policy has been formulated and adopted by constitutional, democratic procedure, it will be accepted and observed by all as an expression of the sovereign will of the people, until such time as the policy is changed by constitutional methods. Even those who disagree with it should do their part to make it effective. This is the democratic way in peacetime; it is the democratic way in time of war.

Finally, we have a right to expect that attempts to prevent the fulfillment of a policy by sabotage, violence, or subversive activities can and will be dealt with vigorously and according to law. And here we can take our lesson from those democracies abroad that failed to deal vigorously with illegal activities against the democratic process and that now are only memories in the minds of men.

The second thing we need to remember is that an emergency does not abrogate the Constitution or dissolve the federal Bill of Rights. That is not only good sense; it is good constitutional law.

Seventy-three years ago, one year after the Civil War, the Supreme Court declared in the famous Milligan case that "The Constitution of the United States is a law for rulers and people, equally in war and in peace, and covers with the shield of its protection all classes of men, at all times, and under all circumstances." I want to give emphatic assurance that in this emergency, as well as in time of peace, the Department of Justice embraces that policy without reservation. And, because we are convinced that it represents the wishes of the overwhelming majority of the American people, we are determined to apply it and to practice it as thoroughly and intelligently as men are capable of doing.

We are aware, and the people should also be aware, that this will be no simple task. It is a problem of steering an even course that will invade neither of the two boundaries that I have mentioned. In brief, it is a problem of finding a sound basis for maintaining public safety without encroaching on the Bill of Rights. (3)

In enforcing some laws, we must not violate other laws. In upholding the Constitution, we must not infringe on the priceless heritage of civil liberty which the Constitution guarantees. To do that—to suppress or suspend the Bill of Rights—would be to destroy the very democratic principles that we are seeking to preserve. It would be to yield to the same autocratic psychology that we want to keep out of this country. We must not let that come to pass. We must have it understood that, while we will oppose firmly and vigorously any illegal activities, we will do so in a responsible manner and within the orbit of the Constitution. That is the American way.

The immortal Justice Holmes laid down a formula which I believe will help us to keep a true course. In a celebrated wartime case involving the very things discussed here, he wrote these lines:

When men have realized that time has upset many fighting faiths, they may come to believe even more than they believe the very foundations of their own conduct that the ultimate good desired is better reached by free trade in ideas. . . . While that experiment is part of our system, I think that we should be eternally vigilant against attempts to check the expression of opinions that we loathe—unless they so imminently threaten immediate interference with the lawful and pressing purposes of the law that an immediate check is required to save the country.

The willingness, the determination, the ability, to follow that democratic principle, so ably stated by a great friend and interpreter of democracy, will be, in my estimation, a real test of patriotism in this or any future crisis.

The true citizen of America will remember that loyalty to our tradition of civil liberty is as much a part of patriotism as defense of our shores and a hatred for treason. He will never forget that civil liberty under the American system is a legal right in time of war as well as in time of peace—that, whatever the time, it is liberty for all, irrespective of the accident of birth. The true American will remember that, whether it be peacetime or wartime, there could be nothing more unpatriotic in this land of many peoples and many creeds than the persecution of minorities and the fomenting of hatred and strife on the basis of race or religion. He will realize that if, in the atmosphere of war, we allow civil liberty to slip away from us, it may not be long before our recent great gains in social and economic justice will also have vanished. For a nation that is calloused in its attitude toward civil rights is not likely to be sensitive toward the many grave problems that affect the dignity and security of its citizens. We must not let this crisis destroy what we have so dearly won.

Many years ago, in the midst of another great emergency, Abraham Lincoln put this question to the Congress of the United States: "Must a government of necessity be too strong for the liberties of its own people, or too weak to maintain its own existence?" Let us, in this troubled hour, answer that question as befits a great and enlightened democracy. Let us prove for all time that ours is a twofold strength—the physical strength of self-defense and the moral strength of unflinching devotion to our own ideals.

This is a time to strengthen our civil liberties—to freshen our understanding of them and to redouble our efforts to extend them in full to every member of our democracy. This is a time to renew our determination that civil liberty must be protected, with fine impartiality, without prejudice or favor, for everyone —from the poorest laborer to the wealthiest man in the land. That is the American way. It is—this idea that liberty must be for all —the finest thing that America has given to civilization.

In material things, of course, our contribution has been vast and wonderful. To us and our fathers before us, mankind owes inventions by the score that have transformed the character of human living. And justly we are proud of these achievements. Justly we erect a "World of Tomorrow" and a "Golden Gate Exposition" to demonstrate what we have achieved in years gone by and what we hope to achieve in years to come. But, recognizing the splendor of these accomplishments, and without detracting in the slightest from their significance, I venture to suggest that in our faith in the idea of individual liberty we have given to the world something even finer, something more priceless, something so precious, in fact, that dollars cannot buy it.

It is an idea that men—some of them consciously and the vast majority unconsciously—have reached out for all through the ages, seeing in it the realization of their fondest hopes. But never did they see its actual fulfillment until a group of fugitives from Old World tyranny established that idea, like a jewel, in a framework of government, a pattern of social living, that we today call the American democracy.

In all our public discussions, I suppose there is no word we use more often than that term *democracy*. It is fine that we do. I hope that in untold ages to come the American people will still be using that word, and using it with the devotion that men give to their most priceless possession.

But I wonder sometimes if we do not too often use the word *democracy* without thinking what it means. I wonder if we have not become a little numb to the significance of the idea of individual liberty that is the secret of democracy. How often do we profess our faith in democracy and forget to associate it with the things in our own lives that are democracy?

What, exactly, is this idea of individual liberty? What do we mean when we talk about the beauty and the dignity of the human personality?

Why, we mean that unknown fellow, mounted on his soap box in the city street, speaking his piece about the way he thinks the country and the government ought to be run. We mean that editor or author, writing as he pleases, condemning or commending the Administration as his opinions dictate. We mean that little group of Mennonites or Mormons or Quakers worshiping in their own churches in the way that their consciences tell them is right. We mean the ordinary citizen expressing his frank opinions to his mayor or congressman or President, and getting consideration of them. We mean the businessman setting up shop for the kind of business and in the kind of community that he prefers, with nothing but the public welfare to say him nay. We mean the workingman at liberty to choose his own occupation and to move when he pleases into another. We mean the scientist free to search for truth, and the educator free to teach it, unhampered by the fear of some "superman" who makes his own truth and allows no competition.

These are ordinary things to a people that has done them pretty much without interruption for a century and a half. They seem elementary and commonplace—so simple that it seems unnecessary to speak of them. But actually they are not ordinary things. They are the hallmarks of civilization. They stand for the gracious way of living that humanity has always been groping for, through even the blackest nights of tyranny and barbarism that history has recorded. Looking at it that way, we have a powerful, positive argument why we in America must cling to these things with all our strength, no matter how great the cost. In a very definite sense we are trustees of civilization. We are guardians of the idea without which civilization is a hollow shell—the idea that every man, no matter how meek and humble and inconspicuous, shall have his place in the sun. (4)

But, if we want a stronger argument, there are many close at hand. They are negative arguments, but they strike home with the force of a thunderbolt.

What exactly does it mean when a people gives up the idea that the individual's freedom to live his own life is, after all, the most priceless possession of any society? It means the suppression of every one of the "simple, ordinary" things that we are so prone to take for granted. It means, for any man who presumes to speak unkindly of the powers that rule, a concentration camp at hard labor, or perhaps something worse. It means a cringing, servile press that writes not as it pleases, but as some Great Man at Headquarters directs. It means the suppression of religion or the steady, demoralizing persecution of those who refuse to embrace some barbaric creed that makes a god of an all-powerful state. It means the ruthless conscription of industry and labor and business alike, all dancing like marionettes at the direction of the state, for the greater glory of a political doctrine that sees human beings only as nameless cogs in a great machine. It means the debasement of science and education and the arts to the level of tools of an arrogant minority that happens to hold the key to the gun room. Worst of all, it means the enslavement of the human mind and spirit—a slavery that undermines self-respect and slowly destroys moral integrity.

There is no doubt in my mind that, should the American people ever have to choose between these alternatives, they would make the right choice. I believe the habit of a hundred and fifty years is bound to win over any momentary loss of direction. But the unmistakable fact is that the seeds of barbarism have been sown among us, and there are those who would like to see them sprout and grow.

Civil liberty is simply the idea that I have mentioned—the idea of human dignity—translated into actuality. And measurably as we safeguard civil liberty, we enrich human dignity. Measurably as we make real to every member of our democracy the spirit of the Bill of Rights, we demonstrate that we are qualified to be the trustees of civilization.

I do not mean to exaggerate the danger. I do not mean to erect a straw man. I am eager only that we should be on guard against the tendencies and practices that corrode democracy and sap its strength. These things do happen here. They happen every day.

Ever since the Department of Justice established a new unit for the specific purpose of increasing the Federal Government's ability to protect civil rights, it has received a steady deluge of letters complaining that civil liberties have been abridged. Some of the complaints, of course, are unwarranted, but many are not. They indicate clearly that some public officials have used their power arbitrarily; that ordinances have been passed and invoked that are oppressive and unjust and violate common right; that citizens have been denied the right to express freely their opinions and to worship as they please; and that some have been prevented from petitioning their government for the redress of grievances.

We are a tolerant people; yet it has been estimated that some eight hundred organizations in the United States are carrying on definite anti-Jewish propaganda. All told, they claim in the neighborhood of six million followers—no doubt a considerable overstatement. But, even if we reduce the figure by half or more, we face the fact of a large number of our people who subscribe to the philosophy that has reduced the Jews of central Europe to a condition of misery seldom equaled in the world's history.

Almost daily we hear from one quarter or another the familiar suggestion that always accompanies periods of stress and uncertainty—the suggestion that we solve our problems by suppressing those whose talk is out of line with the majority, or by "taking steps" against some group that is supposed to be the source of our troubles. It has been said before, and I believe should be said plainly many times again, that in the last analysis the remedy for that kind of attitude lies in the people themselves. For that attitude will have a very slim chance of survival in the face of a public opinion that will have no traffic with it.

But it is not entirely a matter of public opinion. It is far from that. Public opinion crystallizes slowly, and in times like this, when there is so much that is confusing and misleading, the process is abnormally slow. And, until public opinion does reach the point where it will not tolerate violation of civil liberties, there can and will be such violation—unless government takes a hand and refuses to permit it.

In a sense, the part that government can play is purely negative. But it would be a serious mistake to conclude that it is therefore of little significance. Let government play its part vigorously, and with a clear understanding of its responsibility, and it is bound to be a powerful bulwark of civil liberty, not only as an agency that imposes penalties but as an influence on public thinking. (5)

Each of the states is equipped to protect civil liberties through its own constitution and bill of rights. The Fourteenth Amendment of the federal Constitution and the federal civil rights statutes, all products of the Civil War, have enabled the Federal Government to take a much more vigorous part than it could formerly under the federal Bill of Rights alone. I believe the new Civil Liberties Unit of the Department of Justice will make that part more significant than ever before.

Today every dweller in our land, no matter how humble, can look to the state for defense of his liberties, and, if that should fail, then to the Constitution and laws of the United States.

But it is an inescapable fact—and one that no one knows better than mayors and municipal law officers—that the first battle-ground of civil liberties is the local communities. It is they who man the front-line trenches. It is they who decide, in the first instance, whether to suppress the individual who criticizes the mayor or the President, or who wants to hire a hall, or who walks up and down the street with a sign on his back, or who spreads some alien doctrine in his newspaper, or who preaches some strange and unorthodox religion. It is they who decide whether to silence him or let the democratic process run its course.

I have been a mayor myself during three of the bitterest years that the American people have ever suffered. I know that this responsibility is often a heavy one. I know that sometimes the pressure to turn one's back on the democratic faith in civil liberty for all seems to be almost irresistible. In moments of great tension, well-meaning people, gripped by hysteria, are likely to insist that the "realistic" way to meet the threat of extremist philosophies is to deny to their advocates the liberty that they themselves, given the power, would take away from all others.

Superficially, it is an appealing argument. It seems to be a common-sense method of fighting fire with fire. But it will quickly lose its appeal if we remember this simple truth: You do not and cannot strengthen or protect democracy by undermining it. And you begin to undermine democracy the moment you begin to draw the line and say that this or that person or group shall not have civil liberty. Draw the line against one group, and it is an easy step to draw it against another and then another.

And every such step is another attack on the concept through which democracy functions—the concept that Justice Oliver Wendell Holmes spoke of as "free trade in ideas." Simply stated, that concept means that democracy gives a hearing to every idea. It gives every philosophy the opportunity to get itself accepted in the competition of the market. And ultimately—as our history shows—the true idea, the right policy, comes out on top.

I do not mean to say that we should not be on guard against dangerous and extremist notions that get into the market place. We should and must be on guard, and not just some of the time, but all of the time.

We have criminal laws that protect us against violence and incitement to violence. We should be ready and able to use them. We have legitimate methods of bringing propaganda groups into the open and exposing their nature and their origin to the light of day. We ought to know not only what they preach but who their sponsors are and where they get their funds. But as devotees of democracy we cannot crush them and deny them a place in the market. We need not do this. We have no reason to fear their competition. We have a better article to sell. And, because we have a better article, we can do a better job of salesmanship—a job of salesmanship that will endure long after the terrorism and the coercion of the autocrats have been proved the futile methods that they are. (6)

It may seem that I have stressed the evils that will come to us if we fail to meet our duty of preserving civil liberty. But we do not owe it merely to ourselves. We owe it to the generation after ours and to unborn generations yet to come. And we owe it to the generations past that did fulfill their trusteeship. Especially we owe it to that small band of inspired men who forged a state on a foundation of civil liberty out of the raw materials of a wilderness and a people who knew liberty mainly in their hopes and aspirations. We owe it to Roger Williams, whose courage was equal to his conviction that freedom of thought was not freedom of thought until it was shared by all. We owe it to men of the stamp of Patrick Henry and the noble Jefferson, who fathered the Bill of Rights.

They fought to gain civil liberty, confident that those who followed, seeing its pricelessness, would never let it go. It is for us to prove ourselves worthy of that trust.

One hundred and fifty-one years ago, a group of American citizens, meeting in the colonial community of Concord, New Hampshire, voted by fifty-seven to forty-seven to ratify the federal Constitution which had been written at Philadelphia one year before. We do not formally celebrate the day, but it was an event of tremendous significance. It meant that the required majority of nine states had ratified, and that the Constitution was in full legal effect. It meant that the American people had cast their lot together under the guidance of a document that Gladstone once described as the most remarkable political work produced by the human intellect in modern times.

That document—our federal Constitution—is remarkable in many ways. But there is one thing, above all, that makes it remarkable—one quality on which all the others depend—and that is the singular emphasis it places on personal liberty. In the very first sentence we read that the American people established the Constitution to secure, among other things, "the blessings of liberty" to themselves and their posterity. And the history books tell us that they were so very concerned about their liberties that many of the states refused flatly to ratify the Constitution unless they were assured that a bill of rights would be added. When that assurance was given, they ratified, but not before.

Obviously, the Bill of Rights was not an accident. It was not the product of a whim or a passing fancy. The people were in deadly earnest about it. They had shed blood and suffered hardship to gain liberty, and they were determined to give it the best protection they could devise. And so, when it came to the job of framing the Bill of Rights, they did not mince words. They did not hedge it around with restrictions or weaken it with qualifications and conditions. They said in plain English: "Congress shall make no law respecting an establishment of religion, or prohibiting the free exercise thereof; or abridging the freedom of speech or of the press; or the right of the people peaceably to assemble and to petition the Government for redress of grievances."

In virtually every one of the forty-eight state constitutions we find the same bold guarantees of civil and religious liberty, expressed in the same blunt language. The constitution of New Jersey, for example, declares with beautiful simplicity: "No law shall be passed to restrain or abridge the liberty of speech or of the press." Recently the Supreme Court declared that the federal courts would protect the fundamental rights of the individual from encroachment not only on the part of the Federal Government but on the part of the state and local governments as well. In his opinion, Mr. Justice Stone reminded us again how much the Bill of Rights means to our democracy. "No more grave and important issue," he said, "can be brought to this Court than that of freedom of speech and assembly."

Why is this so? Why this remarkable emphasis on freedom of speech and assembly and religion?

Because the wise men who wrote the federal Bill of Rights and the New Jersey Bill of Rights were doing more than stating legal prohibitions on the legislature. They were expressing a philosophy of human living. They were defining the spirit of a free and sovereign people. They were putting into words the meaning of democracy itself. They were determined to put an end in this country to the kind of government that tells the individual he may not speak as he pleases; that tells the newspapers what they may or may not print; that denies the citizen the right to practice whatever religion his conscience chooses; and that, in general, treats the individual as the servant of an all-powerful state. They were so bent on ending that kind of government that they started a revolution and never gave it up until their objective was won.

We could destroy all their work if we wanted to do it. We could uproot this whole democratic structure overnight simply by going back to the ancient notion that government knows what is best for the people and that the people must not question the wisdom of what the government does for them or to them or with them. But, if we did that, we would be striking a heavier blow at civilization than it has ever suffered in the history of mankind. What, after all, is civilization? Is it our great skyscrapers and our long bridges? Is it our huge factories and marvelous automobiles? Is it the radio and the airplane and all the rest of the wonderful inventions that make life easier and smoother and faster? Those things are part of it, of course—an important part of it. But they aren't all of it.

The heart of civilization, the thing that gives it a soul, is exactly that spirit of freedom that runs all through our Bill of Rights. It is the idea that the individual has a natural right to be free up to that point where he injures the interests of the people as a whole. Take that idea away from our government, or build a government without it, and you have a government that is something less than civilized. (7)

It may seem that I have constructed a straw man so that I might have the satisfaction of pushing it down. It may seem pointless to talk about the Bill of Rights when obviously the overwhelming majority of our people believe the Bill of Rights is a good thing and want it kept in our Constitution. I wish that the problem were as simple as that, but it isn't.

It is one thing to believe in civil liberty and another thing to practice it in all the daily relationships of man to man. And I am fraid the facts are that some of us have been for civil liberty in theory but not very careful about practicing it in our daily lives.

Some of us, under the tension of political and economic conflicts, have let ourselves forget that civil liberty is not just for those whom we agree with but also for those whose ideas are hateful to us. We have forgotten that civil liberty is not just a problem for the federal and state governments, but something that must be protected first of all by every individual citizen. The Federal Government, for example, cannot effectively protect the civil liberty of the individual unless public-spirited citizens in every community have the courage to come forward and coöperate with the Federal Government in seeing that the rights of the humblest and most unpopular minority are scrupulously protected.

Because some of us have at times forgotten these things, we

have condoned infractions of the Bill of Rights that Thomas
Jefferson and Patrick Henry and Benjamin Franklin would never
have condoned.

What is the evidence? It comes to the Department of Justice
every day in a steady stream. Every day the newly created Civil
Liberties Unit reads the tragic story in letters and telegrams
from all parts of the country. We hear of municipal officials
aiding in the provocation of race conflict, even though government in a democracy is intended to be for all and not just some
of the people. We hear of arbitrary ordinances and arbitrary
police action that deny workmen the right of peaceful picketing,
even though our courts have recognized that peaceful picketing
is a just and proper right of working people. We hear of local
authorities and private citizens manhandling union organizers,
even though the Supreme Court long ago recognized that it is
proper and desirable for labor to unite in organizations. We
hear of groups arbitrarily denied the right to distribute literature,
even though the Bill of Rights leaves no doubt that freedom
of speech and of the press are fundamental to our political
system.

But there is no need to go to the Department of Justice for
proof. The citizen who looks carefully can see it all around him,
near at hand. He can see it in the type of mind that believes labor
or industry, as the case may be, ought to be punished for its
sins by terrorism and coercion; in that distorted mentality that
blames the Jew for all our troubles; and in the discrimination
practiced against those who happened to be born with a darker
skin than most people possess.

What are these tendencies and practices, after all, but forms
of intolerance? And what is there more completely opposed to
the Bill of Rights and to all our American traditions than intolerance? It is the most un-American, unconstitutional, un-
Christian, and undemocratic thing in our life today.

There is no room for intolerance in the America that our
fathers planned. It belongs in those other countries where freedom has been all but forgotten and where human slavery is the
common lot. It belongs in those other lands where men hardly
dare to whisper their thoughts and where they hold meetings

by stealth under cover of the night. It belongs in those places on earth where fine literature and art and music have been destroyed and where the schools spread propaganda for those in power.

Intolerance has no place here, and those who embrace it are following not the fathers but someone else. They are not following Jefferson, for it was he who sponsored the Bill of Rights. They are not following Benjamin Franklin, for it was Franklin who deliberately wrote into the Declaration of Independence the phrase "*one* people." Such individuals forget that America became great because it was created and has remained spiritually one people.

Go down in the subway of the great metropolis, walk the crowded streets and the market places, stand near the factory gates at closing time, and what do you see? Not Englishmen or Italians alone, or Gentiles or Jews alone, or white people or black alone, or conservatives or progressives alone. You see the children of every race and every nation and every creed under the sun. You see America and America's future. If you are disheartened by what you see, if these people of other races and national origins seem alien to you, then America's future and your own will not be happy. But, if you see them all as being of the stock that built this great nation from a wilderness, if you look at them as fellow servants of democracy, then our future is bright and full of hope.

America is not one hundred per cent Puritan or one hundred per cent Cavalier. America is an amalgam of men and women of different kin with a common passion for liberty and tolerance. And with them all rests the future of American democracy.

In many ways the period we live in is like the period that followed the Civil War. There has been no Gettysburg or Bull Run, but, in the manner of war, the depression has inflicted wounds and brought hardships to many. Today, as in 1865, the nation faces a tremendous job of reconstruction.

We need to place the economic system in such order that men may have the chance to work and to earn a living wage. We need to find ways to bring health and decent shelter to those who lack them. We must take care that the aged are adequately insured against want and the worker against unemployment. We must protect the quality of government service by weeding out the incompetent, and protect its integrity by eliminating those who violate their public trust. We must cut the alliances between politics and corruption wherever they exist.

Just as it was with Lincoln in 1865, we need "to bind up the nation's wounds"; to care for those who have borne the modern battle; "to do all which may achieve and cherish a just and lasting peace." And now, as never before, we need to do our work, as Lincoln advised, "with malice toward none, with charity for all." We need to do it with tolerance for those with whom we disagree; with compassion for those who are less fortunate than we; with sympathy and understanding for those who speak a different tongue or whose background is in a different land. We need to do it with a constant understanding that the things we have in common are far bigger and more important than any difference that may seem to keep us apart.

It is in such a spirit, and such a spirit alone, that peace is won, justice achieved, and the sons of men made free. (8)

QUESTIONS

I

1. What, in Mr. Murphy's opinion, is the finest possession of the American people? What must we guard against in controlling internal aggression? (1)
2. What regrettable abuse of civil liberties occurred in America during the World War? Why does the author believe that similar happenings need not reoccur in the present crisis? (2)
3. What two principles should we keep in mind by which to guide our policy toward unpatriotic activities? (3)
4. What must the Bill of Rights guarantee to citizens of the United States? What, according to the author, does civil liberty mean in practice? (4)
5. What are the negative arguments against abridging civil liberty? (5)
6. What are the duties of the states and local units of government in defending civil liberty? What legal protection do we have against actual violence? (6)

7. What are the historical backgrounds in the creation of civil liberty? Why is it necessary to put so much emphasis on freedom of speech and assembly and religion? (7)
8. What is the real test of our belief in civil liberty? What is the proof that civil liberty is in constant jeopardy? (8)

II

1. Have you ever known, from your own experience, a case in which a person's civil liberties were denied? Have you heard older people tell of such cases happening during the World War?
2. Would you allow a political radical, a labor agitator, or a religious fanatic to speak on street corners? What would you do if you heard a pacifist violently denouncing the government when a war was in progress?
3. Do you think our present governmental agencies are able to protect us against the misuse of free speech and the danger of espionage and sabotage?
4. Discuss the following quotations: "An emergency does not abrogate the Constitution or dissolve the federal Bill of Rights" (3); "The heart of civilization, the thing that gives it a soul, is exactly that spirit of freedom that runs all through our Bill of Rights" (7).
5. Mr. Justice Murphy sees the future America peopled by "children of every race and every nation and every creed under the sun." Do you accept this prophecy? Are you disheartened by the prospect or encouraged by it?
6. Can you cite a case of flagrant violation of civil rights by the mayor of an American city? by an automobile company in obstructing the distribution of labor "literature"?

III

1. Show that the first sentence of this essay is an epitome of its central trend of thought.
2. This essay is a cool, dispassionate, almost legal discussion of the subject. Observe the length of the sentences, the arrangement and abstractness of the ideas, the historical references, the objective attitude of the writer, as contributing to the lofty tone of the essay.
3. Where, in the essay, does the author make references to himself as a public servant? Do you uphold or condemn his record, as Mayor of Detroit, in relation to the "sit-down" strikes in the automobile industry?

WORDS

From the right-hand column, choose the correct synonym for each
word in the left-hand column. Many of these words you have had
before; so you should be able to do this exercise with considerable
speed.

1. virility (*1*)	1. despotic
2. imbued (*2*)	2. strain
3. rancor (*2*)	3. high-handedly
4. espionage (*2*)	4. scope of influence
5. formulated (*3*)	5. impregnated
6. abrogate (*3*)	6. haughty
7. autocratic (*4*)	7. compound
8. orbit (*4*)	8. arranged
9. fomenting (*4*)	9. forms into a unit
10. arrogant (*5*)	10. strength
11. corrode (*5*)	11. hatred
12. arbitrarily (*5*)	12. instigating
13. crystallizes (*5*)	13. abolish
14. tension (*8*)	14. spying
15. amalgam (*8*)	15. rust

THEME TOPICS

1. My Right to Say What I Please
2. Civil Rights in War Time
3. Down with the Opposition!
4. Civil Liberty: The Cornerstone of American Democracy
5. Vigilante Activities in America
6. Anti-Semitism in America
7. Racial Intolerance: America's Shame
8. America: Still the Melting Pot of the World
9. War Hysteria
10. I Uphold (Oppose) Pacifists and Conscientious Objectors

ARE WE FIT TO KEEP OUR DEMOCRACY?

HARRY EMERSON FOSDICK

TWO kinds of questions face our lives, one kind very familiar, the other critically needing emphasis. How can I become rich? is commonly asked. Am I fit to become rich? is less frequently faced. We want to be married—many say that. Are we fit to be married?—far fewer ask that. This kind of contrast today faces our public life also. How can we save democracy?—we all are thinking about that. But are we fit to keep our democracy?—we had better face that too, for it is the crux of the matter.

It is natural today that our attention should be absorbed with the external military assault on the democracies. We hang over the radio; we wait for each new edition of the paper; our first thought in the morning concerns the war; and all America is talking about military measures. But democracy essentially is an order of life that never can be defended by military measures alone. Democracy is basically inward, moral, spiritual; its foundations are not even political; politics is its superstructure; its foundations are in the qualities of its citizens. The question, therefore, that everybody is asking, How can we save our democracy? implies another question that goes deeper than the first and will outlast it, namely: Are we ourselves personally and nationally fit to keep our democracy? (1)

For one thing, there has been an obvious deterioration among us in this respect: that once democracy was a sacrificial cause to be served, but to multitudes of our people it has now become much more like a public picnic to attend. Make no mistake about what we who believe in democracy face in this modern world. In our anger we call our pet devils, Hitler and Mussolini, un-

A sermon delivered at the Riverside Church, New York, June 2, 1940. Copyrighted. Used by permission of the author.

pleasant names, but when we have called Hitler a madman, Mussolini a jackal, and all the rest, we may still miss the real significance of our problem unless we go behind the way these movements and their leaders look to us from the outside to the way they look to themselves from the inside. The Nazis, the Fascists, and the Communists are honestly persuaded that democracy is, as Mussolini once called it, "a putrescent corpse." They think that democracy was a temporary aberration, and that now—especially in view of new industrial techniques, with the collectivism that they entail—the day has dawned for another order of society altogether, solidified, regimented, totalitarian, ruled from the top down and not from the bottom up. That idea they take seriously. It is to them a cause. They think the future belongs to it. They have idealized it as the hope of the world, and to it they are ready to give the last full measure of their devotion. However Nazism may look to us from the outside, never forget the way it looks to the Nazis from the inside!

Remember, then, that democracy was once a cause like that. To our fathers it was a new way of living that contained the hope of the future. To it they gave their creative faith. On its behalf they disciplined themselves. To its successful procedure they dedicated time, energy, thought, life. When Lincoln pled that government of the people, by the people, and for the people might not perish from the earth, he was thinking of a sacrificial cause.

Whether we are the children of the founding fathers or comparative newcomers to this land, how long is it since some of us have so thought of democracy? With many of us it has ceased being a cause and become a picnic. The spectacle in Washington during these last twenty years has been in some of its aspects downright scandalous—one pressure group after another coming up to Congress, not in the least interested in whether government of, by, and for the people perishes from the earth, but interested only in getting its special privilege, tariff, concession, pension, handout, what-you-will, from a compliant and often cowardly legislature. The government of the republic has become in the imagination of multitudes a great cow to be milked, and that attitude toward the republic has spread far and wide, and high and low.

As for our non-governmental life, how often it has become a grab bag! The most popular idea of democracy, I suspect, is that it is a place where every one can do as he pleases. Each man for himself, and the devil take the hindmost—that is the popular idea of democracy. Can anybody seriously question that this kind of deterioration has taken place among us? (2)

Behind this war is a conflict of ideas that will be here when the war is over. The Nazis believe with desperate moral earnestness in another order of society than ours—regimented, totalitarian. They think they can solve some of the most insistent problems of man's economic life by their means. They think we are fools to suppose that we can make the democracies as efficient as they are. If we have no response to make to them except an aggrieved and disturbed selfishness, as though to say, But you are spoiling our picnic, history will sit in judgment on us that in the end we lost our democracy because we were not fit to keep it.

This leads us to the further statement that democracy is not something to be taken for granted, as though because it has been once created that is the end of the matter. Democracy cannot in any real sense be inherited. It must be reborn in each new generation in the hearts of its citizens. Dictatorship can, in a way, be inherited. That rests on coercion and tyranny, and, if the tyrant be powerful and skillful enough, he can hand on to his successor the régime he has established. But democracy must be spiritually engendered in each new generation in the hearts of its people. It depends on voluntary qualities of personal character—the responsible use of freedom, the willingness to hear diverse opinions debated and weighed within the state, inner devotion to the common weal that makes coercion needless, and voluntary assumption of the duties that democracy entails. So, because the democratic way of life depends upon qualities that cannot be coerced, it must be reborn each new generation or it goes to pieces. (3)

We may well, for a few moments, turn our thoughts away from the external enemies of democracy to those enemies we meet inside—doubts, for example, prevalent, insidious doubts, everywhere running through the democracies.

Doubt number one. Democracy works, some people say, in small areas where everybody knows everybody and understands for whom and for what he is voting, but when we expand its operation to cover an immense continent like this, with its complicated problems, how can we expect it to work? Egypt, they say, always was an empire, while Greece was made up of small, democratic states, and for a plain reason. Egypt was tied together by the River Nile into a vast, but unified area that had to be handled imperially, but Greece was broken by its rugged mountain ranges into small communities where everybody knew everybody, and so democracy could work. So, they say, we may make the democratic way of life operate in small areas, but it dies, as another put it, "five miles from the parish pump."

Doubt number two. Democracy, some say, is an essentially bungling and ineffective way to get anything important done. To carry on a modern war under democracy is impossible. Macaulay wrote long ago, "Armies have triumphed under leaders who possessed no very eminent qualifications. But what army commanded by a debating club ever escaped discomfiture and disgrace?" Well, some say, are not the economic problems of mankind as complicated as war? How can we make democracy work?

Doubt number three. It is foolish, some say, to suppose that the common people ever will be fit for self-government. Intelligence tests are not everything, but they indicate that the average mental age of Americans is about fourteen years. In simpler days, with a smaller, more homogeneous population, one might have been enthusiastic about equality at the ballot box, and Whittier could even grow lyrical on Election Day:

> The rich is level with the poor,
> The weak is strong today;
> And sleekest broadcloth counts no more
> Than homespun frock of gray.

But in view of subsequent events, who of us feels like bursting into a song when we go to the polls—if we go to the polls—and how can we turn over the complicated affairs of a vast nation like this, men think, to millions of fourteen-year-old children, half of whom do not care enough to vote? Talk about Trojan horses and fifth columns! Doubts like these run all through the democracies, and it is going to take more than airplanes to settle them.

Democracy is a great and difficult faith; it is not to be taken for granted. But I ask you, in spite of all the difficulties, how do you like the alternative? The outlines of the alternative are being drawn across the world with unmistakable clarity. My soul! What an alternative it is! In days like these I understand afresh the significance of Thomas Huxley's words that "The most sacred act of a man's life is to say and to feel, 'I believe.'" Well, despite the difficulties, I believe in the democratic way of life. At any rate, America's destiny is there. A nation is more than its geography; the essence of a nation is its idea, its mission, what it spiritually symbolizes and stands for. America's mission has been, and is, democracy. Its only major reason for existence is to make democracy succeed. If it fails there, it fails altogether. So history will judge us; so we should judge ourselves. These are days for a profound rebirth of faith in the democratic way of life, and a profound moral and spiritual rededication among our citizens. (4)

This leads us to the further statement that democratic liberty is not simply being free from something, but being free for something. So Paul said long ago, "For freedom did Christ set us free . . . only use not your freedom for an occasion to the flesh, but through love be servants one to another." That admonition faces us as a free nation. We have been liberated *from* many crushing coercions, but what have we used our freedom for? Here in America we do not suffer from some coercions that if imposed on us would steal from us the most cherished values we possess. For in the deepest areas of life, liberty is not a luxury; it is the essence of the business. Coerced thought is not really thought. Coerced science is not science. In Nazi Germany where no anthropologist could reach a pro-Semitic conclusion, or in Russia where no economist could come out for an anti-Stalinist economy, scientific research in those realms is not scientific research. A coerced conscience is no longer conscience. Coerced religion is not religion, for anything in religion that is not voluntary is not real. When it comes to being a soul, liberty is not a luxury; it is the essence of the business. We may well thank God and our fathers for some of our liberties. But see how, like spendthrifts, receiving a great legacy, we have taken this unspeakable boon and have forgotten what it was supposed to be used for. (5)

To our fathers, at their best, democracy consisted not alone in liberty. Liberty, they thought, must pass into fraternity, and fraternity into equality, and it took all three—liberty, fraternity, and equality—to make a fortunate democracy. Do not try to evade that by laughing off the phrase in the Declaration of Independence about all men being created free and equal. The founding fathers were no fools; they did not suppose that all men have the same intelligence quotients. But that phrase meant to them something real, substantial, practicable, not in theory alone but in experience, namely, that in approximate equality of opportunity, of right to justice and of general economic condition, lay the hope of a free nation. When de Tocqueville visited this country in the early days he wrote this: "Amongst the novel objects that attracted my attention during my stay in the United States, nothing struck me more forcibly than the general equality of condition among the people." So political democracy came up out of economic democracy, and a general condition of equality. Remember Daniel Webster saying in 1820: "With property divided, as we have it, no other government than that of a republic could be maintained, even were we foolish enough to desire it." So, a basic equality of conditions made the republic possible.

Then, only a little more than a century after Daniel Webster's remark, we read the report of the Brookings Institution on the income of American families: "Thus it appears that 0.1 per cent of the families at the top received practically as much as 42 per cent of the families at the bottom of the scale." In that gross inequality, and the resentment that comes from it, is the tinder inside the democracies that the Communists put their torch to; that is the breach in the democratic wall that the Trojan Horse goes through; that is the road the fifth column marches on. We have been freed from many coercions, but we have not used our freedom to build a community of people living together in liberty, fraternity, and approximate equality of opportunity and condition. Mark this! We never can make the Declaration of Independence and *The Grapes of Wrath* lie permanently down in peace together.

Today all of us are concerned about the defense of American democracy. We had better be. But it is going to take more than militarism to save it. The bulwarks of democracy are in the fidelities of all the people to the democratic way of living, and that concerns every one of us, every day, in every personal and social relationship, and it involves the well-being of every citizen of the republic. (6)

Finally, when thus we look at the inner qualities of democracy, how inextricably Christianity is tied up with it. That ought not to need a long argument. Under what totalitarian régime is Christianity having even a decent chance? Not in Russia! Not in Italy, where even the Pope himself is hard put to it! As for Germany, deliberate anti-Christianity is rampant there as well as anti-Semitism. And the reason for this unavoidable conflict between the totalitarian states and Christianity is plain: under the totalitarian régime the state itself becomes God; there is no higher loyalty. But to a Christian, no state can be God, and the Christian's conscience must never enslave itself to the dictates of any human government. So, long ago in Rome the first Christians went to the lions rather than burn incense to Caesar.

Far too prevalent among us is the idea that the essence of democracy is the rule of the majority. That is not true. A dictatorship also can be the rule of the majority. Does any one suppose that if a free election were held today in Germany, Italy, Russia, or Japan, there would not be a majority on behalf of the dictator? Such dictatorships can claim to be the régime of the majority, but they utterly lack the distinctive quality of democracy—not the rule of the majority, but the rights of the minorities. That is the peculiar quality of the democratic way of life. Nowhere on earth today has any important minority any rights except in the democracies, and that means something basic for Christianity. It means that in a democracy the Christian conscience can say, even to the nation, We must obey God rather than men.

See, what I am trying to say, whether you agree with the details or not. There are grave dangers to democracy today from without, but the crux of that battle for us will be mainly inside America, with the question rising, Are we morally and spiritually fit to keep democracy? Can we make it efficient enough to survive? (7)

QUESTIONS

I

1. Where should the emphasis be placed in the questions about democracy which we ask ourselves? Why cannot democracy be defended by military measures alone? (*1*)
2. What was democracy once and what has it become? What has government become to most people? What is the popular idea of democracy? (*2*)
3. What problems will face democracy after the war? Why can democracy not be inherited? (*3*)
4. What three doubts do many people have about the working of democracy? What is the alternative to democracy? (*4*)
5. Why cannot scholarship and religion function in a dictatorship? (*5*)
6. In what way did our forefathers think of democracy? In what ways has it failed to fulfill their hopes? (*6*)
7. In what way is the spirit of democracy the same as that of Christianity in defending the rights of the minority? What is the real problem we face about democracy? (7)

II

1. Have you ever applied Mr. Fosdick's query to yourself: Am I fit for democracy? Have you ever felt democracy to be a moral and spiritual, rather than a political, matter?
2. What is the difference between our forefathers' spirit, which won democracy, and ours? Do you think that democracy has to be won anew by every generation?
3. Is Mr. Fosdick right in saying that many people regard the government as "a great cow to be milked"?
4. From your own observations, refute the "doubts" which many people have raised against democracy.
5. Why are scholarship, science, and conscience free only in a democracy?

6. Do you think the unequal distribution of wealth the most dangerous problem facing democracy? Have you any suggestions for a solution?
7. Do you find yourself in fundamental agreement with Mr. Fosdick's thesis that the inner dangers to democracy are greater than those from without? Which are likely to be the more immediate dangers? which the more lasting?

III

1. What device for attracting and holding the reader's interest does the author use in his opening paragraph? How is the real subject for discussion introduced and emphasized?
2. Point out a geographical parallel used as proof, the use of the alternative to prove a point, and a figure of speech, almost ludicrous, yet graphic and powerful.
3. How does the author warn the reader not to allow his objection to minor details in the discussion to interfere with his open-mindedness toward the main thesis of the article—that the real dangers to democracy are from within?

WORDS

First, without a dictionary, give a working definition of as many of the following words as you can. Over half of them, in one form or another, you have already had. Be careful not to define "in a circle," as *sacrificial* (2), "making sacrifices." Finally, look up the words you do not know.

1. crux (1)
2. deterioration (2)
3. putrescent (2)
4. aberration (2)
5. entail (2)
6. regimented (2)
7. coercion (3)
8. régime (3)
9. engendered (3)
10. insidious (4)
11. imperially (4)
12. eminent (4)
13. discomfiture (4)
14. homogeneous (4)
15. clarity (4)
16. mission (4)
17. admonition (5)
18. anthropologist (5)
19. boon (5)
20. bulwarks (6)
21. fidelities (6)
22. inextricably (7)
23. rampant (7)
24. prevalent (7)

THEME TOPICS

1. I Believe in Democracy
2. Enemies to the Democracies from Without (from Within)
3. Freedom of Conscience (Thought) in a Democracy
4. The Spiritual Quality of Democracy

Making Democracy Work

DEMOCRACY

DAVID CUSHMAN COYLE

IN ancient times, a "foot" was the length of a person's foot.
To be exact, it was the length of the King's foot; but a
carpenter, not usually having the King handy, was apt to
use his own. When business and science began to feel the need
for more exact measurements, they had to agree on a standard
definition of the unit, independent of both King and carpenter.
So it is with our political catchwords. Democracy, as a political
measuring-rod, goes to whatever length the speaker may find
convenient. In order to use the word for constructive purposes,
it has to be tied down to some definite meaning.

Democracy may mean "government by the people," as in
the old-fashioned New England town meeting, which was a descendant of the ancient tribal assembly of the Saxons. This form
of democracy is found, of course, only in small communities.
Plato in his *Republic* noted that the state could not properly
contain more citizens than could assemble and hear the voice
of a speaker. The radio has now extended this possibility to the
whole civilized world, but has not yet provided any practical
method by which millions of people can discuss among themselves and take action in open meeting.

Democracy is often taken to mean a form of government in
which the smaller units have most of the power, and the central
government is weak. This use of the word is common in federal
nations like the United States, where the states were the original
sovereigns.

Another important definition of democracy is a literal translation from the Greek: "The power of the people." This is the

principle declared by our Declaration of Independence, not that the people make the laws or govern themselves, but that they have power to change the lawmakers or the form of the government at their pleasure.

All three of these meanings can be justified by history and by public opinion, but they have to be kept separate if we want to be clear about how any proposed policy is related to democracy. (1)

In the first sense of the word, "government by the people," the United States is, of course, not a democracy. We are too numerous and too widely scattered to govern ourselves; we are governed by agents elected or appointed for that purpose. Even in electing a President, which is our nearest approach to direct action, we are counted by states, so that a minority of voters, suitably distributed, can win an election, and have done so. We do not make the laws: there is no direct national referendum on legislation, or even on amendments to the Constitution. Representation is not even uniform. Nevada has two senators for 41,000 citizens who voted in 1932, while New York has two to represent 4,650,000. A lady who stays in Reno long enough to acquire a voting residence can have theoretically 113 times as much influence on the Senate of the United States as her ex-husband on Long Island.

In 1930 there were about seventy-two million people of voting age living in the United States, but in 1932 less than forty million voted for President, and Mr. Roosevelt was elected by less than one-third of the adults in the country. Aside from aliens, there are millions of citizens who are not interested, and other millions who are excluded because of race, or because they have recently changed residence, or merely because they are away from home and forget to obtain an absentee ballot.

These facts are noted, not to prove that the United States is something different from a democracy, but to illustrate the fact that no such thing as 100 per cent democracy, in all possible senses of the word, exists here or is likely to exist. The American people want as much democracy as they can conveniently get, but they are not enough interested in absolute perfection to do anything drastic about it. (2)

Democracy in its second meaning, as a form of government in which the smaller units have most of the power, was not the ideal that directed the framing of our Constitution. The purpose of the Constitution was to strengthen the central government at the expense of the States. The provisions limiting the federal power were put in to allay fears of the opposition that the centralization might be without limit. The Federalists believed that a strong national government was essential for the promotion of prosperity and for national defense.

The form of the Constitution was also influenced by a strong feeling, among the leaders of political opinion, that the common people were not to be trusted. Although the sovereignty of the people had been proclaimed in the Declaration of Independence, the word "democracy" was not in favor as it is today. It corresponded more nearly to our words "mob rule" or "demagoguery." When the French Revolution came, bringing the horrors of the guillotine, public opinion throughout the world was affected in much the same way as it was by the Russian Revolution in our day. In 1800, to call a man a "democrat" meant about the same that calling him a "red" means to us. At that time Jefferson was not calling himself a democrat, and if he had been told that one hundred and thirty-five years later a group of conservatives would speak of themselves as Jeffersonian Democrats, he would have been surprised.

There were, accordingly, two aspects of the Constitution, which may be called the federalist and the aristocratic. The federalist aspect consisted in strengthening the central Government. The aristocratic aspect appears in the various provisions for keeping the Government as far removed from popular control as possible.

The federalist principle, by which many of the powers of the states were given to the Federal Government, was the chief obstacle to the adoption of the Constitution. Washington and Hamilton, Madison, and even Jefferson, who was abroad at the time, were in favor of ratification. In violent opposition were a mass of local politicians, who felt their powers to be in danger. George Mason, Luther Martin, and other leaders of the common people opposed the Constitution because of its aristocratic tinge.

At that time the principles of federalism and aristocracy were closely bound together, so much so that the Bill of Rights was not even included in the original Constitution, but was added in the first ten amendments as a concession to the people in order to obtain ratification. Madison and Jefferson, dissatisfied with the aristocratic features that were still attached to Federalism, turned in favor of States' Rights soon after 1789.

With the passage of time, however, the close tie between federalism and aristocracy was weakened. The tariff and slavery questions separated the landed aristocracy of the South from the business leaders of the North, who continued to favor a strong central government. This conflict was only one of many forces that from the beginning have worked to make the Constitution more federalist and less aristocratic. The checkered career of American democracy for a century and a half has moved generally toward centralization and at the same time toward a greater degree of popular control in government. (3)

After the Bill of Rights, the next inroad of democracy was the breakdown of the Electoral College, which had been intended as a free assembly of leading citizens who would use their best judgment in the choice of a President. The people promptly turned the Electoral College into a rubber stamp so thoroughly that no party would think of criticizing this unofficial amendment of the Constitution.

In 1861 the States' Rights controversy flared into war, resulting in the establishment of the Federal power to deny the right of secession. After the war the Constitution was further amended to enlarge the rights and privileges of the common people.

With the growth of large-scale business and finance after 1870, there was increasing criticism of the election of senators by state legislatures—too many senators appeared to be representatives of big business. In 1913, the election of senators was transferred to the people by amendment of the Constitution. In the same year the income tax, which had been constitutional in 1860 and unconstitutional in 1896, was finally validated by an amendment. No doubt the authors of the Constitution would have hesitated to provide specifically for a graduated income tax, which in 1787 had barely been invented in Europe. But the existence of a carriage tax and the other luxury taxes at that time may be taken to indicate a recognition of the principle of taxation by ability to pay. During the nineteenth century the idea that graduated income taxation was an instrument of democracy made its way slowly, until by 1913 there were few to oppose it in principle.

The two amendments of 1913 increased the relative power and influence of the mass of the voters, an effect that was later emphasized by the granting of national suffrage to women.

The place of the Supreme Court was not clearly defined by the founding Fathers; the Court had little dignity during the first twenty years of its existence, and its influence was slow to develop. Its decrees were successfully defied by Jefferson, Jackson, Lincoln, and Grant. The fact remains, however, that no written constitution is permanently workable in the absence of some authoritative power of interpretation, as the Federalists recognized from the start. During the past sixty years, therefore, a custom of respecting the Court's opinions has grown up, a custom that the Roosevelt Administration found too strong to overcome even when those opinions ran contrary to the will of the majority of the voters.

After the election of senators was turned over to the people, the Court stood for a time as a last barrier against rapid changes in federal power and practice, a barrier that was bound to melt away with the passage of time. For better or for worse, the United States, instituted as a strictly limited federalism with strong brakes upon the popular majority, has now become a strongly federalist nation in which a growing power rests with the voting population as a whole.

These various changes have been brought about by shifting tides of public opinion that have finally reversed the positions of the major political parties on the vital question of states' rights. (4)

Hamilton and the other Federalists, representing the large landowners and businessmen, can be considered the ancestors of the present-day Republican Party. They were in favor of the Constitution and opposed to states' rights. Jefferson, on the other hand, stood for the small farmers and the common people generally, and was the grandfather of the Democratic Party. Jefferson was in favor of states' rights after 1790, except while he was President. In the War Between the States, the Republicans were still fighting for federalism—including a protective tariff designed to benefit manufacturers at the expense of farmers. The Democrats were still violently attached to states' rights. Only in the present century have there been increasing signs of a Republican affection for the states, and a Democratic leaning toward strong federal powers. The reason, of course, is that the shoe has gotten on the other foot, indicating that the states' rights principle is not quite so fundamental as both parties have sometimes thought. One effect of this reversal of attitude has been to make the New Deal descend from both Hamilton and Jefferson, while the anti-New Dealers descend from both Jefferson and Hamilton. Ancestors are useful as background, but their opinions, torn from their setting and applied to the present century, can be made to prove both sides of almost any modern question.

Historically, therefore, the controversies over democracy have been little concerned with the first definition given above. It was evident from the beginning that even the three million inhabitants of the original Thirteen States were too many to govern themselves in national affairs. The necessity for representative government can be regarded as settled, at least until radio and television allow us all to meet in one national assembly with a chance for each to have his say.

The development of our democracy has been concerned with the controversies over states' rights and over popular control of government. The tide has run toward stronger government and more popular control, which brings us to the third definition of democracy—"the power of the people." It is here that we meet the clear distinction between democracy and dictatorship, which since 1918 has become the fundamental political question throughout the world. (5)

The distinction between democracy and dictatorship is not a matter of the strength or weakness of the national government. All the democracies are strengthening their governments. The distinction lies in the legal powers of the voters. While our national government is not a government by the people, it is a government by consent of the people. The principle is laid down in the Declaration of Independence. "Governments are instituted among men, deriving their just powers from the consent of the governed, That whenever any Form of Government becomes destructive of these ends, it is the Right of the People to alter or abolish it and to institute new Government." Since the beginning of the Republic, we have altered the form of government twelve times by amending the Constitution—if we count the Bill of Rights as one time. We have abolished the Government only once, in 1788, when the people ratified a new Constitution in complete disregard of the impractical methods of amendment provided in the Articles of Confederation.

The essential difference between dictatorship and democracy is that under a dictatorship the people can alter or abolish their form of government only by armed revolt; in a democracy they can do anything they like by voting. The right of final choice is the right of sovereignty; in a democracy the majority of voters is the final sovereign.

A corollary of the right of sovereignty is the less drastic right to overturn the party in power, by voting them out instead of having to drive them out by armed force. The power to change either the form of the government or the men who make and administer the laws, by legal instead of violent means, is the essence of democracy.

Dictatorship arises not out of a gradual or sudden increase in the powers of government, but out of weakness and ineffectiveness that cannot seemingly be remedied by a change of administration. So long as the people believe that they can improve matters at the next election, they are not likely to throw the whole system out the window as the Italians and Germans did. (6)

Our system of elections coming at stated periods is sometimes awkward, when an administration is seriously at odds with Congress and the people, and no immediate change can be made. Our system is slow; the consent of the governed may get badly out of date. President Wilson was in favor of changing to the parliamentary form, in which there may be an appeal to the people whenever the executive disagrees with the legislature, allowing the voters a closer check on the policies of the government. What Mr. Wilson might have accomplished if the war had not come, no one can say, but there is now no apparent desire among the voters to adopt a parliamentary form.

On the other hand, even though we cling to our regular periodic elections, the contact between the Government and voters is becoming closer, so that legislators and Executive are undoubtedly influenced by the currents of public opinion. There are several kinds of contact that are taking new and vital forms.

The President is required under the Constitution to report to Congress upon the state of the Union and to propose such legislation as he may think desirable. The growth of newspapers and more lately of the radio has extended the President's audience to include the nation and sometimes the world at large. At the same time, any private person with money to pay for printing or radio time can address millions of voters and present arguments for or against proposed legislation. The people respond by sending millions of letters and telegrams to Washington, and after a few experiences the legislators and their secretaries are able to distinguish between spontaneous individual messages and those emanating from headstones in the graveyards. The methods of strawballoting have been improved to the point where considerable confidence is placed in sample polls indicating the public opinion of the day.

All these developments add greatly to the volume of popular discussion and to the ability of legislators to gauge the opinions of their constituents without waiting for the next election, or even for a visit to their home districts. In spite of the danger of abuses and the danger of too rapid swings of public opinion, the effect appears to be to give the people a larger measure of influence over their government. Since the powers of the central government inevitably grow with the emergence of new national needs and problems, a corresponding growth of popular interest and control over government would seem to be healthy and desirable. For the essence of successful democracy is the establishment of a government strong enough to meet all national necessities, but so closely controlled by the people as to be always the servant of the commonwealth and never the master. (7)

QUESTIONS

I

1. What three definitions of democracy does the author give? (*1*)
2. In what sense is the United States not a democracy? (*2*)
3. What were the differences in the "federalist" and the "aristocratic" principles of government, and how have the distinctions between them gradually become less marked? (*3*)
4. By what steps did the government of the United States come closer to being an expression of the will of the people? (*4*)
5. In what ways have the Republican Party and the Democratic Party exchanged places? Toward what two principles has the tide of American democracy constantly run? (*5*)
6. What is the difference between the operation of a democracy and that of a dictatorship? (*6*)
7. What means do the people have to make their wishes felt by their legislators? (*7*)

II

1. What effect do you think radio and television will have upon the future of representative, democratic government in America?
2. Do you believe writing or telegraphing your representative has much effect upon his vote? Do you put much reliance in the polls conducted upon vital issues?
3. Do you feel that you have a clearer understanding of what we mean by the word *democracy* from having read this essay?

III

1. The essay begins with an example, an analogy which is a sort of spring-board to the main thought which the author wishes to advance. Do you consider this beginning effective? (*1*)
2. Read the last sentence of the essay carefully. Is it an effective summary of the thought of the essay and at the same time an effective conclusion? What figure of speech does this sentence contain? (*7*)

WORDS

The words of this essay may be studied for their simplicity and clearness. There is not a single word in the essay that an average student should need to look up in the dictionary.

THEME TOPICS

1. The Democratic Way
2. I Believe (Disbelieve) in Polls and Straw-Votes
3. The Influence of Radio on Government
4. Letters and Telegrams as Political Weapons
5. Government Should (Should Not) Become Constantly Stronger
6. How Dictators Rule
7. When I Cast My First Vote
8. The States' Rights Issue Is Dying (Is Dead)
9. I Believe in (Do Not Believe in) the Income Tax
10. Political Reforms I Am Interested In

THE CHANGING PATTERN OF AMERICA

WILLIAM FIELDING OGBURN

THE zero year of each decade is the time for learning about ourselves as a people, for it is the year when we take the Census. The Domesday Book of William the Conqueror, one of the first great inventories, has evolved now to the point where the Constitution of the United States decrees that such a record be made every ten years. Hence, 1940 is a year for recording our progress in population, in wealth and in a thousand different characteristics. It is a huge undertaking, costing $53,000,000 and requiring an army of statisticians working three years to complete the count. But the results are worth the money and time. The story will not be fully told for several years, but it is being revealed to us item by item for the different population centers as soon as the additions are ready.

The first big news is that the total population of the United States is 131,000,000, as contrasted with 123,000,000 ten years ago. We are larger by only 8,000,000, whereas from 1920 to 1930 we grew 17,000,000. That we would grow only about one-half as fast in the decade between 1930 and 1940 as we did in the decade between 1920 and 1930 was forecast by sociologists quite accurately, which gives added confidence to their prediction that in another thirty years we shall have ceased to increase. (1)

The Far West, where nature is lavish with its beauties, grew the fastest, largely owing to the fact that we continue a 300-year-old practice of moving West. The South was next in growth, because of the high birth rate in that region and because Southerners have not been leaving the South as they did in former years. This latter situation is due to the fact that unemployment in urban areas reduced the incentive for migration. Several States

From *The New York Times Magazine*, October 13, 1940. Copyrighted. Used by permission of The Times Publishing Company and of the author.

in the Dust Bowl area—the Dakotas, Nebraska, Kansas and Oklahoma—lost population, and New England grew only slightly. The center of population will move still further west. (2)

Somewhat unexpected is the knowledge that the big cities have almost stopped growing. New York grew only 6 per cent during the decade and Chicago's population remained stationary, whereas the growth of each city during the previous decade was about 25 per cent. Philadelphia lost population, as did also Pittsburgh, St. Louis, San Francisco, Boston and Cleveland. Buffalo remained the same, Detroit and Milwaukee grew 3 and 2 per cent and Baltimore 6 per cent, while Los Angeles increased 21 per cent. The total growth of these cities of a half million or more population in 1930 was only a sixth of their growth a decade earlier.

Does this fact mean that the big cities are too big? Many sociologists have thought so for some time. There is not much play space in the cities for children, and the birth rate is too low to maintain the population. The death rate is larger than in the country. Rent is high, the streets are crowded, and speeding automobiles are a menace. Even from an economic point of view the costs of production for industry are lower in the small towns.

The people would be expected to find better and more comfortable living conditions elsewhere than in the big cities, but habits are slow to change and buildings last a long time. The expectations of the sociologists that big cities would cease getting bigger did not come true by 1930, but they are being realized by 1940. For the Census does show that people are not flocking to the large cities as they once did and suggests that some are moving away. Perhaps the Census of 1950 will show an actual decrease in all cities of over a half million. If so, they will not dwindle rapidly, they will hardly become the ghost towns one sees more and more frequently in traveling over the land—towns with deserted buildings and streets, echoes and whistling winds, where once were hustling miners and lumbermen. (3)

Further, all cities, large and small, did not grow as fast as the remainder of the nation. All cities which had 25,000 or more inhabitants in 1930 grew only 4.7 per cent, whereas the nation's total population increased 7 per cent. This is the first time in the history of the United States that cities have not grown faster than the farms, villages and towns. For the past two centuries not only the United States but the whole civilized world has been characterized by the astounding mass appearance and growth of cities. Does the Census of 1940 tell us that we are witnessing the reversal of a trend that has been an outstanding phenomenon of the Age of Steam? Can it be that we are returning to the farm and village and turning our backs on the urban way of life? Such an important indication needs to be examined more carefully.

The failure of cities to grow as fast as the rest of the country may be merely a temporary phenomenon due to the business depressions of the Nineteen Thirties and not the reversal of centuries-long trends. These hard times meant ten million unemployed, many of whom were in cities. Hence, during the Nineteen Thirties the cities were not so powerful as magnets in attracting the country boys and girls who wanted to get away from the drudgery and low incomes of the farms.

If the hard times of the past decade did not favor the growth of cities, then they must have meant more people for the farms and small communities. But the Census Bureau has not yet computed the figures to show whether the farms or the small communities grew the faster. An estimate, not an actual count, of the farm population in 1940 has been made by the Bureau of Agricultural Economics. The figure is 32,000,000, an increase of 6.9 per cent over the farm population of 1930. This gain of the farms in population is surprising because the farms had been losing population for twenty years. The farm population was 2,000,000 smaller in 1930 than in 1910. The farms are growing again.

Does this increase of farm population mean a reversal of a trend? Or is it merely a result of the business depression? It is probable that the bad times of the past decade have favored the growth of the farm population. Many families returned to farms—generally to the poorer or abandoned ones—in fear of an economic collapse or to dig in until the economic storm had passed. However, the major increase in population of the agricultural areas comes from their high birth rates. The farm population would double in forty-five years if there were no migration and the present birth and death rates remained the same, while, in the same period under the same provisions, the large cities would lose population and be reduced to 68 per cent of their present size. Farms are the breeding ground of the nation, while the cities are the consumers of the population. (4)

These differentials of urban and farm growth have led some observers to think that perhaps a peasant class would grow up in the United States. This speculation is reinforced by the disparity between urban and rural income, which had been increasing until counteracted in part by the efforts of the United States Department of Agriculture. The very low income of the sharecropper is also supporting evidence of the view that we are likely to develop a class in the rural regions comparable to the peasants of Europe.

The rural poverty of peasants is found where the farm lands are overcrowded, where the ratio of arable land to farm hands is low. It does not seem probable that we shall reach that condition in the United States, for the reason that the farmers are taking up machines driven by mechanical power.

One farmer now feeds eighteen persons. With more machines and more science, he may feed thirty-six. But there will not be thirty-six persons for him to feed, with the population of the United States stationary and possibly decreasing twenty-five or thirty years hence. Machines raise the per capita income, but they will also mean technological unemployment on the farms. They are an invasion of iron men taking away jobs from the farmers and farm laborers. Unemployment on the farms is likely to push along the fall of the birth rate on the farms, which is still high. (5)

If the big cities grow less rapidly and if there is to be less need for farmers, may not the greatest increase be found in the communities of medium size? Indeed, such is one of the most interesting findings from the data so far released. Towns grew at a faster rate than did the cities and faster than the villages and farms combined. Places from 10,000 to 25,000 increased by 9 per cent, while cities beyond this size grew only 4.7 per cent in population, and the smaller communities were larger by only 6.8 per cent.

Why the towns grow at a faster rate is not clear. Perhaps the town dwellers did not migrate to the cities, as in previous decades, while the high birth rate of the farms forced some migration to the towns. The course of migration is not from the farms directly to the big cities, as is supposed. The farm youth generally go first to the towns. In any case, because "our town" is being favored, it should not be concluded that we are all going back to live at Grover's Corners, for the great majority of us still live in rural communities and in the cities. (6)

Is this recrudescence of the town an indication of a trend that will continue through other decades? Perhaps so. A clue to the answer to this sequence is found in another curious discovery from the Census figures of 1940. It is this: the big cities grew less rapidly than did the counties in which these big cities are located. For instance, the population of cities of over 250,000 population increased by only 3.4 per cent, while the counties surrounding the cities grew by 17 per cent, or five times as fast. Why should the county area surrounding a city grow faster than the city? This county area surrounding the city is the place of fine residences, of factory sites, of small family homes, of satellite towns, of bedroom communities.

County territory surrounding a city grows faster than the city because of the automobile, though the electric car and steam railroad have aided the trend. The telephone, moving-picture theatre and chain-store have also favored the growth of the suburbs. The truck and paved highway have enabled light industries to move out from the city to regions of lower rents and wages, while manufacturers can at the same time truck their products to ships and railroads which connect with distant centers. The Census of 1940 shows a remarkable growth of this metropolitan area around the great city.

What the Census records regarding large cities is the population of only a political unit, of an area around which there has been drawn a political boundary line. But a city is not merely a political unit. It is also an economic entity. In fact, the *raison d'être* of a city is economics. Cities were largely created by steam, used in the factories and on the railroads.

There were cities before steam, but only a small percentage

of the population lived in them. The multitude of cities of modern times are made by the railroad. The legislators have drawn lines around these economic areas and they are called cities. Quite compact they are, for people needed to live near where they worked, since local transportation was poor or non-existent.

The electric street cars became widely used only at the close of the last century. Dwellings were piled on top of one another. Then the gasoline engine was invented and gave us excellent local transportation, as the railroad steam engine had given us excellent long-distance transportation. The invention of abundant and speedy means of travelling short distances and then its wide adoption is spreading the city outward, and extending its area greatly. This means that economically the city has spread over a great deal of surrounding territory. But the political boundary line has not been redrawn to make it synonymous with the economic boundary. (7)

If the political boundary of cities had been changed to keep pace with the new economic boundaries, then the Census of 1940 would have shown a greater growth of cities. Instead, this great growth of the metropolitan area is shown in terms of smaller political units—villages, towns and small cities.

A few cities have changed their boundaries to make them fit more nearly the economic area. Los Angeles has extended its limits to include 448 square miles, which is a little less than the area of New York and Chicago combined. Yet the population of Los Angeles is only 1.5 million, while that of New York and Chicago is 10.8 million. Los Angeles grew 21 per cent, while New York and Chicago grew only 4 per cent. Similarly, the area of San Diego encompasses ninety-five square miles, while Cleveland has left her boundary unchanged at seventy-three square miles. The density of San Diego is 2,100 per square mile and Cleveland's is 12,000.

Obviously, the population of political areas, when some cities have widened them to include the economic area and others have not, means little or nothing with regard to the population of the economic area of the city. What does it mean that San Diego grew 37 per cent and Cleveland lost 2 per cent? If they both had included the same per cent of economic area, then the comparisons would be valid. The figures for 1940 merely compare rates of growth between boundary lines of a map.

The less dense the population of the city—that is, the bigger its boundary line—the more likely it is to show large gains in population between 1930 and 1940. The correlation for sixty-five cities over 100,000 in population between density and increase of populations is —.5. It is well for those who fight over the comparisons of the growth of San Francisco and Los Angeles or of other rival cities to remember the lack of economic significance of the political boundary lines.

But the fact that the county outside the city has grown five times as fast as the city does show that the automobile is dispersing the city dwellers outward. It is really destroying the old city as we have known it, the city which the railroad created, and is giving us something else, for which as yet we have no suitable name, but call the metropolitan community.

The growth of the metropolitan community has a good deal of significance for American life. It means the loosening up of the city, the lessening of the overcrowded conditions of the city blocks and the precipitation outward of the city population so that they may have both the advantages of the town and the attractions of the metropolis.

It should be a better world for children, with green lawns and fresher air. It will be a region of wider and faster highways and more parking space for automobiles. It will provide a wonderful opportunity for planning, an opportunity which the cities of the railroad era missed.

Now another opportunity is offered for planning—planning the location of factories, of express highways, of the placing of schools, of the whole metropolitan region, the new economic city, in order that we may have a fuller and a better life. The coming of the helicopter, the autogiro and other steep-flight aircraft will accentuate this whole movement. (*8*)

QUESTIONS

I

1. What facts about the growth and the rate of growth of population in the United States did the 1940 census reveal? (*1*)

2. Why has the Far West increased in population? Why has the South also increased in population? What accounts for the decrease in population in certain Western states? What is the population situation in New England? (*2*)

3. Why have the large cities almost stopped growing? What is the significance of this trend? What is the author's opinion about our cities' becoming "ghost towns"? (*3*)

4. Where were the largest increases in population and why? (*4*)

5. Does the author think America is to have a peasant class? What effect has the introduction of machinery had upon the American farmer? (*5*)

6. What theory is given by the author for the relatively large increase in population of the medium-sized towns? (*6*)

7. What factors in recent years have favored the growth of suburban communities? What is meant by a "metropolitan area"? (*7*)

8. In what way do the political boundaries of many of our larger cities not give a true picture of their population? What promise for better living does Mr. Ogburn see in the "metropolitan community"? (*8*)

II

1. Few facts are more important about a country than the distribution of its population. Do you think the United States would be better off with a greater rural population? small-town population? suburban population? city population?

2. Many sociologists believe that the future trend in this country is to decentralize population and industry. Do you share this belief?

3. Many farmhouses today have every convenience that can be found in a suburban home. Will this fact have any effect upon the trend of population?

4. Do you think more and more young people realize that they leave as many opportunities in small towns as they are likely to find in the large cities to which they go? Where, in your opinion, do your greatest opportunities lie?

5. What do you think were the greatest disadvantages of the place in which you spent your childhood?

III

1. What was the purpose of the author in emphasizing the *importance* of the census in the first paragraph?

2. Explain the references to the Domesday Book of William the Conqueror, to "our town" and "Grover's Corners." Explain *raison d'être*.

WORDS

Answer the following questions.

1. inventories (*1*): In what activity is this word most frequently used?
2. lavish (*2*): Is profuseness or extravagance uppermost in your idea of *lavish?*
3. urban (*2*): What is the word meaning the opposite of *urban?*
4. reversal (*4*): In what direction does a person turn who suffers a *reversal?*
5. phenomenon (*4*): What is the plural of this word?
6. disparity (*5*): Does *disparity* emphasize the likeness or unlikeness of one thing to another?
7. arable (*5*): What is the etymological idea in *arable* as applied to land?
8. recrudescence (*7*): What does the *recrudescence* of an epidemic mean?
9. satellite (*7*): What does this word mean in astronomy?
10. entity (*7*): Is an *entity* a unit or a fraction?
11. synonymous (*7*): Is success *synonymous* with failure?
12. metropolitan (*8*): What does this word tell you about the "city states" of ancient times?
13. valid (*8*): What word of opposite meaning can be made from *valid?*
14. correlation (*8*): What does *cor-* add to the word *relation* in this word?
15. precipitation (*8*): In what way is this word frequently used in meteorology?

THEME TOPICS

1. I Intend to Live in the Country (a Suburb, the City)
2. The Small Town Is Coming into Its Own
3. Neighbors (Gossip, Social Life) in a Small Town
4. I Prefer the Bright Lights
5. Down on the Farm
6. Solving the Problem of the Dust Bowl
7. When the Census Taker Called (humorous)
8. What Population Trends Mean
9. Suburban America
10. My Predictions about the 1950 Census

THE PRICE OF YOUR FREEDOM

HENRY A. WALLACE

WORLD affairs have now taken such a turn that all of us must begin to think about the basis of our democracy, the price of our freedom.

Even before the Nazi peril grew great, it was becoming obvious that our citizens, and our boys and girls, must be taught that every right carries with it a corresponding duty, every privilege a responsibility; that we must talk more and more about individual success in terms of service to the general welfare.

If we could have jogged along as we did in the nineteenth century, with an abundance of new, rich land, and without any threats from the outside world, such ideas might have amounted to little more than pleasant philosophizing.

But now, with our lands fully occupied to our ocean frontiers, and with totalitarian dangers facing us across both of those oceans, we have no alternative but to develop a Bill of Duties, a bill which will maintain, revivify, and fulfill the Bill of Rights. (1)

The Bill of Rights consists of the first ten amendments to the Constitution. It was adopted just 150 years ago. These rights guarantee the great freedoms of religion, speech, press, and person. Their essence is respect for the dignity of the individual human soul.

We take these freedoms for granted. We forget that it has been only in the last 160 years that they have had any real vitality and place in the world. And now, as we see the march of nations in which the State is everything, the individual nothing, we realize that it is possible for liberty in the modern sense to disappear from the world as suddenly as it came. We see that the time has come when our Bill of Rights must be defended by a Bill of Duties.

While the danger from abroad may spur us to this, the need for such a Bill of Duties may be even greater after the peace comes. The tremendous power of modern machinery, large corporations, strong labor organizations, and aggressive pressure groups makes it absolutely essential that there exist some effective counterbalance on behalf of the general welfare.

The Bill of Rights was the product of long thought and discussion by many men and many minds. So must be the Bill of Duties. I hope that the question will come to the front in the forums and discussion groups, in the high schools and colleges, among our citizens everywhere. Because it is vitally important to us all, and in the hope that I may help to stimulate such discussion, I venture to put forth a tentative Bill of Duties, followed by some comment on their meaning:

1. The duty to think, every day, how I can best serve the general welfare; to put it ahead of the welfare of my party, of my group, of my region, and of myself.

2. The duty to make democracy efficient by working harder and more harmoniously every day to produce the products most needed.

3. The duty to provide government mechanisms to enable our power of consumption to equal our power of production.

4. The duty to work for an economic democracy to match our political democracy, where the right to a job will be as definite as the right to a vote.

5. The duty to study and know our country, and to see it as an interdependent whole.

6. The duty of order, not imposed from above, but coming from the individual human heart.

7. The duty of observing the spirit as well as the letter of the Bill of Rights. (2)

Article 1, with its emphasis on the public welfare, contains the essence of the Bill of Duties, just as Amendment One of the Constitution, which grants the freedoms of speech, press, and assemblage, contains the very spirit of the Bill of Rights.

The time is ripe in the United States today for a practical yet religious acceptance of the doctrine of the public welfare in a more complete and understanding manner by each individual than has ever been the case with any nation in any previous time in the world.

All must catch the vision. Workers must learn to look beyond their objective of shorter hours and higher pay to the problem of how best to produce more goods in a balanced way for all workers, and not merely for those who are organized. Farmers must look beyond parity prices to the problem of how best to balance agricultural production and income with city production, so as to bring about the greatest welfare of all in the long run. Businessmen must look beyond the problem of obtaining maximum profits on their invested capital to the job of bringing about a stable increased outflow of goods year after year on a basis which will best serve the welfare of all.

This allegiance to the general good must take the form of a widespread passionate conviction.

But now, the reader is beginning to ask me, "Just what would you have us do?" In reply, I want to give you a formula which has in it more power for the individual's success and the country's success than you will believe until you have tried it. If you are a young person it will prepare channels for you in a manner which will influence your entire future for the better.

Day after day, say to yourself as a kind of prayer, morning, noon, and night: "My purpose is to do everything possible for the general welfare, for the long-time good of all mankind."

This may seem vague and general, but, if you really believe it and make it a part of your very being, you will begin to see the results. You will find persons of like mind to work with you; you will find new opportunities opening for service to your fellows; you will be amazed at how much happier, more useful, and more joyous your life will be. (3)

Article 2, the duty to make democracy efficient, has at this moment a special urgency and meaning: production. Production for defense; production to carry out our resolve to resist aggression.

Boys who have given up good jobs and are serving in our camps at a fraction of the pay they formerly received are complying with the Bill of Duties. Anyone, whether in business, labor, or agriculture, who interferes with the increased supplies of products so vitally needed is violating the Bill of Duties.

In the long run, however, making democracy efficient has a wider meaning. I am certain that the best type of administration is to give as many people as possible the feeling that they belong, that they are really wanted, and that they are *participants* in their own right in serving something enormously bigger than they are. Poverty in the midst of plenty, unemployment for men who are able and eager to work—these are deadly enemies of the efficiency as well as the spirit of democracy.

But efficient production is not enough. In peacetime, a central dilemma of modern democratic capitalism is to get the goods we make into the hands of the people who use those goods. Hence, the imperative duty, in Article 3, to use all our intelligence, ingenuity, and good will in devising government mechanisms to enable our power of consumption to equal our power of production. (*4*)

Article 4 is the duty to work for an economic democracy to match our political democracy. The Bill of Rights 150 years ago granted individual liberty. It meant much in those days when, if hard times came, men could always strike out for rich lands and broadening frontiers.

But can these rights mean what they should to a modern citizen who, entangled in our complex industrial system, finds himself jobless, hungry, in despair at being unable to provide for his family? You cannot eat the Bill of Rights. And we cannot permit unbalances in the economic structure which make liberty meaningless for millions. Capitalism, with its emphasis on thrift, hard work, and new methods of production, has a great contribution to make to the future. But it must be humanized and geared to the public welfare, until we have economic as well as political democracy.

To aid in this we have the further duty, in Article 5, to study and know our varied people; to know all regions and their vast resources; to appreciate the mighty inheritance which comes from the toil of our forefathers; and to understand the interdependence which bids us all to work together.

This is not easy to do. But if you approach life as I have suggested, with a prayerful daily resolve directed toward the general welfare, you will find yourself curious about everything. You will attract information as a magnet attracts iron. Workers, businessmen, and farmers will all tell you how they look at life. If you travel, it will become education. And the hard, dry facts of economics will come alive to you as you see how they affect the good of your fellow men.

You will see the country as a whole. You will see that every eroded acre, every jobless man, every idle factory, every unused talent, is sinful waste of our inheritance, damaging not only to the individuals involved, but to all of us. And thus a responsibility to all of us. (5)

Article 6 is the duty of order. Modern civilization, if it is to continue at all, must have order. In the totalitarian scheme, it is imposed from above. In a democracy, most of the order must and should come from the human heart. The most perfect order in the world will be obtained when the citizens of democracy recognize, instinctively and fully in all of its implications, the fatherhood of God, the brotherhood of man, and the dignity of the individual human soul.

The Bill of Rights guarantees us our rights. But it also clearly implies a duty, Article 7, to observe the spirit as well as the letter of these freedoms. It obligates us to use these fairly and wisely, so as not to injure the general welfare. The forefathers who established our rights knew this. Look back at their debates and see their temperate tone, their attitude of fairness.

Too many, today, have forgotten this obligation. They use our precious freedom of speech as a license for wholesale attack against religions, or races, or classes of other good American citizens. Others distort fact, misplace emphasis, or stir up dissension and controversy for the mere sake of sensationalism.

Not only the freedom of speech and press, but their purity, accuracy, temperance, and fairness are vital to the information and unity of our democracy. (6)

The above, then, are seven tentative suggestions for a Bill of Duties. I do not ask you to agree with them. I do ask your devout thought as to what our duties should be.

For the first time in the history of the world, we have here in the United States the possibility of combining into a harmonious whole all the prerequisites of the good life. The opportunity is ours, but it may not linger. Events abroad or selfishness at home can wreck our dream of building a Kingdom of Heaven here on earth—unless we, every last one of us, look to our duties.

We can't run away. The time of responsibility is upon us. (7)

QUESTIONS

I

1. Why must we face the present in a spirit different from that in which we faced the past? (*1*)
2. Why is there even greater need for a Bill of Duties after the peace than in time of war? (*2*)
3. Why does Mr. Wallace put first in his list of duties "the duty to think, every day, how I can best serve the general welfare"? (*3*)
4. Why has the duty to make democracy work a special meaning "at this moment"? (*4*)
5. What does the author mean by saying that our economic democracy must match our political democracy? (*5*)
6. What is the importance of order in a Bill of Duties? How have the guarantees of the Bill of Rights been abused? (*6*)
7. What does the author think will be our reward for observing the Bill of Duties? (*7*)

II

1. Which of the seven points in Mr. Wallace's Bill of Duties do you consider the most important? Which do you think has the least chance of being fulfilled?
2. Do you think poverty and unemployment are our greatest internal problems? Do they hold the seed for the ultimate destruction of democracy? Do you think we can have "economic democracy"?
3. Do you agree that capitalism must be humanized? Have you any suggestions as to how this can be done?
4. Mr. Wallace says that totalitarian states get order by fiat from above. Can we achieve order in a democracy? By doing so, might we lose more than we should gain?
5. Do you think practising tolerance an easy duty? What is your own most intolerant attitude?

6. Consider the following quotations: "Every right carries with it a corresponding duty, every privilege a responsibility" (*1*); "This allegiance to the general good must take the form of a widespread passionate conviction" (*3*); "We cannot permit unbalances in the economic structure which make liberty meaningless for millions" (*5*).

7. Do you think Mr. Wallace's suggestions are too utopian or do they lie within the possibility of human fulfillment?

III

It is suggested that you study Mr. Wallace's essay as an example of organization.

WORDS

State which of the following sentences are true and which are false.

1. revivify (*1*): To *revivify* is to bring back to life.
2. forums (*2*): *Forums* were arenas in which athletic contests were held.
3. tentative (*2*): A *tentative* plan is one upon which final action has been taken.
4. parity (*3*): *Parity* suggests inequality.
5. dilemma (*4*): A *dilemma* presents a choice between two alternatives.
6. eroded (*5*): *Eroded* land is good for agriculture.
7. temperate (*6*): A *temperate* action is a passionate one.
8. distort (*6*): To *distort* facts is to present them accurately.
9. dissension (*6*): *Dissension* is necessary to a spirit of amity.
10. prerequisite (*7*): A *prerequisite* is a result that follows an action.

THEME TOPICS

1. My Responsibility to the General Welfare
2. Order Should Begin in My Room
3. Poverty Can (Cannot) Be Prevented
4. The Self-Centered (Selfish, Money-Grabbing) American
5. Men Live by Visions
6. Making America a Better Place to Live In
7. My Bill of Duties
8. Toward Economic Democracy
9. Humanized Capitalism
10. It *Can* Happen Here

EFFICIENT DEMOCRACY

W. J. CAMERON

MOST of us probably have discovered that we instinctively dislike the word *defeatism*. We dislike the appearance, the sound, and the spirit of it. All of which should be sufficient evidence that it is not our word. And indeed, it is *not* our word. The nation that coined this word succumbed to it last June. But the spirit the word represents is by no means a stranger to us—it pops up every little while in the most unexpected places.

We had a bad attack of economic defeatism several years ago, when it was the fashion to say that economically we were *finished and done*. The defeatists diagnosed ours as "a dying economy." Well, that had a long and rather fashionable run, until common sense protested that our economy was *not* dying. And so the diagnosis, "our *dying* economy," was streamlined overnight into "our *mature* economy" which meant precisely the same thing, namely, that our American economy had passed its prime and now declined toward old age and death. But in good time all that defeatist phraseology passed away and now is rarely heard.

Those were the days when to many of a certain type among us, almost anything in the world looked better than things American. We were regaled with choruses of admiration for every new political or social experiment *east* of the English Channel. But when the highly lauded alien systems began to divulge their real nature, their American admirers came straggling home to Uncle Sam—things American were not so contemptible after all. (*1*)

Thus, as you will observe, defeatism with us usually takes the

From Seventh Series of Talks by W. J. Cameron, 1940-1941. Copyrighted. Used by permission of R. Renaldy for the author.

form of admiring the alien thing and depreciating the American. That tendency is not altogether abated. Its latest phase was the disparaging comparison of the democracies with the dictatorships on the score of efficiency. It was grudgingly agreed that democracies may be civilized but they are not efficient; if you want to get things done, we were told, you must throw the democratic method overboard. We heard that or read that and then repeated that without analyzing it, thereby becoming phrasemongers, and mongers of foolish phrases at that.

Now, *it is not true* that compared with totalitarian systems, democracy has proved itself delinquent or slow or inefficient, and it is a very simple matter to produce facts to support that statement. The comparison, of course, is not made on the high ground of human freedom, or efficient economic supply, or general progress toward general happiness, for in these high matters everyone admits that the democracies lead; the comparison is made on the lower level of military enterprise. We are asked to behold and be astounded by the dictators' efficiency in the production and use of military equipment, and we are asked to believe that in this field the democracies are helpless children.

Well, if you take time to look and to think you will find that everything attributed to totalitarian efficiency was actually created by democracy. Air force? That is an invention of democracy; the man who gave the world the airplane is living in Dayton, Ohio. The tank? The tank is an invention of democracy; a "secret weapon" in the last war; called a "tank" because people were innocently led to suppose that its purpose was to carry *water* to the troops in the field. Parachute troops? In the year 1784, a man of the American democracy—Benjamin Franklin by name—wrote down the whole *rationale* of parachute troops. You may find it all in his published letters. And Mass Production, by which the militarists got these things in such large quantities, is the gift of the American democracy to the whole world. In view of these facts, and they are only a few out of many, where would you say the credit for *efficiency* rests? The dictators borrowed from us all we had, except our decent regard for human rights. (2)

We shall have to admit that we *are* incompetent in some things.

We could no more train ourselves to utilize a time of peace and the instruments of peace to prepare war for our neighbors than we could persecute human beings because of race or religion—if *doing that* is what you call *efficiency*. We shall have to admit that others can descend to the abyss of violence with much greater facility and with much less reason than we, because we are so constituted that we must take our principles along with us—if that's inferiority and inefficiency, then we are inferior and inefficient. And we certainly must confess that in the matter of surreptitious boring into the vitals of our neighbor nations to demoralize them, we should probably be the most inefficient people in all the world. But we have observed that efficiency in these black arts has brought to the people who are most expert in them nothing but privation, collapse, and world isolation.

There is an efficiency so-called that is the essence of blundering, and there is that the thoughtless call inefficiency that is the height of skill and power. This latter, which thus far is the type of efficiency toward which our people lean, always has had the last word. (*3*)

QUESTIONS

I

1. What is meant by "economic defeatism"? (*1*)
2. What evidence is there that the democracies are really more efficient than the dictatorships? (*2*)
3. In what respects, according to the author, are the democracies incompetent? (*3*)

II

1. Have you ever heard "defeatist" talk about our outworn economic system, the failure of democracy, and other national ills? Did you concur in, or disagree with, these gloomy predictions?
2. Can you add evidence to what the author has given, to prove that democracy is efficient in inventions, industry, business, etc.?

III

1. How far in the introduction to this essay does the general material extend? What is the first sentence which reveals that the real theme of the essay is "efficient democracy"?

2. Point out three figures of speech in this essay. Note how they aid in condensing the thought.

WORDS

Use the following words in the blanks to give satisfactory meaning to the sentences: succumbed (*1*), diagnosed (*1*), mature (*1*), phraseology (*1*), regaled (*1*), lauded (*1*), divulge (*1*), depreciating (*2*), abated (*2*), disparaging (*2*), delinquent (*2*), utilize (*3*), abyss (*3*), facility (*3*), surreptitious (*3*), demoralize (*3*).

1. This company wishes to offer you every —————— it has to help you succeed in your work.
2. The agitation finally ——————.
3. The aviator was —————— for his daring exploit.
4. It is my —————— judgment that this action is wrong.
5. The enemy hoped to —————— the country by a sudden attack.
6. His habit of making —————— remarks caused people to dislike him.
7. All members —————— in their dues will have to pay a fine.
8. We —————— ourselves at the feast.
9. The document was written in a difficult legal ——————.
10. He —————— to an unexpected heart attack.
11. His stocks and bonds were constantly —————— in value.
12. The little child refused to —————— the secret.
13. We shall now —————— many things once considered waste.
14. He became dizzy as he looked over the ——————.
15. The doctor —————— the case as a streptococcic infection.
16. The —————— plan against his friend was not honorable.

THEME TOPICS

1. Free Men Are Better Workers
2. Democracy Is (Is Not) Efficient
3. The Fad of Foreign Superiorities
4. The Actual Deficiencies of Democracy
5. The Democracies and Human Progress
6. Slow-Moving Democracy
7. Defeating Defeatism
8. Admiring Europe Is Out of Date
9. The Black Arts of the Dictators
10. Democracy—the Seed-Bed of Human Talents

THE INDISPENSABLE OPPOSITION

WALTER LIPPMANN

WERE they pressed hard enough, most men would probably confess that political freedom—that is to say, the right to speak freely and to act in opposition—is a noble ideal rather than a practical necessity. As the case for freedom is generally put today, the argument lends itself to this feeling. It is made to appear that, whereas each man claims his freedom as a matter of right, the freedom he accords to other men is a matter of toleration. Thus, the defense of freedom of opinion tends to rest not on its substantial, beneficial, and indispensable consequences, but on a somewhat eccentric, a rather vaguely benevolent, attachment to an abstraction.

It is all very well to say with Voltaire, "I wholly disapprove of what you say, but will defend to the death your right to say it," but as a matter of fact most men will not defend to the death the rights of other men: if they disapprove sufficiently what other men say, they will somehow suppress those men if they can.

So, if this is the best that can be said for liberty of opinion, that a man must tolerate his opponents because every one has a "right" to say what he pleases, then we shall find that liberty of opinion is a luxury, safe only in pleasant times when men can be tolerant because they are not deeply and vitally concerned. (*1*)

Yet actually, as a matter of historic fact, there is a much stronger foundation for the great constitutional right of freedom of speech, and as a matter of practical human experience there is a much more compelling reason for cultivating the habits of free men. We take, it seems to me, a naïvely self-righteous view when we argue as if the right of our opponents to speak were something that we protect because we are magnanimous, noble, and

From *The Atlantic Monthly*, August, 1939. Copyrighted. Used by permission of *The Atlantic Monthly* and by arrangement with the author.

unselfish. The compelling reason why, if liberty of opinion did not exist, we should have to invent it, why it will eventually have to be restored in all civilized countries where it is now suppressed, is that we must protect the right of our opponents to speak because we must hear what they have to say.

We miss the whole point when we imagine that we tolerate the freedom of our political opponents as we tolerate a howling baby next door, as we put up with the blasts from our neighbor's radio because we are too peaceable to heave a brick through the window. If this were all there is to freedom of opinion, that we are too good-natured or too timid to do anything about our opponents and our critics except to let them talk, it would be difficult to say whether we are tolerant because we are magnanimous or because we are lazy, because we have strong principles or because we lack serious convictions, whether we have the hospitality of an inquiring mind or the indifference of an empty mind. And so, if we truly wish to understand why freedom is necessary in a civilized society, we must begin by realizing that, because freedom of discussion improves our own opinions, the liberties of other men are our own vital necessity.

We are much closer to the essence of the matter, not when we quote Voltaire, but when we go to the doctor and pay him to ask us the most embarrassing questions and to prescribe the most disagreeable diet. When we pay the doctor to exercise complete freedom of speech about the cause and cure of our stomach-ache, we do not look upon ourselves as tolerant and magnanimous, and worthy to be admired by ourselves. We have enough common sense to know that if we threaten to put the doctor in jail because we do not like the diagnosis and the prescription it will be unpleasant for the doctor, to be sure, but equally unpleasant for our own stomachache. That is why even the most ferocious dictator would rather be treated by a doctor who was free to think and speak the truth than by his own Minister of Propaganda. For there is a point, the point at which things really matter, where the freedom of others is no longer a question of their right but of our own need.

The point at which we recognize this need is much higher in some men than in others. The totalitarian rulers think they do not need the freedom of an opposition: they exile, imprison, or shoot their opponents. We have concluded on the basis of practical experience, which goes back to Magna Carta and beyond, that we need the opposition. We pay the opposition salaries out of the public treasury.

In so far as the usual apology for freedom of speech ignores this experience, it becomes abstract and eccentric rather than concrete and human. The emphasis is generally put on the right to speak, as if all that mattered were that the doctor should be free to go out into the park and explain to the vacant air why I have a stomachache. Surely that is a miserable caricature of the great civic right which men have bled and died for. What really matters is that the doctor should tell *me* what ails me, that I should listen to him; that if I do not like what he says I should be free to call in another doctor; and that then the first doctor should have to listen to the second doctor; and that out of all the speaking and listening, the give-and-take of opinions, the truth should be arrived at.

This is the creative principle of freedom of speech, not that it is a system for the tolerating of error, but that it is a system for finding the truth. It may not produce the truth, or the whole truth all the time, or often, or in some cases ever. But if the truth can be found, there is no other system which will normally and habitually find so much truth. Until we have thoroughly understood this principle, we shall not know why we must value our liberty, or how we can protect and develop it. (2)

Let us apply this principle to the system of public speech in a totalitarian state. We may, without any serious falsification, picture a condition of affairs in which the mass of the people are being addressed through one broadcasting system by one man and his chosen subordinates. The orators speak. The audience listens but cannot and dare not speak back. It is a system of one-way communication; the opinions of the rulers are broadcast outwardly to the mass of the people. But nothing comes back to the rulers from the people except the cheers; nothing returns in the way of knowledge of forgotten facts, hidden feelings, neglected truths, and practical suggestions.

But even a dictator cannot govern by his own one-way inspiration alone. In practice, therefore, the totalitarian rulers get back the reports of the secret police and of their party henchmen down among the crowd. If these reports are competent, the rulers may manage to remain in touch with public sentiment. Yet that is not enough to know what the audience feels. The rulers have also to make great decisions that have enormous consequences, and here their system provides virtually no help from the give-and-take of opinion in the nation. So they must either rely on their own intuition, which cannot be permanently and continually inspired, or, if they are intelligent despots, encourage their trusted advisers and their technicians to speak and debate freely in their presence.

On the walls of the houses of Italian peasants one may see inscribed in large letters the legend, "Mussolini is always right." But if that legend is taken seriously by Italian ambassadors, by the Italian General Staff, and by the Ministry of Finance, then all one can say is heaven help Mussolini, heaven help Italy.

For at some point, even in a totalitarian state, it is indispensable that there should exist the freedom of opinion which causes opposing opinions to be debated. As time goes on, that is less and less easy under a despotism; critical discussion disappears as the internal opposition is liquidated in favor of men who think and feel alike. That is why the early successes of despots, of Napoleon I and of Napoleon III, have usually been followed by an irreparable mistake. For in listening only to his yes men—the others being in exile or in concentration camps, or terrified—the despot shuts himself off from the truth that no man can dispense with. (3)

We know all this well enough when we contemplate the dictatorships. But when we try to picture our own system, by way of contrast, what picture do we have in our minds? It is, is it not, that anyone may stand up on his own soapbox and say anything he pleases, like the individuals in Kipling's poem who sit each in his separate star and draw the Thing as they see it for the God of Things as they are. Kipling, perhaps, could do this, since he was a poet. But the ordinary mortal isolated on his separate star will have an hallucination, and a citizenry declaiming from separate soapboxes will poison the air with hot and nonsensical confusion.

If the democratic alternative to the totalitarian one-way broadcasts is a row of separate soapboxes, then I submit that the alternative is unworkable, is unreasonable, and is humanly unattractive. It is above all a false alternative. It is not true that liberty has developed among civilized men when anyone is free to set up a soapbox, is free to hire a hall where he may expound his opinions to those who are willing to listen. On the contrary, freedom of speech is established to achieve its essential purpose only when different opinions are expounded in the same hall to the same audience.

For, while the right to talk may be the beginning of freedom, the necessity of listening is what makes the right important. Even in Russia and Germany a man may still stand in an open field and speak his mind. What matters is not the utterance of opinions. What matters is the confrontation of opinions in debate. No man can care profoundly that every fool should say what he likes. Nothing has been accomplished if the wisest man proclaims his wisdom in the middle of the Sahara Desert. This is the shadow. We have the substance of liberty when the fool is compelled to listen to the wise man and learn; when the wise man is compelled to take account of the fool, and to instruct him; when the wise man can increase his wisdom by hearing the judgment of his peers.

That is why civilized men must cherish liberty—as a means of promoting the discovery of truth. So we must not fix our whole attention on the right of anyone to hire his own hall, to rent his own broadcasting station, to distribute his own pamphlets. These rights are incidental; and though they must be preserved, they can be preserved only by regarding them as incidental, as auxiliary to the substance of liberty that must be cherished and cultivated.

Freedom of speech is best conceived, therefore, by having in mind the picture of a place like the American Congress, an assembly where opposing views are represented, where ideas are not merely uttered but debated, or the British Parliament, where men who are free to speak are also compelled to answer. We may picture the true condition of freedom as existing in a place like a court of law, where witnesses testify and are cross-examined, where the lawyer argues against the opposing lawyer before the same judge and in the presence of one jury. We may picture freedom as existing in a forum where the speaker must respond to questions; in a gathering of scientists where the data, the hypothesis, and the conclusion are submitted to men competent to judge them; in a reputable newspaper which not only will publish the opinions of those who disagree but will reëxamine its own opinion in the light of what they say.

Thus the essence of freedom of opinion is not in mere toleration as such, but in the debate which toleration provides: it is not in the venting of opinion, but in the confrontation of opinion. That this is the practical substance can readily be understood when we remember how differently we feel and act about the censorship and regulation of opinion purveyed by different media of communication. We find then that, in so far as the medium makes difficult the confrontation of opinion in debate, we are driven towards censorship and regulation. (4)

There is, for example, the whispering campaign, the circulation of anonymous rumors by men who cannot be compelled to prove what they say. They put the utmost strain on our tolerance, and there are few who do not rejoice when the anonymous slanderer is caught, exposed, and punished. At a higher level there is the moving picture, a most powerful medium for conveying ideas, but a medium which does not permit debate. A moving picture cannot be answered effectively by another moving picture; in all free countries there is some censorship of the movies, and there would be more if the producers did not recognize their limitations by avoiding political controversy. There is then the radio. Here debate is difficult: it is not easy to make sure that the speaker is being answered in the presence of the same audience. Inevitably, there is some regulation of the radio.

When we reach the newspaper press, the opportunity for debate is so considerable that discontent cannot grow to the point where under normal conditions there is any disposition to regulate the press. But when newspapers abuse their power by injuring people who have no means of replying, a disposition to regulate the press appears. When we arrive at Congress we find that, because the membership of the House is so large, full debate is impracticable. So there are restrictive rules. On the other hand, in the Senate, where the conditions of full debate exist, there is almost absolute freedom of speech.

This shows us that the preservation and development of freedom of opinion are not only a matter of adhering to abstract legal rights, but also, and very urgently, a matter of organizing and arranging sufficient debate. Once we have a firm hold on the central principle, there are many practical conclusions to be drawn. We then realize that the defense of freedom of opinion consists primarily in perfecting the opportunity for an adequate give-and-take opinion; it consists also in regulating the freedom of those revolutionists who cannot or will not permit or maintain debate when it does not suit their purposes.

We must insist that free oratory is only the beginning of free speech; it is not the end, but a means to an end. The end is to find the truth. The practical justification of civil liberty is not that self-expression is one of the rights of man. It is that the examination of opinion is one of the necessities of man. For experience tells us that it is only when freedom of opinion becomes the compulsion to debate that the seed which our fathers planted has produced its fruit. When that is understood, freedom will be cherished not because it is a vent for our opinions but because it is the surest method of correcting them.

The unexamined life, said Socrates, is unfit to be lived by man. This is the virtue of liberty, and the ground on which we may best justify our belief in it, that it tolerates error in order to serve the truth. When men are brought face to face with their opponents, forced to listen and learn and mend their ideas, they cease to be children and savages and begin to live like civilized men. Then only is freedom a reality, when men may voice their opinions because they must examine their opinions. (5)

The only reason for dwelling on all this is that if we are to preserve democracy we must understand its principles. And the principle which distinguishes it from all other forms of government is that in a democracy the opposition not only is tolerated as constitutional but must be maintained because it is in fact indispensable.

The democratic system cannot be operated without effective

opposition. For, in making the great experiment of governing people by consent rather than by coercion, it is not sufficient that the party in power should have a majority. It is just as necessary that the party in power should never outrage the minority. That means that it must listen to the minority and be moved by the criticisms of the minority. That means that its measures must take account of the minority's objections, and that in administering measures it must remember that the minority may become the majority.

The opposition is indispensable. A good statesman, like any other sensible human being, always learns more from his opponents than from his fervent supporters. For his supporters will push him to disaster unless his opponents show him where the dangers are. So if he is wise he will often pray to be delivered from his friends, because they will ruin him. But, though it hurts, he ought also to pray never to be left without opponents; for they keep him on the path of reason and good sense.

The national unity of a free people depends upon a sufficiently even balance of political power to make it impracticable for the administration to be arbitrary and for the opposition to be revolutionary and irreconcilable. Where that balance no longer exists, democracy perishes. For unless all the citizens of a state are forced by circumstances to compromise, unless they feel that they can affect policy but that no one can wholly dominate it, unless by habit and necessity they have to give and take, freedom cannot be maintained. (6)

QUESTIONS

I

1. Upon what false assumption does the right to free speech usually rest? (1)
2. What is the real reason for protecting an opponent's right to express his opinion? How does going to a doctor illustrate the author's point? (2)
3. What is the mistake totalitarian despots make when they suppress all opposition? (3)
4. What form must free speech take if we are to discover the whole truth, and in what places is this method effectively used? (4)

5. Why must we regulate those means of spreading ideas that, from their very nature, preclude the possibility of debate? (5)
6. How is an opposition necessary to the working of democracy? (6)

II

1. Do you agree that the whole truth is found, not in the expressing of ideas, but in the clash of argument in actual debate? What part did the old college debating societies play in educating students? Do modern "bull sessions" serve a similar purpose?
2. Are you tolerant of ideas contrary to your own? Have you been enlightened by those who have opposed you?
3. Comment upon the following quotations: "The liberties of other men are our own vital necessity" (2); "This is the creative principle of freedom of speech, not that it is a system for the tolerating of error, but that it is a system for finding the truth" (2); "For experience tells us that it is only when freedom of opinion becomes the compulsion to debate that the seed which our fathers planted has produced its fruit" (5).
4. Do you find yourself in agreement with Mr. Lippmann's thesis that free expression of the opinions of the opposition is indispensable in a democracy?

III

1. Mr. Lippmann devotes the first three paragraphs of this essay to what might be called a "negative beginning." Why does he take such pains to disabuse the reader's mind of preconceived ideas?
2. Why does the author use the analogy of hearing the opposition and of hearing "straight talk" from a doctor? Is the analogy clarifying? Is it sustained?
3. Think of three adjectives that best describe the author's style of writing in this essay.

WORDS

In the following sentences, one other word besides the italicized one comes from the same stem. Point out that word.

1. eccentric (1): *Eccentric* inventors have experimented with centripetal forces for centuries.
2. benevolent (1): The *benevolent* man wrote a voluntary recommendation for the volume.

3. magnanimous (2): A *magnanimous* person will not cast animadversions upon his enemies, no matter how antagonized he may be.

4. irreparable (3): An irresponsible person ignores the fact that an *irreparable* loss cannot be repaired.

5. confrontation (4): The *confrontation* of the spy at the frontier with conclusive evidence of his guilt so confused him that he confessed.

6. hypothesis (4): The hypercritical scholar merely mentioned the *hypothesis* in a parenthetical remark.

THEME TOPICS

1. We Learn from Those Who Oppose Us
2. The Importance of the Minority Party
3. I Enjoy (Dislike) Debating
4. The Value of Clashes of Opinion
5. Moving Pictures Should (Should Not) Be Censored
6. Yes-Men Are Dangerous Counselors
7. Science: The Free Forum of Thought
8. I Like (Dislike) Debates over the Radio
9. The Opposition Preserves Democracy
10. "Shut Up!"

THE FAITH OF AN AMERICAN

WALTER MILLIS

W HAT follows is an essay in autobiography. While a
generation of young Europeans was growing up amid
the catastrophes which Erika Mann describes, a generation of young Americans was finding itself more distantly involved in the same historic processes. We looked on, more or less
consciously, at the European revolution; more or less consciously
we saw our own notions of society and our convictions about
our world shaped or modified by its dimly apprehended lessons.
We, also, made our mistakes; though so far they have exacted
less ferocious penalties. We, also, learned something perhaps by
experience, and though it is true that one's own experience will
never teach another, an account of how many of us thought and
felt under the impact of the great changes of the past quarter
of a century may be not without its interest for those younger
men and women who have so often cited us as supporting witnesses—or as horrible examples.

How far I may be typical of what came to be called the "Lost
Generation" I do not know. Precisely because I bear so few of
the conventional stigmata, I may actually be more typical than
one would suspect. So far as I know, I was never "lost"; but then,
very few of my contemporaries seem to have been either. Though
I was in uniform during the World War, I never saw a battle;
and though I was in Paris from time to time after it, I never
sat at length with Hemingway expatriates on the terrace of the
Dome or the Select, engaging in endless, monosyllabic dialogues
in disillusion. But in these things I suspect that I am by no means
unique. I have had much less direct experience of war than

From *Zero Hour*, edited by Stephen Vincent Benét, and published by
Farrar & Rinehart, Inc. Copyrighted, 1940. Used by permission of the
author and the publishers.

many of my age; to some extent, however, this is counterbalanced by the fact that my professional interests have required me to read and think about it rather more, probably, than most. War, at all events, has formed the ultimate background of my entire active life. Either in its prosecution or its preparation, in its physical horrors or its broader social implications, it has constituted a framework dimly surrounding all other activities, affecting every idea of the purposes of our society, limiting in one way or another every vista of the international or domestic scene. And in this I am not different from any other American in his or her early forties.

The first impact of war on my own consciousness was the romantic one. I was fifteen when the Great War broke over Europe; and it broke with a glamour which the present struggle can scarcely exercise, I imagine, over any fifteen-year-old of today. The vast present literature of mud-and-blood did not then exist. I had seen pictures of contorted corpses in *The Photographic History of the Civil War;* but that work, vivid as it was, conveyed nothing like the pain and futility which darken every page of Stallings' *First World War.* The soldier of my imagination was still a Kipling or a Richard Harding Davis character; and though something of the horrors might look out occasionally through what I had read about the Napoleonic, the Civil or the Spanish-American conflicts, they had been long dimmed by time.

Boys of the same age today have had, I suppose, a much sounder education in the grim subject. I got mine slowly, and with what now seems to be an almost incredible naïveté—until I realize that this very naïveté, which was a product of the censorships and which was shared by grown men and women as well as by children, was one of the significant differences between those times and these. Up until the very end, when the Armistice found me just finishing my preliminary training and with a very raw second lieutenant's commission in my locker trunk, I had never, in all my imaginings as to what "it" would really be like, achieved any picture remotely approaching the reality. Something of the glamour of militarism persisted; and I remember my own shock when, proudly presenting myself to my mother, as a "surprise," in my new officer's uniform, I suddenly saw by her face that to her it was like my death warrant. I had not thought of that side of the matter. I was still picturing myself as a story-book soldier. I was still imagining myself swinging a field battery into action with all the dash and drama of a parade-ground maneuver. I was as raw as that. (1)

But I was not carried away by what afterward came to be called "war hysteria." Perhaps some of my classmates were. A number dropped out early to join up for active service; one or two were killed, several others made war records of great distinction. I wondered a little at the time as to the exact motives by which they were impelled—and I still wonder occasionally. Partly, perhaps, they were swept away by the excitement and the propaganda. But others of us, even then, entertained our doubts; and they were no different from the doubts besetting younger people today. I was, of course, afraid; I may have had no conception of what the Great War was really like, but by 1917 hints were beginning to come through the censorships. If there was still a great deal of the Arthur Guy Empey kind of literature about, there was also Barbusse by that time and a terrible little book, *Men in War*, by the Hungarian, Latzko. I was afraid of being afraid. And I was skeptical. No one with the slightest bent toward an analytical attitude could fail to feel that the propagandas were overdone, the causes of the war obscure, its promised gains uncertain. We were all "liberals" in those days, and believers in the rational life. I remember my inner convictions—running like a thread under the "Squads right!" and the nomenclature of the three-inch field gun—that no people could possibly be so wholly given to rapine and slaughter as the Germans were represented as being. The immediate cause of the American entry into the war—the submarine campaign, which had actually taken only a handful of American lives—seemed somehow inadequate; the menace of a German invasion of the United States, with which this cause was buttressed, seemed farfetched and always rather unconvincing; the greater aims of winning a war to end war and of making the world safe for democracy were much more moving—but I remember that I doubted even then whether they would in fact be realized.

So far as I can recall, it was no sense of burning consecration, no fanatical devotion to a leader or a cause, which overbore these rational doubts and carried me down a path which, save for the ending of the war, would have dropped me unresisting into the agony of the Western Front. It was, rather, a matter of drifting with the tide. I was simply one of my kind, doing as they did, accepting the role for which the social framework of which I was a part had cast me. I did not offer myself heroically before I was called; I never, on the other hand, had any impulse toward the part of a conscientious objector. Possibly I was politically and socially more immature than the better-educated youths of today. Afterwards, at any rate, it seemed to me that this was an irrational and unsatisfactory way in which to go down into the terrible vortex of modern war. To enlist for killing without a deep conviction—or without a signed, sealed and delivered contract to guarantee that the sacrifice would be worth while—seemed the height of foolishness; to offer up one's life to a cause simply for the reason, at bottom, that everyone else was doing it seemed a grotesquely childish proceeding. So it often appeared to me afterward. But today I am not so sure; and much of what follows is by way of explaining why I am not sure.

What kind of soldier I would have made, with this emotional equipment, I was never to learn. At the time I hoped that I would do my duty when the crises came; I still hope that I would have done it. I do not know. But in general (neglecting whatever personal reactions the stress of battle might have brought out in myself) it seems to me that this way of going to war is not a bad foundation for the soldierly virtues. I suspect that men who have enlisted because everyone else is doing it—because, in other words, there is a group job to be done and they are part of their group— are better equipped to stick it in the long run than men driven by such suicidal fanaticisms as the Nazis inculcate in their shock troops, or even than men impelled by great ideals which, in this imperfect world, are nearly always doomed to stultification. I suspect that the front-line soldier who fights because he is there, because his immediate comrades are fighting, because he cannot let down the squad on his left or right or abandon the infantry being covered by his tank guns, will fight better and longer than those guided by less simple, more lofty, more logical and therefore more vulnerable motives. This is, of course, no answer to the question of whether one should fight at all or not. But it contains, perhaps, a hint of the answer. And I found a similar hint in my own feelings as I looked back on it after the war was over. I never for a moment regretted the fact that chance had spared me the suffering and horrors of the battlefield; I was never bothered (even in the earlier post-war days, before we had all grown so cynical over the results) by the thought that I had struck no blows for the new world of peace and democracy. But what I did regret, even while I was glad that I had escaped, was that I had missed one of the great experiences of my generation. An immense and terrible task was performed by my contemporaries. I would have liked to have had a share in the doing of it, quite regardless of what was done. It was a part of the heritage of my age, of the society, the group, in which and by which I lived. I would not have done it for fun; but since, historically, it had to be done, I would have liked to have had a share in it. And therein lies a real hint, I think, not only of the reason why men do fight but of the reason why, at times, they should. (2)

But none of us was thinking about fighting again in those days. We had all suddenly been dumped out into the peace of 1919. The war to end war had been won at last—and for millions of men and women it really had been a war to end war, in spite of all the cheap sneers that have since been flung at that phrase— while few even of the most skeptical among us could have imagined that in fact they would ever live to see another like it. Some of us, as I have said, had found out in the hard way what modern war really is; the rest of us were soon to learn. I forget when Philip Gibbs' *Now It Can Be Told* first blossomed in the book-stores, but no one who had reached the age of literacy in the earlier nineteen-twenties is ever likely to forget the long and terrible procession of the war books which followed on its heels. Perhaps they made a deeper impression upon those who had not been there than upon those who had. I am rather struck by the fact that among men of my acquaintance it is those who saw active service in the last war who are, as a rule, the strongest supporters of a bold foreign policy today and the most ready to risk their lives again if such a policy should fail to avert a conflict; while the man who has made himself the chief national spokesman of the policy of appeasement, safety and scuttle is Colonel Lindbergh, who was too young to take part in the last struggle. But the World War as experienced either directly or in the vast testimonial of pain and courage, horror, suffering, fortitude, weariness and disillusion which it produced, has left on all men and women of my age an impression which is ineradicable.

It is not surprising that for so many of us the strongest impulse that we brought to the consideration of our times and our society was the impulse springing from the simple conviction that this sort of unutterable barbarity should never happen again. In Jules Romains' *Verdun*—one of the best of all the war books, even though it came, or possibly because it came, long after the main mass had been read and buried away in the back of the mind— there is wrung from one of the characters the exclamation that nothing—*nothing*—could be worth all the suffering which he feels and sees around him. But it was not only the suffering, recorded on so many sensitive and courageous pages as well as upon those of the hysterical, of the radical propagandists, or of the merely prurient horror-merchants. Scattered through this great literature —the record of the first major war to be fought by armies almost universally literate and therefore able to record it—were books of another and in a way more dreadful kind. There was, for example, Colonel Repington's chatty, guileless account of the "inside" war—the war of gossip and intrigue, of cosy little tea parties and dinners among the great at which the lives of thousands were juggled on a clever remark, the war of petty ambitions, callousnesses, stupidities, all going on at the centers of power and command while men were dying not far away. There were books like Corday's diary of *The Paris Front*, with its bitterer, more adult cynicism and disillusion, its more acid picture of doubt and uncertainty in the ranks, of selfishness and smallness at the top. The suffering was bad enough. It was what had apparently gone on behind the suffering that made it worse. What, really, had it all been about? What were the real ends which this immense crucifixion of an age had served? (3)

If the war raised the question, in the peace we seemed to have our answer. There were greed and littleness, silly nationalism, paltry personal ambition and plain unwisdom at Paris; and the Treaty of Versailles certainly was not perfect. But for me, and I imagine for a great many of my generation, it was not the Treaty, not anything which happened at Paris, that produced the real disillusion. It was what happened afterward. The statesmen may have been greedy and unwise; it was as nothing compared to the greed and folly and blindness of the peoples who were to pass upon their work. Many have now come to realize that the Treaty of Versailles, for all its faults, was in fact a much greater and nobler document than it was represented as being in the post-war years. But we younger people believed in the Treaty in 1920; most of us, I think, believed in the Covenant and the League, and in the new vistas which Wilson's high rhetoric had opened before us. Our elders pointed out the Treaty's faults. We were not impressed by them. We wanted to accept the great risks; we wanted to help build the new, warless world in which democratic institutions would not only be safe but would demonstrate a creative power beyond anything they had shown before. And we saw this vision dissipated before our eyes by a complicated, somehow grotesque process which we did not understand. We saw it tangled in a partisan political battle about which most of us cared very little. We saw it picked elaborately to pieces by the destructive fingers of legalistic nicety, we saw it involved in absurd disputes about "the" League or "a" league; in manifestoes and reservations; in every kind of passionate inanity, sincere or otherwise. In the end, we did not quite know what had happened. We blamed it on the obstinacy of Wilson or the petty jealousy of Lodge; we wondered whether perhaps we had not been wrong ourselves, or ascribed the whole thing to the mere accidents of politics, to a malevolent chance. But the vision was dead, all right; there was no doubt about that, and not much doubt that, whatever personal contributions the politicians and editors had made to its destruction, it was the people themselves who had let it die. The steam had gone out of them. The ardor had evaporated. They could fight, suffer and win a war; they could put their victory to no intelligible purpose. They fled into "normalcy." They wanted to be let alone; to mumble all the old, easy shibboleths of patriotism and politics and economic reaction.

So it had all been for nothing. The speeches and flag-waving had been meaningless, or had meant only a barren and outworn kind of jingo patriotism. We may not have gone to war *for* an ideal, but an ideal had at least illuminated our course and given it the appearance of reasonableness. This ideal had vanished; in its place we had Warren G. Harding. It was not simply that the ideal had been betrayed by politicians or sold by evil men; it had been abandoned by the whole society of which we were a part. We were told by our elders, including those of unquestioned integrity and eminence, that to imagine that it was possible to eliminate war from international society or create a new world order was to betray a childish naïveté, not to mention a gross ignorance of the Constitution. We supposed that we had been fighting, or preparing to fight, for peace and democracy; it was an absurd notion—what we had really been fighting for was to take vengeance on the Germans for having sunk a few American ships and killed a small number of American citizens, most of whom had been fully warned of their danger. That was a real cause for war. The rest was a windy and impracticable "idealism," which could only affect inexperienced minds. We believed this, most of us—how could we have done otherwise? We might not have believed a Lodge, or even a Borah. But the election returns were unanswerable. The election returns were us; they were the voice of the society in which we were framed, by which alone we had our public existence. So it had all been, somehow, a mistake. (*4*)

With this lesson, or what we could only read as this lesson, we were dumped into the post-war world; and, as I have said, it is not surprising if a good many of us felt that in the elimination of this pointless horror from society there lay the first, the central, problem of our times. The post-war world was in fact a much more confusing place than we knew. Its manners, its politics, its economy alike were in a much greater state of flux than we realized; the ancient issues between the individual and the state, between man and his society, were running so very deep that most of us were but dimly aware that there were any such issues at all. It was easy to fall victim to over-simple solutions. No doubt too many men and women of my generation relapsed into the simplest solution of all; they adopted a purely personal attitude toward their times, took what the day brought, voted the Democratic ticket or the Republican, tried to make a living and let it go at that. Of those troubled by a more restless impulse to understand their age, some simply forgot about the war and—taking up again at the point where everything had been dropped in 1914—concentrated their attention on all the old social issues, political reform, industrial relations, problems of economic and financial organization. But to others among us it seemed as if all that could wait. We forgot about society and concentrated our attention on war.

This loathsome atrocity, appalling in itself, destructive of all social values, with so much seeming baseness in its inspiration and futility in its results—this thing, surely, would have to be done away with. This, surely, was the greatest scourge to which our civilization was still subject, more terrible than poverty, more crushing than injustice, productive of more waste and misery and degradation than all the special ills which formed the stuff of peace-time socio-economic controversy. So a good many of us felt; and we attacked our enemy in our several ways. Some, like Hemingway or Dos Passos or Stallings, reported the horror as they had seen it with a passionate and convincing indignation. Some—Sherwood comes to mind—used the weapons of satire. Some journeyed to Geneva in Shotwell's trail; they gave themselves to the effort of reviving the war-time inspiration, of breathing life into the League of Nations, of elaborating new legal formulae—"outlawries of war," "collective securities," perfected "peace systems" —in which to bind the monster. Others, like Buell, founded or labored in study associations, tried to stimulate thought or spread information, wrote monographs, compiled statistics. It was a war on a wide front. The historical process had demonstrated to us that the original war against war for which we had enlisted had not really been that at all; we had simply allowed ourselves to be bamboozled by the propagandas. But, as Keynes once said of Wilson, we refused to be de-bamboozled. This was our own war against war. Events have proved that it was a misdirected one. But none, I think, who took however small a part in it need be ashamed of having done so.

I had a part in it; I do not pretend that it was a particularly important one, but this is admittedly autobiography. I am using myself simply as an illustration to show that the men and women of the "war generation" have in their own way been through most of the dilemmas that appear to trouble their immediate successors; whatever we may say now is at any rate not said in ignorance of those issues or blindness toward them. Like these others in the middle post-war years I was fascinated by the subject of war; I loathed the business; I thought an attack upon it as good a point as any other at which to attack the general problem of our times. Most of the excuses advanced to justify militaristic preparation and war-like policies seemed to me obviously shallow —the transparent rationalizations of people either blinded by their vested interest in military institutions or incapable of taking more than a childishly narrow, romantic view of human history. I remember the disgust with which I followed for example, the antics of the "Coolidge" naval conference in 1927, at which unthinking jingo nationalism, professional navalist pedantry and a total failure to bring any scientific analysis to the question of what the proposed ships were really for or really capable of doing, succeeded—not, it may be said, without the assistance of the munitions interests—in wrecking any chance of completing the structure of naval limitation which had been begun at Washington in 1921. I was as critical as most of military measures, military appropriations, the whole inspiration and purpose of the military institution. And it occurred to me to write my own kind of book about war.

It was in 1931 that I published a book called *The Martial Spirit*. It was an account of the Spanish-American War, written partly because this seemed to me in itself, a curious and arresting episode in the development of contemporary America, but partly, also, because it seemed a suggestive example of the war process in action. I was inclined to think of war as a disease or aberration of normal society; and though the whole emphasis of this book was satiric rather than solemn, I felt that it might be of use as a kind of practical case-history. Precisely because the scale of the Spanish-American War was small, the physical horrors relatively few, but the historical consequences considerable, it should offer a better subject in which to study the essential pathology than the vaster, more complex and more terrible examples. The book did not go unread. But if it was a case history, it never suggested to me—nor to anyone else so far as I am aware—any hint of the cure.

Perhaps war was not, as I and many others had tended to regard it, a disease of society. Perhaps it was not even a crime, as the authors of the Treaty of Versailles had assumed and as the earnest workers in the Geneva vineyards still seemed to assume. Perhaps it was a stupidity—a failure in logic and sense on the part of peoples and their responsible statesmen, a vast accident compounded out of short-sightedness, ignorance, the inability to relate means to end or cause to effect. So, at any rate, the outbreak of war in 1914 seemed to have been, as it was now appearing to us through the researches of Fay and the other scholars of the "origins." I was struck by the fact that I did not know either how or why the United States had got into the war in 1917; I was even more struck by the fact that no one else seemed to know either. Plenty of people had their explanations, of course, but the explanations were all different; there were any number of reasons, but when they were all added up they did not come to anything very reasonable. I decided that I would try to find out, to my own satisfaction at any rate; and I went to work upon another book, the primary purpose of which was simply to give as full, as intelligible and self-consistent an account as I could of the "origins" of the American intervention.

Again it seemed to me that the attempt might yield a book which would not only be of interest in itself but would be useful. I felt that one great trouble with everyone dabbling in this subject—from the peace-society people at one end with their simple denunciations of war around through the Geneva legalists with their protocols and "peace systems" to the soldiers, whose one prescription was more armaments to preserve the peace—was that they all had an inadequate grasp of the actual process which they were trying to control. They were, so to speak, proposing to regulate a watch with no more imaginative an understanding of its anatomy than could be derived from a cursory glance at the movement. Each was so sure that he knew how the watch ought to work, and therefore how to regulate it, that none was taking time to find out whether the watch really did work that way. In the case of the American intervention in 1917, I wanted to find out how the watch had actually ticked, what had made it go, what kind of mechanisms were involved. Except for a powerful bias against avoidable wars, I really had no bias in this endeavor; I was not committed to any single theory of the war's causation, but I did hope that from a survey of the war mechanisms as a whole there might emerge some practical hints as to how to control these mechanisms—if not for the complete prevention of war, then at least so as to insure that they would yield less socially futile results than seemed to have been achieved in this case.

It was not our entry in the war which I minded so much; it was what I regarded as our complete betrayal afterward of everything which might have justified the sacrifice and made the victory worth while. But the subsequent betrayal might have resulted from an initial confusion as to the purposes for which we had taken up the sword. And the more I looked into it the more was I impressed by how much confusion there had been. Applying the light of after-knowledge to the actual causes of the American entry, I saw everywhere what seemed to me to be shortsightedness, ignorance, passionate emotionalism, personal (if often unconscious) greeds or political ambitions, a reckless, almost frivolous, failure to analyze the actual situation at any given time so as to utilize the great power of the United States in such a way as to achieve concrete results in some degree equivalent to the inevitable costs of any given course of action. When it was completed, my book, *Road to War*, was a pretty severe indictment of the whole process; *that* war, I felt, should have been prevented, and I thought I detected in the analysis not a few points at which better controls might have been applied, not a few ways in which the war mechanism might have been so regulated as either to have avoided the intervention altogether or at least insured that any intervention we might have made would have achieved far more at far less cost. (5)

The book got read. It did seem to influence some people—it may have helped to influence some policies. I never imagined, and would not for a moment claim, that I supplied the inspiration for the neutrality acts of 1935 and later. But *Road to War* appeared at a time when others had begun to reëxamine the 1914-1917 period for suggestions as to how in fact to prevent a repetition of that episode. They had detected much the same points as I thought I found for the application of controls that might have "kept the country out of war" then and that might serve to do so in face of the new storms that by this time were gathering in Europe. A good many abler and more influential minds than my own were concerned with the problem; if I speak of my own share in it, it is again only because this is illustrative autobiography. But whatever my share may have been, the results were not entirely satisfactory to myself. The more it came to the point of trying to translate the suggested controls—embargoes, restrictions on loans, discouragements to propaganda and so on—into concrete legislative policy which would meet a future situation that was beyond exact prediction, the more difficult did the undertaking appear. I wrote some articles and made a number of speeches about neutrality and how to maintain it, but it never seemed to me that I succeeded in saying much. In the end a number of the suggestions implicit in my book (as in other studies of the subject) were written into law. But the several neutrality acts were obviously fumbling and confused creations; they began to be applied, in the Ethiopian, the Far Eastern and the Spanish crisis, in some very peculiar and unexpected ways, and it seemed as if something, somewhere, must have been left out of the demonstration.

It was. In the end about all that this particular line of attack had yielded were some suggestions as to technical devices that would assist in keeping the country out of war—provided it wanted to stay out of the war. They were, in other words, devices which would not really be of much practical use except in conditions under which they would hardly be necessary. They might do something toward preventing an abandonment of neutrality for trivial, frivolous, purely momentary, reasons; they nowhere reached to the basic problem of war itself. They said nothing about the fundamental reasons for which nations do or do not fight. Granting that I had proved in my book (I did to

my own satisfaction, if not to that of others) that the United
States had blundered in a blind and confused way into the last
war, and in so doing had doomed its intervention to a large
measure of futility, I still had not proved that it might not go
clear-sightedly into another war, and thereby achieve results, in
terms of national or human welfare, that would be commensurate
with the cost. For that matter, I had not even proved that it
would not have been an even greater disaster had we stayed out
of the last war than it was to go into it. If I had suggested something as to possible means for controlling the war process, I had
said nothing whatever about the ends to which the controls
should be applied. I had said nothing about the actual role of war
in human society; neither had most others. The very people who
were most vociferous in their determination that the United
States should never under any circumstances enter another European war were the first to assume it as axiomatic that the country
would have to fight if invaded. But why the one and not the
other? The answer was by no means so obvious as it appeared
to be at first sight.

And all the while such questions were growing only more and
not less urgent. While we talked and wrote books and adopted
resolutions and devised "peace systems," the distant thunders
were muttering steadily louder, steadily more insistent. In this
brief sketch of our own private "war to end war" I have scarcely
mentioned what was going on in the world at the same time—the
rise of military Fascism, the slow disintegration of the League of
Nations, the world depression, the invasion of Manchuria, the
enthronement of Nazism in supreme power over Germany. It
might seem as though I were describing a campaign conducted
in a vacuum. It might seem so; and unfortunately that, I believe,
is exactly what it was. As I said before, we forgot about society
to concentrate our attention upon war. It was war in the abstract
we thought about—war in general, an entity to be set aside and
examined and combated in itself. This was true, whether we
thought of it as a disease, a crime, a stupidity or a mechanical
process. In each case we were isolating war from the society in
which it appears; and I think that the hard-bitten economic deter-
minists among us—the Marxists who regarded it as an inevitable

product of the capitalistic system or the radical materialists who ascribed it most rigorously to such alleged social forces as imperialist rivalry, pressures of population and so on—were doing so just as much as the rest of us. However much they may have fallen back on social forces for their explanation, it was still war in the abstract—war as a thing in itself—of which they were thinking. But war is not abstract, nor a thing in itself. It does not simply grow out of society; in a sense, it *is* society. It is certainly the most striking, and the most completely socialized, of all social activities. We were making a double error. We were at the same time both isolating our subject too rigorously from its social context, and generalizing it too loosely, assuming on the one hand that war could be treated as a thing in itself and on the other hand that all wars were the same kind of thing. One phrase has reëchoed now for years through American life: "We must keep the United States out of war." But two obvious questions have rarely been asked: "Who are 'we'?" and "What War?" Had they been asked more often, we might have made more progress. (6)

We did not ask them; but history did. We had been opposing war in the abstract; Herr Hitler, improving enormously upon the initiatives already taken by Mussolini, by the Russians and the rest, abruptly presented it to us in a very concrete form. We had assumed that all reasonable men were one in wishing to eliminate wars from the world. Here were men—I will not say whether they were reasonable or not, but they were men who had raised themselves to absolute power over great nations—who were deliberately cultivating war as the central framework of society. They had made it the operating principle of the state, the primary social institution binding all others together. War was as fundamental to the totalitarian state as the concept of majority rule or legal process was to the democratic type of social organization. Their economy was based on armament orders; their politics on military discipline; their social aims on imperial conquest; their foreign policy on all the cruel myths—racial superiority, survival of the fittest, population pressure, the necessity to expand and so on—which had been used to rationalize warfare in the past and which we had labored so long to expose.

We had hated the physical suffering and horror of war; it meant nothing to these men. We had hated the febrile emotionalism, the propaganda lies and exaggerations essential to its conduct by the complex modern state. They made the lie a main instrument of government and elevated propaganda to a religious dogma. We had hated the intellectual suppressions of war, its barbarous blindness and narrowness. They clapped an iron censorship on their people. We had hated war's release of the most primitive passions, the sadism and blood lust to which it gave expression. They had used sadism as a motivating force of their society, and while foreign enemies were unavailable as victims they had quite deliberately appointed their Jewish communities to the role. We had hated, or thought we had hated, war's complete overriding of the individual, its imposition of an absolute unity. They perceived in this aspect of war one of its deepest and most powerful appeals to the lonely human spirit; and while they jammed their concentration camps with the recalcitrant they put all the rest of their people, down to their girls and babies, into uniform. And out of these elements they compounded a social organization of amazing strength, stability and destructive energy.

Here was war in a concrete form which we had not anticipated. Before this development all our arguments fell to the ground. War is horrible? "Of course," they replied in effect, "what of it?" and they burned all the books, barred all the motion picture films and jammed all the radio broadcasts which might have conveyed this degenerate notion to their own people. Your whole picture of the world is a cruel and grotesque lie? "Naturally," they responded, "so is yours; but ours is a bigger lie and so more readily believed. We will make it bigger still. We will make it such a thundering lie that we shall believe it ourselves and then nothing can touch us." And the trouble was that they were, in a measure, right. Their system worked. It worked to ends that seemed brutal, retrogressive, destructive to us, but it worked; and nothing that we could say—nothing that we had said in the twenty-odd years we had been pondering these problems—had the slightest relevance to the issue.

Here there was not only war in a new form; here was rapidly

developing a specific war. We saw it coming nearer and nearer, in China and Ethiopia and Spain and Austria; and nothing in the armory which we had elaborated against war in general had any effect upon the steady advance of this particular conflict. The final demonstration was slow to arrive. The democratic statesmen used all the weapons against war which we had suggested. They were patient; they were reasonable; they refused to take bellicose action; they were slow to build up their own armaments; they tried to see the other side's point of view; they offered concessions. And still the crisis developed. At last there was Munich. Mr. Chamberlain, in effect, took our advice. He was not going to waste human life for small, uncertain and ignoble ends. What, in any rational system of human accounting, was the fate of Czechoslovakia worth to the young Englishmen who would have to die to save her? What had war ever achieved except disaster and destruction for all? Who could win a modern war, about which the only certain thing was that everyone would be a loser? Mr. Chamberlain applied these principles, which so many of us had so often elaborated, to the case in hand. Mr. Chamberlain did not fight; he did not waste life—and within some eighteen months Europe was filled with the dead bodies of Poles and Finns and Norwegians and Frenchmen and Englishmen and Germans by the hundreds of thousands; the giant bombs were smashing English pubs and churches and homes, the wreck and waste of war was spread over a continent. (7)

Here was the demonstration; and it was convincing. We were no longer facing war in general; here was war, specific and concrete, and it was war offering no quarter, admitting of no compromise. The only way to combat it was to fight it in the literal sense, with its own weapons—bombs, machine-guns, tanks, and a passionate determination however engendered, whether by patriotism, by propaganda, by hope of a better world, by fear of a worse one, or by the simple resolve to do one's share in a common job the doing of which cannot be avoided. Here was the demonstration, and here was the dilemma. One had either to fight war by making oneself warlike—by embracing all the cruelties, the suppressions, the agonies which we had detested—or one had to surrender to it and see it enthroned in the world as the central institution of Western civilization and the world itself organized, directed and controlled by the barbarous men who had built the New Europe around it.

Here was the dilemma; and at the first moment it seemed an appalling one. To many it still seems so. It terrified some, paralyzed others, and drove many more into a weak evasion of the issue which is perhaps worse than paralysis. Those who said that we shall never fight in Europe but will of course defend our national territory against invasion were among them. They merely hoped that there would never be an invasion; and hiding their eyes in this hope, which is none too solid at best, they refused to see that once the possibility of fighting at all is admitted, the question of the point at which to fight becomes almost a technical one—a practical question of achieving maximum gain at minimum cost. Those were also among them who talked of piling our own armaments to the skies while making peace with whoever wins in Europe. They were evading the whole issue as Mr. Chamberlain did when he came back from Munich with "peace in our time" and a redoubled rearmament program. Why armaments if we are to make peace, and why peace if we need armaments? What are the armaments supposed to be for? What are they to defend—a mere geographical entity, or a way of life, a general system of political and social ideas, which any peace with a victorious Hitler would certainly make impossible?

There were many in these past few months who, in all sorts of ways, desperately tried to evade their whole problem or hide it from themselves. They did not want to fight and they did not want to surrender; they were very anxious to prepare, but they did not know what the preparedness was to defend, and they shuddered when practically effective steps were proposed—such as the prompt occupation of bases, an embargo against Japan, an alliance with Canada, the despatch of ships or American air squadrons to Britain—which held out some hope of making the preparedness really effective at minimum long-run cost. But some of us, who after all have lived with this thing a good while now, began to ask ourselves some of these rather fundamental questions. Why, for example, should one be denounced as a blood-thirsty warmonger for suggesting that a few thousand Americans be enlisted to tip the scales of history where they are hanging balanced on the coasts of England; and yet everybody assumed it to be axiomatic that, should the scales go down, we would draft not only New Yorkers but Georgians and Californians to die in far greater numbers for the defense of New York? Why should there be such a determined insistence on the volunteer system of raising an army when no one has ever suggested a volunteer system for raising taxes? Why should we think it admirable to persuade, entice or browbeat our more impressionable young men into dying for us, when if anyone is to be asked to die it can surely only be because this is an imperative duty which each owes equally to the whole?

And in asking such questions as these—I throw them out at random—not only does the dilemma cease to be a dilemma at all, but at last, I think, we begin to approach the heart of this problem with which we have wrestled for twenty-odd years. War loses none of its hideousness or horror. But it is seen clearly to be something which reaches to the very fundamentals of our state and our society. You cannot ask poor men to suffer and die for nothing more than the rich man's profits; you cannot enlist one man to suffer and leave his neighbor free to enjoy in comfort all the benefits of his sacrifice. You cannot adopt a cautious foreign policy in order to save the lives of a few thousand today if by doing so you are going to slaughter hundreds of thousands tomorrow; similarly, you cannot draft millions to exhaust their time and energy in preparation for defense if you are going to give away everything that you have taught them to believe in defending. War challenges virtually every other institution of society—the justice and equity of its economy, the adequacy of its political systems, the energy of its productive plant, the bases, wisdom and purposes of its foreign policy. There is no aspect of our existence as individuals living in and by virtue of a social group which is not touched, modified, perhaps completely altered by the imperatives of war. And that is only to say, as I have said before, that war *is* society. It is society in action, for defense or aggression. Whether we like it or not it is, at the present stage of human history, virtually our one completely social activity;

and so long as it exists in the world we cannot, as social beings, escape it.

We had thought of war as something distinct from the normal operations of society—a special case of disease or crime or stupidity. But while I believe it to partake of all those attributes, it is not special or distinct. It is, as yet, the deepest expression of our social life, and as social beings we have to face it. The young man, for example, who resents being drafted for military service because it will interfere with his career can with justice, I think, be asked why he assumes that he will have a career, if he is uninterested in the common defense of the social framework which alone makes any modern career a possibility. War is society; and there are still times when any social organization—as the French have just demonstrated with terrible completeness—must be willing to fight unless it is to die. I do not think this will always be so. The war to end war must and will go on, and ultimately I believe it will be victorious. But war cannot be conquered by those who are afraid of it; and no great social ends can ever be achieved by those who are unable to act as members of their own society, utilizing when it is unavoidable the forms of expression, however gross or cruel, through which a social group does in fact operate as a society and not merely as a random collection of individuals. (8)

This may seem illogical; I do not care if it does. For if our first error was to approach war as a thing in itself, our second was to approach it as a purely rational issue. We demanded of this horror that it must have a reason to justify it, quite forgetting that almost no aspect of human life ever is reasonable. If governments are to lead their peoples into war, we said, they must do so in the highest wisdom, in complete purity of motive and for ends not only clearly conceived but worth the sacrifice; and when greed or cowardice or littleness appeared here and there behind the lines we flamed with disgust and disillusion. The disgust was appropriate; the disillusion was naïve. Greed and littleness and unwisdom are the commonplaces of all existence; no triumph of peace has ever been achieved without their presence, and while the effort to reduce them should be unrelenting, their existence should neither cause surprise nor be an excuse for defeatism.

The suffering, we said, must have a reason, and were exasperated when we could find none to assign to it. We forgot the amount of quite irrational suffering in all existence. There are disasters, losses, bitter bereavements in peacetime life—completely aimless, unjust and no less difficult to bear than those imposed by war. The suffering of war is a great reason for trying to do away with war; but we will never do away with war by expecting it to be rational, and to say that it is not is no excuse for failing to fight it with its own weapons, the only weapons, as we have been taught, which give any promise of success.

We are not rationalists discussing a problem in logic. We are men and women living social lives, utilizing for ends that seem good to us the instruments which society has developed. There is perfection nowhere, either in means or results, and there is suffering everywhere. But we know that no social life of any sort is possible unless it is informed by convictions—convictions which can never in the end be justified rationally but convictions at least so strong that we are prepared, when there is no alternative, to fight and take the risk of dying for them. And we must be prepared to do this, not as a result of a bargain—I will risk my neck in an airplane if you guarantee that my children will live in peace, security, enlightenment and on a good income—but simply because we are partners in a common, social effort, and the thing has to be done if we are to do anything. I suggested before that perhaps the best of all reasons for enlisting is that everybody else is doing it; the reason that when there is a common job to be done we wish to have our part in its doing. (9)

The American way of life has many faults and blemishes; it also has many things about it that one may hold up as worth fighting for and risking death for—its freedoms, its decencies, its strivings toward a better existence for greater numbers of its people, its effort to utilize as the springs of its social and political system the highest rather than the basest, the most advanced rather than the most primitive, instinctual drives in humanity. But great as these things are, and imminent though the present threat to them may be, I still do not think we can offer them as the sole, or even the primary, reason for again taking up the sword or again being prepared to do so. If our attitude is purely defensive, if we are merely sitting hoarding our liberties against threatened attack, those liberties are only too likely to atrophy anyway. Men's values inevitably differ, and in the last analysis are always irrational, beyond assessment by any form of cost accounting in which such-and-such an amount of pain or death can be equated to such-and-such a quantity of human or social advance. It is not, really, that kind of calculation at all. But suppose we say: "You must be ready to fight; if you are that; if the society of which you are a part has that much cohesion, conviction and energy as a social whole, then perhaps you will have a chance to make good your freedoms, to avoid the crimes of totalitarian retrogression, really to preserve your nation and whatever of its values seem best to you from foreign invasion—and to do all these things probably with far less cost in life and suffering than if you confess your social organization to be a weak and spineless thing, a mere collection of individual selfishnesses." Suppose we say that. I think we are much closer to the facts both of war and of social organization as a whole; I think we are much nearer to putting our hands upon the primary levers that operate the world we live in. We are then moving with, and not in puny revolt against, the main stream of human existence. We are not then merely kicking against the machinery which drives it; we are not, with the totalitarians, developing all the crudest, most primitive and most wasteful elements of that machinery in order easily to establish a barren power; but we are utilizing the basic mechanisms to produce, in time, better machinery, better results, a better ultimate life.

We are doing our part. I have a feeling that it is worth doing for itself, and in that feeling the dilemma seems to me to disappear. If war can only be fought by making war upon it, then I am prepared to make war upon it. And I doubt whether any other great social end can be achieved unless one is ready at least to risk one's life, as a unit in the social mechanism, for its attainment. I have put all this in generalized, one might say philosophical, terms. It seems to me no less true if it is translated into the most rigidly practical ones. Given the existing world situation as of today, I do not know, I am sure, whether the United States can maintain the essentials of liberal-democratic institutions; a reasonably free, full and prosperous life for its people or not. But it seems to me, as a purely practical calculation in politico-diplomatic probabilities, that the United States will have a far better chance of doing all these things, of utilizing its power to achieve maximum gains at minimum costs, if it can now rely upon a people who feel themselves one, who are ready to do any jobs that require doing, who are prepared in the last analysis to fight and die if they must, who do not shudder in humanitarian horror over a small sacrifice of life if it offers any real and practical chance of averting much greater sacrifices, who have first of all the energy to act as a people, and after that the resolve to utilize the action toward great and not little ends. (*10*)

QUESTIONS

I

1. In what way does the author consider himself typical of his generation, and what was his youthful attitude toward war? (*1*)
2. What was the real reason the author entered the Great War? In what aspect of the war does he regret not having had a part? (*2*)
3. What various kinds of books came from the Great War? (*3*)
4. What is the author's opinion of the Treaty of Versailles? What great disillusionment followed it, and who was primarily responsible for its failure? (*4*)
5. In what way did the writers wage war against war? What was the nature of the author's own attack upon war? (*5*)
6. What effect did the author's books have upon our governmental policies? Wherein does he feel that his "solutions" were inadequate and impractical? What double error was he making in his thinking about war? (*6*)
7. In what form did Hitler present war? What weapons did the democratic statesmen use against totalitarian ideas and how effective were they? (*7*)
8. What was the only alternative to surrendering to Hitler's kind of war? In what way is war a matter of *all* of society? (*8*)
9. What basic mistake does a person make who believes that war, or even life, is rational? What, according to the author, is everybody's duty to society in the performance of a common job? (*9*)
10. By what attitudes and actions does the author believe we have the best chance to make good our freedoms? (*10*)

II

1. The author considers one's duty in war as a *social* obligation. Do you accept this idea? If it is so, is there any defense for conscientious objectors?
2. "War is fundamental to the totalitarian state." Is this statement, in your opinion, true?
3. What do you think of the appeasement policy followed by the democratic European nations in 1938 and 1939? What, in the light of after-events, do you think ought to have been done?
4. Can any great social ends be achieved without human sacrifice? Can you think of social gains of the past which were made at the cost of human suffering and loss of life?
5. Retrace in your mind the steps by which Mr. Millis has changed his attitude toward peace and war since 1920. Do you find yourself in agreement with, or in opposition to, his conclusion: we must fight war to end it?

III

1. Note the use of personal details in this essay. Do these autobiographical touches have any value in making the writing effective? Can you see a way to use the same method in your own writing?
2. Discuss the paragraph beginning "We had hated the physical suffering..." (*7*) as an effective use of contrast both in idea and in form; and the paragraphs beginning "We had thought of war..." (*8*), and "The suffering, we said,..." and "We are not rationalists..." (*9*) for their philosophical ideas.

WORDS

If you can give working definitions for the words in this list (many of them you have had), you possess a somewhat better than average vocabulary.

1. vulnerable (*2*)	9. malevolent (*4*)	17. utilize (*5*)
2. literacy (*3*)	10. integrity (*4*)	18. disintegration (*6*)
3. guileless (*3*)	11. eminence (*4*)	19. imperialist (*6*)
4. intrigue (*3*)	12. futility (*5*)	20. rigorously (*6*)
5. paltry (*4*)	13. dilemmas (*5*)	21. primitive (*7*)
6. dissipated (*4*)	14. anatomy (*5*)	22. degenerate (*7*)
7. grotesque (*4*)	15. bias (*5*)	23. ignoble (*7*)
8. obstinacy (*4*)	16. frivolous (*5*)	24. cohesion (*10*)

If you can define the following words (with the aid of the cues given after them), you have a good vocabulary.

1. stigmata (*1*): stigmatize
2. expatriates (*1*): patriots
3. monosyllabic (*1*): monoplane
4. vista (*1*): vision
5. naïveté (*1*): naïve
6. legalistic (*4*): legal
7. inanity (*4*): inane
8. monographs (*5*): telegraph
9. militaristic (*5*): military
10. dogma (*7*): dogmatic
11. equity (*8*): equal
12. humanitarian (*10*): human

If you can define half of the words in the following list without recourse to a dictionary, you have a highly satisfactory vocabulary.

1. nomenclature (*2*)
2. rapine (*2*)
3. vortex (*2*)
4. inculcate (*2*)
5. stultification (*2*)
6. ineradicable (*3*)
7. prurient (*3*)
8. manifestoes (*4*)
9. shibboleths (*4*)
10. jingo (*4*)
11. flux (*5*)
12. rationalizations (*5*)
13. pedantry (*5*)
14. aberration (*5*)
15. pathology (*5*)
16. protocols (*5*)
17. cursory (*5*)
18. implicit (*6*)
19. vociferous (*6*)
20. axiomatic (*6*)
21. entity (*6*)
22. febrile (*7*)
23. sadism (*7*)
24. recalcitrant (*7*)
25. retrogressive (*7*)
26. relevance (*7*)
27. bellicose (*7*)
28. irrational (*9*)
29. instinctual (*10*)
30. atrophy (*10*)

THEME TOPICS

1. The Claims of Society upon Me
2. My Changed Attitude toward War
3. Doing the Job with Others
4. I Am Still a Pacifist
5. Fight War with War
6. War Is Society
7. I Approve (Oppose) Appeasers
8. War Is the Natural Order of a Totalitarian State
9. The World *Can* Be Made Safe for Democracy
10. Our American Heritage Is Worth Fighting For

If you can define the following words (with the aid of the cues given after them), you have a good vocabulary.

1. stigmata ([illegible]): stigmatize
2. expatriates ([illegible]): patriots
3. monosyllabic ([illegible]): monoplane
4. vista ([illegible]): vision
5. naiveté ([illegible]): naïve
6. legalistic (4): legal
7. inanity (4): inane
8. monographs ([illegible]): telegraphs
9. militaristic (5): military
10. dogma ([illegible]): dogmatic
11. equity (8): equal
12. humanitarian (12): human

If you can define half of the words in the following list without recourse to a dictionary, you have a highly satisfactory vocabulary.

1. nomenclature (2)
2. caprice (2)
3. vortex (2)
4. acquiesce (2)
5. stultification (2)
6. ineradicable ([illegible])
7. prurient ([illegible])
8. manifestoes (4)
9. shibboleths (4)
10. purged (4)
11. dint (5)
12. rationalizations ([illegible])
13. pedantry ([illegible])
14. aberration ([illegible])
15. pathology ([illegible])
16. protocols (5)
17. cursory (4)
18. implicit (6)
19. vociferous (6)
20. axiomatic (6)
21. egress ([illegible])
22. febrile ([illegible])
23. sadism (7)
24. recalcitrant (7)
25. retrogressive ([illegible])
26. irrelevance ([illegible])
27. bellicose (7)
28. irrational (9)
29. instinctual ([illegible])
30. atrophy (10)

TWELVE TOPICS

1. The Claims of Society upon Us
2. My Changed Attitude toward War
3. Doing the Job with Others
4. I Am Still a Pacifist
5. Fight War with War
6. War Is Society
7. I Approve (Oppose) Appeasers
8. War Is the Natural Order of a Totalitarian State
9. The World Can Be Made Safe for Democracy
10. Our American Heritage Is Worth Fighting For

Democracy and the Future

MY LOVE AFFAIR WITH FREEDOM

E. B. WHITE

I HAVE often noticed on my trips up to the city that people have recut their clothes to follow the fashion. On my last trip, however, it seemed to me that people had remodeled their ideas too—taken in their convictions a little at the waist, shortened the sleeves of their resolve, and fitted themselves out in a new intellectual ensemble copied from a smart design of the very latest page of history. It seemed to me they had strung along with Paris a little too long.

I confess to a disturbed stomach. I feel sick when I find anyone adjusting his mind to the new tyranny abroad. Because of its fundamental strictures, fascism does not seem to me to admit of any compromise or any rationalization, and I resent the patronizing air of persons who find in my plain belief in freedom a sign of immaturity. If it is boyish to believe that a human being should live free, then I'll gladly arrest my development and let the rest of the world grow up. (*1*)

I shall report some of the strange remarks I heard in New York. One man told me that he thought perhaps the Nazi ideal was a sounder ideal than our constitutional system "because have you ever noticed what fine alert young faces the young German soldiers have in the newsreel?" He added: "Our American youngsters spend all their time at the movies—they're a mess." That was his summation of the case, his interpretation of the new Europe. Such a remark leaves me pale and shaken. If it represents the peak of our intelligence, then the steady march of despotism will not receive any considerable setback at our shores.

Another man informed me that our democratic notion of pop-

ular government was decadent and not worth bothering about—
"because England is really rotten and the industrial towns there
are a disgrace." That was the only reason he gave for the hopelessness of democracy; and he seemed mightily pleased with himself, as though he were more familiar than most with the anatomy
of decadence, and had detected subtler aspects of the situation
than were discernible to the rest of us.

Another man assured me that anyone who took *any* kind of
government seriously was a gullible fool. You could be sure, he
said, that there is nothing but corruption "because of the way
Clemenceau acted at Versailles." He said it didn't make any difference really about this war. It was just another war. Having
relieved himself of this majestic bit of reasoning, he subsided.

Another individual, discovering signs of zeal creeping into my
blood, berated me for having lost my detachment, my pure skeptical point of view. He announced that he wasn't going to be
swept away by all this nonsense, but would prefer to remain in
the role of innocent bystander, which he said was the duty of any
intelligent person. (I noticed, however, that he 'phoned later to
qualify his remark, as though he had lost some of his innocence
in the cab on the way home.)

Those are just a few samples of the sort of talk that seemed to
be going round—talk which was full of defeatism and disillusion
and sometimes of a too studied innocence. Men are not merely
annihilating themselves at a great rate these days, but they are
telling one another enormous lies, grandiose fibs. Such remarks
as I heard are fearfully disturbing in their cumulative effect. They
are more destructive than dive bombers and mine fields, for they
challenge not merely one's immediate position but one's main
defenses. They seemed to me to issue either from persons who
could never have really come to grips with freedom, so as to
understand her, or from renegades. Where I expected to find
indignation, I found paralysis, or a sort of dim acquiescence, as
in a child who is dully swallowing a distasteful pill. I was advised
of the growing anti-Jewish sentiment by a man who seemed to
be watching the phenomenon of intolerance not through tears
of shame but with a clear intellectual gaze, as through a well-
ground lens. (2)

The least a man can do at such a time is to declare himself and tell where he stands. I believe in freedom with the same burning delight, the same faith, the same intense abandon which attended its birth on this continent more than a century and a half ago. Since my attitude is regarded in some circles as a youthful one, I shall address my declaration to the young men and women of America, the upcropping generation. I've always wanted to tell them what I love anyway—ever since I discovered America in a Model T Ford and saw, in every town, the high school building so much bigger and newer than the other buildings, and wondered what was going on behind those walls. My declaration is built on plain lines—nothing fancy. When you know what you love, when you know where you stand, the business of making a declaration is easy and goes along without a hitch. I want to tell something to all the young men and the young women in all the forty-eight States and in the territory of Alaska, the ones that are cropping up and getting going, looking for the jobs, casting the brand new votes, shining up the new guns in the old armories, looking for the answers, reading the ads in the papers, and listening to the bulletins from London. I want to make an affidavit before the generation that is making America go round —the girls getting their first jobs writing the letters that begin "Yours of the fifth instant," the boys showing up at the factory in the early morning, punching the time-clock and taking their places on the assembly line for the first time, the fellows swinging a racquet or a scythe or holding a drill, boys and girls on the banks of the Hudson and the Columbia and the Snake and the Kanawha, sons and daughters of cowhands on the dude ranches in the big States where the bigness is something you can cut with a knife, young fellows and girls in the tank towns and in the cities that make all the noise, boys rafting on ponds and translating Cæsar's Gallic Wars to the thunder of the new wars, playing the slot machines in the drugstores, swimming in the pool below the falls everywhere in America, skiers on the winter hills returning in the twilight down the white lanes to the New England farmhouses, boys in camp and on the trails between lakes, carrying their canoes, American boys hunting jobs and finding them and not finding them, boys on the sand truck sand-ing the tarred roads in the slippery weather in the country places, fellows and girls in the Bluegrass where the big oaks stand on the beautiful lawns where the thoroughbred horses graze, young fishermen in the smelt houses along the frozen Kennebec, boys and girls in Westchester who can hear the foghorn from the Sound when the wind is right, fellows working on lake steamers or walking in the Shenandoah in the soft spring months when the scent of mayflowers searches the heart, in the filling station at the pump checking the oil, working in the big hotels—in Miami, in Atlantic City, in the Adirondacks, hopping the bells and carrying the ice water and on the golf course handing the mashie to the man who wants to make an approach shot, young people who are taking the secretarial courses and the night-school training and who are writing to the manufacturers for the samples and saving the coupons and saving the stamps and writing the new poems and the love letters and the bills of sale all over America from the Atlantic to the Pacific, from the Canadian border to the Gulf of Mexico. There are millions of them; and I think their faces are good alert faces too, and their faces have an inquiring look, which I like, because they haven't been told the answer—haven't been told how to do, with precision, the audacious deed.

I am writing my declaration rapidly, much as though I were shaving to catch a train. Events abroad give a man a feeling of being pressed for time. Actually I do not believe I am pressed for time, and I apologize to the reader for a false impression that may be created. I just want to tell, before I get slowed down, that I am in love with freedom and that it is an affair of long standing and that it is a fine state to be in, and that I am deeply suspicious of people who adjust to fascism and dictators. From such adaptable natures a smell rises. I pinch my nose. (3)

For as long as I can remember I have had a sense of living somewhat freely in a natural world. I don't mean I enjoyed freedom of action, but my existence seemed to have the quality of free-ness. I traveled with secret papers pertaining to a divine conspiracy. Intuitively I've always been aware of the vitally important pact which a man has with himself, to be all things to himself, and to be identified with all things, to stand self-reliant, taking advantage of his haphazard connection with a planet, riding his luck, and following his bent with the tenacity of a hound. My first and greatest love affair was with this thing we call freedom, this lady of infinite allure, this dangerous and beautiful and sublime being who restores and supplies us all.

It began with the haunting intimation (which I presume every child receives) of his mystical inner life; of God in man; of nature publishing herself through the "I." This elusive sensation is moving and memorable. It comes early in life: a boy, we'll say, sitting on the front steps on a summer night, thinking of nothing in particular, suddenly hearing as with a new perception and as though for the first time the pulsing sound of crickets, over-whelmed with the novel sense of identification with the natural company of insects and grass and night, conscious of a faint answering cry to the universal perplexing question: "What is 'I'?" Or a little girl, returning from the grave of a pet bird, leaning with her elbows on the windowsill, inhaling the unfamiliar draught of death, suddenly seeing herself as part of the complete story. Or to an older youth, encountering for the first time a great teacher who by some chance word or mood awakens something and the youth beginning to breathe as an individual and conscious of strength in his vitals. I think the sensation must develop in many men as a feeling of identity with God—an eruption of the spirit caused by allergies and the sense of divine existence as distinct from mere animal existence. This is the beginning of the affair with freedom. (4)

But a man's free condition is of two parts: the instinctive free-ness he experiences as an animal dweller on a planet, and the practical liberties he enjoys as a privileged member of human society. The latter is, of the two, more generally understood, more widely admired, more violently challenged and discussed. It is the practical and apparent side of freedom. The United States, almost alone today, offers the liberties and the privileges and the tools of freedom. In this land the citizens are still invited to write their plays and books, to paint their pictures, to meet for discussion, to dissent as well as to agree, to mount soapboxes in the public square, to enjoy education in all subjects without censorship, to hold court and judge one another, to compose music, to talk politics with their neighbors without wondering whether the secret police are listening, to exchange ideas as well as goods, to kid the government when it needs kidding, and to read real news of real events instead of phony news manufactured by a paid agent of the state. This is a fact and should give every person pause.

To be free, in a planetary sense, is to feel that you belong to earth. To be free, in a social sense, is to feel at home in a democratic framework. In Adolf Hitler, although he is a freely flowering individual, we do not detect either type of sensibility. From reading his book I gather that his feeling for earth is not a sense of communion but a driving urge to prevail. His feeling for men is not that they co-exist, but that they are capable of being arranged and standardized by a superior intellect—that their existence suggests not a fulfillment of their personalities but a submersion of their personalities in the common racial density. His very great absorption in the destiny of the German people somehow loses some of its effect when you discover, from his writings, in what vast contempt he holds *all* people. "I learned," he wrote, "...to gain an insight into the unbelievably primitive opinions and arguments of the people." To him the ordinary man is a primitive, capable only of being used and led. He speaks continually of people as sheep, halfwits, and impudent fools— the same people from whom he asks the utmost in loyalty, and to whom he promises the ultimate in prizes. (5)

Here in America, where our society is based on belief in the individual, not contempt for him, the free principle of life has a chance of surviving. I believe that it must and will survive. To understand freedom is an accomplishment which all men may acquire who set their minds in that direction; and to love freedom is a tendency which many Americans are born with. To live in the same room with freedom, or in the same hemisphere, is still a profoundly shaking experience for me, so that I can't rest till I have tried to tell young men and women about it.

One of the earliest truths (and to him most valuable) that the author of *Mein Kampf* discovered was that it is not the written word, but the spoken word, which in heated moments moves great masses of people to noble or ignoble action. The written word, unlike the spoken word, is something which every person examines privately and judges calmly by his own intellectual standards, not by what the man standing next to him thinks. "I know," wrote Hitler, "that one is able to win people far more by the spoken than by the written word...." Later he adds contemptuously: "For let it be said to all knights of the pen and to all the political dandies, especially of today: the greatest changes in this world have never yet been brought about by a goose quill! No, the pen has always been reserved to motivate these changes theoretically."

Luckily I am not out to change the world—that's being done for me, and at a great clip. But I know that the free spirit of man is persistent in nature; it recurs, and has never successfully been wiped out, by fire or flood. I set down the above remarks merely (in the words of Mr. Hitler) to motivate that spirit, theoretically. Being myself a knight of the goose quill, I am under no misapprehension about "winning people"; but I am inordinately proud these days of the quill, for it has shown itself, historically, to be the hypodermic which inoculates men and keeps the germ of freedom always in circulation, so that there are individuals in every time in every land who are the carriers, the Typhoid Marys, capable of infecting others by mere contact and example. These persons are feared by every tyrant—who shows his fear by burning the books and destroying the individuals. A writer goes about his task today with the extra satisfaction which comes from knowing that he will be the first to have his head lopped off—even before the political dandies. In my own case this is a double satisfaction, for if freedom were denied me by force of earthly circumstance, I am the same as dead and would infinitely prefer to go into fascism without my head than with it, having no use for it any more and not wishing to be saddled with so heavy an encumbrance. (6)

QUESTIONS

I

1. What is the author's attitude toward those who would compromise with fascism? (1)

2. What examples of such compromise did he encounter in New York City? (2)

3. Give typical examples of the young people to whom the author is addressing himself. (3)

4. Why did Mr. White inevitably fall in love with freedom? Does every individualist experience this same love affair? What part does Nature have in the matter? In what sense is the experience religious? (4)

5. Into what two phases does freedom divide itself? Which is the better understood? What is Adolf Hitler's conception of the worth of the individual man? (5)

6. What is Hitler's opinion of the relative power of the spoken and the written word? What does the author believe the written word accomplishes? (6)

II

1. Can you remember any incidents in your own life that made you aware of yourself as an individual? A supreme moment of happiness? A transcending experience? Something beautiful? The revelation of the inner and true meaning of something?

2. "The free spirit of man is persistent in nature; it recurs, and has never successfully been wiped out, by fire or flood." (6) This is Mr. White's settled conviction. Are you in agreement with his belief?

III

1. Do you consider the author's analogy of remodeling ideas like clothes an engaging and amusing beginning for his essay? (1)

2. Note the long paragraph in (3) and the long sentence beginning "I want to make an affidavit. . . ." Do this paragraph and sentence suggest the idea of the speed with which the author later says he is writing? The long sentence is an excellent example of individual yet typical details. Its effectiveness is based on selection. Do you think it is well done?

3. Note the best figures of speech in the essay. Point out sentences or passages which seem to you to have a strongly poetic or dramatic effect.

4. What effect do such expressions as "hopping the bells," "kidding the government," "phony news," and "at a great clip" give to the essay?

5. Point out expressions and incidents of humor and satire in the essay.

WORDS

If you are in doubt about the meaning of any of the words in the following list, look them up in a good dictionary.

1. ensemble (*1*)	11. annihilating (*2*)	21. allergies (*4*)
2. strictures (*1*)	12. grandiose (*2*)	22. planetary (*5*)
3. rationalization (*1*)	13. cumulative (*2*)	23. co-exist (*5*)
4. patronizing (*1*)	14. renegades (*2*)	24. ignoble (*6*)
5. summation (*2*)	15. affidavit (*3*)	25. motivate (*6*)
6. decadence (*2*)	16. audacious (*3*)	26. inordinately (*6*)
7. anatomy (*2*)	17. tenacity (*4*)	27. hypodermic (*6*)
8. gullible (*2*)	18. intimation (*4*)	28. inoculates (*6*)
9. subsided (*2*)	19. vitals (*4*)	29. infinitely (*6*)
10. berated (*2*)	20. eruption (*4*)	30. encumbrance (*6*)

THEME TOPICS

1. Freedom and Human Dignity
2. What I Think of Appeasers
3. My Affidavit for Democracy
4. Kidding the Government
5. When I Discovered Myself as an Individual
6. An Experience I Shall Always Remember
7. My Dog and Me
8. What Adolf Hitler Thinks of Me
9. I Love Freedom, Too, Mr. White
10. The Free Spirit of Man Persists

STILL "THE HOPE OF THE HUMAN RACE"

HENRY STEELE COMMAGER

THIS people," wrote Turgot of Americans in 1778, "is the hope of the human race." It was a note that had been sounded before—from the very beginning, indeed, of settlement in the New World; it was a note that was to be sounded again and again in the years to come, by Europeans and Americans alike, by statesmen and by poets and by the plain people who sailed hopefully to the Promised Land or who followed "fair freedom's star" over the mountains and across the plains and prairie lands of the West. We hear it in Jefferson's celebration of this Republic as "the world's best hope," in Lincoln's appeal for the maintenance of the "last best hope of earth"; we hear it in those lines of Longfellow—"Sail on, O Ship of State" —which Winston Churchill read to us so dramatically, or better yet in the proud boast of Walt Whitman—

Thou holdest not the venture of thyself alone, not of the Western
    Continent alone;
With thee Time voyages in trust, the antecedent nations sink or swim
    with thee,
Theirs, theirs as much as thine, the destination-port triumphant.

What was the hope to be fulfilled, what was it the Old World expected from the New? It was, of course, what we have recently come to speak of as the Four Freedoms. It was liberty, democracy, equality, economic opportunity and security. It was the right of men to live their own lives, in peace and in comfort, to worship as they would, to marry whom they would, to follow such careers as their talents permitted, to make and unmake their own governments, to be subject to equal laws. (1)

That this hope has been in large part fulfilled is clear. It is well for us to remember that it was not fulfilled without effort and struggle. The United States has faced, from its beginning, many dangers; has survived many and serious threats. It won independence against overwhelming odds and against odds defended it; it maintained national integrity only at the cost of the greatest war of the nineteenth century. For two centuries, and more, Americans faced the test of the frontier—of a wilderness which might have barbarized men if men did not first tame it, of continuous uprooting and transplanting, continuous accommodation of men to environment and adaptation of environment to men. They faced, for an equally long period, the test of the melting pot—of the assimilation of millions of newcomers with different and often discordant backgrounds, cultures, faiths, and they fused out of these varied elements a unified people. They faced the test of continuous economic readjustments—the abrupt impact of the industrial revolution, the shift from a national to a world agricultural economy, the swift rise of the cities, successive depressions. All of these dangers the nation has surmounted, all of these tests—the military, the social, the economic —it has survived, preserving the essentials of liberty, democracy and security.

Now, at the height of our power, we are confronted with a new threat—one more ominous than any we have yet known. That threat was vaguely foreshadowed a quarter-century ago, but victory then lulled us into the belief that we could retain our own liberty and democracy and security regardless of what occurred elsewhere in the world. During the decade of the Thirties that illusion was gradually exposed; within the last three years it has been shattered. It is clear now that our whole way of life has been challenged. (2)

What is the nature of that danger? It is no mere military threat; there are graver perils than the military, more insidious forms of conquest; as the Knights of Aristophanes proclaimed many centuries ago,

There are things, then, hotter than fire, there are speeches more shameless still
Than the shameless speeches of those who rule the City at will.

What is at stake now is the vindication of that hope which we had thought fulfilled—the maintenance, for ourselves and for the peoples of the world, of liberty, democracy and security. Our ideal of democracy is condemned now by those who announce that democracy is the weakest of all systems of government and who oppose it for systems that appear far more effective. Our economic individualism is threatened by economic collectivism or by the complete subordination of economy to political purposes. Our traditional ethics is confronted by a new ethical system which denies in large part the values which we have always cherished and always taken for granted. Our faith in man is challenged by a new faith—a faith in the organic state or in the party or in a collective humanity.

It is difficult for the average American to grasp the nature of this challenge, for it is a new thing to us—new and for the most part incomprehensible. We are an easy-going people, we have never really known defeat, we have never known disillusionment —as Santayana observed, the notion of evil is foreign to our minds. Yet we must come to recognize that what we are in the midst of now is not just another imperialist war, not just a continuation of the scramble for natural resources, not just the violent expression of the megalomania of one man, but a death-struggle between two philosophies of government.

The core of the American philosophy of goverment is the individual. The individual is the source of government, he makes government, he can unmake government. The individual has rights and liberties—rights and liberties in society, to be sure, but nevertheless individual rights: the right to worship, to speak, to write, to go about his own affairs undisturbed by the State. No matter how socialized our thinking, our administration, our business, has become, it is still true that the ultimate objective of our government is the creation and protection of the free man. (3)

To this philosophy nazism and communism oppose a diametrically different one. Nazi and Communist philosophy, differing in many things, agree in subordinating the individual to something larger—in one case the state, in the other society as organized in the Soviet. In these philosophies the individual is unimportant, his liberties, his property, his ambitions and hopes, his social and family relationships, negligible. And this profound difference in the point of departure of the democratic and the Nazi-Communist philosophies has affected the whole system of values which they cherish. It is because we have failed to realize this that we are so naïvely shocked by what has occurred on the Continent of Europe in the last three years: by broken promises, by ruthless invasion and conquest, by religious and racial persecution, by the regimentation of life, by Fifth Column activities, by the whole strategy of terror.

By our standard of values these things are wicked, and we wonder how they could come to pass. To the Nazis and the Communists, who repudiate our standard of values and subscribe to a very different standard, they are not wicked at all; they are logical. For in that philosophy the end inevitably justifies the means, and because the practitioners are without experience and without wisdom, the justification is a short-range one.

The means are different, that much is clear, and the democracies have not yet schooled themselves to imitate them; it is a sorry joke that this war is being lost on the playing fields of Eton. Democracy appeals to reason, nazism to authority; democracy depends on coöperation, nazism exacts obedience; democracy has faith in education, nazism perverts emotions through propaganda; democracy exalts tolerance, nazism exploits intolerance—racial, religious, political.

But let it be emphasized, too, that the ends are different. The ends are not, as with us, the liberty and the happiness of the individual. The ends are the power and the wealth and the glory of the state or the party, or of some abstract and distant humanity. The means reject the age-long habits of society; the ends repudiate human values and life itself. The Nazi embraces the fallacious concept of the superman and the slave; it rests on the brutalizing pseudo-scientific notion of the survival of the fittest. It is a negation rather than an assertion of philosophy: it is anti-liberal, anti-democratic, anti-Semitic, anti-capitalist, anti-rational, anti-Christian, anti-human. It is, in short, as Rauschning has pointed out, a philosophy of nihilism. (4)

If these new philosophies are successful in the present conflict their success will give them immense prestige and power. They have already spread to the Far East; they have taken root in some parts of Latin America, they are not without adherents even in this country. They are, in their very nature, progressive and aggressive. They are, by their nature, totalitarian. They are at war not only with democratic politics but with democratic economy, society and morals. If they succeed, then indeed that danger which Woodrow Wilson saw—and fought—will have materialized: the world will no longer be safe for our democracy, not in our time.

This, then, is the challenge which confronts us, the challenge of vindicating everything that we have stood for for three centuries. To those for whom the history of mankind has meaning, America is once more the hope of the human race.

Everywhere in the world plain men and women recognize this. They know it in the concentration camps of Germany, in the devastated towns of Poland, in anguished France, in occupied Denmark and Norway, in war-torn China, in the frightened States of South America, in England, embattled and heroic. When we come to realize the nature of the conflict and the issues that are at stake, we too will know that we have still to fulfill our promise to mankind. We will know that now, more truly than when Lincoln spoke, "we shall nobly save or meanly lose the last, best hope of earth." (5)

QUESTIONS

I

1. What is the nature of the beliefs of poets, philosophers, and statesmen as to the part America was destined to play in world history? (1)
2. Name at least five of the threats and adjustments which the United States has overcome. (2)
3. What is the new threat to the survival of democracy? (3)
4. What are the fundamental differences, both in means and in ends, between Nazism and democracy? (4)
5. What function, according to the author, must America play in the future of the world? (5)

II

1. This essay brings up the fundamental question of whether America in the future is to pursue an isolationist or an international policy. To what extent is the present world situation the result of the policy we did pursue? What is your personal stand on this issue? Give reasons for whichever view you take.
2. In Mr. Wallace's essay ("The Price of Your Freedom," page 442), the expression "economic democracy" is used. In this essay we find the phrase "economic collectivism." Analyze and discuss the full import of these two expressions.
3. "The core of the American philosophy of government is the individual." Do you subscribe to this belief?
4. Why is it impossible for a democratic civilization to believe in the concept of a superman or a super-race?
5. Mr. Commager says all the democratic nations of the world look to us to preserve and reëstablish the four freedoms. What is your opinion about the necessity, or the advisability, of our accepting this gigantic task?

III

1. The author begins by giving several quotations as proof that other men have thought of America in the same way as he proposes to discuss America in this essay. Does this method win the reader's acceptance of the thesis? Where does he end his introduction and begin the essay proper?
2. Interpret the two lines of verse from Aristophanes. What twentieth-century meaning do you read into these lines? (3)
3. Does the author's device of closing the essay with a quotation, and thereby in form and spirit connecting the end with the beginning, give unity to this piece of writing? Are the author's quotations apt? Do they illuminate his thought? Do they add weight, as proof, to his argument?
4. Section (4) has some excellent examples of paragraph transitions. To what does "To this philosophy" refer in the preceding paragraph? To what does "these things are wicked" refer? To what does the sentence "But let it be emphasized, too, that the ends are different" refer?
5. Note the effective use the author has made of parallelism in the sentence beginning "Democracy appeals to reason..." (4)
6. Observe how the author, in the paragraph beginning "If these new philosophies," has gained the effect of climax. (5)

WORDS

Almost all of the following words you should know. *Megalomania* may give you trouble, but you know *mania* as a kind of "frenzy" or "insanity," and you know *megaphone*. What does a megaphone do to the human voice? You likely now have the cue to the word *megalomania*. Write sentences in which you use these words.

1. barbarized (2)	8. ethics (3)	15. repudiate (4)
2. assimilation (2)	9. imperialist (3)	16. fallacious (4)
3. discordant (2)	10. megalomania (3)	17. concept (4)
4. ominous (2)	11. naïvely (4)	18. negation (4)
5. illusion (2)	12. regimentation (4)	19. nihilism (4)
6. insidious (3)	13. perverts (4)	20. prestige (5)
7. vindication (3)	14. exploits (4)	21. adherents (5)

THEME TOPICS

1. I Believe in Isolationism (Internationalism)
2. America: The Hope of the World
3. Fundamental Differences between Democracy and Nazism
4. Crises in American History
5. America's Political (Economic, Social) Adjustments
6. The New Threat to America
7. Is Individualism Doomed?
8. The False Logic of Nazism
9. The Myth of the Superman
10. What Kind of World Is Coming?

AMERICAN YOUTH LOOKS AT ITS FUTURE

EDMUND E. DAY

BOLD, indeed, would be the man who undertook to speak authoritatively these days for American youth; and for a man past fifty to speak at all for American youth may appear to be plainly presumptuous. Nevertheless, that is what I propose to do. Middle life may have its disadvantages in this connection, but many years of association with school and college youth should have offsetting advantages. Fortified with such confidence as may be drawn from this long and wide acquaintance with young people, I am going to act for a little while as youth's spokesman, bringing to your attention certain views which, I have every reason to believe, are much on the minds of a host of young people in America today.

There are at least three good reasons for undertaking this rather difficult task. In the first place, youth is badly handicapped in getting its views effectively before the American public. Youth is relatively unorganized. Youth has not learned to operate through pressure groups. On many subjects it appears to be strangely inarticulate. Thus far it has not had effective access to the instruments of propaganda. Here and there the voice of youth is being heard; by and large even when raised it is drowned in the clamor of other parties. It is time to make an effort to give youth a chance to have its say.

In the second place it is clear that a somewhat sharper competition of age groups looms in the immediate future of American life. Already in some states the question has arisen whether old-age pension or public school costs are going to be covered

From *School and Society*, March 18, 1939. Copyrighted. An address before the American Association of School Administrators, Cleveland, Ohio, February 27, 1939. Used by permission of the author.

by the diminishing public funds that are available. There is every reason to think that the aged and infirm will make increasing demands upon the national income. Evidences accumulate that the adult population will increasingly restrict the opportunities for youthful employment in industry. In still another quarter, a steadily rising burden of benefits for the veterans of the Great War promises to draw diverse lines of interests between our age groups. More and more it becomes clear that among the stresses and strains of the present social order are those which stem not from the conflicts of classes but from the competing interests of successive generations.

The changing age composition of the American population is almost certain to accentuate all this. The number of young people between sixteen and twenty years of age will reach its maximum of about 12½ million in the early 1940's. Within the next twelve years the total in this age group will probably drop about 2,000,000. In 1930 there was in the continental United States, according to the decennial census of that year, a total of approximately 123,000,000 people. Of this number about 48,300,000 were under nineteen years of age and about 6,600,000 were sixty-five years of age or older. The young people outnumbered the old more than seven to one. It is conservatively estimated that in 1960 there will be a total population of approximately 140,000,000 people, of whom about 37,000,000 will be under nineteen and 15,000,000 will be sixty-five or over. The young people of all ages from birth to eighteen years inclusive will then outnumber the old folks by only two and a half to one. In other words, over the next twenty years, the number of children and young people is expected to decline about 11,300,000 and the number of old people to increase about 8,400,000. As this fundamental shift in the age composition of our population takes place, the competing interests of the generations may be expected to become more and more sharply drawn. Under these circumstances it is important that measures be adopted to secure most effective presentation of the desires and interests of our young people.

In the third place, I venture to act as spokesman for American youth because I believe it to be one of the privileges of the teaching profession to serve as mediator between each on-coming generation and those that have gone before. In times of relative economic stability and little social change, the reconciliation of the differences between the generations is not likely to prove troublesome. But in times like our own in which profoundly important changes are taking place with disconcerting speed, age groups separated by no more than fifteen or twenty years may live in totally unsympathetic worlds. Thus the Great War may be said to have created a deep and almost unbridgeable chasm between those who fought in the trenches and those who carried on at home in their accustomed places. The lack of understanding between parents and their offspring during the decade following the Great War was a matter of common note. The great depression has had like divisive effects. The adult population has been too engrossed in its own troubles to give much heed to the correlative perplexities and difficulties of youth. Herein lies a part of the opportunity and obligation of the great company of educators: to make more widely known the interests and aspirations of American youth in the troubled times through which we are passing. (1)

It has to be admitted at the outset that, with reason, youth might have a sharply critical attitude toward the legacy of our times. From the perspective of the late 1930's, there is a bitter, almost ridiculous irony about the idea that the Great War was fought "to end all wars" or "to make the world safe for democracy." Youth knows that, whoever claims to have won that war, civilization certainly lost it. Within our own country the national economy after several years of treatment remains sadly confused. A mounting public debt poses to youth the problem of later repayment. The burden of caring for the unemployed, the destitute, the sick, the aged and infirm, not to mention the veterans of foreign wars, assumes larger and larger proportions. Meanwhile the natural resources upon which the national economy is based are not what they used to be, with free land gone, forest land largely denuded, millions of tons of topsoil washed to the sea, and mineral deposits substantially reduced. No, youth would be within its rights if it commented rather caustically upon the job which has been done by its predecessors. Upon the whole, the attitude which youth has taken with regard to these matters is extraordinarily free of resentment. Happily youth concentrates its attention on the future, not on the past.

The significant views of American youth as it looks at its future relate to a wide variety of subjects, many of which I cannot undertake to consider. In the brief time available to me, I propose to confine my reporting to the views of American youth with regard to the schools, employment, and democracy. These are all very large subjects, and all I can hope to do is to give you in barest outline some of the views which I believe American youth to be entertaining. (2)

The attitude of youth toward the schools has been profoundly affected by the fact that the secondary school, as well as the elementary, has become well-nigh inescapable. Time was—and not so very long ago—when those who did not like formal education could avoid it after a limited sentence in the elementary grades; there was always some kind of job to which to escape. That time seems to have passed, with little prospect of its return. It now looks as if, up to age eighteen, or possibly nineteen or twenty, young people in America will be compelled to go to some kind of school. The high school can no longer be thought of as a school for the more academically disposed minority of young Americans; it has become a school for all young Americans of whatever disposition.

The attitude of youth toward the schools is widely variant, of course, and reflects great diversity of youthful interests, attitudes, and aspirations. It is safe to say, however, that by the time they are well along in their teens the great bulk of our young people wish to have the school programs exhibit clear and fairly direct bearing upon the life interests of the learners. What are some of the primary roles these young people expect shortly to be playing? Obviously they wish to become workers or producers—in other words, job-holders; the great bulk of them wish to become home and family builders; less uniformly and less fervently, they wish to be effective citizens. Here are approaching responsibilities for which they would like to prepare. They are not inclined to accept the doctrine that no specific preparation is in order; that the only suitable course of training is indirect and is solely concerned with the cultivation of intellectual and moral virtues.

No thoughtful person is going to question the importance of these intellectual and moral virtues. No one is suggesting that society try to dispense with these virtues. On the contrary, everyone wants a more ample supply of them, and the only serious question is how to get it. One answer is to return to the traditional academic disciplines; the other is to reorganize the curriculum with specific reference to the evolving life interests of the learners. It is reasonably clear that youth leans to the latter view of the matter. By some this is thought to be due to a softening of the intellectual and moral fiber of youth. Frankly it does not seem to me that this is a fair interpretation. We must realize that the secondary school is dealing with a new kind of school population, and that young Americans of secondary school age are facing a new kind of world. It would be surprising, indeed, if under these circumstances no change of school program were in order.

Youth, then, is somewhat critical of the American school of today and is looking, rather confidently, I believe, for certain changes for the better. Without seeking any softening of the school program, youth expects the American school of the future to cope more successfully with vocational training and adjustment, with preparation for home and family life, with training for effective citizenship in a truly democratic America. Here is a challenge from youth to the schoolmen that cannot be brushed aside.

One further idea about education gains wider and wider circulation among our young people. Increasingly it is held that individuals of exceptional promise should not be kept from realizing their promise through lack of financial means. It is argued, and soundly so, that there is inexcusable social as well as individual wastage in our failure to provide means by which these more gifted young Americans can obtain full development. Some system of wise selection and subsequent financial aid should be devised and supported. Where are those who will seriously question the soundness of this proposal? (3)

It is when dealing with the problem of employment that American youth is most likely to show traces of resentment. To young people, the full-time job is final and convincing evidence that at last adulthood has been achieved and independence established. The psychological value to youth of satisfactory employment is incalculable. Normal home and family living only so become possible. Self-respect only so can be achieved. It is not at all surprising that youth views the future so largely in terms of the prospects of employment.

American youth has thus far met the problem of unemployment rather stoically, but it is too much to expect that it will continue to do so indefinitely. It is high time that we all recognize that no society can long endure that leaves its young men in idleness. Measures should be promptly devised for dealing more constructively with this whole problem. Capital and labor, the schools and government should all join forces in closing the present gap between the school and the job. Possible extensions of the idea of the civilian conservation corps should be explored. Local communities should deal more earnestly and imaginatively with the possibilities of local community work programs. If undertakings along these lines cost money, let it not be forgotten that maintenance for the aged is no more indispensable than employment for the youthful. In the matter of opportunities for work, youth must be served.

Given employment, what does American youth expect of its future? In the first place, it does not look for opportunities to accumulate large means; it recognizes that the day of the great American fortunes has passed, probably never to return. But as an offset, a measurable increase in security is looked for, in fact demanded. At times it would appear as if American youth had grown prematurely old in its insistence upon guarantees of security rather than upon chances for adventure. Presumably this attitude springs from fear that the chances of successful adventure have ceased to be reasonable. But the spirit of adventure which always lies latent in youth will return to life. After all, the world remains an extraordinarily interesting place. Science and technology continue to perform their miracles, and thrilling careers of invention and discovery remain open. Service to one's times still carries rich rewards. The opportunities for social participation are expanding. Increasing leisure time lies at our disposal. If youth can come to see adequate meaning in life, if it can develop its inner resources and not attach too much importance to the material implements of daily living, it can come to view its prospects with renewed satisfaction. (4)

Young Americans regard democracy with an attitude not of skepticism, but of frank questioning. They can see—as can all of us—that democracy is in a measure of distress, and they are led to wonder how serious the complications will turn out to be. Their ideas of just what democracy means are somewhat vague and remote from their own day-to-day living. They are likely to think of democracy as a bookish ideal of government rather than as a concrete system of close-at-hand human relationships. They wonder whether democracy can maintain a satisfactory level of economic efficiency; whether it can solve the problem of unemployment. They hope they will not have to choose between freedom and a decent job. (Heaven forbid that they should have to!) They are impressed with the fact that great inequalities of human circumstance continue to challenge the concept of social justice that lies at the heart of democracy. On every hand they observe a distressing lack of social unity or of any consolidated social purpose. In short, they are troubled about democracy, and despite an underlying belief and loyalty, cannot but wonder what lies ahead.

Let us be thankful that American youth no longer takes democracy in childlike faith. The time has arrived for dealing more openly and constructively with those phases of American life which belie our democratic ideals. After all, democracy is not a blessing conferred for all time on the American people by the founding fathers; it is an aspiring purpose to be achieved only as the generations succeed in really establishing peace on earth and good will among men. Eternal vigilance is required for the preservation of such democracy as we have; unending endeavor for its improvement. If youth with its frank questioning leads America to replace its complacency toward democracy with honest concern for its future, youth will have served well those democratic purposes for which we all stand. (5)

Early manhood and womanhood is not an easy period of life;

it is, in fact, one of life's most difficult periods. Youth needs sympathetic counsel and wise coöperation in working out its problems. I am not one of those who would subordinate adult living to the demands of the oncoming generation; on the contrary, I am convinced that each generation in its prime is entitled to its own time in the saddle. But while there and living in the present, each succeeding generation is under obligation to keep an eye on the future, and the rights and interests of youth—of the generation to come—are to be respected even if the shift of political force carries in other directions. Youth has its part to play in social planning, and let not its failure to speak be taken as a sign of either indifference or complacency. After all, civilizations, like parents, may be judged in part by the thought and care they give to their young. Let us make sure that in this respect American civilization of the middle twentieth century is not found wanting. (6)

QUESTIONS

I

1. What three reasons does the author give for undertaking the difficult task of acting as spokesman for youth? Which of the three do you consider most important? (1)
2. Why do young people today have good reason to be critical of the legacy which their elders have passed on to them? (2)
3. How does youth view the function in America of the public high school? What does the author believe should be done for students of exceptional promise who have no financial resources? (3)
4. What expectations has youth the right to demand in the matter of employment? Why does present-day youth not expect to make great fortunes similar to those in the past? (4)
5. What is the attitude of young Americans toward democracy? In what way is this attitude salutary? (5)
6. What should be the attitude of each generation toward its own times? toward the generation that is to follow it? (6)

II

1. Do the competing interests of different age groups seem to you an important factor in American life? What is your attitude toward old-age pensions? toward soldier bonuses?

2. What do you think is right and what is wrong with the education you have received to date? Have you any ideas as to how the average American youth should be educated?
3. What do you think of CCC camps and public works as a solution of unemployment? How can America, in normal times, make employment more steady and secure?
4. Has the author expressed your views toward democracy? If not, wherein do your views differ from his?

III

1. Analyze the essay for clearness of outline.
2. What qualities has the first paragraph as an opening for the essay? What qualities has the last section as a close? Read the essay down to (5). Are you "satisfied" to stop there?

WORDS

Give working definitions for the following words. For very few of them should you need the aid of a dictionary.

1. inarticulate (*1*)	5. correlative (*1*)	9. stoically (*4*)
2. decennial (*1*)	6. denuded (*2*)	10. latent (*4*)
3. mediator (*1*)	7. caustically (*2*)	11. skepticism (*5*)
4. divisive (*1*)	8. incalculable (*4*)	12. complacency (*5*)

THEME TOPICS

1. Mistakes of the Generation before Me
2. I Want a Job (a Home, Security)
3. I Expect (Do Not Expect) to Make a Fortune
4. Wherein My Education Is Deficient
5. Toward More Practical Education in America
6. Flaws I See in American Democracy
7. Youth Is Not an Easy Period of Life
8. Debts (The Aged, War, Unemployment) as a Problem for Youth
9. No Longer a Young Man's World
10. What I Would Say as Youth's Spokesman

"I AM AN AMERICAN"

R. L. DUFFUS

I AM an American. The things I shall say about myself may seem at first to contradict one another, but in the end they add up. I am almost always recognized at once wherever I go about the world. Some say it is my clothes that give me away. Some say it is my way of talking. I think it is more than that.

I have had an unusual history. My ancestors came over in the *Mayflower*. They also came over during the hungry Forties of the last century, in the hopeful Eighties, in the troubled Nineties. Or I came five years ago and have just become a citizen. Name any race—I belong to it.

I have been around. I have seen the earth. No plain, no river, no mountain, no ocean, no race is alien to me, but now *I am an American. I am an American* because my father, or his father, or some other one of my ancestors, grew tired of being ordered about by persons no better or wiser than himself; or had more ambition or more energy than there was room for in the place where he was born; or was eager for new experience, or was hungry for land.

I, or some one for me, bought my share of America at a price. I have known hardships, sickness and danger.

I could not be held within the limits set for me by kings and lordlings on the other side of the water. I pushed forward. I hunted far beyond the mountains. I returned and took my wife and our brood and our wagons over. I crossed the great river and the little rivers. I crossed the ocean of plains. I crossed the deserts and the further ranges.

From *The New York Times Magazine*, May 18, 1941. Copyrighted. Used by permission of The Times Publishing Company and of the author.

The life I lived shaped me into a new kind of human being. I will not say a better kind, only a different kind. (*1*)

I have not loved arrogant authority. I have not respected any man because of the accident of birth. I have judged my fellows by what they were and what they did. I have relied upon myself. I have hoped greatly.

Out of the hate for power not answerable to the people, out of the bravest words and the boldest acts of my ancestors in other lands, out of the necessities of a new and untamed world, out of the knowledge learned by pioneers, that no man lives to himself alone; out of the desire for freedom, for peace and moderation, I have tried to create my government. I have not been wholly successful. I hope to be. I shall be.

In my struggle with this continent, out of my dreams, out of my griefs, out of my sins, I have laid by a great store of memories. They are a part of what I am. No torrent of words can tell of them. Some of them are too deeply hidden for words. But no new world, no new order in the world, can wipe them out.

I remember great men and great deeds. I remember great sayings.

But I remember, also, sayings that were never written down and deeds known only to a few: the pioneer greeting his wife as he came in from his new cornfield, in the dappled shade of ringed and dying trees; the strong surge of discussion in remote crossroads stores; the young man in Georgia or Ohio kissing his mother good-bye as he goes to enlist; a Mississippi Negro, a Texas cowboy, a round-house wiper making a song; a small-town William Tell standing up to a petty tyrant; all manner of men and women planning, working, saving, seeing that the children had better schooling than the parents; reformers crying out against brutality and corruption; dreamers battling against the full tide of materialism.

I remember all these things. They help to steady me when I lie awake at night, or when I walk the streets or go about the countryside in the darker night of injustice and violence that has come over the earth.

I stand up straighter. These are my people that have said and done these things.

I am an American. I am of one race and of all races. I am heir to a great estate. I am free and bound to the wheel of a great responsibility.

I turn. I look back across the oceans. Are they not my people, too, all of them? (*2*)

Have we come so far, done so much, suffered so much, hoped so much—and does it mean nothing? Is this New World to become an Old World? Were the brave words and the braver deeds in vain? Shall men stand straight and proud, manful and just, courageous and tender, building and sharing, on but one continent and for but a little time?

I am an American. I say, no!

On this continent, in God's good time, was brought forth "a new nation, conceived in liberty and dedicated to the proposition that all men are created equal." What was proved three centuries ago, a century and a half ago, three-quarters of a century ago, is not the less true now.

Freedom is not a lie. The brotherhood of man is not a lie. The kindly help given by neighbor to neighbor does not rest on a lie. "These truths we hold to be self-evident." Challenged, they are none the less true.

I am an American. I cannot let the challenge drop. I cannot say, I am not as other men and their tribulations do not concern me. I cannot say, free—let others be slaves for all of me.

I am an American and the inheritor of this continent. But the deed of gift was not handed to me without a codicil. There are stipulations and conditions. What was won by courage must be kept by courage. What was won in pain will have to be defended in pain. What was achieved cannot be enjoyed without new achievement.

I cannot rest upon my memories. I shall make new and proud memories for my children. I shall say to tyrants, as they said, "Stand aside!" Over vast prairies, beyond loftier mountains than my pioneer fathers crossed, I see a new vision: all who struggle anywhere for liberty are my countrymen, and no spot where blood has been shed for conscience' sake is foreign ground to me.

After the years, the centuries, I begin to know what it means to be an American. (*3*)

QUESTIONS

I

1. What are the backgrounds of persons becoming Americans, and what are the reasons for their becoming Americans? (*1*)
2. What experiences in America make men Americans? (*2*)
3. What is the American's answer to a challenge to his freedom? (*3*)

II

1. Is there any relation, in your opinion, between the American character today and the fact that our ancestors were the bold, the restless, the freedom-loving among their contemporaries?
2. "The brotherhood of man is not a lie." (*3*) Why is the American particularly stirred when this truth is challenged?
3. "All who struggle anywhere for liberty are my countrymen, and no spot where blood has been shed for conscience' sake is foreign ground to me." (*3*) Do you fully accept this doctrine of America's international responsibility?

III

1. To whom does the "I" throughout the essay refer?
2. The two distinctive features of the style of this essay are short staccato sentences and repetition. Could these devices of "force" be used successfully in a long essay?
3. Point out five good figures of speech in this essay.
4. How does the last sentence summarize the whole essay?

WORDS

Use the following words in original sentences of your own: arrogant (*2*), dappled (*2*), tribulations (*3*), codicil (*3*), stipulations (*3*).

THEME TOPICS

See list of Theme Topics for the following essay.

A CREED FOR AMERICANS

STEPHEN VINCENT BENÉT

WE believe in the dignity of man and the worth and value of every living soul, no matter in what body housed, no matter whether born in comfort or born in poverty, no matter to what stock he belongs, what creed he professes, what job he holds.

We believe that every man should have a free and equal chance to develop his own best abilities under a free system of government, where the people themselves choose those who are to rule them and where no one man can set himself up as a tyrant or oppress the many for the benefit of the few. (1)

We believe that free speech, free assembly, free elections, free practice of religion are the cornerstones of such a government. We believe that the Declaration of Independence, the Constitution and the Bill of Rights of the United States of America offer the best and most workable framework yet devised for such a government.

We believe in justice and law. We do not believe in curing an evil by substituting for it another and opposite evil. We are unalterably opposed to class hatred, race hatred, religious hatred, however manifested, by whomsoever instilled. (2)

We believe that political freedom implies and acknowledges economic responsibility. We do not believe that any state is an admirable state that lets its people go hungry when they might be fed, ragged when they might be clothed, sick when they might be well, workless when they might have work. We believe that it is the duty of all of us, the whole people, working through our democratic system, to see that such conditions are remedied, whenever and wherever they exist in our country. (3)

We believe that political freedom implies and acknowledges personal responsibility. We believe that we have a great and priceless heritage as a nation—not only a heritage of material resources but of liberties, dreams, ideals, ways of going forward. We believe it is our business, our right and our inescapable duty to maintain and expand that heritage. We believe that such a heritage cannot be maintained by the lacklustre, the selfish, the bitterly partisan or the amiably doubtful. We believe it is something bigger than party, bigger than our own small ambitions. We believe it is worth the sacrifice of ease, the long toil of years, the expense of our heart's blood. (4)

We know that our democratic system is not perfect. We know that it permits injustices and wrongs. But with our whole hearts we believe in its continuous power of self-remedy. That power is not a theory—it has been proven. Through the years, democracy has given more people freedom, less persecution and a higher standard of living than any other system we know. Under it, evils have been abolished, injustices remedied, old wounds healed, not by terror and revolution but by the slow revolution of consent in the minds of all the people. While we maintain democracy, we maintain the greatest power a people can possess —the power of gradual, efficient, and lawful change. (5)

Most of all, we believe in democracy itself—in its past, its present and its future—in democracy as a political system to live by—in democracy as the great hope in the minds of the free. We believe it so deeply rooted in the earth of this country that neither assault from without nor dissension from within can ever wipe it entirely from that earth. But, because it was established for us by the free-minded and the daring, it is our duty now, in danger as in security, to uphold and sustain it with all that we have and are. We believe that its future shall and must be even greater than its past. And to the future—as to the past of our forebears and the present of our hard-won freedom—we pledge all we have to give. (6)

QUESTIONS

I

1. What aspects of the democratic way of life are referred to in the first two paragraphs? (*1*)
2. What legal guarantees are embodied in the next two paragraphs? (*2*)
3. What is the economic responsibility of America? (*3*)
4. What is the personal responsibility of each citizen in a democracy? What sacrifices are involved in citizenship? (*4*)
5. What are the most obvious imperfections in the functioning of our American democracy? (*5*)
6. What is the hope of democracy for the future? (*6*)

II

1. "We believe in something bigger than party." Do you know individuals in our government, or in private life, who are more loyal to their political party than to their country? What is your attitude toward political parties?
2. In your opinion, has the "power of gradual, efficient, and lawful change" really proved itself in the century and a half of the American democratic experiment? (*5*)
3. Do you agree with Mr. Benét that democracy is too deeply rooted ever to be exterminated either by assault from without or by dissension from within?

III

1. Note the cumulative force of repeating "We believe" at the beginning of each of the first six paragraphs. What nice variation of this formula does the author use in the last paragraph?
2. Does this poetic and eloquent creed move you to a warmly emotional glow of acceptance of Mr. Benét's point of view? If it does, analyze the source of the appeal in the eight short paragraphs of this essay.

WORDS

The entire essay may profitably be studied as an example of simplicity in diction. Note how these plain words give this piece of writing the quality of unquestionable sincerity and honesty. Also observe how many of the sentences are simple sentences, which give the Creed a directness that is challenging and convincing. The good writer makes both his words and his sentences accomplish the purpose he has in mind.

THEME TOPICS

1. The Brotherhood of Man
2. The Folly of Racial Hatreds
3. The Advantages of the Party System
4. Americans—Old and New
5. The American Tradition of Freedom
6. America's Responsibility for a Free World
7. Strange Americans I Have Met
8. Our Blood Relation to Europe
9. Government and Social (Economic) Problems
10. Democracy Cannot Be Rooted Up

Corrective Handbook

CHART OF CORRECTIVE HANDBOOK

1. THE SENTENCE	a. Frag-ment	b. Comma Fault	c. Choppy Sen-tences	d. Subor-dina-tion
2. GRAMMAR	a. Case	b. Agree-ment	c. The Verb	d. Modi-fiers
3. PUNCTUA-TION	a. The Comma	b. The Semi-colon	c. The Colon	d. Quota-tion Marks
	e. Paren-theses	f. Italics	g. The Dash	h. The Period
	i. Ques-tion Mark	j. Excla-mation Point	k. Capitals	l. The Hyphen
4. SPELLING	a. Your Spell-ing List	b. Spelling by Ob-serva-tion	c. Spelling by Rules	
5. DICTION	a. Idiom	b. Provin-cialisms	c. Vulgar-isms	d. Slang
	e. Trite-ness	f. Fine Writing	g. Sound of Words	h. Wordi-ness
6. STYLE	a. Unity	b. Clear-ness	c. Empha-sis	d. Co-herence
	e. Ambi-guity	f. Vague-ness	g. Parallel-ism	h. Repeti-tion
	i. Mis-placed Words	j. Awk-ward-ness	k. Dan-gling Modi-fiers	l. Double Nega-tives, Compar-isons

SYMBOLS FOR CORRECTING THEMES

For teachers who wish to use the generally accepted symbols for correcting themes instead of those in the "Corrective Handbook" (for instance, *Frag.* instead of 1a, *K* instead of 6j), the following list is given. The student can readily refer, from these symbols, to the treatment given the error in the "Corrective Handbook."

A.	Ambiguous	Sp.	Spelling
Agr.	Faulty agreement	Syl.	Wrong syllable division
Awk. or K	Awkward	T.	Tense
Cap.	Capitalize	Tr.	Transpose
Cf.	Comma fault	Trans.	Transition needed
Cl.	Not clear	U.	Unity lacking
Coh.	Coherence lacking	V.	Vague
Col.	Colloquialism	W.	Wordiness
D.	Diction	Wk.	Weak sentence, etc.
Dlng.	Dangling modifier	,/;/⊙/	Punctuate with the mark indicated
Frag.	Sentence fragment	¶	New paragraph
Gr.	Faulty grammar	No ¶	No paragraph division
Hk.	Hackneyed expression	#	More space
Ital.	Italics needed	◡	Close up
l.c.	Use lower-case letter	∧	Insert omitted letter, word, or punctuation mark
Ns.	New sentence	δ	Omit, delete
Obs.	Obscure	/-/	Insert hyphen
P.	Wrong punctuation	‖	Parallel structure needed
Pf.	Period fault	ﾞ	Insert apostrophe
R.	Repetition	" "	Insert quotation marks
Ref.	Faulty reference	X	Careless; obvious error
S.	Faulty sentence	?	Query by reader
Sl.	Slang	——	Italics (for word underscored)

1. THE SENTENCE

a. Fragment (or Period Fault)

A sentence fragment is a group of words—usually a phrase or subordinate clause—which does not express a complete thought. Correction:

1. The fragment may be incorporated in the sentence of which it is logically a part.
2. It may be expanded into an independent sentence.

Wrong: He paid the bill. An almost forgotten account of long standing.
Right: He paid the bill, an almost forgotten account of long standing.
Right: He paid the bill. It was an almost forgotten account of long standing.

Wrong: James struggled with the problem. Believing he could find the solution.
Right: James struggled with the problem, believing he could find the solution.
Right: James struggled with the problem. He believed that he could find the solution.

Wrong: Tom had to walk three miles to a filling station. Because he had run out of gas.
Right: Tom had to walk three miles to a filling station, because he had run out of gas.
Right: Tom had to walk three miles to a filling station. He had run out of gas.

Wrong: I like to travel. To see the places I have always heard about.
Right: I like to travel in order to see the places I have always heard about.
Right: I like to travel. Traveling gives me an opportunity to see the places I have always heard about.

Wrong: Our car is hard to start. Especially in cold weather.
Right: Our car is hard to start, especially in cold weather.
Right: Our car is hard to start. It is especially difficult to start in cold weather.

Wrong: He flicked on the light. Turned it off and tiptoed across the room.

Right : He flicked on the light, turned it off, and tiptoed across the room.

Right: He flicked on the light. Then he turned it off and tiptoed across the room.

b. Comma Fault

The comma fault results when two or more sentences are joined by only a comma. Correction:

1. Write as separate sentences.
2. Insert a coördinating conjunction (*and, or, but, nor, for*) after the comma.
3. Substitute a semicolon (occasionally a colon) for the comma.
4. Subordinate one of the sentences to the other, thereby making a complex sentence.
5. Reduce one of the sentences to a phrase.
6. Make a single sentence of the two sentences.

Any of these corrections will make the sentence technically right, but the best one to use will depend upon the exact thought the writer wishes to convey.

Wrong: The singer waited for the applause to stop, then she began her solo.

Right: The singer waited for the applause to stop. Then she began her solo.

Right: The singer waited for the applause to stop, and then she began her solo.

Right: The singer waited for the applause to stop; then she began her solo.

Right: When (*or* After) the applause had stopped, the singer began her solo.

Right: The singer waited for the applause to stop before she began her solo.

Right: The applause having stopped, the singer began her solo.

Right: After the applause, the singer began her solo.

Right: The applause stopped the singer from beginning her solo.

Wrong: The dormitory was noisy, he could not study.

Right: The dormitory was noisy. He could not study.

Right: The dormitory was noisy, and he could not study.

Right: The dormitory was noisy; he could not study.
Right: The dormitory was noisy; so he could not study.
Right: The dormitory was so noisy that he could not study.
Right: There was so much noise in the dormitory that he could not study.
Right: He could not study because the dormitory was so noisy.
Right: Since the dormitory was noisy, he could not study.
Right: Because of the noise in the dormitory, he could not study.
Right: Studying in the dormitory was impossible because of the noise.
Right: The dormitory being noisy, he could not study.
Right: The noise in the dormitory prevented him from studying.

c. Choppy and Stringy Sentences

A series of short, choppy sentences is likely to be unpleasing to the reader and to give him the impression that the writer is mentally immature. Note the following examples:

Choppy: The wood was in the yard. He had to carry it into the kitchen. He carried it into the kitchen in his arms.
Improved: He carried the wood in his arms from the yard into the kitchen.

Choppy: It was a rainy day. He felt depressed. He always felt that way when it was rainy.
Improved: Whenever it was rainy, as it was today, he felt depressed.

The opposite effect results from stringy sentences. In such sentences, the mind runs on without any realization of the true relationship of the ideas in the sentence. Observe the following illustrations:

Stringy: We came to the bend in the road and there before us was the town and we had been hoping to get to it before dark.
Improved: At the bend in the road was the town which we had been hoping to reach before dark.

Stringy: He liked detective stories, but he disliked love stories, and he didn't care for serious books either.
Improved: Since he disliked love stories and serious books also, he confined his reading to detective stories.

d. Subordination

A person who subordinates the less important ideas in a sentence to the more important ones reveals a clear and discriminating mind. Subordination is usually the solution for loose, undistinguished sentences, as can be seen from the following:

Poor: He had bought a new car, and he didn't have any money left.
Better: Since he had bought a new car, he didn't have any money left.

Poor: He had won the state spelling contest, and he was only twelve years old.
Better: Although he was only twelve years old, he had won the state spelling contest.
Better: In spite of the fact that he was only twelve years old, he had won the state spelling contest.

Poor: Her name was Jane, and she was the most beautiful girl I had ever seen.
Better: Jane was the most beautiful girl I had ever seen.
Better: I had never seen a girl as beautiful as Jane.

2. GRAMMAR

a. Case

For nouns, the possessive case presents almost the only source of difficulty. Correct possessives may be made by observing the following examples:

Singular	Plural	Singular
boy's	boys'	Dickens' or Dickens's
father's	fathers'	Keats' or Keats's
lady's	ladies'	Burns' or Burns's
enemy's	enemies'	
monkey's	monkeys'	*Joint Possession*
turkey's	turkeys'	Mary and Susan's mother
man's	men's	Procter and Gamble's soap
woman's	women's	The secretary and treasurer's report
child's	children's	(one officer)
ox's	oxen's	
goose's	geese's	*Separate Possession*
beau's	beaus' *or* beaux'	Mary's and Susan's mothers
		Altman's and Gimbel's stores
		The secretary's and the treasurer's reports (two officers)

With the gerund the possessive case of the noun is usually used.

Wrong: They insisted on *Henry* taking the examination.
Right: They insisted on *Henry's* taking the examinations. (Emphasis on *taking*.)
Right: There I saw *Henry* taking a picture. (Emphasis on *Henry*, not on *taking*, which is here a participle.)

With pronouns, errors occur most frequently with the nominative and objective cases. The following sentences illustrate the most common of these errors.

Wrong: *Him* and *me* roomed together.
Right: *He* and *I* roomed together. (Subjects of *roomed*.)

Wrong: John and *her* bought the house.
Right: John and *she* bought the house. (Part of compound subject.)

Wrong: It was *them*.
Right: It was *they*. (Subjective complement.)

Wrong: If I were *him*, I would not go.
Right: If I were *he*, I would not go. (Subjective complement.)

Wrong: John saw you and *she* in the restaurant.
Right: John saw you and *her* in the restaurant. (Object of *saw*.)

Wrong: Mrs. Martin sent her mother and *she* an invitation.
Right: Mrs. Martin sent her mother and *her* an invitation. (Indirect object.)

Wrong: They asked Mary and *I* to come early.
Right: They asked Mary and *me* to come early. (Objective case, subject of the infinitive *to come*.)

Wrong: They thought the successful candidate to be *he*.
Right: They thought the successful candidate to be *him*. (Objective complement.)

Wrong: The winners, Robet and *him*, are to make speeches.
Right: The winners, Robert and *he*, are to make speeches. (Apposition with subject.)

Wrong: Let's you and *I* go to the movies.
Right: Let's you and *me* go to the movies. (Apposition with objective *us*: Let's = Let us.)

Wrong: All of *we* girls belong to the club.
Right: All of *us* girls belong to the club. (Object of preposition *of*.)

Wrong: There should be no secrets between you and *I*.
Right: There should be no secrets between you and *me*. (Object of the preposition *between*.)

Wrong: I shall leave the matter to you and *he*.
Right: I shall leave the matter to you and *him*. (Object of the preposition *to*.)

Wrong: This is the boy *whom*, I believe, won the scholarship.
Right: This is the boy *who*, I believe, won the scholarship. (Subject of *won*.)

Wrong: He is the man *who*, I remember, I met in Honolulu.
Right: He is the man *whom*, I remember, I met in Honolulu. (Object of *met*.)

Wrong: Give the prize to *whomever* deserves it.
Right: Give the prize to *whoever* deserves it. (Subject of *deserves*.)

Wrong: Mary is older than *me*.
Right: Mary is older than *I*. ("...than I am old.")

Wrong: He thinks he's just as good as *them*.
Right: He thinks he's just as good as *they*. ("...as they are.")

Wrong: *Who* are you looking for?
Right: *Whom* are you looking for? (Object of *for*.)
Right: For *whom* are you looking?

Wrong: *Who* is he calling?
Right: *Whom* is he calling? (Object of *is calling*.)

The apostrophe is never used with personal pronouns or relative pronouns to express possession. Hence write *ours, yours, hers, its, theirs,* and *whose,* but never *our's, your's, her's, it's, their's,* and *who's* for the possessive. Attention must also be paid not to use *there* for *their*.

Right: The owl had *its* nest in the hollow tree. (Possessive pronoun.)
Right: *It's* a chance in a lifetime. (Contraction of *it is*.)

Right: *Their* house is in the country. (Possessive pronoun.)
Right: *There* are several ways to view the problem. (Expletive.)
Right: *There's* no more sugar in the bowl. (Expletive.)
Right: Put the bundle down *there*. (Adverb of place.)
Right: *They're* coming by airplane. (Contraction of *They are*.)

Right: *Your* idea is sound. (Possessive pronoun.)
Right: *You're* responsible for the tickets. (Contraction of *You are*.)

Right: The girl *whose* grades were highest won the prize. (Possessive relative pronoun.)
Right: *Who's* going to drive the car? (Contraction of *Who is*.)

With the gerund the possessive case of the pronoun is usually used.

Wrong: The authorities objected to *him* obstructing the sidewalk.
Right: The authorities objected to *his* obstructing the sidewalk. (Emphasis on *obstructing*.)
Right: I saw *him* running down the street .(Emphasis on *him*, not on *running*, which is here a participle.)

535

b. Agreement

A verb agrees with its subject in number. It also agrees with its subject in person, but errors in person are relatively infrequent.

Wrong: You *was* late this morning.
Right: You *were* late this morning. (*Are* and *were* used with *you*, even when one person is addressed.)

Wrong: He *don't* answer my letters.
Right: He *doesn't* answer my letters. (*Don't* is equivalent to *do not*.)

Wrong: There *was* abundant supplies for the refugees.
Right: There *were* abundant supplies for the refugees. (*Supplies* is the subject.)

Wrong: On the other bank of the river *stands* the fortifications.
Right: On the other bank of the river *stand* the fortifications. (*Fortifications* is the subject.)

Wrong: The pay of all workers in factories *have* been increased.
Right: The pay of all workers in factories *has* been increased. (*Pay* is the subject.)

Wrong: Buildings in the old section of the town *was* razed.
Right: Buildings in the old section of the town *were* razed. (*Buildings* is the subject.)

Wrong: Each of the winners in the district contests *have* received a prize.
Right: Each of the winners in the district contests *has* received a prize. (*Each* is the subject.)

Wrong: The captain, as well as the team, *were* elated by victory.
Right: The captain, as well as the team, *was* elated by victory. (*Captain* is the subject.)

Wrong: The president, together with the other officers of the bank, *were* indicted.
Right: The president, together with the other officers of the bank, *was* indicted. (*President* is the subject.)

Wrong: The jury *were* unanimous in voting conviction.
Right: The jury *was* unanimous in voting conviction. (Collective noun, singular in idea.)

Wrong: The jury *was* locked up in their hotel rooms for the night.
Right: The jury *were* locked up in their hotel rooms for the night.
(Individual members referred to.)

Wrong: The greatest annoyance *were* the noises made by traffic.
Right: The greatest annoyance *was* the noises made by traffic.
(*Annoyance* is the subject. A verb does not agree with its subjective complement—here *noises*.)

Right: She and I *are* old friends. (Compound subject.)
Right: The lessee and manager *was* Mr. Brown. (One person.)

Right: Every man and every woman *has* a right to vote. (Separateness emphasized.)
Right: Either Mary or her sister *was* the winner. (Alternate choice.)
Right: Either the shipping clerk or his helpers *were* negligent. (Verb agrees with nearer subject.)
Right: Neither the members nor the chairman *was* ready for the report. (Verb agrees with nearer subject.)
Right: The foreman, and not the workmen, *was* responsible. (Verb agrees with affirmative subject.)
Right: Fish *were* plentiful in those waters. (Subject plural in idea.)
Right: Twenty-five dollars *is* cheap for that suit. (Subject a sum.)

A frequent error, especially with *kind* and *sort*, is the attraction of *this* and *that*, into *these* and *those*, by the following noun.

Wrong: I would not answer *these* kind of letters.
Right: I would not answer *this* kind of letters.

Wrong: I admire *those* sort of antiques.
Right: I admire *those* sorts of antiques.

A pronoun agrees with its antecedent in person and number. Errors most frequently occur in the lack of agreement in number.

Wrong: Everyone had *their* own opinion.
Right: Everyone had *his* own opinion. (*Everyone* is singular.)

Wrong: Each boy had *their* chance.
Right: Each boy had *his* chance. (Antecedent is singular.)

Wrong: The delegate or the alternate will take *their* place.
Right: The delegate or the alternate will take *his* place. (Singular by alternate choice.)

Wrong: Neither the star nor the leading lady knew *their* parts.

Permissible: Neither the star nor the leading lady knew *his* or *her* part.

Better: The star did not know *his* part, nor did the leading lady know *hers*.

Wrong: Every man and every woman will do *their* duty.

Permissible: Every man and every woman will do *his* or *her* duty.

Better: Everyone will do *his* duty.

Wrong: Every time a beggar asks for money, Father gives *them* a dime.

Right: Every time a beggar asks for money, Father gives *him* a dime. (Antecedent is singular.)

Wrong: Either of the boys *are* trustworthy.

Right: Either of the boys *is* trustworthy. (Alternate choice.)

Wrong: Anyone has the right to express *their* own ideas.

Right: Anyone has the right to express *his* own ideas. (Antecedent is singular.)

Wrong: Nobody should eat *their* dessert until all are served.

Right: Nobody should eat *his* dessert until all are served. (Antecedent is singular.)

Wrong: He is one of the greatest orators who *has* spoken here.

Right: He is one of the greatest orators who *have* spoken here. (*Orators* is the antecedent, not *one*.)

c. The Verb

Tense expresses the time of the action of a verb. A few errors in relation to tense must be guarded against, especially in the sequence of tenses.

Wrong: Then she *began* and *sings* a most beautiful solo.

Right: Then she *began* and *sang* a most beautiful solo. (Both verbs should be in the same tense—here past.)

Wrong: He *showed* the doctor his hand which he *burned*.

Right: He *showed* the doctor his hand which he *had burned*. (Past perfect tense needed to indicate action antecedent to that in *showed*.)

Wrong: He could find no one to do the work; so he *done* it himself.
Right: He could find no one to do the work; so he *did* it himself.
(Past tense is *did*.)

Wrong: Even though prices have advanced, he has *began* to build
his new home.
Right: Even though prices have advanced, he has *begun* to build
his new home. (Past participle required with *has, have, had*.)

Wrong: Last summer I wanted *to have gone* to California.
Right: Last summer I wanted *to go* to California. (At the time of
wanting, my desire was *to go*.)

Wrong: We hoped you *would have accepted* the invitation.
Right: We hoped you *would accept* the invitation.

Wrong: If he *would have apologized*, I should have forgiven him.
Right: If he *had apologized*, I should have forgiven him. (The
apology required before the forgiving.)

Wrong: *Setting* the table in the afternoon, she had dinner ready in
a few minutes.
Right: *Having set* the table in the afternoon, she had dinner ready
in a few minutes. (Perfect participle needed to express antecedent
time.)

Errors in mood are concerned chiefly with the subjunctive,
which expresses doubt or uncertainty, condition contrary to fact,
wishing, and necessity or obligation.

Right: If he *were* sure of their coming, he would rent the house.
(Doubt.)
Right: If I *were* she, I should take the trip. (Contrary to fact.)
Right: I wish I *were* at the party. (Wish.)
Right: The law requires that one *stop* at the intersections. (Obli-
gation.)

The verb *may* expresses permission or wish; the verb *can* expresses ability or possibility.

Right: *May* I go with you? (Permission.)
Right: *May* you never face such a danger again. (Wish.)
Right: *Can* you read Spanish? (Ability.)
Right: This coal *can* be burned in a stoker. (Possibility.)

To avoid errors in use of *sit-sat-sat*, *lie-lay-lain*, and *rise-rose-risen*, remember that these verbs are intransitive. *Set-set-set*, *lay-laid-laid*, and *raise-raised-raised* are transitive.

Right: I *sat* under that old tree years ago.
Right: I *lay* on the couch yesterday afternoon.
Right: I *rose* before daylight on Christmas morning.
Right: She *set* the dessert in the icebox several hours ago.
Right: She *laid* her cloak on the bed.
Right: The boy *raised* his hand.

Other errors common in the use of the verb are illustrated by the following examples.

Wrong: He always *has* and always *will be* stubborn.
Right: He always *has been* and always *will be* stubborn. (*Be* cannot be used with *has*.)

Wrong: He *could of beat* the record if he had tried.
Right: He *could have beaten* the record if he had tried. (*Of* is no part of a verb.)

Wrong: He *had ought* to bought the house.
Right: He *ought* to have bought the house. (*Had* is never to be used with *ought*.)

d. Modifiers

Adjectives modify nouns and, occasionally, pronouns; adverbs modify verbs, adjectives, and other adverbs. If this basic distinction is kept clearly in mind, errors in the use of modifiers will be eliminated.

The adjective is used as the subjective complement after all forms of the verb *to be*, and usually with such verbs as *seem*, *become*, *appear*, *look*, *feel*, *smell*, *taste*, and the like.

Wrong: She looked *stylishly* in a blue ensemble.
Right: She looked *stylish* in a blue ensemble. (*Stylish* modifies *she*.)

Wrong: The patient felt *badly* this morning.
Right: The patient felt *bad* this morning. (*Bad* modifies *patient*.)

Wrong: This flower smells *sweetly* when in bloom.
Right: This flower smells *sweet* when in bloom. (*Sweet* modifies *flower*.)

The modifier is an adverb when it indicates the manner of the action in the verb.

Wrong: She looked *thorough* in every corner of the room.
Right: She looked *thoroughly* in every corner of the room. (Manner of *looking*.)

Wrong: The lady felt the goods *careful* before buying.
Right: The lady felt the goods *carefully* before buying. (Manner of *feeling*.)

Wrong: The druggist smelled the bottle *cautious*.
Right: The druggist smelled the bottle *cautiously*. (Manner of *smelling*.)

Wrong: He could read Spanish as *easy* as he could read English.
Right: He could read Spanish as *easily* as he could read English. (Manner of *reading*.)

Wrong: The rain fell hard and *steady*.
Right: The rain fell hard and *steadily*. (Manner of *falling*.)

The modifier after the object of a verb is an adjective if it modifies the object of the verb and an adverb if it indicates the manner of the action of the verb.

Right: He held the lever *firm*. (*Firm* lever.)
Right: He held the lever *firmly*. (Manner of *holding*.)

Right: Fasten the bolt *tight*. (*Tight* bolt.)
Right: Fasten the bolt *tightly*. (Manner of *fastening*.)

An adjective must not be used when an adverb is required.

Wrong: He did *bad* in mathematics.
Right: He did *badly* in mathematics. (Manner of *doing*.)

Wrong: He speaks English *good* for a foreigner.
Right: He speaks English *well* for a foreigner. (Manner of *speaking*.)

Wrong: *Most* every man has some good in him.
Right: *Almost* every man has some good in him. (*Every* is an adjective and cannot be modified by an adjective.)

Wrong: I am *sure* glad you told me that.
Right: I am *surely* glad you told me that. (*Glad* is an adjective.)

Wrong: His speech was *real* convincing.
Right: His speech was *really* (or *very*) convincing. (*Convincing* is a participle, hence an adjective.)

Errors frequently occur in the use of the comparative and superlative degrees of adjectives and adverbs.

Wrong: John was the *tallest* of the two Smith boys.
Right: John was the *taller* of the two Smith boys. (Comparative degree used of two.)

Wrong: Mary is the *most* intelligent of the twins.
Right: Mary is the *more* intelligent of the twins. (Comparative degree used of two.)

Wrong: Solomon was wiser than any man that ever lived.
Right: Solomon was wiser than any other man that ever lived. (Solomon was a man and he once lived.)

Wrong: Texas is the largest of any state in the Union.
Right: Texas is the largest of all the states in the Union.
Right: Texas is the largest state in the Union.

Wrong: His sense of color is better than a painter.
Right: His sense of color is better than that of a painter.
Right: His sense of color is better than a painter's.

Wrong: Our house is as large, if not larger, than theirs.
Right: Our house is as large as, if not larger than, theirs.
Better: Our house is as large as theirs, if not larger.

Wrong: This chair is smaller but fully as comfortable as that one.
Right: This chair is smaller than that one, but fully as comfortable.

Wrong: Your answer is different *than* mine.
Right: Your answer is different *from* mine. (No comparison but idea of distinction between.)

Other errors in the use of adjectives are illustrated in the following examples.

Wrong: Chicago is *further* from New York City than Buffalo.
Right: Chicago is *farther* from New York City than Buffalo.
(*Farther* and *farthest* are used of distance.)

Wrong: He made no *farther* effort.
Right: He made no *further* effort. (*Further* and *furthest* are used of degree—here means "additional.")

For misplacement of adverbs and the misuse of the double negative, see STYLE i and l.

3. PUNCTUATION

a. The Comma

The comma is the most frequently used mark of punctuation. The following sentences illustrate the uses of the comma.

We had run completely out of gas, and there was no town within ten miles. (With a coördinating conjunction making a compound sentence.)

The highway was closed for repairs, but there was a little dirt road by which to detour. (With a coördinating conjunction making a compound sentence.)

A tall, dark, handsome man came upon the stage. (With words in series.)

Hammers, saws, and chisels were scattered on the bench. (With words in series.)

He knocked at the front door, at the back door, and on the windows. (With phrases in series.)

We want a man who is intelligent, who is industrious, and who is trustworthy. (With clauses in series.)

After eating, the old lady removed the dishes. (To avoid misreading.)

They shouted, for the janitor was hard of hearing. (To avoid misreading.)

However, they still had some hope of reaching their destination by night. (To set off introductory words.)

Tom, stop tapping your foot on the floor. (To set off a word in direct address.)

Oh, how I regretted having spoken so hastily. (To set off a mild interjection.)

Completely discouraged, he was ready to give up. (To set off a participle at the beginning of a sentence.)

He talked in a loud voice, speaking his words very fast. (To set off a participle at the end of a sentence.)

The rain having stopped, we continued our walk. (To set off a nominative absolute.)

In a manner of speaking, the weather is a great social asset as a ready topic of conversation. (To set off an introductory, nonrestrictive phrase.)

To come to the point, we will not grant your request. (To set off an introductory, non-restrictive phrase.)

When the weather was pleasant, they often had picnics in the woods. (To set off a subordinate clause that precedes the main clause.)

Although he had run for office many times, he had never been elected. (Same reason as above.)

She said, "I shall come without fail." (To set off a direct quotation.)

That you have done such a thing, I can scarcely believe. (To set off a part of a sentence out of its natural order.)

The other persons, too, want to have their share. (To set off a parenthetical word within a sentence.)

There are, on the other hand, some extenuating circumstances. (To set off a parenthetical phrase within a sentence.)

This book, as everyone knows, was originally written for the author's own children. (To set off a parenthetical clause within a sentence.)

You know, Peggy, I have often thought of the good times we used to have. (To set off a word in direct address within a sentence.)

Miss McCord, the speaker of the evening, had a charming voice. (To set off words in apposition.)

The old man, weary from hard work, walked home slowly in the evening. (To set off a non-restrictive modifier within a sentence.)

Lincoln, who had little formal education, became a master of English. (To set off a non-restrictive clause within a sentence.)

"There is," he said, "not a moment to lose." (To set off the words governing a direct quotation.)

In December, 1895, my father was born. (To set off the year in a date.)

Cleveland, Ohio, is on Lake Erie. (To set off a state from a city.)

b. The Semicolon

There was no way to avoid the question; they had to consider it. (To separate the independent clauses of a compound sentence when no coördinating conjunction is present.)

His query had been answered very curtly; consequently, he did not carry the conversation any further. (To separate the independent clauses of a compound sentence when no coördinating conjunction is present.)

c. The Colon

This year he is taking the following studies: chemistry, psychology, history, and English. (To introduce explanatory items.)

d. Quotation Marks

"This is," he said, "the last offer I shall make." (To set off a direct quotation.)

545

"Where did you put my hat and coat?" he asked. (The question mark is put within the quotation marks when the quotation is a question.)

Did he say, "Read three chapters for the next time"? (The question mark is put outside of the quotation marks when it is not part of the quotation.)

e. Parentheses

This man (he had once been wealthy) was little better than a beggar. (To enclose matter loosely connected with the thought of the sentence.)

f. Italics

Italics are used for the names of books, plays, magazines, newspapers, ships, for words discussed as words, and for emphasis. In writing, italics are indicated by drawing a line under the word or words to be italicized.

g. The Dash

I think I shall read a little before I go to bed—where is that book anyway? (To indicate an abrupt change in thought.)

To have a secure position, to own a little home, to give his children some educational advantages—these were the simple ambitions of Mr. Todd. (Used before the summarizing part of a sentence.)

Mr. Joyce—he is the man you met last summer—has just written a novel. (Used as a less formal substitute for parentheses.)

h. The Period

Everything considered, this has been a successful day. (To end a declarative sentence.)

Take more time with your work. (To end a mildly imperative sentence.)

Mr. Smith has gone to Buffalo, N. Y. (Used with abbreviations.)

i. The Question Mark

When do you want this report handed in? (To end an interrogative sentence.)

546

j. The Exclamation Point

Stop annoying me! (To end a strongly imperative sentence.)
Goodness! That must be the fire whistle. (Used after a strong
interjection.)

k. Capitals

Capitals are used with the first word of every sentence, the
pronoun *I* and the interjection *O*, all proper nouns and adjectives,
the important words in the titles of books, plays, etc., the titles
of high officials when the word refers to a specific person, words
of personal relationship (like Father, Uncle) when they refer to
a specific person and are not preceded by a personal possessive
pronoun, directions when they refer to a specific part of the
country or the world but not when they refer to points of the
compass, names of languages (English, Spanish) but not other
studies unless the name refers to a specific course, and the names
of seasons only when they are personified.

l. The Hyphen

The hyphen is used in many established word combinations,
as: *warm-blooded, hard-shelled, fire-eater, moon-struck, water-
soaked*. Whether to hyphenate a word or to write it as a solid
word or as separate words needs constant care on the part of the
writer. There are no absolute rules to serve as a guide; in all
doubtful cases a good dictionary should be consulted.

The hyphen is used for compound adjectives placed before
nouns, as: a *first-class* investment, a *round-faced* man, *ready-to-
wear* cloth, a *now-or-never* attitude. However, if the words are
of more than two syllables, and especially if the first is an adverb
ending in *-ly*, the hyphen is not used, as: a *hopelessly outnumbered* army, *quickly prepared* plans. If the adjective follows the
noun, it is not hyphenated unless it is itself a hyphenated word,
as: "His chances seem to be *first class*," but "His prejudices are
deep-seated."

The hyphen is used with all compound numbers from twenty-
one to ninety-nine and with all fractions except *one half*, as:
forty-six, nine-tenths.

The hyphen is used with all compounds of *self* in which it stands as the first element of the word, as: *self-examination, self-conscious.*

A hyphen is used to indicate the division in a word that comes at the end of a line. If you are in doubt about the division of any word, you should unfailingly consult a dictionary. Note the following general principles of syllabication:

1. Words of one syllable must not be broken even though they are long words. The following represent wrong syllabication: *thro-ugh, glimp-se, talk-ed, stop-ped.*

2. Do not set off a single letter, and preferably do not set off two letters, of a word, as: *i-tem, o-mit, tast-y, test-ed.*

3. A double consonant is usually divided, unless the consonant has the sound of a single letter, as: *hap-pen, intel-ligent, swim-ming,* but *tell-ing, will-ing.*

4. A safe rule is to divide a word where a prefix or suffix is joined, as: *dis-loyal, under-handed, mother-hood, scholar-ship, advance-ment.*

4. SPELLING

a. Your Own Spelling List

On a separate page in your notebook give the correct spelling of every word you misspell in your themes. It would be advisable to include words misspelled in other papers that you write. If a word is misspelled a second time, you should face the truth: you are not trying hard enough. Do not deceive yourself by saying, "I can't spell." Spelling may be difficult for you, but that is all the more reason for conquering the difficulty. Anyone can spell correctly who has the *will to spell*.

b. Spelling by Observation

Many words are misspelled because they are pronounced carelessly or slovenly. Among the most important of these words are the following, in which the troublesome letter or syllable is indicated by italics.

accident*a*lly	incident*a*lly	reco*g*nize
bound*a*ry	lab*o*ratory	su*r*prise
Feb*r*uary	lib*r*ary	temper*a*ment
gover*n*ment	occasion*a*lly	us*u*ally

Sometimes an extra letter is inserted in a word, as is illustrated by the following:

Wrong	*Right*	*Wrong*	*Right*
argu*e*ment	argument	hind*e*rance	hindrance
ath*e*letics	athletics	hop*e*ing	hoping
com*m*ing	coming	interfe*r*red	interfered
disast*e*rous	disastrous	judg*e*ment	judgment
dis*s*appear	disappear	light*e*ning	lightning
dis*s*appoint	disappoint	mischiev*i*ous	mischievous
du*e*ly	duly	rememb*e*rance	remembrance
griev*i*ous	grievous	simil*i*ar	similar

Sometimes words are misspelled by the omission of a letter. In the following words the letter which is sometimes wrongly omitted is indicated by italics.

acom*m*odate	entire*l*y	neces*s*ary
ac*q*uired	excel*l*ent	notic*e*able
begin*n*ing	fa*s*cinate	oc*c*asion
chang*e*able	forgot*t*en	of*t*en
dis*s*atisfied	me*a*nt	recom*m*end
embar*r*ass	mis*s*pell	writ*t*en

Sometimes the letters are transposed, as in the following words:

Wrong	*Right*	*Wrong*	*Right*
ang*el*	angle	irreve*l*ant	irrelevant
Brit*ia*n	Britain	p*r*espiration	perspiration
C*e*asar	Caesar	tra*de*gy	tragedy
ca*lv*ary	cavalry	vill*ia*n	villain
hund*e*rd	hundred	Wed*en*sday	Wednesday

Other words have an amazing uniformity in the way in which they are misspelled.

Wrong	*Right*	*Wrong*	*Right*
acros*t*	across	pa*y*ed	paid
conquer*er*	conqueror	pred*u*jice	prejudice
defin*a*te	definite	pre*p*eration	preparation
di*s*cribe	describe	priv*a*lege	privilege
d*i*spair	despair	privil*edg*e	privilege
d*e*vide	divide	r*e*dicule	ridicule
d*e*vine	divine	r*e*ligious	religious
exist*a*nce	existence	shin*n*ing	shining
extre*a*mly	extremely	s*e*nce	since
famil*a*r	familiar	spea*c*h	speech
gramm*e*r	grammar	tr*y*s	tries
hum*e*rous	humorous	tru*e*ly	truly
independ*a*nt	independent	writ*t*ing	writing

Words having the same or closely similar sound but a different spelling and meaning require special attention. Among the most common of these are the following.

accent	ascent	altar	alter
accept	except	altogether	all together
advice	advise	born	borne
affect	effect	canvas	canvass
already	all ready	coarse	course

council	counsel	prophecy	prophesy
dying	dyeing	respectfully	respectively
forth	fourth	site	cite
hole	whole	staid	stayed
holy	wholly	stationary	stationery
lead	led	than	then
lessen	lesson	there	their
loose	lose	to	too
pain	pane	weather	whether
peace	piece	whose	who's
principal	principle	your	you're

c. Spelling by Rules

A word which ends in silent *e* usually drops the *e* before a suffix beginning with a vowel, but retains the *e* before a suffix beginning with a consonant. (In the past tense of a word like *arrange*, it is to be remembered that the suffix -*ed* is added; therefore the *e* has been dropped or there would be a double *e*.)

arrange	arranging	arranged	arrangement
care	caring	cared	careful, careless
hope	hoping	hoped	hopeful, hopeless
love	loving	loved, lovable	lovely, loveliness

An exception to this rule is that after *c* and *g* the *e* is retained if the suffix begins with *a* or *o*.

peace	peaceable	manage	manageable
service	serviceable	outrage	outrageous

If a word of one syllable or a word of two or more syllables accented on the last syllable ends in a single consonant preceded by a single vowel, the consonant is doubled before a suffix beginning with a vowel.

drop	dropping	dropped	dropper
plan	planning	planned	planner
commit	committing	committed	committee
control	controlling	controlled	controller
occur	occurring	occurred	occurrence
regret	regretting	regretted	regrettable

Note that the consonant is not doubled if the final syllable is not accented.

benefit	benefited	confer	conference
cancel	canceled	equip	equipage
signal	signaled	prefer	preference

Words with the diphthongs *ie* and *ei*, when the sound is long ē, have *i* before *e*, except after *c*. Hence:

achieve	chief	grief	relieve	wield
believe	field	piece	siege	yield

but after *c* we have *ei* (the same order as in Ce*li*a.)

ceiling	conceit	deceive	perceive	receive

Words ending in *y* preceded by a consonant change *y* to *i* before adding a suffix unless the suffix itself begins with *i*.

copy	copies	copied	copying
deny	denies	denied	denying
try	tries	tried	trying

With words ending in *y* preceded by a vowel, the suffix is added without change in the word.

alley	alleys	destroy	destroying
money	monkeys	enjoy	enjoying
delay	delays	joy	joyful

The following difficult words can best be learned in groups.

supersede	exceed	accede
	proceed	concede
	proceeds	intercede
	proceedings	precede
	succeed	procedure
		recede
		secede

5. DICTION

a. Idiom

Language, to be good, must not violate the idiom peculiar to it. The most frequent errors in idiom occur in the use of prepositions with certain nouns, verbs, and adjectives. For instance, say angry *with* a person and *at* a thing; agree *to* (not *with*) a suggestion; comply *with* (not *to*) a request; part *from* a person and *with* a thing; take exception *to* (not *with*) a remark; possessed *of* (not *with*) talent; independent *of* (not *from*); in search *of* (not *for*); different *from* (not *than*); *between* (not *among*) two contestants.

b. Provincialisms and Colloquialisms

Unless a writer is attempting to show the characteristic language or speech of a locality, words and expressions that have only local acceptance or even understanding—that is, words not national in use—should be avoied. Examples of provincialisms are *clever* in the sense of "hospitable"; *tote* for "carry"; *calculate* or *reckon* for "think."

Although colloquialisms are often permissible in informal writing, and certainly in conversation, they should be avoided in literary writing. For instance, for "It is *funny* why he *didn't* come" one had better substitute *strange, puzzling*, or *inexplicable*, and *did not;* and for "He is a *funny* old man" one had better say *queer, peculiar*, or *eccentric*.

All such contractions as *don't, he'll, isn't, won't* give a colloquial tone to writing and should be used only when they are appropriate.

c. Vulgarisms and Improprieties

Language that is used by illiterate or grossly ignorant people certainly has no place in either formal or informal writing. For instance, a person would not wish to be identified with the people who say *could a, would of, hisself, them* houses, *boughten* goods, where is he *at*, and scores of similar expressions.

Improprieties in language are less reprehensible than vulgarisms, but they should, nevertheless, be avoided. The following sentences illustrate improprieties in the use of language: "He was *mad* at his roommate"; "Will you *loan* me your typewriter?"; "We shall very gladly *except* your offer"; "Do not act *like* you *was* interested in his offer."

d. Slang

The use of slang in writing must be determined by the writer's sense of fitness. Slang certainly should not be used in formal writing as the expression of the writer's own thought, and it is all too frequently used in informal composition. True, slang often gives writing a graphic, timely, racy quality, but its use readily runs into excess, and there is the danger that it will make the writing seem common and cheap. The justification in employing slang lies with the user; he should be able to *defend* slangy expressions in any particular sentence. Moreover, slang changes so rapidly and passes out of use so quickly that the current slang of last year seems stale, that of several years ago is meaningless, and that of a decade ago is almost a dead language.

e. Triteness

Avoid trite or hackneyed expressions in your writing. The real objection to such expressions is not that they have often been used or that they are old, but that they are vague or inaccurate in conveying thought. They are, in fact, a kind of substitute for clear and concise thinking. Your writing will be improved by the omission of such trite expressions as "along these lines," "last but not least," "when all is said and done," "poor, but proud," "in the wee hours of the morning," "dressed in conventional black," "happy as a lark," "our feathered friends," and thousands of similar antiquated clichés.

f. Fine Writing

Many persons, who speak simply and naturally enough, have the peculiar notion that writing should be "elevated." To sound as unlike their natural selves as possible, they write in a stilted,

artificial style which brings great satisfaction to themselves and amazement to the normal reader. Society columns in city papers and the personal items in the country press are frequently characterized by an outlandish jargon which masquerades as "elegance." "The lovely bride, radiant in beauty and carrying a fragrant bouquet of white roses, treaded her way slowly down the aisle to the dulcet chords of the melodious organ" is enough to make the judicious weep. Writing should no more attract attention to itself, as *writing*, than a person should make himself conspicuous by flamboyant colors and bizarre cuts of clothes. Neither is in good taste.

g. Sound of Words

Words should not only express the writer's exact meaning, but they should not offend the reader's ear. Harsh combinations of sounds should be avoided, as: "The new art creation was a sensation throughout the nation."

Also avoid the use of alliteration in such sentences as the following: "The lovely ladies lingered on the lawn."

Furthermore, avoid, in prose, words that rhyme, as: "This rose grows almost till the snow blows."

The reader's attention should not be distracted by verbal tricks from *what* is being said. Naturally enough, "conscious writing" often arouses the reader's resentment, because he feels that the writer is trying to be clever. Worse still, such writing lacks sincerity.

h. Wordiness

Wordiness in writing, as in speaking, is annoying and wearisome. Since superfluous words "dilute" the thought, redundant or verbose writing will likely be flat and uninteresting. The following sentences are improved by the omission of the italicized words: "He jumped *down* off *of* the high bank"; "Be sure to return that hammer *back again*"; "The old lady *was very old; she* had lived *to be* almost a hundred years *old*"; "*There were* five of us *who* wanted to take the trip."

6. STYLE

a. Unity

Unity is an essential of all good writing. It begins with the sentence, which should have oneness or singleness of thought. A sentence may, of course, embody two or more *ideas*, but these ideas should be closely and logically related. Such is not the case in the following sentence: "The house burned completely down, and the fire department did not receive adequate funds from the town council." Now there may have been some connection between these two ideas in the writer's mind, but the connection is not clear to the reader. Possibly the writer meant something like this: "The house burned completely down. The responsibility for such wanton destruction of buildings should be placed upon the town council which had not voted adequate funds to safeguard property."

The paragraph, as well as the sentence, should exemplify the principle of unity. To do this, each paragraph should concentrate upon a definite segment of the complete development of the topic and treat this one part as a unit of the larger whole. The paragraph should not wander off into a discussion of loosely related ideas, no matter how interesting, *in themselves*, such ideas may be. Paragraphs lacking unity usually result from crowding too many ideas, each inadequately treated, into one paragraph. After writing each paragraph, apply to it this test: *Exactly what does it say?* If you cannot state the answer in a single, concise sentence, there is only one logical, and surely only one artistic, thing for you to do—rewrite the paragraph.

Lack of unity in the whole composition usually results from the choice of a subject too broad or too general for development in a short time. Choose a simple, concrete subject. Avoid such subjects as "Loyalty," "The Story of Civilization," "The Development of the United States as a Nation." You will be deceived if you think such topics will be easy to write about because they are "big." You had better confine your writing to something with which you are familiar, in which you are interested, and about which you feel a sincere desire to express your own opinions.

b. Clearness

Clearness of thought is the absolutely irreducible requirement of good writing. Clearness requires not merely that the reader can understand but that he cannot misunderstand. Clear writing means clear thinking; muddy writing results from vague, confused, *uninterested* thinking. Clearness is, at heart, a matter of sincerity; if you don't care enough to write clearly, the chances are you won't. The lack of clearness usually results from illogical order of ideas, dangling modifiers, indefinite or wrong antecedents of pronouns, mixed constructions, and changes in point of view. The more important of these hindrances to clear writing will be treated in detail below.

c. Emphasis

Writing, to attain its full effectiveness, must have the proper emphasis. Emphasis depends on *how* the ideas are expressed in the sentence and *where* they are placed in the sentence, the paragraph, and the whole composition.

Concrete words are usually more emphatic than general words, as:

His attitude toward *the matter* was known to only a *few* persons.
His attitude toward *the consolidation of the two banks* was known only to *the directors*.

Graphic words are more likely to be emphatic than generic words, as:

He *came* wildly into the room.
He *rushed* wildly into the room.

The important idea can be made more emphatic by subordinating the less important ideas, as:

He was industrious, and he soon became an executive in the company.
Because he was industrious, he soon became an executive in the company.
Because of his industry, he soon became an executive in the company.
Being industrious, he soon became an executive in the company.

The loose sentence is usually less emphatic than the periodic sentence, as can be seen from the following:

The car came to an abrupt bend, and it was going at great speed.
The car, going at great speed, came to an abrupt bend.

The passive voice is usually less emphatic than the active voice, as the following illustrations will show:

A deer was shot by the hungry men and eaten.
The hungry men shot a deer and ate it.

Inquiries about our services are welcomed by us.
We welcome inquiries about our services.

A series should be built up through a logical sequence or to an effective climax:

The little boy was peevish, hungry, and tired.
The little boy was tired, hungry, and peevish.

A rescue at last! There was a ship approaching. They had been on the water three days. They had given up hope.
They had been on the water three days. They had given up hope. Then they saw a ship approaching. A rescue at last!

The inversion of the natural order of a sentence is sometimes used to gain emphasis:

No one could deny that he had done everything humanly possible.
That he had done everything humanly possible, no one could deny.

Repetition, if it is *intentional*, can be a very effective means of gaining emphasis:

She saw the mail man drop the letter in the box—a letter she had anxiously waited for, and now that it had come, a letter she dreaded to receive.
Questions, questions, questions. She thought she would go insane if anyone asked her again how it had happened.

The use of parallel constructions as a means of attaining emphasis is illustrated in section g, below.

Emphasis by position can be succinctly explained by pointing out that the beginning and the end of sentences, paragraphs, and whole compositions are the places of importance. If emphasis is desired, weak phrases, parenthetical expressions, and loosely joined ideas should be taken from the beginning or the end of a sentence and incorporated in the body of it, as:

> To be classed as literature, a book must have universal and permanent appeal.
> A book, to be classed as literature, must have universal and permanent appeal.

> In my opinion, loyalty is the finest quality a human being can possess.
> Loyalty, in my opinion, is the finest quality a human being can possess.

> I believe it was Voltaire, but some one has said that he would die to defend a person's right to free speech.
> Some one—I believe it was Voltaire—has said that he would die to defend a person's right to free speech.

> I demand to know who is to be allowed to vote, as a first point of order.
> I demand, as a first point of order, to know who is to be allowed to vote.

You will readily find examples of emphasis, by position, in paragraphs and whole compositions from your reading of selections in this book.

d. Coherence

The sentences within a paragraph must be joined clearly, smoothly, and logically so that the thought *flows* from one sentence to another, and the paragraphs themselves must be connected so that there are no abrupt breaks between them. A good writer naturally works in terms of chronological sequences, or from a consistency of viewpoint, or by the logical relationship of ideas. Even a good writer, however, will not attain coherence without concentrated and persistent effort.

There are many mechanical means by which to attain coherence, both in joining sentences and in joining paragraphs. If the thought is accumulative, such words and phrases as *again, also, furthermore, in addition, indeed, in like manner, in particular, in short, in truth, likewise, moreover, next, of course, similarly, subsequently, too, ultimately* may be used. If the thought is adversive, *contrarily, conversely, however, nevertheless, none the less, notwithstanding, on the contrary, on the other hand, otherwise, yet* may be employed. If the thought is causal, *consequently, therefore, thus* are useful connectives. Coherence may also be obtained by repetition of words, by the skilful use of pronouns, and by condensed reference to the preceding idea. In joining paragraphs, sometimes a whole sentence, called a transition sentence, is the best means of insuring coherence. It must be understood that all these ways of procuring coherence are mechanical, and the writer's method is not entirely concealed from the observant reader. However, it is better to have a little of the skeleton of writing peep through than to have the writing disjointed, jarring, or chaotic.

A finer, maturer, yet far subtler kind of coherence results from that perfection of thinking which causes one sentence to flow into the next by what may be called, for want of a better name, the *fusion* of thought and form. This is the coherence that characterizes superior writing. Such coherence comes only with continued practice in writing; its attainment may be taken as an almost unfailing test that one writes well.

Excellent examples of coherence may be found in any of the selections of this book.

e. Ambiguity

To attain clearness, the writer must avoid ambiguity of any kind.

> Ambiguous: Jane told Mary to eat *her* cake.
> Improved: Jane told Mary to eat *her own* cake.
> Better: Jane said, "Mary, eat *your* cake."
> Better: Jane said, "Mary, eat *my* cake."

> Ambiguous: They brought the dog into the house, which had been hit by an automobile.

Clear: They brought the dog, which had been hit by an automobile, into the house.

Ambiguous: Mrs. Thomas bought an old house from a real estate dealer that she had admired for years.
Clear: From a real estate dealer, Mrs. Thomas bought an old house that she had admired for years.

Ambiguous: He recognized her as she came up and stopped the car.
Clear: He recognized her and stopped the car as she came up.

Ambiguous: The young man who loved her weekly sent letters.
Clear: The young man who loved her sent letters weekly.

f. Vagueness

The following sentences lack one of the essentials of all good writing—clearness. Carefully note why these sentences are not clear and how they have been corrected.

Vague: The campus, unless they keep people off the grass, you will have paths all over it.
Clear: Unless people keep off the grass, the campus will have paths all over it.

Vague: Wolves eat meat as well as dogs.
Clear: Wolves, as well as dogs, eat meat.

Vague: Man breathes through his pores as well as his lungs.
Clear: Man breathes through his pores as well as through his lungs.
Clear: Man breathes through both his pores and his lungs.

Vague: The chairman and speaker sat on the platform.
Clear: The chairman and the speaker sat on the platform.

Vague: They have rebelled in Jugoslavia.
Clear: The Jugoslavs have rebelled.

Vague: It says in the papers that cold weather may be expected.
Clear: The paper predicts that cold weather may be expected.

Vague: We found the roads so rough.
Clear: We found the roads so rough that driving was difficult.
Clear: We found the roads very rough.

Vague: He thinks his themes are better.
Clear: He thinks his themes are better than those of other students.

g. Parallel Structure

Parallel structure is often the best form to use for the expression of ideas that are similar, as can be seen from the following sentences:

He enjoyed very much to ski in winter and swimming in warm weather.
He enjoyed very much to ski in winter and to swim in summer.

You can go to Lexington by bus or you can take the train there.
You can go to Lexington by bus or by train.

The trees suffered from drought and because insects ate the leaves.
The trees suffered from drought and from defoliation by insects.

I like dogs, but I don't like cats. In my opinion, cats are sneaky animals, but dogs are noble and loyal.
I like dogs, but I dislike cats. In my opinion, dogs are noble and loyal, but cats are sneaky animals.
I like dogs because they are noble and loyal, but I dislike cats because they are sneaky.

h. Repetition

Repetition, although it can be useful as a means of emphasis, is usually a blemish in writing. Often the omission of an unnecessary word will correct the error, as in the following sentences:

Wrong: The doorkeeper *he* let us in for nothing.
Right: The doorkeeper let us in for nothing.

Wrong: This *here* cup is cracked.
Right: This cup is cracked.

Wrong: That *there* desk is locked.
Right: That desk is locked.

To correct faulty repetition, a synonym may sometimes be substituted for the repeated word, but care must be taken not to make your writing artificial or strained by *forced* synonyms.

Poor: He was *old*, and *persons* should be kind to *old persons*.
Better: He was *old*, and *one* should be kind to *aged persons*.

Poor: The grass was *green;* in fact, everything was *green* with the first touch of spring.

Better: The grass was *green;* in fact, everything was *verdant* with the first touch of spring.

Poor: Some people disapprove of *dancing,* but I have always enjoyed *dancing.*

Forced: Some people disapprove of *dancing,* but I have always enjoyed the *terpsichorean art.*

Better: Although some people disapprove of *dancing,* I have always enjoyed *it.*

Repetition is often corrected by the use of a pronoun, as in the following sentence:

Undesirable: I had Mary's permission; so I wore *Mary's* coat.

Better: I had Mary's permission; so I wore *her* coat.

Omission of unnecessary words will often cure repetition. Indeed, many sentences are made more forceful by the omission of overworked intensives:

Undesirable: It was *very* hot that afternoon, and I was *very* tired; so I was not *very* much interested in what Susan was trying to tell me.

Better: It was hot that afternoon, and I was very tired; so I was not much interested in what Susan was trying to tell me.

Sometimes the best method by which to correct repetition is to recast the entire sentence.

Poor: It *began* to *rain, so* that we *just* had to get out of the yard; *so* we went into the house and *began* to dance *just* as if the *rain* had not spoiled the picnic.

Better: In the midst of our picnic it began to rain. Even though we were driven into the house, we had about as much fun dancing.

i. Misplaced Words

Modifying words, especially adverbs, should be placed close to the words they modify. Note the following examples:

Illogical: We *only* saw three rabbits during the hunting trip.

Right: We saw *only* three rabbits during the hunting trip.

Illogical: He was *even* shunned by his friends.
Right: He was shunned *even* by his friends.

Illogical: I *scarcely* had any flowers this year.
Right: I had *scarcely* any flowers this year.

Illogical: We *just* answer the important letters.
Right: We answer *just* the important letters.

Illogical: That is the tallest building I *almost* ever saw.
Right: That is *almost* the tallest building I ever saw.

Illogical: I do not *ever* expect to see him again.
Right: I do not expect *ever* to see him again.

Illogical: The apprentice tried to learn *hard*.
Right: The apprentice tried *hard* to learn.

j. Awkwardness

An awkward sentence is very much like a clumsy person—both may be fundamentally good, but need improvement. Sometimes an awkward sentence can be improved by changing a word or two, but usually such a sentence must be recast.

Awkward: This subject, the subject of inflation, is important; in fact, it is so important a subject that I want to talk to you about it tonight.
Better: The importance of the subject of inflation is justification enough for my speaking to you about it tonight.
Better: I feel justified in speaking to you tonight about inflation because the subject is so important.

k. Dangling Modifiers

A modifier must be logically as well as grammatically attached to the correct word in a sentence.

Confused: He kept shooting at the rabbit, running around in all directions.
Better: He kept shooting at the rabbit, which was running around in all directions.

Faulty: Entering the town, the city hall loomed before us.
Right: As we entered the town, the city hall loomed before us.

Faulty: After studying the problem for a while, the solution became clear.

Right: After studying the problem for a while, he clearly saw the solution.

Faulty: The theme was closed by quoting a verse from Longfellow.

Better: He closed the theme by quoting a verse from Longfellow.

Better: The theme was closed by the quotation of a verse by Longfellow.

Faulty: To drive safely, the wheel should be held with both hands.

Better: To drive safely, one should hold the wheel with both hands.

Faulty: My pipe always goes out when talking about something interesting.

Better: My pipe always goes out when I am talking about something interesting.

Faulty: Personally, jazz music is not to my liking.

Better: Personally, I do not like jazz music.

1. Double Negatives and Comparisons

Double negatives and double comparisons are no longer accepted as good English.

Wrong: The refugees *scarcely* had *no* time to gather their belongings.

Right: The refugees *scarcely* had time to gather their belongings.

Wrong: He *wasn't* in *no* mood to tolerate foolishness.

Right: He wasn't in *any* mood to tolerate foolishness.

Right: He was in *no* mood to tolerate foolishness.

Wrong: I do not *doubt but* that you tried hard.

Right: I do not *doubt* that you tried hard.

Wrong: He was *less harder* hit by the depression than the other merchants.

Right: He was hit *less hard* by the depression than the other merchants.

Right: He was *not so hard* hit by the depression as the other merchants.

(1)